CASTES AND TRIBES OF SOUTHERN INDIA
(VOLUME VII)

CASTES AND TRIBES OF SOUTHERN INDIA
(VOLUME VII)

EDGAR THURSTON,
K. RANGACHARI

ISBN: 978-93-90058-92-1

Published: 1909

LECTOR HOUSE LLP
E-MAIL: lectorpublishing@gmail.com

CASTES AND TRIBES OF SOUTHERN INDIA (VOLUME VII)

BY

EDGAR THURSTON, C.I.E.,

Superintendent, Madras Government Museum; Correspondant Étranger,
Société d'Anthropologie de Paris; Socio Corrispondante,
Societa, Romana di Anthropologia.

ASSISTED BY
K. RANGACHARI, M.A.,

of the Madras Government Museum.

VOLUME VII—T TO Z

1909.

CONTENTS

LIST OF ILLUSTRATIONS

CASTES AND TRIBES OF SOUTHERN INDIA

T

Tābēlu (tortoise).—A sept of Aiyarakulu, and section of Gāzula Kāpu and Koppala Velama.

Taccha Kurup.—Barbers who shave Malabar Kammālans.

Tacchan.—The name of the carpenter sub-division of Kammālans, and further returned, at the census, 1891, as an occupational sub-division by some Paraiyans. Taccha Karaiyān has been recorded as a name for some members of the Karaiyān fishing caste. The Tacchasāstram, or science of carpentry, prescribes in minute details the rules of construction.

Tacchanādan Mūppan.—Recorded, in the Madras Census Reports, 1891 and 1901, as a sub-division of Kuricchans, and of Kurumbas of the Nīlgiris.

Tādan.—*See* Dāsari.

Tagara.—A section of Poroja.

Takru.—A class of Muhammadan pilots and sailors in the Laccadive islands. (*See* Māppilla.)

Talaivan (a chief).—A title of the Maravans. Jādi or Jāti Talaivan is the name of the hereditary chief of the Paravas of Tinnevelly, who, at times of pearl fisheries, receives a fixed share of the 'oysters.'

Talamala.—A sub-division of Kānikar.

Talayāri.—The Talayāri (talai, head) or chief watchman, or Uddāri (saviour of the village), is a kind of undepartmental village policeman, who is generally known as the Talāri. Among other duties, he has to follow on the track of stolen cattle, to act as a guard over persons confined in the village choultry (lock-up), to attend upon the head of the village during the trial of petty cases, to serve processes, and distrain goods. In big villages there are two or three Talayāris, in which case one is a Paraiyan, who officiates in the Paraiya quarter. In parts of the Telugu country, the Mutrāchas, who are the village watchmen, are known as Talārivallu, or watchman people, and, in like manner, the Bēdars are called Talārivāndlu in the Kurnool and Bellary districts.

It is noted, in the Gazetteer of the Tanjore district (1906), that "from the earliest years of the British occupation of the country, fees were paid to the talaiyāri or village watchman. He was probably survival of a state of society in which kāvalgars did not exist, and his duties were, it seems, to look after the villagers' fields and threshing floors. At any rate, he continued in existence even after the abolition of the kāval system (*see* Maravan), and was declared by the early Police Regulation (XI of 1816) to be part of the regular police establishment. Practically he did little real police duty, and in 1860, when the mufassal police was reorganised, all claims to the services of the talaiyāri as a servant of the State were formally abandoned, the Inspector-General of Police having reported that any attempt to utilise the talaiyāri body would be fruitless and unpopular. Talaiyāris still continue to be employed and paid by the ryots (cultivators) as the private guardians of their crops and harvested grain. Recently, however, the district was brought into line with the rest of the Presidency by the creation of a new force of talaiyāris, who now perform the police duties assigned to such persons elsewhere. They are provided with lathis (sticks) and badges, and are a useful auxiliary to the police."

Tāli.—"The tāli," Bishop Caldwell writes,[1] "is the Hindu sign of marriage, answering to the ring of European christendom. I have known a clergyman refuse to perform a marriage with a tāli, and insist upon a ring being used instead. A little consideration will show that the scrupulous conscience can find no rest for itself even in the ring; for, if the ring is more Christian than the tāli, it is only because its use among Christians is more ancient. Every one knows that the ring has a Pagan origin, and that, for this reason, it is rejected by Quakers." "The custom," Wagner informs us,[2] "of wearing the wedding ring on the fourth finger of the left hand had unquestionably a Pagan origin. Both the Greeks and the Romans called the fourth left-hand finger the medicated finger, and used it to stir up mixtures and potions, out of the belief that it contained a vein, which communicated directly with the heart, and therefore nothing noxious could come in contact with it, without giving instant warning to that vital organ."

The marriage badge, as it occurs in Southern India, is, broadly speaking, of two types. The one in use among the Tamil castes is oblong in shape, with a single or double indentation at the base, and rounded at the top. The corresponding bottu or sathamanam of the Telugu and Canarese castes is a flat or cup-shaped disc. The tāli in use among various Malayālam castes at the tāli-kettu ceremony is a long cylinder.

Tāli-kettu kalyānam (tāli-tying marriage).—A ceremony gone through by Nāyar girls, and girls of some other Malayālam castes, in childhood. Of those who gave evidence before the Malabar Marriage Commission, some thought the tāli-kettu was a marriage, some not. Others called it a mock marriage, a formal marriage, a sham marriage, fictitious marriage, a marriage sacrament, the preliminary

---

[1] Ind. Ant. IV, 1875.
[2] Manners, Customs, and Observances.

part of marriage, a meaningless ceremony, an empty form, a ridiculous farce, an incongruous custom, a waste of money, and a device for becoming involved in debt. "While," the Report states, "a small minority of strict conservatives still maintain that the tāli-kettu is a real marriage intended to confer on the bridegroom a right to cohabit with the bride, an immense majority describe it as a fictitious marriage, the origin of which they are at a loss to explain. And another large section tender the explanation accepted by our President (Sir T. Muttusami Aiyar), that in some way or other it is an essential caste observance preliminary to the formation of sexual relations." In summing up the evidence collected by him, Mr. Lewis Moore states[3] that it seems to be proved beyond all reasonable doubt that "from the sixteenth century at all events, and up to the early portion of the nineteenth century, the relations between the sexes in families governed by marumakkathāyam (inheritance in the female line) were of as loose a description as it is possible to imagine. The tāli-kettu kalyānam, brought about by the Brāhmans, brought about no improvement, and indeed, in all probability, made matters much worse by giving a quasi-religious sanction to a fictitious marriage, which bears an unpleasant resemblance to the sham marriage ceremonies performed among certain inferior castes elsewhere as a cloak for prostitution (*see* Dēva-dāsi). As years passed, some time about the opening of the nineteenth century, the Kērala mahatmyam and Kēralolpathi were concocted, probably by Nambūdris, and false and pernicious doctrines as to the obligations laid on the Nāyars by divine law to administer to the lust of the Nambūdris were disseminated abroad. The better classes among the Nāyars revolted against the degrading system thus established, and a custom sprang up, especially in North Malabar, of making sambandham a more or less formal contract, approved and sanctioned by the Karnavan (senior male) of the tarwad[4] to which the lady belonged, and celebrated with elaborate ceremony under the pudamuri (female cloth cutting) form. That there was nothing analogous to the pudamuri prevalent in Malabar from A.D. 1500 to 1800 may, I think, be fairly presumed from the absence of all allusion to it in the works of the various European writers." According to Act IV, Madras, 1896, sambandham means an alliance between a man and woman, by reason of which they, in accordance with the custom of the community to which they belong, or either of them belongs, cohabit or intend to cohabit as husband and wife.

Tambala.—The Tambalas are summed up, in the Madras Census Report, 1901, as "Telugu-speaking temple priests. Their social position differs in different localities. They are regarded as Brahmans in Godāvari, Kistna and Nellore, and as Sūdras in the other Telugu districts." It is noted, in the Census Report, that the Tambalas are described by C. P. Brown as a class of beggars, who worship Siva, and who beat drums; secular priests, etc. These men are generally Sūdras, but wear the sacred thread. "It is said that, during his peregrinations in the north, Sankarāchārya appointed Tamil Brāhmans to perform temple services in all the Saiva shrines. Hence the Telugu people, in the midst of whom the Tamilians lived, called them the Tambalas (Tamils). They are not now, however, regarded as Brāhmans,

[3] Malabar Law and Custom, 1905.
[4] Tarwad: a marumakkathāyam family, consisting of all the descendants in the female line of one common female ancestor.

whatever their original position may have been. They will eat only with Brāhmans. Most of them are Saivites, and a few are Lingayats. The Smarta Brāhmans officiate as their priests at birth, marriage, and death ceremonies. They do not eat animal food, and all their religious rites are more or less like those of Brāhmans. Their usual titles are Aiya and Appa."

Tambān.—One of the divisions of Kshatriyas in Travancore. (*See* Tirumalpād.)

Tambi (younger brother).—A term of affection in the Tamil country, used especially when a younger person is being addressed. It is also recorded as an honorific title of Nāyars in Travancore, and a suffix to the names of Nāyar sons of Travancore sovereigns.

Tambirān.—The name for Pandāram managers of temples, *e.g.*, at Tiruvādudurai in Tanjore and Mailam in South Arcot.

Tamburān.—For the following note on the Rājahs or Tamburāns, I am indebted to the Travancore Census Report, 1901. "They form an endogamous community of Kshatriyas, and live as seven families in Travancore. They are distinguished by the localities in which they reside, viz., Mavelikkara, Ennaikkāt, Kartikapalli, Mariappalli, Tiruvalla, Prāikkara, and Aranmula. They are all related by blood, the connection between some of them being very close. Like the Kōiltampurāns, all the members of their community observe birth and death pollution with reference to each other. Their original home is Kōlattunāt in North Malabar, and their immigration into Travancore, where the reigning family is of the Kōlattunāt stock, was contemporaneous, in the main, with the invasion of Malabar by Tippu Sultan. The first family that came into the country from Kōlattunāt was the Putuppalli Kōvilakam in the 5th century M.E. (Malabar era). The Travancore royal family then stood in need of adoption. The then Rājah arranged through a Koiltampurān of Tattārikkōvilakam to bring from Kōlattunāt two princesses for adoption, as his negotiations with the then Kōlattiri were fruitless. The Puttuppali Kōvilakam members thus settled themselves at Kartikapalli, the last of whom died in 1030 M.E. The next family that migrated was Cheriyakōvilakam, between 920 and 930 M.E. They also came for adoption. But their right was disputed by another house, Pallikkōvilakam. They then settled themselves at Aranmula. The third series of migrations were during the invasion of Malabar by Tippu in 964 M.E. All the Rājahs living there at the time came over to Travancore, of whom, however, many returned home after a time.

The Rājahs, like the Kōiltampurāns, belong to the Yajurvēda section of Dvijas, but follow the sūtra laid down by Baudhāyana. Their gōtra is that of Bhargava, *i.e.*, Parasurāma, indicating in a manner that these are Kshatriyas who were accepted by Parasurāma, the uncompromising Brahmin of the Hindu Purānas. They have all the Brahminical Samskāras, only the Brahmin priest does most of them on their behalf. Chaulam, or tuft ceremony, is performed along with Upanāyanam. The Samāvartanam, or termination of the pupil stage, is celebrated on the fourth day of the thread investiture. Instruction in arms is then given to the Kshatriya boy, and is supposed to be kept up until the requisite skill has been obtained. The tāli-tying (mangalya dhāranam or pallikkettu of a Rāja lady) is done by a Kōiltampurān, who thereafter lives with her as her married husband. The Kanyakādānam, or giving away of the bride, is performed by the priest who attends also to the other Sāstraic rites. The males take Sūdra consorts. If the first husband leaves by death or otherwise, another Kōiltampurān may be accepted. This is not called marriage, but kūttirikkuka (living together).

At Srādhas (memorial services), the Kartā, or performer of the ceremony, throws a flower as a mark of spiritual homage at the feet of the Brahmins who are invited to represent the manes, and greets them in the conventional form (namaskāra). The priest does the other ceremonies. After the invited Brahmins have been duly entertained, oblations of cooked rice are offered to the ancestors by the Kartā himself.

They are to repeat the Gāyatri ten times at each Sandhya prayer, together with the Panchākshara and the Ashtākshara mantras.

Their caste government is in the hands of the Nambūtiri Vaidikas. Their family priests belong to the class of Malayāla Pōttis, known as Tiruveli Pōttis.

Besides the ordinary names prevalent among Kōiltampurāns, names such as Martānda Varma, Āditya Varma, and Udaya Varma are also met with. Pet names, such as Kungāru, Kungappan, Kungōman, Kungunni, Unni and Ampu are common. In the Travancore Royal House, the first female member always takes the name of Lakshmi and the second that of Parvati.

Tāmoli.—A few members of this North India caste of betel-leaf sellers have been returned at times of census. I am unable to discover in what district they occur. Tāmbuli or Tāmuli is recorded as a caste of betel-leaf sellers in Bengal, and Tāmboli as a caste carrying on a similar occupation in the Bombay Presidency.

Tānamanādu.—A sub-division of Valaiyan.

Tanda.—The word literally refers to a settlement or encampment of the Lambādis, by some of whom it is, at times of census, returned as a tribal synonym.

Tandan.—It is recorded, in the Madras Census Report, 1891, that "in Walluvanād and Pālghat (in Malabar) Tandan is a distinct caste. The ceremonies observed by Tandans are, in general outline, the same as those of the southern Tiyyans, but the two do not intermarry, each claiming superiority over the other. There is a custom which prohibits the Tandan females of Walluvanād from crossing a channel which separates that tāluk from Mankara on the Pālghat side." The Tandans of Malabar are described by Mr. F. Fawcett as a people allied to the Izhuvans, who observe the custom of fraternal polyandry, which the Izhuvans abhor.

For the following note on the Tandans of Travancore, I am indebted to Mr. N. Subramani Aiyar.

The castemen are known as Urālis to the south of Varkallay, and Tandans to the north of it. In some places to the east of Kottarakaray, they were popularly termed Mutalpattukar, or those who receive the first perquisite for assistance rendered to carpenters. In the days when there were no saws, the rough instruments of the Tandan served their purpose. Hence some members of the caste were called Tacchan (carpenter). Tandan is derived from the Sanskrit dandanam or punishment, as, in ancient times, men of this caste were employed to carry out the punishments that were inflicted by the authorities upon offenders. For the execution of such punishments, the Tandans were provided with swords, choppers and knives. As they were also told off to guard the villages (ūr) of which they happened to be inhabitants, they acquired the title of Urāli. In some places, Tandans are also called Vēlans. Males and females have respectively the title Mūppan and Mūppatti, meaning an elder. In addressing members of higher castes, the Tandans call themselves Kuzhiyan, or dwellers in pits.

The Tandans are said to have once belonged to the same caste as the Izhuvans, but to have fallen away from that position. They must, in times gone by, have joined the military service of the various States in Malabar. They were, in some places, given rent-free lands, called Urāli parambu, in return for the duties they were expected to perform. With the return of peaceful times, their occupation changed, and the climbing of palm trees, to extract the juice thereof, became their most important calling. They are also largely engaged in the manufacture of ropes. Many families still receive the mutalpattu, or allowance from the carpenters.

The Tandans are divided into four endogamous sections, called Ilanji, Puvar, Irunelli, and Pilakkuti.

The ornaments of the women are, besides the minnu, wreaths of red and red and black beads. Nowadays the gold gnāttu of the Nāyars is also worn. Tattooing is popular. Even males have a crescent and a dot tattooed on the forehead, the corresponding mark in females being a line from the nasal pit upwards. Among the devices tattooed on the arms are the conch shell, lotus, snake, discus, etc. In their food and drink the Tandans resemble the Iluvans.

The priests of the Tandans are called Tanda Kuruppus, and they are also the caste barbers. The chief deity of the Tandans is Bhadrakāli, at whose shrines at Mandaikkad, Cranganore, and Sarkkaray, offerings are regularly made. At the last place, a Tandan is the priest. The chief days for the worship of this deity are Bharani asterism in March and Pattāmudayam in April. November is a particularly religious month, and the day on which the Kartikay star falls is exclusively devoted to worship. The first Sunday in January is another religious occasion, and on that day cooked food is offered to the rising sun. This is called Pogala. Maruta, or the spirit of smallpox, receives special worship. If a member of the caste dies of this disease, a small shed is erected in his memory either at his home or near the local Bhadrakāli shrine, and offerings of sweetmeats and toddy are made to him on the 28th of Makaram (January-February). Chitragupta, the accountant of Yama, the god of death, is worshipped on the full-moon day in April-May. Ancestor worship is performed on the new-moon day in July.

A girl's tāli-tying ceremony, which is called kazhuttukettu, takes place when she is between seven and twelve years old. The bridegroom is a relative called Machchampi. The Kuruppu receives a money present of 2½ fanams for every tāli tied in his presence. Though more than one girl may go through the ceremony in the same pandal (booth), each should have a separate bridegroom. The relations between the bride and bridegroom are dissolved by the father of the former paying the latter sixteen rāsi fanams. The daughter of a man's paternal aunt or maternal uncle may be claimed as murappen or lawful bride. The sambandham, or actual marriage, takes place after a girl has reached puberty. A family is regarded as out-caste, if she has not previously gone through the tāli-tying ceremony.

Only the eldest member of a family is cremated, the rest being buried. Death pollution lasts for ten days. The anniversary of a death is celebrated at the seashore, where cooked food, mixed with gingelly (*Sesamum*) is offered to the departed, and thrown into the sea.

Tandān.—The Tandān is the hereditary headman of a Tiyan tara (village), and is a Tiyan by caste. He is appointed by the senior Rāni of the Zamorin's family, or by some local Rāja in territories outside the jurisdiction of the Zamorin. The Tandān is the principal person in the decision of caste disputes. He is expected to assist at the tāli-tying, puberty, marriage and pregnancy ceremonies of members of the caste. His formal permission is required before the carpenter can cut down the areca palm, with which the shed in which the tāli is tied is constructed. In cases of divorce, his functions are important. When a new house is built, a house-warming ceremony takes place, at which the Tandān officiates. Fowls are sacrificed, and the right leg is the Tandān's perquisite. He is a man of importance, not only in many affairs within his own caste, but also in those of other castes. Thus, when a Nāyar dies, it is the Tandān's duty to get the body burnt. He controls the washerman and barber of the tara, and can withdraw their services when they are most needed. He officiates, moreover, at marriages of the artisan classes.

Tangalān.—A sub-division of Paraiyan. The word indicates one who may not stand near, in reference to their belonging to the polluting classes.

Tangēdu.—Tangēdu or Tangēdla (*Cassia auriculata*) has been recorded as an exogamous sept of Kāpu and Padma Sālē. The bark of this shrub is one of the most valuable Indian tanning agents, and is, like myrabolams (*Terminalia* fruits), used in the manufacture of indigenous dyes.

Tantuvāyan (thread-wearer).—An occupational name used by various weaving castes.

Tapodhanlu.—The name, meaning those who believe in self-mortification as wealth, adopted by some Telugu mendicants.

Tārakan.—*See* Mūttan.

Tartharol.—The name, recorded by Dr. W. H. R. Rivers,[5] of a division of the Todas. Tartāl is also given by various writers as a division of this tribe.

Tarwād.—Defined by Mr. Wigram[6] as a marumakkathāyam family, consisting of all the descendants in the female line of one common female ancestor.

Tāssan.—A Malayālam synonym for the Telugu Dāsari.

Tattān.—The goldsmith section of the Tamil and Malayālam Kammālans.

---

[5] The Todas, 1906.
[6] Malabar Law and Custom.

Teivaliol.—The name, recorded by Dr. W. H. R. Rivers,[7] of a division of the Todas.

Telaga.—"The Telagas," Mr. H. A. Stuart writes,[8] "are a Telugu caste of cultivators, who were formerly soldiers in the armies of the Hindu sovereigns of Telingana. This may perhaps account for the name, for it is easy to see that the Telugu soldiers might come to be regarded as the Telugus or Telagas *par excellence*. The sub-divisions returned under this name show that there has been some confusion between the Telagas proper, and persons who are members of other Telugu castes. The Telagas are Vaishnavites, and have Brāhmans for their priests. Their customs closely resemble those of the Kāpus. They eat flesh, but are not allowed to drink liquor. They are usually farmers now, but many still serve as soldiers, though their further recruitment has recently been stopped. Their common titles are Naidu and Dora."

In a note on the Telagas and Vantaris (strong men), it is suggested that they should be classed with the Kāpus, of which caste they are an offshoot for the following reasons:—"(1) Members of the three classes admit that this is so; (2) a collation of the intipērulu or septs shows that the same names recur among the three classes; (3) all three interdine, and intermarriage between them is not rare. A poor Telaga or Vantari often gives his daughter in marriage to a rich Kāpu. The Telagas and Vantaris are highly Brāhmanised, and will have a Brāhman for their guru, and get themselves branded at his hands. A Kāpu is generally content with a Sātāni or Jangam. Though they do not differ in their marriage and funeral rites from the Kāpus, they usually marry their girls before puberty, and widow remarriage and divorce are disallowed. A Kāpu is invariably a cultivator; a Vantari was in olden days a sepoy, and, as such, owned inām (rent-free) lands. Even now he has a prejudice against ploughing jirāyati (ordinarily assessed) lands, which a Kāpu has no objection to do. Similarly, a Telaga takes pride in taking service under a Zamindar, but, unlike the Vantari, he will plough any land. Kāpu women will fetch their own water, and carry meals to the fields for their fathers and husbands. The women of the other classes affect the gōsha system, and the men carry their own food, and fetch water for domestic purposes, or, if well-to-do, employ Kāpus for these services. It may be added that rich Kāpus often exhibit a tendency to pass as Telagas."

Tēlikula.—The Tēlikulas are summed up, in the Madras Census Report, 1901, as "a Telugu oil-presser caste, which should not be confused with Tellakula, a synonym for Tsākala, or with Telli, a caste of Oriya oil-pressers." Telikula is a synonym for the Gāniga or Gāndla caste of oil-pressers, derived from the oil (gingelly: *Sesamum indicum*), whereas the names Gāniga and Gāndla refer to the oil-mill. In the Northern Circars, the name Tēlikula is used in preference to Gāniga or Gāndla, and the oil-pressers in that part of the country are known as Tēlikula-vāndlu. The Tēlikulas are Onteddu, *i.e.*, use a single bullock for working the oil-mill, whereas, among the Gānigas, there are both Onteddu and Rendeddu sections, which employ one and two bullocks respectively.

Tellakula (white clan).—Recorded, in the Census Report, 1901, as a synonym

[7] The Todas, 1906.
[8] Madras Census Report, 1891.

for Tsākala. According to the Rev. J. Cain,[9] the Tellakulas are Telugu washermen (Tsākalas), who, in consequence of having obtained employment as peons in Government offices, feel themselves to be superior to other members of their caste.

Telli.—The Tellis are the oil-pressers of the Oriya country, whose caste name is derived from telo, oil. They are apparently divided into three endogamous sections, named Holodia, Bolodia, and Khadi. The original occupation of the Holodias is said to have been the cultivation and sale of turmeric. They may not carry turmeric and other articles for sale on the back of bullocks, and consequently use carts as a medium of transport thereof. And it is further contrary to their caste rules even to assist in loading or unloading packs carried by bullocks. The Bolodias receive their name from the fact that they carry produce in the form of oil-seeds, etc., on pack bullocks, bolodo being Oriya for bullock. The Khadis are mainly engaged in expressing various oils in oil-mills, and this occupation is also carried on by some members of the other sections. All Tellis seem to belong to one gōtra, called Karthikēswara. The caste title is Sāhu. In social position the Tellis, unlike the Tamil Vāniyans (oil-pressers), are on a par with the agricultural castes, and are one of the panchapātako, or five castes from which individuals are selected to decide serious issues which arise among the Badhōyis. The headman of the Tellis is called Bēhara, and he is assisted by a Bhollobaya, and in some places apparently by another officer called Pento.

It is considered by the Tellis as a breach of caste rules to sail in a boat or ship. If a cow dies with a rope round its neck, or on the spot where it is tethered, the family which owned it is under pollution until purification has been effected by means of a pilgrimage, or by bathing in a sacred river. The Holodias will not rear male calves at their houses, and do not castrate their bulls. Male calves are disposed of by sale as speedily as possible. Those Holodias who are illiterate make the mark (nisāni) of a ball of turmeric paste as a substitute for their autograph on documents. In like manner, the nisānis of the Bolodias and Khadis respectively are the leather belt of a bullock and curved pole of the oil-mill. Among nisānis used by other Oriya castes, the following may be noted:—

> Korono (writer caste), style.
> Rāvulo (temple servants), trident.
> Bāvuri (basket-makers and earth-diggers), sickle.
> Dhōba (washermen) fork used for collecting firewood.
> Brāhman, ring of dharba grass, such as is worn on ceremonial occasions.

In their marriage ceremonies, the Tellis observe the standard Oriya type, with a few variations. On the day before the wedding, two young married women carry two new pots painted white on their heads. To support the pots thereon, a single cloth, with the two ends rolled up to form a head-pad, must be used. The two women, accompanied by another married woman carrying a new winnowing basket, and mokkuto (forehead chaplet), proceed, to the accompaniment of the music of a chank shell and pipes, to a temple, whereat they worship. On their way home, the two girls, according to the custom of other Oriyas castes, go to seven houses, at each of which water is poured into their pots. During the marriage ceremony,

[9] Ind. Ant., VIII, 1879.

after the ends of the cloths of the bride and bridegroom have been tied together, they exchange myrabolams (*Terminalia* fruits) and areca nuts. Until the close of the ceremonies, they may not plunge into a tank (pond) or river, and, in bathing, may not wet the head.

Most of the Tellis are Paramarthos, and follow the Chaitanya form of Vaishnavism, but some are Smartas, and all worship Tākurānis (village deities).

Telugu.—Telugu or Telaga is used as a linguistic term indicating a person who speaks that language. It has, at recent times of census, been returned as a sub-division of various classes, *e.g.*, Agasa, Balija, Banajiga, Bēdar, Bestha, Dēvānga, Holeya, Kumbāra, Rāchewar, Tsākala, and Uppara. Further, Telugu Vellāla appears as a synonym of Velama, and Telugu Chetti as a synonym of Saluppan.

Tēn (honey).—Tēn or Jēn has been recorded as a sub-division or exogamous sept of jungle Kurumbas and Holeyas. Some Irulas style themselves Tēn Padaiyāchi or Tēn Vanniyan, Padaiyāchi and Vanniyan being a title and synonym of the Pallis.

Tendisai (southern country).—Recorded as a division of Vellālas in the Madura and Coimbatore districts.

Tenē (millet: *Setaria italica*).—An exogamous sept of Holeya.

Tengina (cocoanut palm).—The name of a section of Halēpaiks, who tap the cocoanut for extracting toddy.

Tennam.—Tennam (cocoanut) or Tennanjānar (cocoanut tappers) is recorded as the occupational name of Shānan. Tenkāyala (cocoanut) occurs as an exogamous sept of Yānādi, and the equivalent Tennang as a tree or kothu of Kondaiyamkōtti Maravans.

Tennilainādu.—A territorial sub-division of Kallan.

Terkattiyar (southerner).—A term applied to Kallan, Maravan, Agamudaiyan, and other immigrants into the Tanjore district. At Mayāvaram, for example, it is applied to Kallans, Agamudaiyans, and Valaiyans.

Tertal.—A division of Toda.

Teruvān.—A synonym of the Malabar Chāliyans, who are so called because, unlike most of the west coast castes, they live in streets (teru).

Tēvadiyāl (servant of god).—The Tamil name for Dēva-dāsis. Tēvan (god) occurs as a title of Maravans.

Tēyyambādi.—A section of Ambalavāsis or temple servants in Malabar, the members of which dance and sing in Bhagavati temples, and perform a song called nāgapāttu (song in honour of serpents) in private houses, which is supposed to be effective in procuring offspring.[10]

Thādla.—Thādla or Thālla, meaning rope, is an exogamous sept of Dēvānga and Karna Sālē.

Thākur.—About a hundred members of this caste are returned, in the Madras

[10] Gazetteer of Malabar.

Census Report, 1901, as belonging to a Bombay caste of genealogists and cultivators. It is recorded, in the Bombay Gazetteer, that "inferior in rank to Marāthas, the Thākurs are idle and of unclean habits. Though some of them till and twist woollen threads for blankets, they live chiefly by begging and ballad singing. At times they perform plays representing events mentioned in the Purāns and Rāmayan, and showing wooden puppets moved by strings."

Thalakōkala (female cloths).—An exogamous sept of Dēvānga.

Thālam (palmyra palm).—An exogamous sept or illam of Kānikar.

Thāmballa (sword bean: *Canavalia ensiformis*).—An exogamous sept of Tsākalas, members of which will not eat the bean.

Thambūri.—A class of people in Mysore, who are Muhammadans, dress like Lambādis, but do not intermarry with them. (*See* Lambādi.)

Thanda Pulayan.—For the following note, I am indebted to Mr. L. K. Ananthakrishna Aiyar.[11] The Thanda Pulayans constitute a small division of the Pulayans, who dwell in South Malabar and Cochin. The name is given to them because of the garment worn by the females, made of the leaves of a sedge, called thanda (apparently *Scirpus articulatus*), which are cut into lengths, woven at one end, and tied round the waist so that they hang down below the knees. The following story is told with regard to the origin of this costume. A certain high-caste man, who owned lands in those parts, chanced to sow seeds, and plant vegetables. He was surprised to find that not a trace of what he sowed or planted was to be seen on the following day. With a view to clearing up the mystery, he kept a close watch during the night, and saw certain human beings, stark naked, come out of a hole. They were pursued, and a man and a woman were caught. Impressed with a sense of shame at their wretched condition, the high-caste man threw his upper garment to the male, but, having nothing to give as a covering for the woman, threw some thanda leaves over her. The Thanda Pulayans are also called Kuzhi Pulayans, as they were found emerging from a pit (kuzhi). The leafy garment is said to be fast going out of fashion, as Māppillas, and others who own the Pulayans, compel them to wear cotton cloths. According to the Rev. W. J. Richards, a division of the Pulayans, who are called Kanna Pulayans, and found near Alleppey, wear rather better, and more artistically made aprons.[12]

The following legend is current regarding the origin of the Thanda Pulayans. In the south, the Pulayans are divided into the eastern and western sections. The former were the slaves of Duryodhana, and the latter were attached to the Pāndus. These formed the two rival parties in the war of the Mahābaratha, and the defeat of Duryodhana was the cause of their degradation.

The Thanda Pulayans appear to have been the slaves of the soil till 1854, when they were emancipated. Even now, their condition has not undergone much material improvement. Though they are left more to themselves, they still work for farmers or landlords for a daily wage of paddy (unhusked rice). If they run away,

[11] Monograph Eth. Survey, Cochin No. 1, 1905.
[12] Ind. Ant., IX, 1880.

they are brought back, and punished. There is a custom that, when a farmer or landlord wants a few Pulayans to work in the fields, he obtains their services on payment of fifteen to twenty rupees to them, or to their master. When a Pulayan's services are thus obtained, he works for his new master for two edangalis of paddy a day. They can obtain their liberation on the return of the purchase-money, which they can never hope to earn. Having no property which they can claim as their own, and conscious perhaps that their lot will be the same wherever they go, they remain cheerful and contented, drudging on from day to day, and have no inclination to emigrate to places where they can get higher wages. The Cherumars of Palghāt, on the contrary, enjoy more freedom. Many go to the Wynād, and some to the Kolar gold-fields, where they receive a good money-wage. The Thanda Pulayans work, as has been said, for some landlord, who allows them small bits of land. The trees thereon belong to the master, but they are allowed to enjoy their produce during their residence there. When not required by the master, they can work where they like. They have to work for him for six months, and sometimes throughout the year. They have little to do after the crop has been garnered. They work in the rice-fields, pumping water, erecting bunds (mud embankments), weeding, transplanting, and reaping. Men, women, and children may be seen working together. After a day's hard work, in the sun or rain, they receive their wages, which they take to the nearest shop, called mattupitica (exchange shop), where they receive salt, chillies, etc., in exchange for a portion of the paddy, of which the remainder is cooked. The master's field must be guarded at night against the encroachment of cattle, and the depredations of thieves and wild beasts. They keep awake by shouting aloud, singing in a dull monotone, or beating a drum. Given a drink of toddy, the Pulayans will work for any length of time. It is not uncommon to see them thrashed for slight offences. If a man is thrashed with a thanda garment, he is so much disgraced in the eyes of his fellow men, that he is not admitted into their society. Some improve their condition by becoming converts to Christianity. Others believe that the spirits of the departed would be displeased, if they became Christians.

The Thanda Pulayan community is divided into exogamous illams, and marriage between members of the same illam is forbidden. Their habitations are called matams, which are miserable huts, supported on wooden posts, sometimes in the middle of a paddy field, with walls of reeds, bamboo mats or mud, and thatched with grass or cocoanut leaves. A few earthen pots, bamboo vessels, and cocoanut shells constitute their property. They are denied admission to the markets, and must stand at a distance to make their purchases or sales.

Pulayan girls are married either before or after attaining puberty, but there is special ceremony, which is performed for every girl during her seventh or eighth year. This is called thanda kalyānam, or thanda marriage. It consists in having the girl dressed at an auspicious hour in the leafy garment by a woman, generally a relative, or, in her absence, by one selected for the purpose. The relations and friends are entertained at a feast of curry and rice, fish from the backwater, and toddy. Prior to this ceremony, the girl is destitute of clothing, except for a strip of areca bark.

At the marriage ceremony, the tāli (marriage badge) is made of a piece of a conch shell (*Turbinella rapa*), which is tied on the bride's neck at an auspicious hour. She is taken before her landlord, who gives her some paddy, and all the cocoanuts on the tree, beneath which she happens to kneel. When the time has come for her to be taken to the hut of the bridegroom, one of her uncles, taking her by the hand, gives her into the charge of one of her husband's uncles. On the third morning, her paternal and maternal uncles visit her at the hut of the bridegroom, by whom they are entertained. They then return, with the bride and bridegroom, to the home of the former, where the newly-married couple stay for three days. To ascertain whether a marriage will be a happy one, a conch shell is spun round. If it falls to the north, it predicts good fortune; if to the east or west, the omens are favourable; if to the south, very unfavourable.

The Thanda Pulayans follow the makkathāyam law of inheritance (from father to son). They have their tribal assemblies, the members of which meet together on important occasions, as when a woman is charged with adultery, or when there is a theft case among them. All the members are more or less of equal status, and no superior is recognised. They swear by the sun, raising their hands, and saying "By the sun I did not." Other oaths are "May my eyes perish" or "May my head be cut off by lightning."

Every kind of sickness is attributed to the influence of some demon, with whom a magician can communicate, and discover a means of liberation. The magician, when called in professionally, lights a fire, and seats himself beside it. He then sings, mutters some mantrams (prayers), and makes a discordant noise on his iron plate (kokkara). The man or woman, who is possessed by the demon, begins to make unconscious movements, and is made to speak the truth. The demon, receiving offerings of fowls, sheep, etc., sets him or her free. A form of ceremonial, called urasikotukkuka, is sometimes performed. At a place far distant from the hut, a leaf, on which the blood of a fowl has been made to fall, is spread on the ground. On a smaller leaf, chunam (lime) and turmeric are placed. The person who first sets eyes on these becomes possessed by the demon, and sets free the individual who was previously under its influence. In the event of sickness, the sorcerer is invited to the hut. He arrives in the evening, and is entertained with food, toddy, and betel. He then takes a tender cocoanut, flower of the areca palm, and some powdered rice, which he covers over with a palm leaf. The sick person is placed in front thereof, and a circle is drawn round him. Outside the circle, an iron stylus is stuck in the ground. The demon is supposed to be confined within the circle, and makes the patient cry out "I am in pai (influence of the ghost) and he is beating me," etc. With the promise of a fowl or sheep, or offerings thereof on the spot, the demon is persuaded to take its departure. Sometimes, when the sorcerer visits a house of sickness, a rice-pan containing three betel leaves, areca nuts, paddy, tulsi (*Ocimum sanctum*), sacred ashes, conch and cowry (*Cypræa moneta*) shells, is placed in the yard. The sorcerer sits in front of the pan, and begins to worship the demon, holding the shells in his hands, and turning to the four points of the compass. He then observes the omens, and, taking his iron plate, strikes it, while he chants the names of terrible demons, Mullva, Karinkāli, Aiyinar, and Villi, and utters incantations. This is varied by dancing, to the music of the iron plate, sometimes from evening till noon on the following day. The sick person works himself up into the belief that he has committed some great sin, and proceeds to make confession, when a small money fine is inflicted, which is spent on toddy for those who are assembled. The Thanda Pulayans practice maranakriyas, or sacrifices to certain demons, to help them in bringing about the death of an enemy or other person. Sometimes affliction is supposed to be brought about by the enmity of those who have got incantations written on a palm leaf, and buried in the ground near a house by the side of a well. A sorcerer is called in to counteract the evil charm, which he digs up, and destroys.

THANDA PALAYAN.

When a member of the tribe has died an unnatural death, a man, with a fowl and sword in his hands, places another man in a pit which has been dug, and walks thrice round it with a torch. After an hour or two, the man is taken out of the pit, and goes to a distance, where certain ceremonies are performed.

The Thanda Pulayans worship the gods of Brāhmanical temples at a distance of nearly a quarter of a mile. A stone is set up in the ground, on which they place tender cocoanuts and a few puttans (Cochin coins). A temple servant takes these to the priest, who sends in return some sandal paste, holy water, and flowers. They worship, as has been already hinted, demons, and also the spirits of their ancestors, by which small brass figures of males and females representing the pretas (ghosts) are supposed to be possessed. They worship, among others, Kandakarnan, Kodunkāli, Bhairavan, and Arukola pretas, who are lodged in small huts, and represented by stones. In the month of May, they celebrate a festival, which lasts for several days. Chrysanthemum and thumba (apparently *Leucas aspera*) flowers are used in the performance of worship, and paddy, beaten rice, tender cocoanuts, toddy, etc., are offered up. There is a good deal of singing, drum-beating and devil-dancing by men and women, who on this occasion indulge liberally in toddy. The Pāndavas, whom they call Anju Thamburakkal, are favourite deities. They devise various plans for warding off the evil influence of demons. Some, for example, wear rolls of palm leaf, with incantations written on them, round their necks. Others hang baskets in the rice fields, containing peace offerings to the gods, and pray for the protection of the crop. Wherever there is a dense forest, Mātan and Kāli are supposed to dwell, and are worshipped. From the end of November to April, which is the slack season, the Thanda Pulayans go about dancing from hut to hut, and collecting money to purchase fowls, etc., for offerings. Club-dancing is their favourite amusement, and is often indulged in at night by the light of a blazing fire. The dancers, club in hand, go round in concentric circles, keeping time to the songs which they sing, striking each other's clubs, now bending to ward off a blow on the legs, or rising to protect the head.

The dead are buried, and lighted torches are set up all round the grave, on to which the relations of the dead person throw three handfuls of rice. Near it, squares are made in rice flour, in each of which a leaf with rice flour and paddy, and a lighted torch or wick is placed. The chief mourner, who should be the son or nephew, carrying a pot of water, goes several times round the grave, and breaks the pot over the spot where the head rests. A few grains of rice are placed at the four corners of the grave, and a pebble is laid on it, with mantrams to keep off jackals, and to prevent the spirit from molesting people. Every morning the chief mourner goes to the grave, and makes offerings of boiled rice, gingelly (*Sesamum indicum*) seeds, and karuka grass. On the fourteenth day, he has an oil-bath, and, on the following day, the Pulayans of the village (kara) have a feast, with singing and beating of drums. On the sixteenth day, which is pulakuli or day of purification, the chief mourner makes offerings of rice balls, the guests are fed, and make a present of small coin to the songster who has entertained them. Similar offerings of rice balls are made to the spirit of the deceased person on the new-moon day in the month of Kartigam. During the period of pollution, the chief mourner has to cook his own food. The spirits of deceased ancestors are called Chavar (the dead), and are said to manifest themselves in dreams, especially to near relations, who speak in the morning of what they have seen during the night. They even say that they have held conversation with the deceased. The Rev. W. J. Richards informs us that he once saw "a little temple, about the size of a large rabbit-hutch, in which was a plank for the spirits of the deceased ancestors to come and rest upon. The spirits are supposed to fish in the backwaters, and the phosphorescence, sometimes seen on the surface of the water, is taken as an indication of their presence."[13]

The Thanda Pulayans will not eat with the Ulladans or Parayans, but stand at a distance of ninety feet from Brāhmans and other high-caste people. They are short of stature and dark-skinned. Like the Cherumans, the women adorn their ears, necks, arms and fingers with masses of cheap jewellery.

Thappata (drum).—An exogamous sept of Oddē.

Thāthan (a Vaishnavite mendicant).—The equivalent of the Telugu Dāsari.

Thātichettu (palmyra palm).—An exogamous sept of Karna Sālē and Oddē.

Thāvadadāri.—The name of a section of the Valluvans (priests of the Para-iyans), who wear a necklace of tulsi beads (thāvadam, necklace, dhāri, wearer). The tulsi or basil (*Ocimum sanctum*) is a very sacred plant with Hindus, and bead necklaces or rosaries are made from its woody stem.

Thēlu (scorpion).—Thēlu and Thēla are recorded as exogamous septs of Padma Sālē and Mādiga. The Canarese equivalent Chēlu occurs as a sept of Kuruba.

Thenige Būvva.—A sub-division of Mādigas, who offer food (buvva) to the god in a dish or tray (thenige) at marriages.

Thikka (simpleton).—A sub-division of Kuruba.

Thippa (rubbish heap).—An exogamous sept of Karna Sālē.

Thogamalai Korava.—Recorded[14] as a synonym of a thief class in the southern districts of the Madras Presidency. In a recent note on the Koravas, Mr. F. Fawcett writes that "a fact to be noted is that people such as the members of the well-known Thogamalai gang, who are always called Koravas by the police, are not Koravas at all. They are simply a criminal community, into which outsiders are admitted, who give their women in marriage outside the caste, and who adopt children of other castes."

Thogaru (bitter).—An exogamous sept of Mūsu Kamma.

Thōka (tail).—An exogamous sept of Yerukala.

Thonda (*Cephalendra indica*).—An exogamous sept of Mūsu Kamma, and gōtra of Janappans, members of which abstain from using the fruit or leaves of the thonda plant.

Thumma (bābūl: *Acacia arabica*).—An exogamous sept of Māla and Padma Sālē. The bark, pods, and leaves of the bābūl tree are used by tanners in the prepa-

[13] Ind. Ant., IX. 1880.
[14] F. S. Mullaly. Criminal Classes of the Madras Presidency.

ration of hides and skins, or as a dye.

Thūmu (iron measure for measuring grain).—An exogamous sept of Mutrācha.

Thupa (ghī, clarified butter).—An exogamous sept of Kuruba.

Thūrpu (eastern).—A sub-division of Yerukala and Yānādi.

Thūta (hole).—An exogamous sept of Dēvānga.

Tigala.—Tigala is summed up, in the Madras Census Report, 1901, as "a Canarese synonym for the Tamil Palli; applied also by the Canarese people to any Tamil Sūdras of the lower castes." In parts of the Mysore country, the Tamil language is called Tigalu, and the Canarese Mādhva Brāhmans speak of Tamil Smarta Brāhmans as Tigalaru.

Some of the Tigalas, who have settled in Mysore, have forgotten their mother-tongue, and speak only Canarese, while others, *e.g.*, those who live round about Bangalore, still speak Tamil. In their type of cranium they occupy a position intermediate between the dolichocephalic Pallis and the sub-brachy cephalic Canarese classes.

The difference in the type of cranium of the Tigalas and Tamil Pallis is clearly brought by the following tabular statements of their cephalic indices:—

a. Tigala—

68	◆
69	
70	
71	◆
72	◆◆◆◆◆
73	◆◆◆◆
74	◆
75	◆
76	◆◆◆◆◆
77	◆◆◆◆
78	◆◆◆◆◆
79	◆◆◆
80	◆◆◆
81	◆◆◆◆
82	◆
83	
84	◆◆

b. Palli—

64 ◆
65
66
67 ◆◆
68 ◆
69 ◆
70 ◆
71 ◆◆◆◆
72 ◆◆◆◆◆
73 ◆◆◆◆◆◆◆
74 ◆◆◆◆
75 ◆◆◆◆◆◆◆◆
76 ◆
77 ◆
78 ◆
79 ◆◆
80 ◆

The Tigalas are kitchen and market gardeners, and cultivate the betel vine. They apparently have three divisions, called Ulli (garlic or onions), Elē (leaf), and Arava (Tamil). Among the Ulli Tigalas, several sub-divisions, and septs or budas named after deities or prominent members of the caste, exist, *e.g.*:—

I. Lakkamma—

Tōta dēvaru (garden god).
Dodda dēvaru (big or chief god).
Dodda Narasayya.
Dodda Nanjappa.

II. Ellammā—

Narasayya.
Muddanna.

III. Sidde dēvaru.

The Tigalas have a headman, whose office is hereditary, and who is assisted by a caste servant called Mudrē. Council meetings are usually held at a fixed spot, called gōni mara kattē or mudrē gōni mara kattē, because those summoned by the Mudrē assemble beneath a gōni (*Ficus mysorensis*) tree, round which a stone platform is erected. The tree and platform being sacred, no one may go there on wearing shoes or sandals. The members of council sit on a woollen blanket spread before the tree.

Like the Pallis or Vanniyans, the Tigalas call themselves Agni Vanni, and claim to be descended from the fire-born hero Agni Banniraya. In connection with the Tigalas who have settled in the Bombay Presidency, it is noted[15] that "they are a branch of the Mysore Tigalas, who are Tamil Palli emigrants from the Madras Presidency, and, like the Palli, claim a Kshatriya origin." The Tigalas possess a manuscript, said to be a copy of a sasana at Conjeeveram (Kānchi), from which the following extracts are taken. "This is a Kānchi sasana published by Aswaththa Narayanswāmi, who was induced to do so by the god Varadarāja of Conjeeveram. This sasana is written to acquaint the descendants of the Mahāpurusha Agni Banniraya with the origin, doings, and gōtra of their ancestor Banniraya. This Banniraya sprang from fire, and so is much beloved by Vishnu the many-armed, the many-eyed, and the bearer of the chank and chakram, and who is no other than Narayana, the lord of all the worlds great and small, and the originator of the Vēdas and Vedanta.... All those who see or worship this sasana relating to Agni Banniraya, who obtained boons from the Trimurthis, Dēvatas, and Rishis, and who is the ancestor of the Tigalas, will be prosperous, and have plenty of grain and children. Those who speak lightly of this caste will become subject to the curses of Banniraya, Trimurthis, Rishis, and Dēvas. The glory of this sasana is great, and is as follows:—The keeping and worshipping of this purāna will enable the Tigalas of the Karnataka country to obtain the merit of surapadavi (the state of Dēvas), merit of doing pūja to a thousand lingams, a lakh of cow gifts, and a hundred kannikadānams (gifts of virgins for marriage)." The sasana is said to have been brought to the Canarese country because of a quarrel between the Pallis and the Tigalas at the time of a Tigala marriage. The Tigalas were prevented from bringing the various biruthus (insignia), and displaying them. The sasana was brought by the Tigalas, at an expenditure of Rs. 215, which sum was subsequently recovered from the Pallis.

Tigala occurs further as the name of a sub-division of Holeya.

Tikkē (gem).—A gōtra of Kurni.

Ti (fire) **Kollan.**—A sub-division of Kollan.

Tinda (polluting).—A sub-division of Kanisan. Tinda Kuruppu, meaning a teacher who cannot approach, is a synonym of the Kāvutiyan barber caste.

Tiperum (tī, fire).—A sub-division of Kollan blacksmiths.

Tiragati Gantlavallu (wandering bell hunters).—Stated, in the Manual of the Vizagapatam district, to repair hand-mills, catch antelopes, and sell the skins thereof. In hunting, they use lights and bells.

Tirlasetti (the name of a Balija Chetti).—An exogamous sept of Yānādi.

Tirumalpād.—Tirumalpād has been summed up as "one of the four divisions of Kshatriyas in Travancore. The term, in its literal sense, conveys the idea of those who wait before kings. In mediæval times the Tirumalpāds were commanders of armies." By Mr. Wigram[16] Tirumalpād is defined as a member of a Royal Family. In the Madras Census Report, 1891, it is stated that "there are two Tirumalpāds,

[15] Monograph, Eth. Survey, Bombay, No. 93, Tigala, 1907.
[16] Malabar Law and Custom.

one a Sāmanta, and the other a so-called Kshatriya. The former observes customs and manners exactly similar to Erādis and Nedungādis. In fact, these are all more or less interchangeable terms, members of the same family calling themselves indifferently Erādi or Tirumalpād. The Kshatriya Tirumalpād wears the sacred thread, and the rites he performs are similar to those of Brāhmans, whose dress he has also adopted. He has, however, like Nāyars, tāli-kettu and sambandham separately. His females take Nambūdiri consorts by preference, but may have husbands of their own caste. Their inheritance is in the female line, as among Nāyars and Sāmantas. Generally the females of this caste furnish wives to Nambūdiris. The touch of these females does not pollute a Nambūdiri as does that of Nāyars and Sāmantas, and, what is more, Nambūdiris may eat their food. The females are called Nambashtādiri."

For the following note on Tampāns and Tirumalpāds, I am indebted to the Travancore Census Report, 1901. "The Tampāns and Tirumalpāts come under the category of Malabar Kshatriyas.The word Tampān is a contraction of Tampurān, and at one time denoted a ruling people. When they were divested of that authority by the Ilayetattu Svarūpam, they are said to have fallen from the status of Tampurāns to Tampāns. Their chief seat is the Vaikam tāluk. The Tirumalpāts do not seem to have ruled at all. The word Tirumulpātu indicates those that wait before kings. There is an old Sanskrit verse, which describes eight classes of Kshatriyas as occupying Kērala from very early times, namely (1) Bhūpāla or Mahā Rāja, such as those of Travancore and Cochin, (2) Rājaka or Rājas, such as those of Mavelikara and Kotungallūr, (3) Kōsi or Kōiltampurān, (4) Puravān or Tampān, (5) Srīpurōgama or Tirumulpāt, (6) Bhandāri or Pantārattil, (7) Audvāhika or Tirumalpāt, (8) Chēta or Sāmanta. From this list it may be seen that two classes of Tirumulpāts are mentioned, namely, Srīpurōgamas who are the waiters at the Rāja's palace, and the Audvāhikas who perform Udvāha or wedding ceremony for certain castes. Both these, however, are identical people, though varying in their traditional occupations. The chief seats of the Tirumulpāts are Shertallay and Tiruvalla."

The Tampāns and Tirumulpāts are, for all purposes of castes, identical with other Malabar Kshatriyas. Every Tampān in Travancore is related to every other Tampān, and all are included within one circle of death and birth pollution. Their manners and customs, too, are exactly like those of other Kshatriyas. They are invested with the sacred thread at the sixteenth year of age, and recite the Gāyatri (hymn) ten times thrice a day. The Nambūtiri is the family priest, and (death) pollution lasts for eleven days. The Kettukālyanam, or tāli-tying ceremony, may be performed between the seventh and the fourteenth year of age. The tāli is tied by the Āryappattar, while the Nampūtiris recite the Vēdic hymns. Their consorts are usually Nampūtiris, and sometimes East Coast Brāhmans. Like all the Malabar Kshatriyas, they follow the marumakkathāyam system of inheritance (through the female line). Tampāns and Tirumulpāts are often the personal attendants of the Travancore Maharājas, whom they serve with characteristic fidelity and devotion. The Tirumulpāts further perform the tāli-tying ceremony of the Nāyar aristocracy.

The names of the Tirumulpāts and Tampāns are the same as those of other classes of Kshatriyas. The title Varma is uniformly added to their names. A few families among these, who once had ruling authority, have the titular suffix Bhandārattil, which is corrupted into Pantārattil. The Tampāns call themselves in documents Kōviladhikārikal, as they once had authority in kōvils or palaces.

Tirumān (holy deer).—An exogamous section of Kallan.

Tirumudi (holy knot).—Recorded, in the Madras Census Report, 1901, as "bricklayers, whose women are usually prostitutes; found chiefly in Salem and Coimbatore. They are either Vēttuvans or Kaikōlans. Kaikōlan women, when they are dedicated to the temple, are supposed to be united in wedlock with the deity.

Tiruvalluvan.—A sub-division of Valluvan. Tiruvalluvar, the author of the Kurāl, is said to have belonged to the Valluva caste.

Tiru-vilakku-nagarattar (dwellers in the city of holy lamps).—A name assumed by Vāniyans (oil-pressers).

Tiyadi.—A synonym of the Tiyāttunni section of Ambalavāsis (*see* Unni).

Tiyan.—The Tiyans, and Izhuvans or Iluvans, are the Malayālam toddy-drawing castes of Malabar, Cochin, and Travancore. The following note, except where otherwise indicated, is taken from an account of the Tiyans of Malabar by Mr. F. Fawcett.

The Tiyans in Malabar number, according to the census returns, 512,063, or 19·3 per cent. of the total population. The corresponding figures for the Izhuvans are 101,638, or 3·8 per cent. The Tiyans have been summed up[17] as the middle class of the west coast, who cultivate the ground, take service as domestics, and follow trades and professions—anything but soldiering, of which they have an utter abhorrence.

The marumakkatāyam system (inheritance through the female line), which obtains in North Malabar, has favoured temporary connections between European men and Tiyan women, the children belonging to the mother's tarvad. Children bred under these conditions, European influence continuing, are often as fair as Europeans. It is recorded, in the Report of the Malabar Marriage Commission, 1894, that "in the early days of British rule, the Tiyan women incurred no social disgrace by consorting with Europeans, and, up to the last generation, if the Sūdra girl could boast of her Brāhman lover, the Tiyan girl could show more substantial benefits from her alliance with a white man of the ruling race. Happily, the progress of education, and the growth of a wholesome public opinion, have made shameful the position of a European's concubine; and both races have thus been saved from a mode of life equally demoralising to each." On this point, Mr. L. K. Anantha Krishna Iyer writes as follows.[18] "It is true that there is an elevation both physically and mentally in the progeny of such a parentage. On making enquiries about this, I learn from a respectable and educated Tiyan gentleman that this union is looked upon with contempt by the respectable class of people, and by the orthodox community. I am further informed that such women and children, with

[17] Lieutenant-General E. F. Burton. An Indian Olio.
[18] Monograph Ethnog. Survey of the Cochin State, No. 10, Izhuvas, 1905.

their families, are under a ban, and that respectable Tiya gentlemen who have married the daughters of European parentage are not allowed to enjoy the privileges of the caste. There are, I hear, several such instances in Calicut, Tellicherry, and Cannanore. Women of respectable families do not enter into such connection with Europeans."

It is commonly supposed that the Tiyans and Izhuvans came from Ceylon. It is recorded, in the South Canara Manual, that "it is well known that both before and after the Christian era there were invasions and occupations of the northern part of Ceylon by the races then inhabiting Southern India, and Malabar tradition tells us that some of these Dravidians migrated again from Īram or Ceylon northwards to Travancore and other parts of the west coast of India, bringing with them the cocoanut or southern tree (*tengina mara*), and being known as Tīvars (islanders) or Īravars, which names have since been altered to Tīyars and Ilavars. Dr. Caldwell derives Īram from the Sanskrit Simhala through the Pali Sihala by the omission of the initial S." It is noted by Bishop Caldwell[19] that there are traces of a common origin of the Iluvans and Shānars, Shānar (or Shēnēr), for instance, being a title of honour amongst the Travancore Ilavars. And it is further recorded[20] that there is a tradition that the Shānars came originally from Ceylon. The Izhuvans are supposed to derive their caste name from Izha dwipa (island) or Simhala dwipa (both denoting Ceylon). In a Tamil Puranic work, quoted by Mr. Anantha Krishna Iyer, mention is made of a King Illa of Ceylon, who went to Chidambaram in the Tamil country of Southern India, where a religious discussion took place between the Buddhist priests and the Saivite devotee Manickavachakar in the presence of King Illa, with the result that he was converted to the Saivite faith. From him the Iluvans are said to be descended.

The Tiyans are always styled Izhuvan in documents concerning land, in which the Zamorin, or some Brāhman or Nāyar grandee, appears as landlord. The Tiyans look down on the Izhuvans, and repudiate the relationship. Yet they cannot but submit to be called Izhuvan in their documents, for their Nāyar or Brāhman landlord will not let them have the land to cultivate, unless they do so. It is a custom of the country for a man of a superior caste to pretend complete ignorance of the caste of an individual lower in the social scale. Thus, in the Wynād, where there are several jungle tribes, one is accustomed to hear a man of superior caste pretending that he does not know a Paniyan from a Kurumba, and deliberately miscalling one or the other, saying "This Paniyan," when he knows perfectly well that he is a Kurumba. It is quite possible, therefore, that, though Tiyans are written down as Izhuvans, the two were not supposed to be identical. State regulations keep the Izhuvans of Cochin and Travancore in a position of marked social inferiority, and in Malabar they are altogether unlettered and uncultured. On the other hand, the Tiyans of Malabar provide Magistrates, Sub-Judges, and other officials to serve His Majesty's Government. It may be noted that, in 1907, a Tiya lady matriculate was entertained as a clerk in the Tellicherry post-office.

A divagation must be made, to bring the reader to a comprehension of the

[19] The Tinnevelly Shānars, 1849.
[20] Madras Census Report, 1871.

custom surrounding māttu, a word signifying change, *i.e.*, change of cloth, which is of sufficient importance to demand explanation. When a man or woman is outcasted, the washerwoman (or man) and the barber of the community (and no other is available) are prohibited from performing their important parts in the ceremonies connected with birth, death, and menstruation. A person who is in a condition of impurity is under the same conditions; he or she is temporarily outcasted. This applies to Nambūtiris and Nāyars, as well as to the Tiyans. Now the washerwoman is invariably of the Tiyan caste. There are Mannāns, whose hereditary occupation is washing clothes for Nambūtiris and Nāyars, but, for the most part, the washerwoman who washes for the Nāyar lady is of the Tiyan caste. A woman is under pollution after giving birth to a child, after the death of a member of her tarvad, and during menstruation. And the pollution must be removed at the end of the prescribed period, or she remains an outcaste—a very serious thing for her. The impurity is removed by receiving a clean cloth from the washerwoman, and giving in exchange her own cloth to be washed. This is māttu, and, be it noted, the cloth which gives māttu is one belonging to the washerwoman, not to the person to be purified. The washerwoman gives her own cloth to effect the purification. Theoretically, the Tiyan has the power to give or withhold māttu, and thus keep any one out of caste in a state of impurity; but it is a privilege which is seldom if ever exercised. Yet it is one which he admittedly holds, and is thus in a position to exercise considerable control over the Nambūtiri and Nāyar communities. It is odd that it is not a soiled cloth washed and returned to the person which gives purification, but one of the washerwoman's own cloths. So the māttu may have a deeper meaning than lies in mere change of cloth, dressing in a clean one, and giving the soiled one to a person of inferior caste to wash. This māttu is second in importance to no custom. It must be done on the last day of pollution after birth and death ceremonies, and menstruation, or the person concerned remains outcasted. It is noteworthy that the Izhuvans know nothing of māttu.

An Izhuvan will eat rice cooked by a Tiyan, but a Tiyan will not eat rice cooked by an Izhuvan—a circumstance pointing to the inferiority of the Izhuvan. A Nāyar, as well as a Tiyan, will partake of almost any form of food or drink, which is prepared even by a Māppilla (Malabar Muhammadan), who is deemed inferior to both. But the line is drawn at rice, which must be prepared by one of equal caste or class, or by a superior. An Izhuvan, partaking of rice at a Tiyan's house, must eat it in a verandah; he cannot do so in the house, as that would be defilement to the Tiyan. Not only must the Izhuvan eat the rice in the verandah, but he must wash the plates, and clean up the place where he has eaten. Again, an Izhuvan could have no objection to drinking from a Tiyan's well. Further, there is practically no mixture in the distribution of Tiyans and Izhuvans. Where there are Izhuvans there are no Tiyans, and *vice versâ*. [In a photograph of a group of Izhuvan females of Palghat eating their meal, which was sent to me, they are all in a kneeling posture, with the buttocks supported on the heels. They are said to assume the same attitude when engaged in grinding and winnowing grain, and other occupations, with a resultant thickening of the skin over the knees.]

Differences, which might well come under the heading marriage, may be considered here, for the purpose of comparison between the Tiyans and Izhuvans. During the preliminaries to the marriage ceremony among the Tiyans, the date of the marriage having been fixed in the presence of the representatives of the bride and bridegroom, the following formula is repeated by the Tandān or headman of the bride's party. Translated as accurately as possible, it runs thus. "The tara and changati of both sides having met and consulted; the astrologer having fixed an auspicious day after examining the star and porutham; permission having been obtained from the tara, the relations, the illam and kulam, the father, uncle, and the brothers, and from the eight and four (twelve illams) and the six and four (ten kiriyams); the conji and adayalam ceremonies and the four tazhus having been performed, let me perform the kanjikudi ceremony for the marriage of ... the son of ... with ... daughter of ... in the presence of muperium." This formula, with slight variations here and there, is repeated at every Tiyan marriage in South Malabar. It is a solemn declaration, giving validity to the union, although, in the way that custom and ritual survive long after their original significance has been forgotten, the meaning of many of the terms used is altogether unknown. What, for instance, is the meaning of muperium? No one can tell. But a few of the terms are explainable.

Tara. The tara was the smallest unit in the ancient government system, which, for want of a better term, we may style feudal. It was not exactly a village, for the people lived apart. Each tara had its Nāyar chieftain, and also its Tiyan chief or Tandān, its astrologer, its washerman, its goldsmith, and other useful people, each serving the community for the sake of small advantages. Each tara was its own world.

Changati (friend). The friends of both parties which negotiated the marriage.

Porutham (agreement). Examination of the horoscopes of the boy and girl makes it possible to ascertain whether there is agreement between the two, and the union will be propitious.

Illam. Here intended to mean the father's family.

Kulam. The name, derived from kula a branch, here denotes the mother's family.

Twelve illams, ten kiriyams. The word illam, now used exclusively for the residence of a Nambūtiri, is supposed to have been used in days of old for the house of a person of any caste. And this supposition is said to find support in the way that a Tiyan coming from the south is often greeted in South Canara. Thus, a Malabar Tiyan, travelling to the celebrated temple at Gokarnam in South Canara, is at once asked "What is your illam and kiriyam?" He has heard these terms used in the foregoing formula during his own or another's marriage ceremony, but attached no meaning to them. To the man of South Canara they have genuine meaning. One should be able to answer the question satisfactorily, and thus give a proper account of himself. If he cannot, he gets neither food nor water from the South Canara Tiyan. This also holds good, to some extent, in the case of a southern Tiyan visiting the northern parts of the Cherakal tāluk of Malabar.

The ten illams of South Malabar are as follows:—

Tala Kodan.

Nellika (*Phyllanthus Emblica*).

Paraka or Varaka.

Ala.

Ten Kudi or Tenan Kudi.

Padayan Kudi.

Kannan.

Varakat.

Kytat

Puzhampayi or Bavu   } inferior.

The illams of North Malabar are said to be—

Nellika.
Pullanhi.
Vangeri.
Koyikkalan.
Padayam Kudi.
Tenan Kudi.
Manan Kudi.
Vilakkan Kudi.

Marriage is strictly forbidden between two persons belonging to the same illam. The bride and bridegroom must belong to different illams. In fact, the illams are exogamous. Members of some of the illams were allowed certain privileges and dignities. Thus, the men of the Varakat illam (Varaka Tiyans) were in the old days permitted to travel in a mancheel (a hammock-cot slung on a pole). They were allowed this privilege of higher caste people, which was prohibited to the Tiyans of other illams. But, should one of them, when travelling in a mancheel, happen to see a Rājah or a Nāyar, he was obliged to hang one of his legs out of it in token of submission. The Varaka Tiyans were further allowed to wear gold jewels on the neck, to don silken cloths, to fasten a sword round the waist, and to carry a shield. The sword was made of thin pliable steel, and worn round the waist like a belt, the point being fastened to the hilt through a small hole near the point. A man, intending to damage another, might make an apparently friendly call on him, his body loosely covered with a cloth, and to all appearances unarmed. In less than a second, he could unfasten the sword round his waist, and cut the other down. The well-known Mannanar belonged to the Varakat illam. Those who know Malabar will recall to mind the benevolent but strange institution which he initiated. He provided a comfortable home for Nambūtiri women who were thrown out of caste, and thus in the ordinary course of events doomed to every misery and degradation to be found in life. On being outcasted, the funeral ceremonies of Nambūtiri women were performed by her own people, and she became dead to them. She went to the Mannanar, and her birth ceremonies were performed, so that she might begin life anew in a state of purity. If, on arrival, she entered by the left door, she was his wife, if by the front door, his sister. It is said that, when their chief, Mannanar of the Aramana, is destitute of heirs, the Tiyans of Kolattanād go in procession to the Kurumattūr Nambūtiri (the chief of the Peringallūr Brāhmans) and demand a Brāhman virgin to be adopted as sister of Mannanar, who follows the marumakkatāyam rule of succession. This demand, it is said, used to be granted by the Nambūtiris assembling at a meeting, and selecting a maiden to be given to the Tiyans.

Kiriyam is said to be a corrupt form of the Sanskrit word griham (house), but this seems rather fanciful. There are said to have been about two kiriyams for each village. The names of only three are known to me, viz., Karumana, Kaita, and Kampathi. There is a village called Karumana, near the temple of Lakshmipuram in South Canara. Karumana is applied as a term to signify a Tiyan during the ordinary devil-dancing in temples, when an oracular utterance is delivered. The oracle always addresses the Tiyan as "my Karumana," not as "my Tiyan." The only other use of the word is in Karumana acharam (the customs of the Tiyans).

Other outward and visible differences between Tiyan and Izhuvan marriages are these. The South Malabar Tiyan bridegroom, dressed as if for a wrestling match, with his cloth tied tight about his loins, carries a sword and shield, and is escorted by two companions similarly equipped, dancing their way along. The Izhuvan does not carry a sword under any circumstances. The chief feature of his wedding ceremony is a singing match. This, called the vatil-tura-pāttu, or open the door song, assumes the form of a contest between the parties of the bridegroom and bride. The story of Krishna and his wife Rukmini is supposed to be alluded to. We have seen it all under slightly different colour at Conjeeveram. Krishna asks Rukmini to open the door, and admit him. She refuses, thinking he has been gallivanting with some other lady. He beseeches; she refuses. He explains, and at length she yields. The song is more or less extempore, and each side must be ready with an immediate answer. The side which is reduced to the extremity of having no answer is beaten and under ignominy.

I pass on to the subject of personal adornment of the Tiyans:—

(*a*) North Malabar, Males—

> 1. A horizontal dab made with white ashes on either side of the forehead and chest, and on the outside of each shoulder.

> 2. Two gold ear-rings (kadakkan) in each ear. A silver chain hanging from the sheath of his knife, and fastened with a boss. Two tambak (copper, brass and silver) rings on the ring finger of the left hand.

> 3. A gold kadakkan in each ear, and an iron ring on the ring finger of the left hand.

> 4. A thorn in each ear (another was similarly ornamented). Not married.

> 5. A gold ear-ring in each ear. An iron ring on the little finger of the left hand. Two silver rings, in which is set a piece of hair

from an elephant's tail, on the little finger of the right hand.

A few individuals wore brass rings, and some had ear-rings, in which a red stone was set. Amulets were worn by some in little cylindrical cases on a string, to protect the wearer against enemies, the evil eye, or devils. One man wore a silver girdle, to which an amulet in a case was fastened, underneath his cloth, so that it was not in view to the public. One individual only is noted as having been tattooed, with a circular mark just above his glabella. The arms of a good many, and the abdomen of a few, bore cicatrices from branding, apparently for the purpose of making them strong and relieving pains.

(*b*) South Malabar, Males.

In the country parts, the waist cloth is always worn above the knee. About a third of the individuals examined wore ear-rings. The ears of all were pierced. Those who were without ear-rings had no scruples about wearing them, but were too poor to buy them.

1. Blue spot tattooed over the glabella.

2. Silver amulet-case, containing fifteen gold fanams, at the waist. He said that he kept the coins in the receptacle for security, but I think it was for good luck.

3. Ear-ring (kadakkan) in each ear. A copper amulet-case, containing a yantram to keep off devils, at the waist.

4. Four silver amulet-cases, containing yantrams on a copper sheet for curing some ailment, at the waist.

5. Two gold kadakkans in each ear. A white spot over the glabella.

(*c*) North Malabar, Females.

In olden days, the women used to wear coloured and striped cloths round the waist, and hanging to the knees. The breast was not covered. The body above the waist was not allowed to be covered, except during the period of death pollution. Nowadays, white is generally the colour to be seen, and the body is seldom covered above the waist—never one may say, except (and then only sometimes) in the towns. The Izhuvan women in Malabar always wear blue cloths: just one cloth rolled tightly round the waist, and hanging to the knees. Of late, they have taken to wearing also a blue cloth drawn tight over the breast.

Ornaments. The thōdu, which is now sometimes worn by Tiyan women, is not a Tiyan ornament. The ear-rings, called kathila and ananthod, are the Tiyan ornaments, and look like strings of gold beads with pendants. Discs of white metal or lead are used to stretch and keep open the dilated lobes of the ears, in which gold ornaments are worn when necessary or possible. Venetian sequins, real or imitation, known in Malabar as amāda, are largely used for neck ornaments. There is a Malabar proverb that one need not look for an insect's burrow in amāda, meaning that you cannot find anything vile in a worthy person.

Turning now to the subject of marriage. In the ordinary course of things, a marriage would not be made between a Tiyan girl of South Malabar and a Tiyan man of North Malabar, for the reason that the children of such a marriage would inherit no property from the family of either parent. The husband would have no share in the property of his family, which devolves through the women; nor would the wife have any share in that of her family, which is passed on through the men. So there would be nothing for the children. But, on the other hand, marriage between a girl of the north and a man of the south is a different thing. The children would inherit from both parents. As a rule, Tiyans of the north marry in the north, and those of the south in the south.

It was generally admitted that it was formerly the custom among the Tiyans in South Malabar for several brothers—in fact all of them—to share one wife. Two existing instances of this custom were recorded.

The arrangement of a marriage, and the ceremonial which will now be described, though pertaining strictly to the Calicut tāluk of South Malabar, are sufficiently representative of a Tiyan marriage anywhere. There is, however, this difference, that, in North Malabar, where inheritance through females obtains, and the wife invariably resides in her own tarwad or family home, there is never any stipulation concerning a girl's dowry. In South Malabar, where inheritance is through the males, and where the wife lives in her husband's house, the dowry in money, jewels, or furniture, is as a rule settled beforehand, and must be handed over on the wedding day. In the Calicut tāluk, we find an exception to this general rule of South Malabar, where the subject of the dowry is not usually mentioned. In North Malabar, gifts of jewels are made in proportion as the bride's people are wealthy and generous. What is given is in the way of a gift, and forms no feature in the marital agreement.

The first step to be taken in connection with marriage is examination of the horoscopes of the boy and girl, in order to ascertain whether their union will be one of happiness or the reverse. While this is being done by the Panikkar (Malabar astrologer), the following persons should be present:—

(*a*) On the part of the bridegroom—

    1. Tandān, or chief of the tara.

    2. Father, or other elder in the family.

    3. Uncle, *i.e.*, the mother's brother. In Malabar the word uncle means maternal uncle.

    4. Sisters' husbands.

    5. Four or more friends or companions.

    6. Any number of relations and friends.

(*b*) On the part of the bride—

    1. Tandān of her tara.

    2. Father, or other guardian.

    3. Uncle.

4. Four or more friends.

5. The astrologer of her tara.

6. Friends and relations.

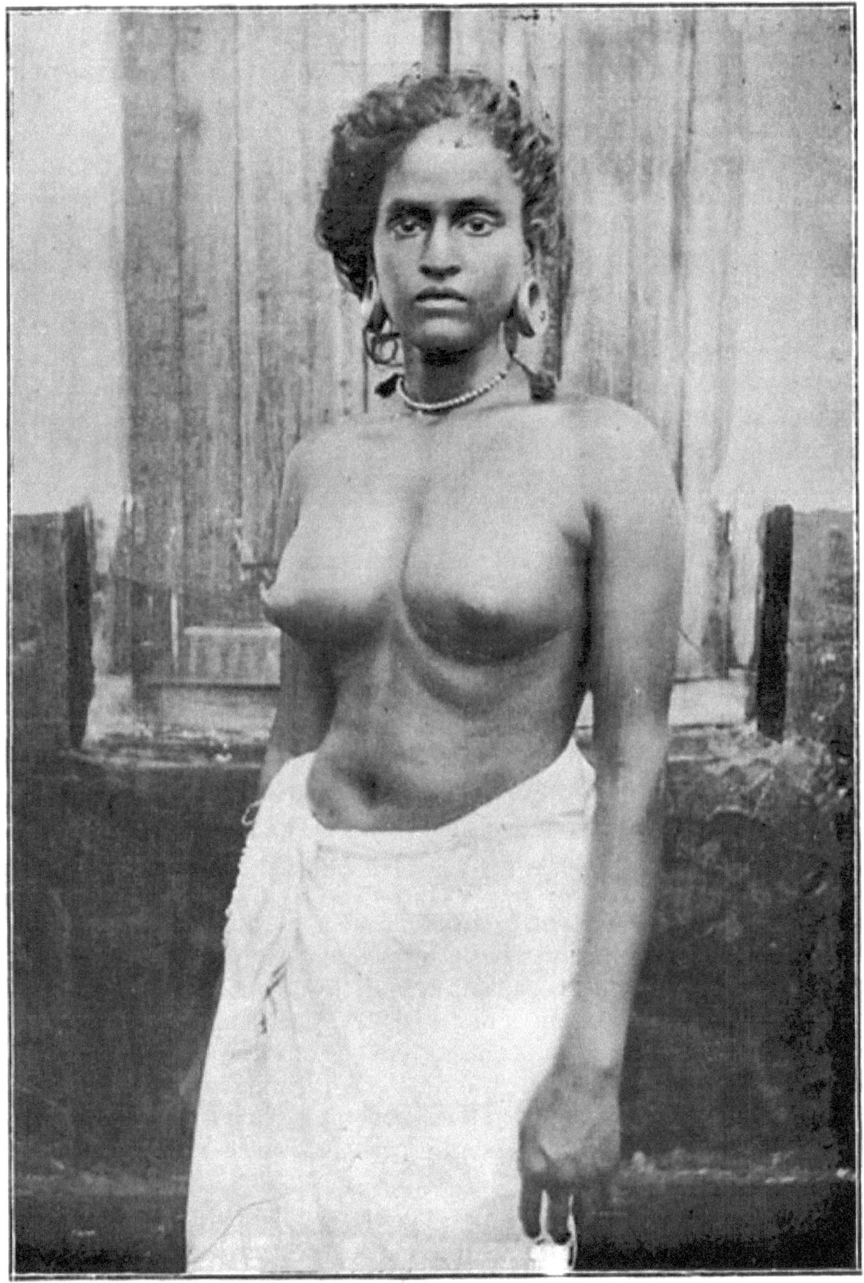

TIYA WOMAN.

The ceremony must be performed at the house of the girl's family. Her father's consent is necessary, but his presence is not essential at this or the two subsequent ceremonies in connection with the marriage. The Tandān, it may be noted, is the caste governmental head in all matters affecting his own caste and the artisans. He is a Tiyan, and his office, which is authorised by the local Rājah, or rather by his senior Rāni, is hereditary. In exceptional cases, however, the hereditary right may be interrupted by the Rāni appointing some one else. The Tandān of the tara is required to assist at every ceremony connected with marriage, at the ceremony when a girl attains puberty, at that of tying the tāli, and at the fifth and seventh months of pregnancy. His formal permission is required before the carpenter can cut down the areca palm, with which the little shed in which the tāli is tied is constructed. In cases of divorce, his functions are important. When a new house is built, there must be a house-warming ceremony, at which the Tandān officiates. Fowls are sacrificed, and the right leg is the Tandān's perquisite. He is a man of importance, not only in many affairs within his own caste, but also in those of other castes. Thus, when a Nāyar dies, it is the Tandān's duty to get the body burnt. He controls the washerman and barber of the tara, and can withdraw their services when they are most needed. He officiates, moreover, at marriages of the artisan class—carpenters, braziers, goldsmiths and blacksmiths.

A group of taras forms what is called a dēsam, the koyma or "sovereignty" of which is represented by a Nāyar tarwad. It is through the head or Karnavan (really the chieftain) of this tarwad that the Tandān approaches the Rāja in matters of appeal, and the like. The Tandān is to some extent under his guidance and control, but he must provide the Tandān with a body-guard of two Nāyars on occasions of marriages. In the old days, it may be mentioned, the Tandāns of the taras within the rule of the Zamorin were always appointed by his senior Rāni. The term Tandān must not be confounded with the Tandars, a people of the Palghāt tāluk, who appear to be allied to the Izhuvans. These Tandars observe the custom of paternal polyandry, while the Izhuvans abhor it.

The procedure observed in the examination of horoscopes is as follows. The Tandān of the bride's tara gives a grass or palmyra palm leaf mat to the astrologer to sit on, and supplies mats or seats for the bridegroom's party. The common sleeping mat of wild pine leaves, or a wooden stool, must, on no account, be given for the astrologer to sit on. It may be day or night when the ceremony takes place, but, whatever the hour may be, a lamp having five, seven, nine, or eleven cotton wicks, must be burning in front of the astrologer. The Tandān's wife puts it in its place. Then the boy's uncle hands over the boy's horoscope to his Tandān, who passes it on to the girl's Tandān. The girl's father hands her horoscope to their Tandān, who, when he has received them both, passes them on to the astrologer. The two horoscopes should agree on twenty-one points—a requirement which might prove awkward, were it not that a balance in favour of beneficent influences is generally allowed to admit of the marriage taking place. In the case of agreement, the boy's uncle, through his Tandān, then pays two fanams[21] (eight

---

[21] A fanam is a small gold coin, worth about four annas, which was formerly current in Southern India, but is no longer in circulation.

annas)—one for each horoscope—to the astrologer. When there is disagreement, the girl's uncle pays the money. The horoscopes (which have been privately examined beforehand to make sure of no disagreement) are returned to their respective owners. After the examination of the horoscope, there is a feast with plenty of sweetmeats. The next item is the conjee (rice gruel) ceremony, at which the following should be present:—

(*a*) On the part of the boy—

    1. Father, his brother, or some one representing him.

    2. Husbands of all married sisters.

    3. Uncle.

    4. Tandān of his tara.

    5. Neighbours and friends.

(*b*) On the part of the girl—

    1. Uncle.

    2. Relations of married sisters.

    3. Relations of married brothers.

    4. Tandān of her tara.

    5. Astrologer of her tara.

    6. Relations and friends.

The horoscopes are again formally examined by the astrologer, who announces that their agreement augurs a happy wedded life. The boy's uncle pays him two fanams. The girl's uncle takes the two horoscopes, which have just been tied together, from the astrologer, and hands them to the Tandān of the girl's tara, who passes them on to the Tandān of the boy's tara. They are handed by him to the boy's uncle. The astrologer then writes on a palmyra leaf a note for each party to the marriage, stating the auspicious day and hour for the final ceremony, the hour at which the bride should leave her house, and the hour for her arrival at the house of the bridegroom. The following programme is then gone through. In the verandah, facing east, before the front door, is spread an ordinary sleeping mat, over it a grass mat, and over that a plain white cloth which has been washed and is not a new one. On the floor close by, the following articles are placed:—

A lamp, having an odd number of cotton wicks, which is kept lighted whatever the hour of day it may be;

A measure, called nāzhi, made of jak tree (*Artocarpus integrifolia*) wood, filled to overflowing with rice, and placed on a flat bell-metal plate (talika);

A plain white cloth, washed but not new, neatly folded, and placed on the metal plate to the right (south) of the rice;

A small bell-metal vessel (kindi), having no handle, filled with water.

The lamp is placed on the south side of the mat, the plate next to it (to the north), and the kindi at a little distance to the left (the north). The people who sit on the mat always face the east. The mat having been spread, the various articles just mentioned are brought from the central room of the house by three women, who set them in their places. The Tandān's wife carries the lamp, the eldest woman of the house the bell-metal plate, and some other woman the kindi. The Tandān of the boy's tara, the boy's sister's husband, and a friend then sit on the mat covered with a cloth. If the boy has two brothers-in-law, both sit on the mat, to the exclusion of the friend. The senior woman of the house then hands three plates of rice conjee to the Tandān of the girl's tara, who places them in front of the three persons seated on the mat. To the right of each plate, a little jaggery (unrefined sugar) is placed on a piece of plantain leaf. Each of those seated takes about a spoonful of conjee in his right hand. The Tandān repeats the formula, which has already been given, and asks "May the conjee be drunk"? He answers his question by drinking some of the conjee, and eating a little jaggery. All three then partake of the conjee and jaggery, after which they rise from the mat, and the plates and mat are removed. The place is cleaned, and the mats are again put down, while betel is distributed. The two Tandāns then sit on the mat. The girl's Tandān picks up a bundle of about twenty-five betel leaves, and gives half to the boy's Tandān. The Tandāns exchange betel leaves, each giving the other four. The boy's Tandān then folds four fanams (one rupee) in four betel leaves, which he hands to the girl's Tandān, saying "May the conjee ceremony be performed"? The Tandāns again exchange betel leaves as before, and distribute them to all the castemen present, beginning with the uncles of the boy and girl. The proceedings in the verandah are now over. The next part of the ceremony takes place in the middle room of the house, where the mats, lamp, and other articles are arranged as before. The two Tandāns sit on the mat with the boy on the right and the girl on the left, facing east. The boy's uncle stands in front of the Tandāns, facing west, and the girl's uncle behind them, facing east. The boy's father gives to the boy's uncle two new plain white cloths, with twenty-one fanams (Rs. 5–4) placed on them. When presenting them, he says "Let the Adayalam be performed" three times, and the girl's uncle says thrice "Let me receive the Adayalam." The Tandāns again exchange betel leaves, and distribute them among the castemen. Then follows a feast, and more betel. The date of the wedding has now to be fixed. They congregate in the middle room once more, and the Tandāns sit on the mat. The girl's Tandān shares a bundle of betel leaves with the boy's Tandān, who, taking therefrom four leaves, places two rupees on them, and gives them to the girl's Tandān. The boy's party supplies this money, which is a perquisite of the Tandān. When handing over the leaves and the coins, the boy's Tandan says "On ... (naming a date) ... and ... (the bride and bridegroom), and friends, and four women will come. Then you must give us the girl, and you must prepare the food for that day." The other Tandān replies "If you bring six cloths and forty-two fanams (Rs. 10–8) as kanam, and two fanams for the muchenan (the girl's father's sister's son), the girl will be sent to you." The cloths should be of a kind called enna kacha, each four cubits in length, but they are not now procurable. Kanam is a term used in land tenures, for which there is no precise equivalent in English. It is a kind of mortgage paid by a tenant to a landlord. The former is liable to eviction by the latter, when he obtains better terms for his land from another tenant—a condition of modern growth breeding much mischief and bad blood. But, when a tenant is evicted, he is entitled, according to law, to the value of certain improvements on the land, including eight annas for each tree which he has planted. The kanam is paid by the boy's sister or sisters. His Tandān addresses his brother-in-law or brothers-in-law in the words "On ... (mentioning a date), you must come early in the day, with Rs. 10–8 as kanam," and gives him or them four betel leaves. Those assembled then disperse. The boy's people may not go to the girl's house before the day appointed for the marriage.

The next item in connection with a marriage is the issue of invitations to the wedding. The senior women of the boy's house, and the Tandān, invite a few friends to assemble at the house of the bridegroom. The mat, lamp, and other articles are placed in the middle room. The bridegroom (manavālan) sits on the mat, with a friend on either side of him. He has previously bathed, and horizontal daubs of sandal paste have been placed on his forehead, breast, and arms. He wears a new cloth, which has not been washed. His Tandān has adorned him with a gold bracelet on his right wrist, a knife with a gold or silver handle at the waist, and a gold or silver waist-belt or girdle over the loin-cloth. The bracelet must have an ornamental pattern, as plain bracelets are not worn by men. The girdle is in the form of a chain. Besides these things, he must wear ear-rings, and he should have rings on his fingers. His sister who pays the kanam dresses in the same style, but her cloths may be of silk, white without a pattern in the border, and she wears gold bracelets on both wrists. All enjoy a good meal, and then set out, and visit first the house of the Tandān. He and his wife walk in front, followed by the boy's elder sisters, if he has any. Then comes the bridegroom with a friend before and behind him, with a few women bringing up the rear. At the Tandān's house there is another meal, and then three, five, or seven houses are visited, and invitation to the wedding given in person. The proceedings for the day are then over, and, after three days, the brother-in-law, uncle, and all others receive invitations.

On the occasion of the marriage ceremony, the barber first shaves the bridegroom's head, leaving the usual forelock on the crown, which is never cut. He performs the operation in a little shed to the east of the house, and a plantain leaf is placed so that the hair may fall on it. As a rule, the barber sits in front of the person whose hair he is shaving, while the latter, sitting cross-legged on the ground, bends forward. But, on this occasion, the bridegroom sits on a low wooden stool. Close by are a lamp and a measure of rice on a plantain leaf. The barber also shaves the two friends of the bridegroom (changathis), and receives a fanam and the rice for his trouble. The three youths then bathe, smear themselves with sandal paste, and proceed to dress. The bridegroom must wear round the loins a white cloth, new and unwashed. Round the top of the loin cloth he wears a narrow waist-band (kacha) of silk, from 14 to 21 cubits in length, with the ends hanging in front and behind. Over the shoulders is thrown a silk lace handkerchief. He puts in his ears gold ear-rings, round the neck a necklace called chakra (wheel) mala,[22] on the

---

[22] Other kinds of necklaces are the mullapu (jasmine flower) mala, avil (beaten rice) mala, so called from the shape of the links, mani mala or bead necklace, and pavizham (coral) mala. These are all worn by women.

right wrist a gold bracelet, gold rings on the fingers, a gold or silver chain round the loins, and a gold or silver-handled knife with a sheath of the same metal. The two companions are dressed in much the same way, but they wear neither necklace nor bracelet. The women wear as many ornaments as they please. Sisters of the bridegroom must wear bracelets on both wrists, a necklace, and a silk cloth (virāli) on the shoulders. The bracelet worn by men is called vala, and must be made of one piece of metal. Those worn by women are called kadakam, and must be made in two pieces. When all are ready, mats, and other things are once more placed in the middle room, and the bridegroom and his two companions sit on the mats. They at once rise, and proceed to the little shed which has been erected in the front yard, and again seat themselves on the mats, which, with the other articles, have been brought thither from the middle room. Then the Tandān gives betel to the bridegroom and his two companions, who must chew it. The Tandān's wife, the elder woman of the house, and the bridegroom's sisters sprinkle rice on their heads. The Tandān gives a sword to the bridegroom and each of his companions. The procession then starts. In front walk two Nāyars supplied by the Koyma of the dēsam (represented by the Nāyar landlord). Then come the Tandān and a few elders, followed by the Tandān's wife and some of the elder women, the bridegroom with his two companions, his sisters, and finally the general crowd. As the procession moves slowly on, there is much dancing, and swinging of swords and shields. At the bride's house, the party is received by the wife of the Tandān of the tara holding a lighted lamp, the oldest woman of the family with a plate containing a measure of rice and a folded cloth, and another woman, who may be a friend, with a kindi of water. They sprinkle a little rice on the heads of the party as they enter the yard. The bridegroom sits on a mat, close to which the lamp and other articles are set. The bride's Tandān takes charge of the swords, betel is distributed, and a hearty meal partaken of. The six cloths, which the bridegroom is required to bring are in reality three double cloths, one of which is for the use of the bride. It is the privilege of the bridegroom's sisters and the Tandān's wife to dress her. Her waist-cloth is tied in a peculiar way for the occasion, and she is enveloped from head to foot in a silken cloth, leaving only the eyes visible. The bridegroom, after his arrival at the bride's house, has to put on a peculiar turban of conical shape, made of a stiff towel-like material, tied round with a silk handkerchief. The bridegroom's sister leads the bride to the little shed (pandal) in the yard, and seats her behind the bridegroom. The kanam, and the remaining four cloths are then given by the bridegroom's sister to the bride's mother, and they, having tied a silk handkerchief across the body like a Brāhman's thread, stand behind the bridegroom, the mother to the right and the sister to the left. The latter says three times "Let the kanam be given," and hands it to the bride's mother, who, as she receives it, says thrice "Let me receive the kanam." The mother at once hands it over to her husband, or the senior male member of the family. The Tandān then places plantain leaves, for use as plates, before the bridegroom and his two companions, and, facing the bridegroom, holds a vessel of cooked rice in front of him. The bride's mother, standing behind him, serves out thrice some rice out of the pot on to the leaf in front of the bridegroom, and the Tandān does the same for his two companions. The bride's mother then mixes some plantains, pappadams (large thin biscuits), sugar, and ghī (clarified butter) with the rice on the bridegroom's leaf-plate, and offers the food to him three times. She will not, however, allow him to taste it. It is taken from his lips, and removed by the washerwomen. The bridegroom's sister has the same play with the bride. The rice, which has thus been made a feature of the ceremony, is called ayini. A few days prior to the marriage, two small bundles of betel leaves, each containing areca nuts, half a dozen tobacco leaves, and two fanams are given by the bridegroom to the Nāyar chieftain of the dēsam as his fee for furnishing an escort. In return for these offerings, he gives a new cloth to the bridegroom. Three measures of raw rice, ten or twelve pappadams, plantains, a cocoanut, and some dry uncooked curry-stuff are given by the bridegroom to each of the Nāyars provided as escort on the eve of the marriage. When they arrive on the scene on the wedding day, they are given some beaten rice, rice cakes, cocoanuts, plantains, and a drink of arrack (spirit). When the bride's parents and relations come for the Vathil ceremony, the same escort is provided, and the same presents are given. Just as the bridegroom and all are ready to leave, the bride's father's sister's son called the machunan, steps forward, and demands two fanams from the bridegroom's party in return for permission to take away the bride. He gets his money, and the party starts for the bridegroom's house, after rice has been sprinkled over the heads of the contracting couple, the sisters of the bridegroom leading the bride. The swords, which have been returned by the Tandān, are again used in flourishing and dancing *en route.*

It is a prevalent custom throughout Southern India that a girl's father's sister's son has the first right to her hand in marriage. This obtains not only among the Dravidian peoples, but also among Brāhmans. The Malayālam word for son-in-law (marumakan) means nephew. If a stranger should marry a girl, he also is called nephew. But the unmarried nephew, having the first admitted right to the girl, must be paid eight annas, or two fanams, before he will allow her to be taken away. The argument is said to be as follows. A sister pays forty-two fanams as kanam for her brother's wife. When the product, *i.e.,* a daughter, is transferred to a stranger, the son claims compensation on his mother's investment at the same rate as that at which a cocoanut tree is valued—eight annas. At all events, the nephew has the first right to a girl, and must be compensated before she can be taken away by another.

At the bridegroom's house, the party is received by the wife of the Tandān and the lady of the house. Following the bride should come her parents and other relations, two Nāyars representing the chieftain, and the Tandān of his tara. The formalities with mats and rice are gone through as before. Rice is sprinkled over the heads, the Tandān receives the swords, and all sit in the shed. The ayini rice ceremony is repeated for the bride by the bridegroom's mother and sisters. The happy pair then proceed to the inner room of the house, where sweetmeats are served to them. Then is observed, as a rule, the asaram or gift ceremony. Relations are expected to give 101 fanams (Rs. 25–4), but the poorest of them are allowed to reduce the gift to 21 fanams (Rs. 5–4), and the others give according to their means. These gifts are supposed to be repaid with interest. The Tandān sees that a regular account of all the gifts is made out, and handed over to the bridegroom, and receives eight annas for his trouble. The accountant who prepares the accounts, and the person who tests the genuineness of the coins, each receives a bundle of betel leaves, four areca nuts, and two tobacco leaves. Betel leaves, areca nuts, and tobacco, are also given to each giver of gifts. After this, there is the vatil or house ceremony. Two large bundles of betel leaves are prepared, each of which contains a thousand or fifteen hundred leaves, and with them are placed forty or fifty tobacco leaves, and seventy to a hundred areca nuts. The bride's Tandān pays two or four rupees as vatil kanam to the Tandān of the bridegroom, who hands the money to the bridegroom's father. The bridegroom then places one bundle of betel leaves, with half the tobacco and areca nuts, before the bride's father, and the other before her mother, and they are distributed by the Tandān of the girl's tara and his wife among the men and women who are present. Sweetmeats are then distributed, and the marriage ceremony is concluded. A formal visit must be made subsequently by the women of the bride's house to the bridegroom's, and is returned by the bride and bridegroom. The first visit is paid by a party consisting of the bride's mother, her uncle's and brother's wives, the wife of the Tandān, and other relations. They are expected to bring with them plenty of sweetmeats and bread for general distribution. When the return visit is made by the bride and bridegroom, the sister of the latter, and other relations and friends, should accompany them, and they should take with them a lot of betel leaves, areca nuts, tobacco, and sweetmeats. This exchange of visits does not, however, complete those which are *de rigueur*. For, at the next Ōnam and Vishu festivals, the newly married couple should visit the house of the bride's family. Ōnam is the beginning of the first harvest, and Vishu the agricultural new year. On these occasions, the bridegroom takes with him the inevitable betel leaves, and presents a new cloth to the parents of the bride and every one else in the house. When the annual Tiruvathira festival takes place between the betrothal and marriage ceremonies, the bridegroom is expected to send to the temple, through his Tandān and one of his own relations, a quantity of ripe and unripe plantains.

The ceremonies which have been described differ considerably from those of the Tiyans of North Malabar, where the marumakkatāyam law of inheritance obtains. These are very simple affairs.

In the Calicut tāluk, a man can marry only one wife at a time. But, when a wife is barren, a leper, or suffering from incurable disease, her husband may, with her formal permission, marry another wife. A bride may be of any age. Where there is no stipulation as to dowry, it is a point of honour to give the girl as many jewels as the bridegroom can afford. Widows may remarry.

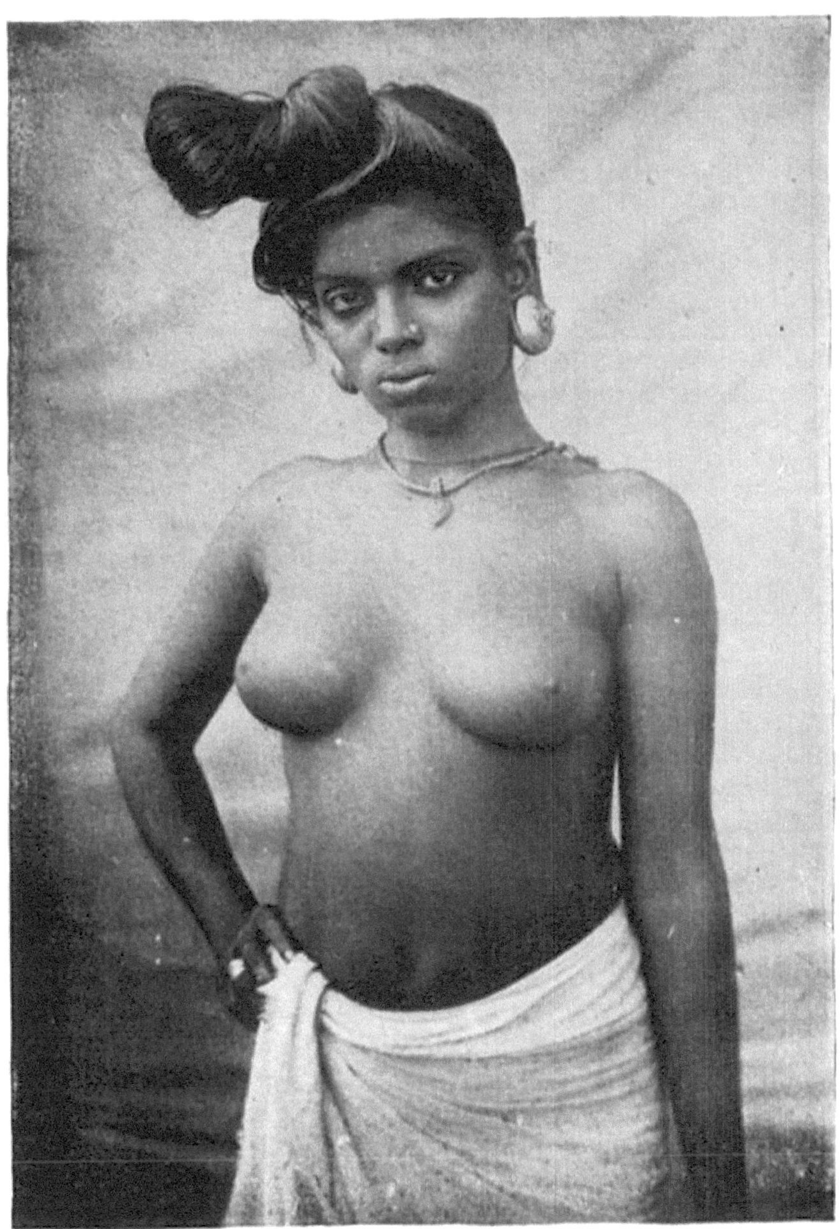

TIYA WOMAN.

Divorce is admissible, when the grounds for it are sufficient. And, when we find that incompatibility of temper is among these, it is safe to say that it is fairly easy of accomplishment. No specific reason need, in fact, be assigned. When it is the man who wishes to get rid of his wife, he must pay her all her expenses towards the marriage, as assessed by persons of the caste who fill the rôle of mediators. He has to give up jewels received from his wife's family, and must, in some cases, pay the discarded wife something on account of her loss of virginity—a circumstance, which might make it difficult for her to obtain another husband. If the wife wishes to get rid of her husband, she must pay up all his expenses towards the marriage. The party found to be in the wrong must pay a fee of five to twenty rupees to the Tandān and all present, the relations excepted. The amount is distributed then and there. The procedure to be adopted in effecting divorce is as follows. The Tandāns of both sides, uncles and relations, and sometimes the fathers, assemble at the house of the wife, the Tandān, or one of the relations. To the left of a burning lamp are placed two small wooden stools. On one of these are laid a small towel with four fanams (one rupee) tied up in a corner of it, and another towel with a little rice and four fanams tied up in it. Close by is the other stool, on which the wife's uncle stretches a single thread taken from his own cloth. The husband carries this stool to the gate, and says three times to the wife's brother, father, or uncle—"Your sister's (daughter's or niece's) matrimonial connection is severed." He then blows away the thread, throws the stool down, and departs for ever. This little ceremony cannot be performed at the husband's house, as it would involve perpetual banishment from his own house. The coins in the cloths go to the Tandāns. It is the uncle who gives these cloths, because it was he who received the two cloths at the conjee ceremony. A marriage cannot be dissolved unless both parties agree.

A girl is under pollution for four days from the commencement of the first menstrual period. During this time she must keep to the north side of the house, where she sleeps on a grass mat of a particular kind, in a room festooned with garlands of young cocoanut leaves. Round the mat is a narrow ridge made of paddy (unhusked rice), rice, and flowers of the cocoanut and areca palms. A lamp is kept burning, near which are placed the various articles already described in connection with marriage. Another girl keeps her company and sleeps with her, but she must not touch any other person, tree or plant. She further must not see the sky, and woe betide her if she catches sight of a crow or cat. Her diet must be strictly vegetarian, without salt, tamarinds, or chillies. She is armed against evil spirits with an iron knife carried on her person, or placed on the mat. On the first day, she is seated on a wooden stool in the yard to the east of the house. The fresh spathe of a cocoanut is cut in front of her. The bunch of blossoms is placed in a copper pot painted with perpendicular lines of chunam (lime), and a horizontal line at the top and bottom. The spathe of an areca palm is similarly treated, and, if the contents of both spathes are plentiful, it is regarded as a good augury of fertility. The wife of the girl's uncle, or, if she is married, her husband's sister pours some gingelly (*Sesamum*) oil over her head, on the top of which a gold fanam has been placed. Failing such relations, the wife of the Tandān officiates. The operation is repeated by two other women, relatives if possible. The oil is poured from a little cup made from a leaf of the jāk tree (*Artocarpus integrifolia*), flows over the forehead, and is received with the fanam in a dish. It is a good omen if the coin falls with the obverse upwards. Rice is cooked with jaggery, and given to the girl. The other women partake thereof, and then have a feast by themselves. The anointing with oil is the only bath the girl has until the fourth day. On the third day, she is not allowed to eat rice in any form, but she may partake of any other grain in the form of cakes. Her uncle's wife, husband's sister, and other relations, give her presents of cakes and bread. During the night, the māttu, or cloth-changing ceremony, takes place. First of all, the washerman comes along with the washerwoman, carrying two washed cloths. In the front yard of the house a lamp with an odd number of wicks is burning. In a bamboo basket are a small measure (edangāli) of paddy heaped up on a plantain leaf, a measure of rice on another leaf, two separate quarter measures thereof, a piece of turmeric, a little straw, a piece of coir (cocoanut fibre), and a cocoanut. As soon as he enters, the washerman, using the straw and coir skilfully, makes a bundle of the contents of the basket, and places it near the lamp, which is standing on a wooden stool. A cocoanut is cut in half, and placed, half on each side, by the stool. Thereon is set a flat bell-metal dish, containing a little rice and seven rolls of betel leaves and areca nuts. The washerwoman, having received the māttu from the woman, places it on his head and proceeds to sing a song, at the conclusion of which he says solemnly three times "Let me place the māttu." He then places the cloths on the bundle, which is on the stool. The girl's uncle's wife, and four other women, have by this time emerged from the middle room of the house, carrying a lighted lamp, a plate with a measure of rice, and a kindi as before. The uncle's wife, having covered her breast with a silk cloth, and wearing all her ornaments, leads the other four women as they walk thrice round the māttu. She then places a fanam (or a four-anna piece) on the māttu, lifts the stool, bundle and all, with one hand on the māttu and the other below the stool, and leads the procession of the women, with the lamp and other articles, to the room where the girl has been sleeping. She deposits her burden near the spot where the girl has laid her head. A general feast then takes place, and the washerman appropriates the fanam, and the paddy and rice spread in the yard. So ends the third day of these strange observances. On the fourth day, the girl bathes in a neighbouring pool, with some ceremonial. Before she leaves the house, the washerman fixes in the ground a branch of a certain tree, to the top and bottom of which he ties the two ends of a long line of thin coir rope or yarn. This is supposed to represent the bow of Kāma, the Indian Cupid. He erects a miniature temple-like structure of young cocoanut leaves, with the stems of young plantains near it, by the side of the pool. Close to it, he places a burning lamp, and a small quantity of rice and paddy, each on a separate plantain leaf. Near them he sets a cocoanut, which has been blackened with charcoal, on some rice spread on a plantain leaf, a cocoanut reddened with turmeric and chunam on raw rice, and another on a leaf, containing fried paddy.[23] He further deposits a few plantains, and two other cocoanuts. Before the girl leaves the house, clad in one of the cloths brought on the previous night, she is well rubbed all over with oil, and the four or six women[24] who accompany her are similarly treated. Leading the way, they are followed by a number of women to the pool, where the girl and her companions bathe. After the bath, they stand by the side of the pool, facing east and holding lighted cotton-wicks in their hands, and go round the miniature temple three times, throwing the wicks into it. The washerman again breaks out into song, accompanying himself by strik-

[23] Ordinarily, paddy is partly boiled before it is pounded to remove the husk. Raw rice is obtained by pounding the paddy, which has not undergone any boiling.

[24] There must in all be five or seven females.

ing a bell-metal plate with a stick. When he has finished, and gone through a little more business on his own account, the girl's husband or brother (if she is unmarried) appears on the scene. He holds aloft the coir string, under the lower end of which a cocoanut has been placed on the ground. The girl passes three times forwards and backwards without touching it. Two cotton wicks, lighted at both ends, are laid on the cocoanut, and the girl should cut the wicks and the cocoanut through, completely severing them, with one blow of a strong knife or chopper. If she is successful, the omen is considered good. The girl, with her party, then bathes a second time. As she comes out of the water, she kicks out backwards like a mule, and sends the stem with the single cocoanut attached flying into the water with her right foot. The second māttu cloth is then brought, and she is clad in it. Then she is full dressed and ornamented and led back to the house with a silk canopy over her head. She is taken to the middle room, and cakes and rice are given to her to eat. A feast is then held. The girl has so far been purified as regards most affairs of life, but she cannot touch any cooking-vessel until she has undergone yet another ceremony. This takes place on the seventh or ninth day after the first appearance of the menses. Every day until then the girl is rubbed with gingelly oil and turmeric. Three ordinary earthenware cooking-pots are piled, one above the other, in the kitchen. The uppermost pot contains cooked rice, the middle one rice boiled with jaggery, and the lowest curry. The pots must be new, and are marked with perpendicular daubs of chunam. Seated on a low wooden stool to the west of the pots, the girl, facing the east, touches each pot with a knife. When the first of all these menstruation ceremonies has taken place at the house of the girl's husband, her mother brings some cakes on this last day. If it has been performed at her father's house, her husband's sister should bring the cakes. They are distributed among all present, and a small meal is partaken of. All the expenses of the first, and seventh or ninth day ceremonies, are borne by the people of the house, who may be those of the family of the girl's father or husband. The expenses of the ceremonial of the fourth day are defrayed by the girl's husband if they have been performed at her father's house, and *vice versâ*.

The young wife has an easy time of it until the fifth month of her pregnancy, when she must again submit to becoming the subject for ceremonial. Then takes place the Belikala, for the purpose of appeasing some of the many malignant spirits, who are unceasing in their attempts to destroy infants in the womb. This consists for the most part of offerings, which are repeated in the seventh month. They are performed by members of the Mannān (washerman) and Pānan (exorcists and devil-dancers) castes. At the commencement thereof, there is a feast. A structure, in shape something like a Muhammadan taboot,[25] about five feet in height, is erected in the front yard of the house. It is made of stems of young plantain trees, and festooned with leaves of young cocoanut palms. The floor of the little edifice, and the ground outside it to the west, are strewn with charcoal made from paddy husk, on which are made magic squares of white rice flour, intermingled with red, green, and yellow, each colour being compounded with specified substances. The squares are not always the same, but are prepared for each occasion, so as to suit

[25] The taboot is a model of a Muhammadan mausoleum, intended to represent the tomb of Husain, which is carried in procession during the Moharram festival.

the particular spirit which is to be invoked and appeased. The pregnant woman, with six female companions, leaves the middle room of the house, carrying the usual lamp and other articles, and they walk seven times round the edifice. Before completing the last round, each throws into it a burning wick. They then stand to the west of it, facing east, and sit down. The Mannāns invoke the spirit in song, accompanied by the clang of metal plates beaten with sticks. Drums must not be used. The music and weird devil-dancing go on more or less all night, and by morning some of the most nervous of the women, overcome by the spirit, go into fits. The fees for the devil-dancing are paid by the pregnant woman's father. Last of all, a live cock is held against the forehead of the woman, mantrams (magical formulæ) are repeated, and rice is thrown over her head. If she should have a fit, the head of the cock is cut off, and the blood offered to the demon spirit. If, however, she does not suffer from undue excitement, the cock is simply removed alive. She is left in peace for the next two months, when she goes to her father's house, at which there is more devil-dancing at another Belikala ceremony. The fees are paid by the woman's husband. They vary from five to thirty-two rupees, according to the cost of the edifice which is erected, and the quality of the dancing. The invocation of some of the devils requires specially trained dancers who must be paid high fees. On the morning following the dance, the tamarind juice drinking ceremony takes place at the house of the woman's father. The fees in connection with this are debited to the husband. Taking advantage of an auspicious moment, the husband and two companions bathe in the early morning, and make a neat toilette, the husband wearing a necklace. They then go to the nearest tamarind, and pluck three small leafy twigs, which they bring to the house. The husband's sister pounds the leaves in a mortar in a little shed or pandal in the front yard. The juice is then strained through a new double cloth eight cubits in length by the husband's sisters. If he has no sisters, this should be done by his and his wife's mothers. Rice conjee is then prepared with water, in which the tamarind juice has been mixed. The husband, and his two companions, sit under the pandal, where the usual lamp and other articles have been placed, with the wife behind him. Her brother then feeds him thrice with the conjee from a small gold spoon. The husband's sister feeds the wife in like manner. One of the three twigs is planted by the husband in the front yard, and his wife waters it every day until the child is born. In the ninth month, the husband's sister presents his wife with a couple of pounds of cummin seed and jaggery. The woman who brings this little gift should be given some cakes and sweetmeats. During pregnancy, a woman always wears an amulet concealed within a cylindrical tube on her neck, to protect her against malignant spirits.

The young wife's child is born at her father's house, where she is under the care of her mother. When the child is born, the brother of the newly made mother goes out into the yard, and strikes the ground three times with the stem of a dry cocoanut palm leaf. If the child is a boy, he emits a long drawn out ku-u-u-u in high falsetto as he does so. It is then the duty of the brother and the midwife to go and inform the father of the event. The midwife receives from him her fee, and a present of a cloth, and other presents from his sisters. If the child is a boy, the brother receives a cloth, and, if a girl, a cloth and a bell-metal plate.

The event of the birth of a child carries with it, as in the case of death, pollution to every one in the house. This is partially removed by ceremonies on the third day, and wholly by further ceremonies on the ninth or eleventh day, whichever happens to be the more auspicious—a Tuesday for example. Any one coming to the house before the first ceremonies have taken place must bathe and wash his or her cloth to remove the pollution. Any one visiting the house after the first, but before the second ceremony, need not bathe, but cannot eat any food in the house. The men of the household can get no rice at home until after the second ceremony has been performed, and they are consequently compelled to board elsewhere for the time being. A washerwoman carries out the purification rites, assisted by a barber woman. First of all, the floors of all the rooms are smeared with cow-dung. All clothes in use are given to the washerwoman. The women rub their bodies all over with oil, and the washerwoman brings māttu for them. The barber woman sprinkles a mixture of cow's milk and karuka grass leaves over the women, who then go to a pool and bathe. When the milk is about to be sprinkled, the usual lamp, rice on a metal plate, and kindi of water are produced. The barber woman takes the rice and one fanam, and receives also some cocoanut and gingelly (*Sesamum*) oil. Much the same things are given to the washerwoman. The second ceremony is just like the first, but, even after its completion, the women of the house cannot touch any cooking-vessels until after the fifteenth day. The ceremony of touching the cooking pots, as at the time of the first menstrual period, is then performed. These three purificatory ceremonies must be performed after every birth.

On the twenty-seventh or fortieth day after the birth of a child, the mother and the infant are taken back to the husband's house, and cow's milk is for the first time given to the child. This event, which has all the solemnity of a regular function, takes place in the middle room, where the lamp, mat and other articles have been arranged. The child's paternal grandfather, father's elder brother, or other senior man administers the milk, which has been boiled. A gold bracelet is dipped in it, and the drops of milk are made to fall into the child's mouth. As this is being done, the celebrant whispers in the child's right ear the name which will be formally given to it in the sixth month. The eldest son is always named after the paternal grandfather, and the second after the father. In like manner, the eldest girl is named after its own mother. Relations and friends take this opportunity to make presents of bracelets and other articles to the infant. A feast is then held. After the ceremony is over, the parents of the child's mother have to send about half a bag of rice flour mixed with jaggery to her husband's house.

For the first six months of its life, a child's food consists of nature's fount and cow's milk. It is then, before the sixth month is over, given boiled rice for the first time. The ceremony takes place either in the middle room of its father's house, or at a temple. The child's grandfather, or the eldest male member of the family, sits on a mat, and takes the child in his lap. With a gold ring he applies honey three times to its mouth, and then gives it a little rice three times. Female relations who are present follow his example, giving the child first honey, and then rice. Several women, with the lighted lamp and other articles, carry the child into the yard, to show it the sky. They go round a cocoanut tree, and stand before the front door, facing west. An elder among the women of the house stands at the front door, calls out the name of the child three times, and asks it to come inside. The relations give little presents of ornaments, and there is a feast.

It will be observed that even a child's life is not entirely free from ceremonial. When it has grown up, it undergoes more of it, and, when it has lived its course on earth, is the subject of still more ceremonial long after it is dead. All these affairs involve some expenditure, but the one which literally runs away with money is marriage. The others are not extravagances, nor are they as costly as might be implied from the continual feasting of a large number of people. We must not think of these feasts as of a banquet at the Carlton, but as simple affairs, at which simple people are content with simple though pleasing fare.

When a child is provided by nature with teeth, it is the subject of a little ceremony, during which it is expected to disclose its natural propensities. The usual mat and other articles are arranged, and there are in addition a large flat bell-metal plate containing a rice cake, a knife, a palmyra leaf grantham (book), a cocoanut, and a gold ornament. The child is let loose, and allowed to pick out anything from the plate. If it takes the cake, it will be greedy; if the knife, brave; if the book, learned; if the cocoanut, a landlord; and, if the gold ornament, rich.

A child's head is shaved in the third or fifth year. The barber, who performs the operation, is allowed to take away the rice which, with the lamp, is at hand. He also receives a fanam and a new cloth. The people of the child's mother bring rice cakes.

The last day of the Dasara festival in the fifth year of a child's life is that on which instruction in the alphabet begins. A teacher, who has been selected with care, or a lucky person holds the child's right hand, and makes it trace the fifty-one letters of the Malayālam alphabet on raw rice spread on a plate. The fore-finger, which is the one used in offering water to the souls of the dead and in other parts of the death ceremonies, must not be used for tracing the letters, but is placed above the middle finger, merely to steady it. For the same reason, a doctor, when making up a pill, will not use the fore-finger. When, later on, the child goes to the village school, the fifty-one letters are written one by one on its tongue with a gold style, if one is available. As each letter is formed, the child has to repeat the sound of it.

The lobes of both a child's ears are bored with a golden pin or a thorn. The helix of the ear is not bored for the purpose of inserting ornaments in it, but is sometimes bored as a remedy for disease, *e.g.*, hernia. Everywhere else in Southern India, it is common for people of almost every class to have the helix of the left ear bored.

The tāli-tying ceremony must be performed before a girl attains puberty. The Tiyan tāli is usually of gold, and worth about half-a-crown. It is not the one which is worn in every day life, but the one which is used in the ceremony about to be described. Throughout Southern India, the tāli is the ordinary symbol of marriage among Hindus, and it is even worn by Syrian Christians. In Malabar, and the Native States of Cochin and Travancore, it is a symbol of marriage, with which a girl is ceremoniously adorned, as a rule before she is affianced. The ceremony occupies three days, on the last of which the tāli is tied. On the first day, a shed or pandal is erected in the front yard. Within it a similar structure is prepared with the leaves of an areca palm, which has been cut down at an auspicious moment, and with the formal sanction of the Tandān of the tara. This inner pandal is tastefully decorated with pictures and flowers. It is important to note that this little pandal must not be begun until the first day of the ceremony. On this day, the carpenter of the tara brings a low wooden seat, rather long and narrow, made from the pala tree (*Alstonia scholaris*), which must be cut at an auspicious moment, for which he receives one fanam. This seat is called mana.[26] A grass mat is spread in the middle room of the house, with a white cloth over it, on which the mana is placed. A lamp, vessel of water, and the usual paraphernalia are arranged on the ground to the south close by. When these preliminaries have been completed, the girl is brought by the uncle's wife to the pandal, and seated on a stool. In front of her, a lamp, and other things which are a feature in all ceremonials, and a measure of paddy are placed on the ground, a gold fanam is put on her head, and over it gingelly oil is poured. As the coin falls from the forehead, it is caught in a cup. It is important which side falls uppermost. The girl is then taken to a pool for bathing, and returns to the pandal. She is conducted to the middle room of the house in procession, with a silk canopy over her head and women carrying lamps, etc. She is confined in this room, which is decorated in the manner described when speaking of the menstruation ceremony, until the third day. She sleeps on a mat, surrounded by a little ridge of rice and paddy, cocoanut and areca palm flowers, and near her head is a copper pot marked with vertical daubs of white. The blacksmith of the tara brings a little stick, called charathkot, with an iron blade at one end, which is supposed to represent an arrow of Kāma. This the girl keeps constantly at her side, and carries in her hand when compelled by nature to leave the room. While confined in the room, she is not allowed to eat fish, flesh, or salt, or see any animals, especially a cat, dog, or crow. On the third day, the tāli is prepared on the spot by the village goldsmith. The girl's uncle gives him the gold, which he melts, and works at in the pandal at an auspicious moment. The paddy and rice, which, with the lamp and vessel of water, have been in evidence during the operations, are given to the goldsmith, with a fanam for his labour. A weaver brings two new cloths, of a particular kind called mantra-kodi, for which the girl's uncle pays. One is worn by the girl, and the mana is covered with the other. The girl is taken to bathe, and, after the bath, is richly dressed and ornamented, and brought in procession, with a canopy over her head, to the house, where she is conducted to the inner room. The mana is then placed, with the cloth near it, on a grass mat in the inner pandal. The uncle's wife sits on the mat, and the uncle lifts the girl, carries her three times round the pandal, and deposits her in his wife's lap. The astrologer, who is present, indicates the moment when the tāli should be tied. The girl's father gives him a fanam, and receives from him a little rice, called muhurtham (auspicious time). When the psychological moment has arrived he sprinkles the rice on the girl's head, saying "It is time." The tāli is then tied round the girl's neck by the uncle's wife. At the upper end of the tāli is a ring, through which the thread passes. The thread which is used

---

[26] Manavalan = bridegroom; Manavati = bride.

for the purpose is drawn from the cloth with which the mana has been covered. [It is odd that there are some families of Nāyars, who are not allowed to use a tāli with a ring to receive the string, and are therefore obliged to make a hole in the tāli itself.] As soon as the tāli has been tied on the girl's neck, a number of boys burst into song, praising Ganapathi (the elephant god), and descriptive of the marriage of King Nala and Damayanti, or of Sri Krishna and Rukmani. Every one joins in, and the song ends with shouts and hurrahs. A mock feeding ceremony is then carried out. Three plantain leaves are spread in front of the girl in the pandal, and rice, plantains, and pappadams are spread thereon. The uncle's wife offers some of each to the girl three times, but does not allow her to touch it with her lips. The girl is then taken to a temple, to invoke the God's blessing.

The description which has just been given is that of the ceremony which is performed, if the girl has not been affianced. If a husband has been arranged for her, it is he who ties the tāli, and his sister takes the place of the uncle's wife. Otherwise the ceremony is the same, with this difference, however, that, when the husband ties the tāli, there can be no divorce, and the girl cannot remarry in the event of his death.

In North, as in South Malabar, the tāli-tying ceremony is always performed before puberty, and occupies four days. This is the orthodox procedure. The girl wears a cloth provided by the washerwoman. She is taken from the middle room of the house to the yard, and there seated on a plank of pala wood. Placed in front of her are a small measure of rice and paddy, a washed white cloth, and a small bell-metal vessel (kindi) on a bell-metal plate. The barber pours cocoanut water on her head, on which a silver and copper coin have been placed. One of her relations then pours water from a vessel containing some raw rice over her head, using two halves of a cocoanut as a spout. The girl is then taken back to the middle room, where she remains for three days. There is a feast in the evening. On the fourth day, a pandal is erected in the front yard, and decorated. The girl is taken to bathe at a neighbouring pool, preceded by women carrying a lamp, a kindi of water, and other things which have been already described. During her absence, the barber performs pūja to Ganapathi in the pandal. After bathing, she cuts a cocoanut in half, and returns in procession, with a silk canopy over her head, amid music and singing, and enters the middle room of the house. The barber woman ties a gold ornament (netti pattam) on her forehead, which she marks with sandal paste, and blackens her eyes with eye-salve. The uncle's wife, preceded by women bearing a lamp and other articles, carries the mana, covered with cloth, from the middle room to the pandal. She walks three times round the pandal, and places the mana on a grass mat, over which has been spread some paddy and some rice where the girl will put her foot. The women who have carried the lamp, etc., return to the room, and escort the girl to the pandal. She walks thrice round it, and takes her seat on the mana. The barber hands her a little rice, which she throws on the lighted lamp, and articles which have been used in the pūja to Ganapathi, and on the post supporting the south-west corner of the pandal. This post should be of pala wood, or have a twig of that tree tied to it. More rice is handed to the girl, and she throws it to the cardinal points of the compass, to the earth, and to the sky. A small earthen pot containing rice, a cocoanut, betel, and areca nuts, is placed near the girl. Into this a variety of articles, each tied up separately in a piece of plantain leaf, are placed. These consist of a gold coin, a silver coin, salt, rice, paddy, turmeric, charcoal, and pieces of an old cadjan leaf from the thatch of the house. The mouth of the pot is then covered over with a plantain leaf tied with string. The girl sprinkles rice three times over the pot, makes a hole in the leaf, and picks out one of the articles, which is examined as an augur of her destiny. Betel leaves and areca nuts are then passed twice round her head, and thrown away. She next twists off a cocoanut from a bunch hanging at a corner of the pandal. Then follows the presentation of cloths called mantra-kodi. These must be new, and of a particular kind. Each of her relations throws one of these cloths over the girl's head. Half of them (perhaps ten or twelve) go to the barber, who, at this point, pours cocoanut water from the leaf of a banyan tree on her head, on which a silver and copper coin have been placed. The astrologer is then asked whether it is time to tie the tāli, and replies three times in the affirmative. The barber woman hands the tāli strung on a thread to the girl's uncle's wife, who ties it round the girl's neck. The barber woman then pours water on the girl's hands. Three times the water is flung upwards, and then to the east, west, south, and north. A cotton wick, steeped in oil, is then twisted round a piece of bamboo, and stuck on a young cocoanut. The girl is asked if she sees the sun, looks at the lighted wick, and says that she does. She is then taken to a cocoanut tree, preceded by the lamp, etc. She walks three times round the tree, and pours water over the root. The ceremony is now concluded, and the girl is marched back to the middle room.

A variation of the tāli-tying ceremony, as performed in Chavakad on the coast between Calicut and Cochin, may be briefly described, because it possesses some interesting features. It is always done by the intended husband, or some one representing him. Seven days prior to the beginning of the ceremony, the carpenter of the tara, with the permission of the Tandān (here called Avakāsi), cuts down an areca palm, and fixes part of it as the south-east post of the booth, at which the tāli will be tied. On the sixth day, the girl is formally installed in the middle room of the house. The carpenter brings a mana of pala wood, the cost of which is paid by the father, and does pūja to it. The bridegroom's party arrive. A lamp is lighted in the booth, which is at this time partly, but not entirely, made ready. Near the lamp are placed a measure of paddy, half a measure (nāzhi) of rice, a looking-glass, a kindi of water, and a wooden cheppu (a rude vessel with a sliding cover). The wives of the Tandān and uncle, together with some other women, bring the girl, and seat her on the mana. The uncle's wife parts her hair, and places a gold fanam on her crown. The Tandān's wife then pours a little oil on it over a leaf of the jāk tree three times. The other women do the same. The girl is then taken to a pool, and bathed. Before her return, the mana should be placed ready for her in the middle room of the house. In the evening there is a feast. On the day but one following, the tāli is tied. The last post of the booth is put up, and it is completed and decorated on the tāli-tying day. A lamp, looking-glass, and other things are put in it. A grass mat is spread on the floor, and a kambli (blanket) and a whitewashed cloth are placed over it. On either side of it is placed a pillow. The bridegroom and his party wait in an adjoining house, for they must not appear on the scene until the psychological moment arrives. The Tandān of the bridegroom's tara, with a few friends, comes first, and hands over two cloths and ten rupees eight annas to the bride's Tandān. The girl is dressed in one of these cloths, and led to the booth, the bridegroom's sister holding her by the hand. She sits on the mana, which has been brought, and placed on the cloth, by her uncle. The bridegroom comes in procession, carried on his uncle's shoulders. The girl is still a child, and he is only a few years her senior. His uncle puts him down on the right side of the girl, after walking thrice round the booth. The girl's uncle's wife sits close to her, on the other side, on the mana. Her father asks the astrologer three times if it is the proper time to tie the tāli, and is answered thrice in the affirmative. Then the boy bridegroom ties the tāli on the girl's neck. The boy and girl sing out a chorus in praise of Ganapathi, and end up with three loud shouts and hurrahs. Then the boy seats himself on the ground, outside the pillow. The girl is taken inside the house, and, after a general feast, is brought back, and seated on the mana, and rice and flowers are sprinkled. No money is paid to the uncle's son, as at Calicut. The boy bridegroom pays eight annas to his sister for leading the bride by the hand. When the marriage has been done by proxy, the boy bridegroom is selected from a tarwad into which the girl might marry. He stays at the girl's house for three days, and, on the fourth day, the boy and girl are taken to a temple. A formal divorce is effected, and the boy is taken away.

TIYANS.

It will not be worth while to attempt a description of the marriage ceremony of the Tiyans of North Malabar, because there is none, or next to none. There the Tiyans and all classes, including even the Muhammadan Māppillas, follow the rule of marumakkatāyam, or inheritance through females from uncle to nephew. The children have no right to their father's property. Either party may annul the marital union at will, without awarding any compensation; and, as its infraction is easy and simple, so is its institution. Nor is there any rigid inquiry as to the antecedents of either party. It is an affair of mutual arrangement, attended with little formality. Proceeding to the girl's house, accompanied by a few friends, the intending husband takes with him a couple of cloths, one for the girl, and the other for her mother. In parts of North Malabar, the Tiyan women wear an ornament called chittu (ring) in a hole bored in the top of the helix of each ear. The holes are bored in childhood, but the chittu is not worn until the girl forms a marital union with a man. The chittus are made on the spot at the time, in the marriage pandal erected for the occasion, the girl's uncle providing the gold. They are never removed during life, except in cases of dire distress. "To sell chittu" is equivalent to having become a pauper. It is supposed that, in olden days, the marriage ceremonies lasted over seven days, and were subsequently reduced to seven meals, or three and a half days, and then to one day. Now the bridegroom remains the first night at the bride's house, and then takes her to his home. Before they leave, a cocoanut, the outer husk of which has been removed, is placed on a stool of pala wood, and one of the bridegroom's party must smash it with his fist. Some of the more orthodox in North Malabar observe the formality of examining horoscopes, and a ceremony equivalent to the conjee-drinking ceremony which has been described, called achāra kaliāna, and the payment of kanam in the shape of forty-one fanams, instead of forty-two as in South Malabar. In connection with fanams it may be noted that the old gold fanam is reckoned as worth four annas, whereas five silver or velli fanams make a rupee. Everywhere in rural Malabar, calculations are made in terms of velli fanams thus: —

10 pice ($\frac{1}{12}$ of an anna) = 1 velli.
5 vellis = 1 rupee.

Bazaar men, and those who sell their small stock at the weekly markets all about the country, arrange their prices in vellis.

When the death of a Tiyan is expected, all the relations draw near, and await the fateful moment. The person who is about to die is laid on the floor of the middle room, for it is inauspicious to die on a cot. We will suppose that the dying man is a parent and a landlord. Each of the sons and daughters gives him a little conjee water, just before he passes away. At the moment of death, all the women bawl out in lamentations, giving the alarm of death. The Cheruman serfs in the fields join in the chorus, and yell out an unintelligible formula of their own. Absent relations are all formally invited. From the houses of the son's wife and daughter's husband are sent quantities of jāk fruits, unripe plantains, and cocoanuts, as death gifts. One half of the husks of the cocoanuts is removed, and the other half left on the shell. After the cremation or burial, these articles are distributed among those present by the Tandān, who receives an extra share for his trouble. When life is extinct, the body is placed with the head to the south, and the thumbs and big toes are tied together. It is then taken out into the yard, washed, bathed in oil, dressed in a new cloth, and brought back to the middle room. A cocoanut is cut in two, and the two halves, with a lighted wick on each, are placed at the head and foot. The house-owner spreads a cotton cloth over the corpse, and all the relations, and friends, do the same. Any one who wishes to place a silk cloth on the corpse may do so, but he must cover it with a cotton cloth. The body is then removed for burial or cremation, and placed near the grave or funeral pyre. It is the rural rule that elderly persons and karnavans of tarwads are cremated, and others buried. The barber, whose function it is to perform the purificatory rites, now removes, and retains as his perquisite, all the cloths, except the last three covering the corpse. As it is being borne away to the place of burial or cremation, water mixed with cow-dung is sprinkled behind it in the yard. The eldest son, who succeeds to the property and is responsible for the funeral ceremonies, then tears crosswise a piece of the cloth which has been placed over the corpse by the people of the house, and ties it round his forehead. He holds one end of the cloth while the barber holds the other, and tears off the piece. The barber then cuts three holes in the remainder of this cloth covering the body, over the mouth, navel, and pubes. A little water and rice are poured over a gold fanam through the slit over the mouth. All who observe the death pollution, *i.e.*, sons, grandsons, nephews, younger brothers and cousins, offer water and rice in the same manner, and walk three times round the grave or pyre. The barber then breaks a pot of water over the grave. No other ceremonial is observed on this day, on which, and during the night, rice must not be eaten. If the body has been cremated, a watch is kept at the burning ground for five days by Pānans, who beat drums all night to scare away the evil spirits which haunt such spots. Early on the second day, all who are under pollution are shaved. The operation is attended with some ceremonial, and, before it is commenced, a lighted lamp, a measure of rice and paddy on a plantain leaf must be at hand. The paddy and rice are a perquisite of the barber. Those who have been shaved bathe, and then follows the crow-feeding ceremony. Rice is boiled in a bell-metal vessel over a hearth prepared with three young cocoanuts. The eldest son, who tore the cloth of succession from the corpse, makes the rice into two little balls, places them on a plantain leaf, and offers them to the spirit of the departed by pouring libations of water on them over a blade of karuka grass. Men and women who are under pollution then do the same. The rice balls are eaten by crows. This little ceremony is performed daily until the eleventh or thirteenth day, when the period of death pollution comes to an end. If the eleventh day happens to fall on a Tuesday or Friday, or on any inauspicious day, the period is extended to the thirteenth day. When the period of death pollution is partly in one month, and partly in another, another death in the house within the year is expected. Preceding the sanchayanam, which occupies the fifth day, there is the lamp-watching on the previous night. In the south-east corner of the middle room, a little paddy is heaped up, and on it is placed a bell-metal plate with an iron lamp having five or seven lighted wicks on it. Under the lamp is a little cow-dung, and close to it is a bunch of cocoanut flowers. The lamp must be kept burning until it is extinguished on the following day. In the case of the death of a male, his niece watches the lamp, and in that of a female her daughter, lying near it on a grass mat. The sanchayanam is the first stage in the removal of death pollution, and, until it is over, all who come to the house suffer from pollution, and cannot enter their own house or partake of any food without bathing previously. When the body has been cremated, the fragments of calcined bones are collected from the ashes, and carried in procession to the sea, or, if this is far away, into a river. The members of the family under pollution then rub their bodies all over with oil, and the barber sprinkles a mixture of cow's milk over their heads, using a blade of karuka grass as a spout. They then bathe, and the eldest son alone observe māttu. The crow-feeding ceremony follows, and, when this is over, the three cocoanuts which were used as a hearth are thrown away. A large bell-metal vessel filled with water is now placed in the front yard before the door of the house. The barber carries the still burning lamp from the middle room, and sets it on the ground near the pot of water. The women who are under pollution come from the middle room, each carrying a lighted wick, walk thrice round the pot, and throw the wicks into the water. The woman who has watched the lamp puts four annas into the pot, and the others deposit a few pies therein. The eldest son now lights a wick from the iron lamp which is about to be extinguished, and with it lights a lamp in the middle room. The barber then dips the iron lamp in the water, and picks out the money as his perquisite. The water is poured on the roots of a cocoanut tree. The bell-metal vessel becomes the property of the woman who watched the lamp, but she cannot take it away until she leaves the house after the pula-kuli ceremony. When the lamp has been extinguished, a woman, hired for the occasion, is seated on a cocoanut leaf in the front yard. The Tandān pours oil on her head three times, and she receives a little betel and two annas. She rises, and leaves the place without turning back, taking the pollution with her. Betel is then distributed. Those who provided the death gifts on the day of the death must on this day bring with them a bag of rice, and about four rupees in money. They have also to give eight annas to the barber. A folded handkerchief is first presented to the barber, who formally returns it, and receives instead of it the eight annas. Before the people disperse, the day of the pula-kuli is settled. Pula-kuli, or washing away the pollution, is the final ceremony for putting off the unpleasant consequences of a death in a family. First of all, the members thereof rub themselves all over with oil, and are sprinkled by the barber with cow's milk and gingelly oil. They then bathe. The barber outlines the figure of a man or woman, according to the sex of the deceased, with rice flour and turmeric powder, the head to the south, in the middle room of the house. The figure is covered with two plantain leaves, on each of which a little rice and paddy are heaped. Over all is spread a new cloth, with a basket containing three measures of paddy upon it. The eldest son (the heir) sits facing the south, and with a nāzhi measures out the paddy, which he casts to the south, east, and west—not the north. He repeats the performance, using the fingers of the left hand closed so as to form a cup as a measure. Then, closing the first and fourth fingers firmly with the thumb, using the left hand, he measures some paddy in the same manner with the two extended fingers. Rice is treated in the same way. A nāzhi of paddy, with a lighted wick over it, is then placed in a basket. The eldest son takes the nāzhi in his left hand, passes it behind his body, and, receiving it with his right hand, replaces it in the basket. The wick is extinguished by sprinkling it with water three times. At the head of the figure on the floor is placed a clean cloth—the washerman's māttu. It is folded, and within the folds are three nāzhis of rice. On the top of it a cocoanut is placed. In the four corners a piece of charcoal, a little salt, a few chillies, and a gold fanam are tied. The eldest son, who is always the protagonist in all the ceremonies after death, lifts the cloth with all its contents, places it on his head, and touches with it his forehead, ears, each side and loins, knees and toes. He does this three times. The plantain leaves are then removed from the figure. A little turmeric powder is taken from the outline, and rubbed on the forehead of the eldest son. He then bows thrice to the figure, crossing his legs and arms so that the right hand holds the left ear, and the left the right ear, and touches the ground with the elbow-joints. It is no joke to do this. All this time, the eldest son wears round his forehead the strip torn from the cloth which covered the corpse. There is nothing more to be done in the middle room for the present, and the eldest son goes out into the yard, and cooks the rice for the final feed to the crows. Three nāzhis of this rice must be pounded and prepared for cooking by the woman who watched the lamp on the fourth night after death. Having cooked the rice, the eldest son brings it into the middle room, and mixes it with some unrefined sugar, plantains and pappadams, making two balls, one large and one small. Each of these he places on a plantain leaf. Then some pūja is done to them, and offerings of rice are made over a gold fanam. The balls are given to the crows in the yard, or, in some cases, taken to the sea or a river, and cast into the water. When this course is adopted, various articles must be kept ready ere the return of the party. These comprise a new pot containing water, a branch of areca blossoms, mango leaves, a kindi containing a gold fanam or gold ring, a little salt and rice, each tied up in a piece of cloth, and a few chillies. The mouth of the pot is covered with a plantain leaf, and secured. There are also two stools, made of pala and mango wood. The eldest son sits on one of these, and places his feet on the other, so that he does not touch the ground. The water in the pot is sprinkled with mango leaves by the barber to the north, south, east and west, and on the head of the son. The remainder of the water is then poured over his head. The barber then sprinkles him with cocoanut water, this time using areca blossoms, and makes him sip a little thereof. The barber makes a hole in the plantain leaf, and picks out the contents. The eldest son bathes, and after the bath there is a presentation of gifts. The barber, sitting in the verandah beside the son, first gives to each person under pollution a little salt and raw rice, which they eat. He then gives them a little betel leaf and a small piece of areca nut, and receives in return a quarter of an anna. The eldest son chews the betel which he has received, and spits into a spittoon held by the barber, whose property it becomes. Then to the barber, who has been presented with a new mat to sit on and new cloth to wear before he seats himself in the verandah, are given an earring such as is worn by Tiyan women, a silk cloth, a white cotton cloth, and a few annas. If the deceased has been cremated he is given six fanams, and, if buried, five fanams as the fee for his priestly offices. On an occasion of this kind, several barbers, male and female, turn up in the hope of receiving presents. All who help during the various stages of the ceremonial are treated in much the same way, but the senior barber alone receives the officiating fee. It is odd that the barbers of the four surrounding villages are entitled to receive gifts of new cloths and money. Those under death pollution are forbidden to eat fish or flesh, chew betel, or partake of jaggery. The restriction is removed on the pula-kuli day. The last act for their removal is as follows. The barber is required to eat some jaggery, and drink some conjee. After this, the eldest son, the Tandān, and a neighbour, sit on a mat spread in the middle of the house, and formally partake of conjee and jaggery. The pula-kuli is then over.

It is a sacred duty to a deceased person who was one of importance, for example the head of a family, to have a silver image of him made, and arrange for it being deposited in some temple, where it will receive its share of pūja (worship), and offerings of food and water. The new-moon day of the months Karkitakam (July-August), Tulam (October-November), and Kumbham (February-March) is generally selected for doing this. The temples at Tirunelli in Wynād and Tirunavayi, which are among the oldest in Malabar, were generally the resting-places of these images, but now some of the well-to-do deposit them much further afield, even at Benares and Rāmēsvaram. A silver image is presented to the local Siva temple, where, for a consideration, pūja is done every new-moon day. On each of these days, mantrams are supposed to be repeated a thousand times. When the image has been the object of these mantrams sixteen thousand times, it is supposed to have become eligible for final deposit in a temple. It is this image which rests in the temple at Tirunavayi, or elsewhere.

An annual srādh ceremony is performed for the sake of the spirit of the deceased, at which crows are fed in the manner already described, and relations are fed. On the night of this day, some sweetmeats or cakes, such as the deceased was fond of during life, are offered to the spirit. A lamp is placed on a stool, and lighted in the middle room of the house, with a kindi of water and a young cocoanut near it. The cakes or sweetmeats are placed in front of the stool. Children sprinkle rice over it, and the door is shut for a quarter of an hour. The individual who feeds the crows should partake of only one meal, without fish or flesh, on the previous day. Another ceremony, which is necessary for the repose of the dead, is called badha-velichatu-variethal, or bringing out the spirit. It cannot be performed until at least a year after death, for during that period the spirit is in a sort of purgatory. After that, it may be invoked, and it will answer questions. The ceremony resembles the nelikala pregnancy ceremony. The performers are Pānans or washermen. Some little girls are seated in front of a booth in the yard. The celebrant of the rite sings, invoking the spirit of the deceased. Late at night, one of the girls becomes possessed by the spirit, and, it is said, talks and acts just like the deceased, calling the children, relations and friends by name, talking of the past, and giving commands for the future conduct of the living members of the family. After this, the spirit is severed from earthly trammels, and attains heavenly bliss.

The wood used for the purpose of cremation is that of a mango tree, which must be cut down after the death. A little sandalwood and cuscus (grass) roots are sometimes added to the pyre. In these days, when the important and interesting features of ceremonial are fast disappearing, it is not surprising that dried cakes of cow-dung are superseding the mango wood.

Among other ceremonies, there is one called kutti pūja, which is performed when a newly built house is taken charge of. Vastu Purusha is the name of the supreme being which, lying on its back with its head to the north-east and legs to the south-west, supports the earth. Or rather the earth is but a small portion of this vast body. Forests are its tiny hairs, oceans its blood-vessels, and the wind its breath. In this body are fifty-three deities, who are liable to disturbance when the surface of the earth is dug, when trees are felled, foundations laid, and a house built. These angry beings must be propitiated, or there will be untimely deaths, poverty, and sickness among the inmates. The ceremony is performed in the following manner. A square with fifty-three columns is made with rice flour in the middle room of the house, and each column is filled with yellow, red, and black powder. A plantain leaf is placed over it, and a few measures of paddy are set on the top of the leaf. On this is placed another leaf, with various kinds of grain, plantains, cocoanuts, and jaggery on it. The carpenter, who is the architect and builder of the house, then performs pūja with flowers, incense and lights, and the troublesome imp-spirit Gulikan is propitiated with toddy and arrack, and a fowl which is decapitated for him. Then all the workmen—carpenters, masons, and coolies—walk thrice round the house, breaking cocoanuts on the walls and doors, and howling in order to drive away all evil spirits which may by chance be lurking about the place. After this, they are all fed until they cry out "We are satisfied, and want no more." They are given cloths and other presents, and the chief feature of the ceremony takes place. This is the formal handing over of the house by the carpenter. He hands it over to a third person, and never directly to the owner. It is not always easy to find a third person who is willing to undertake the responsibility, and who is at the same time suitable for the Gulikan who is dispossessed of the house, and pursues him henceforth, following him who first receives charge of the house. He should be a man who brings luck, cheerful and contented, having a family, and not labouring under any disorder or sickness of body. There is, or was a few years ago, an old Nāyar living not far from Calicut, who was much sought after to fulfil the functions of third person on these occasions, and all the houses he received prospered. The third person is generally a poor man, who is bribed with presents of cloths, money and rice, to undertake the job. He wears one of the new cloths during the ceremony. When the carpenter's ceremonies have been completed, this man is taken to the middle room of the house, and made to stand facing the door, with each foot on a plantain leaf. Pieces of the thatch are tied to the four corners of his cloth. He shuts the door, opens it, and shuts it again. The carpenter calls from without, asking him whether he has taken charge of the house. He replies evasively "Have the carpenters and workmen received all their wages? If they have, I take charge of the house." The carpenter does not answer the question, for, if he did so, the mischief would be transferred to him through the house-owner. So he says "I did not ask you about my wages. Have you taken charge of the house?" The man inside answers as before, adding "otherwise not." The carpenter again says "I did not ask you about my wages. Answer me straight. Have you, or have you not taken charge of the house?" The man inside replies "I have taken charge of the house," and opens the door. Taking in his hands the plantain leaves on which he stood, he runs away as fast as he can without looking back. This he must not do on any account. The people pelt him with plantains, and hoot at him as he runs, and water mingled with cow-dung is sprinkled in his path. After all this, cow's milk is boiled with a little rice in the house, of which every one partakes, and the owner assumes charge of his house.

In the pre-British days, a few of the well-to-do families of Tiyans lived in houses of the kind called nalapura (four houses), having an open quadrangle in the centre. But, for the most part, the Tiyans—slaves of the Nāyars and Nambūtiris—lived in a one-roomed thatched hut. Nowadays, the kala pura usually consists of two rooms, east and west.

Toddy-drawing, and every thing connected with the manufacture and sale of arrack (country liquor) and unrefined sugar, form the orthodox occupation of the Tiyan. But members of the community are to be found in all classes of society, and in practically all professions and walks of life. It is interesting to find that the head of a Tiyan family in North Malabar bears the title Cherayi Panikar, conferred on the family in the old days by a former Zamorin. A title of this kind was given only to one specially proficient in arms. Even in those days there were Tiyan physicians, bone-setters, astrologers, diviners, and sorcerers.

It is easy to identify the toddy-tapper by the indurated skin of the palms, fingers, inner side of the forearms, and the instep. The business of toddy-tapping involves expert climbing, while carrying a considerable paraphernalia, with no adventitious aid other than can be got out of a soft grummet of coir to keep the feet near together, while the hands, with the arms extended, grasp the palm tree. The profession is rarely adopted before the age of eighteen, but I have seen a man who said he began when he was twelve years old. It is very hard work. A tapper can work about fifteen trees, each of which he has to climb three times a day. In the northern districts of the Madras Presidency, among the Telugu population, the toddy-drawers use a ladder about eight or nine feet in length, which is placed against the tree, to avoid climbing a third or a fourth of it. While in the act of climbing up or down, they make use of a wide band, which is passed round the body at the small of the back, and round the tree. This band is easily fastened with a toggle and eye. The back is protected by a piece of thick soft leather. It gives great assistance in climbing, which it makes easy. All over the southernmost portion of the peninsula, among the Shānāns and Tiyans, the ladder and waist-band are unknown. They climb up and down with their hands and arms, using only the grummet on the feet. The Tiyan toddy-tapper's equipment consists of a short-handled hatchet, about seven inches square, of thin iron, sheathed in a wooden case, and fastened to a waist-belt composed of several strings of coir yarn, to which is hung a small pot of gummy substance obtained by bruising the leaves of the aichil plant. A vessel holding a couple of gallons, made out of the spathe of the areca palm, is used for bringing down the toddy. Tucked into the waist-belt is a bone loaded with lead at either end, which is used for tapping the palm to bring out the juice. A man once refused to sell at any price one of these bones—the femur of a sāmbar (*Cervus unicolor*), which had such virtue that, according to its owner, it would fetch palm juice out of any tree. The garb of the tapper at work consists of a short cloth round the loins, and (always during the rains, and often at other times) a head-covering somewhat pointed in shape, made of the leaves of the cocoanut palm placed together as in a clinker-built boat, or of a rounded shape, made out of the spathe of the areca palm. The toddy-tapper should go through the show of reverence by touching the cocoanut tree with the right hand, and then applying his hand to the forehead, every time he prepares to climb a tree.

In connection with toddy-drawing, the following note occurs in the Gazetteer of Malabar. "The tapper and the toddy shopkeeper are generally partners, the former renting the trees, paying the tree-tax, and selling the toddy at fixed prices to the latter. Sometimes the shopkeeper pays both rent and tax, and the tapper is his servant paid by the bottle. The trees are rented half yearly, and the rent varies between Re. 1 and Re. 1–8–0 per tree. They are fit for tapping as soon as they come into bearing, but four years later and in the succeeding decade are most productive. They are seldom tapped for more than six months in the year, and the process, though it shortens the life of the tree, improves the yield of nuts in the rest of the year. The tapper's outfit is neither costly nor elaborate. A knife in a wooden case, a bone weighted with lead (the leg bone of a sambhur for choice), a few pots, and two small rings of rope with which to climb complete the tale. Operations begin when the spathe is still enclosed by its sheath. Once a day the spathe is gently bruised on either side with the bone, and on the third and following days a thin slice is cut off the end twice a day. On the fifteenth day drawing begins, and the bruising ceases. Sheath and spathe are swathed for the greater part of their length in a thick covering of leaves or fibre; the ends are still cut off twice or three times a day, but, after each operation, are smeared with a paste made of leaves and water with the object, it is said, of keeping the sap from oozing through the wound and rotting the spathe. The leaves used for this purpose are those of the éechal or vetti tree, which are said to be one and the same (*Aporosa Lindleyana*); but in British Cochin, where the tree does not grow, backwater mud is utilised. Round the space between the end of the sheath and the thick covering of leaves a single leaf is bound, and through this the sap bleeds into a pot fastened below. The pot is emptied once a day in the morning. The yield of sap varies with the quality of the tree and the season of the year. In the hot months the trees give on an average about a bottle a day, in the monsoon and succeeding months as much as three bottles. In the gardens along the backwaters, south of Chēttuvāyi, Messrs. Parry & Co. consider that in a good year they should get a daily average of three bottles or half a gallon of toddy per tree. A bottle of toddy sells for three or four pies."

In connection with the coir industry, it is noted, in the Gazetteer of Malabar, that "the husks of the cocoanuts are buried in pits as near as possible to the water-line of rivers, backwaters and creeks, and are left to soak for six months, a year, or even eighteen months—the longer the better. The colour of the yarn, and thereby the quality, depends very much on the water in which the husks are steeped. It should be running water, and, if possible, fresh water. If the water be salt, the yarn may at first be almost white, but in a damp climate it soon becomes discoloured and blotchy. As soon as the husks are taken out of the pits, the fibre is beaten out with short sticks by Tiyattis (Tiyan females) and women of the Vēttuvan caste. It is dried in the sun for twelve hours, and is then ready for sale to native merchants at Calicut and Cochin, who in their turn deal with the European firms. The fibre is twisted into yarn by Tiyattis and other women, and in that form the greater part of the coir made in Malabar is exported from Cochin to all parts of the world, but chiefly to the United Kingdom and Germany."

TIYA FEMALES AT A COIR FACTORY.

It has been said that "in North Malabar the preparation of coir is a regular cottage industry of the most typical kind. Throughout the year, wherever one goes, one hears the noise of the women hammering out the fibre, and sees them taking, in the evening, that part of it which they have rolled into yarn to the nearest little wayside shop, to be exchanged for salt, chillies, paddy, etc. But, in the north of the district, nothing of the kind goes on, and the coir is commonly used as fuel."

It has been already stated that marumakkatāyam, or inheritance through nephews, is the invariable rule in North Malabar, being followed even by the Muhammadan Māppillas. In South Malabar, where the Tiyans do not observe marumakkatāyam, the property devolves through the sons. All sons share alike. Daughters have no share. The practice of polyandry, which still exists in Malabar among the Tiyans (and other classes), and which was probably once general, tends to prevent dispersion of the family property. Although theoretically all sons share the property of their father, it is the eldest son who succeeds to possession and management of the tarwad property. The others are entitled to maintenance only, so long as they remain in the same tarwad house. It is the same among the Izhuvans.

Beef, as in the case of all Hindus, is forbidden as an article of diet. The staple food is rice with fish curry. The common beverage is conjee, but this is being supplanted by tea, coffee, lemonade, and soda-water.

A loin-cloth, which should not reach to the knees, with a Madras handkerchief on the shoulders, is the orthodox dress of the males, and a double loin-cloth that of females. Women were not allowed to wear anything above the waist, except when under death pollution. Any colour might be worn, but white and blue are most common. A ring, composed of hollow gold beads, called mani-kathila, is the proper ornament for a Tiyan woman's ear. Twenty or thirty, with a pendant in the middle, might be worn. Gold or silver bracelets could be worn. Hollow silver bracelets were worn by girls until the birth of their first child. But times have changed, and nowadays Tiyan women wear the ornaments which, strictly speaking, appertain to Nāyar and Brāhman women. Their mode of tying the hair, and even their dress, which is inclined to follow the fashion of the Christians, has changed. In olden days, a Tiyan woman could wear an ornament appropriate for a Nāyar on a special occasion, but only with the permission of the Nāyar landlord, obtained through the Tandān, on payment of a fee.

In North Malabar a good round oath is upon Perumāl Iswaran, the God of the shrine at Kōtiyūr. In South Malabar it is common to swear by Kodungallūr Bhagavati, or by Guruvayūr Appan, local deities.

The Tandān is the principal person in the tara, to decide all caste disputes. In South Malabar, he is, as a rule, appointed by the senior Rāni of the Zamorin. A fee of anything up to 101 fanams (Rs. 25–4–0) must be paid to this lady, when she appoints a Tandān. When there is a problem of any special difficulty, it is referred to her for decision. In territories other than those within the power of the Zamorin, the local Rāja appoints the Tandān, and gives the final decision in special cases. As we have seen, the Tiyan is always to some extent subordinate to a Nāyar overlord, but he is not bound to any particular one. He can go where he likes, and reside anywhere, and is not bound to any particular chief, as is the Nāyar. It is noted by

General E. F. Burton,[27] in connection with bygone days, that "such was the insolent pride of caste that the next (and very respectable) class of Hindus, the Teers, were not allowed to come near the Nairs, under penalty of being cut down by the sword, always naked and ready."

In connection with the religion of the Tiyans, I may commence with an old tradition, which is no doubt from a Brāhmanic source. Once upon a time there were seven heavenly damsels, who used to bathe every day before dawn in a lake situated in a forest. Siva found this out, and appeared as a fire on the bank, at which the girls warmed themselves. Having thus lured them, the God made all of them mothers. Seven beautiful boys were born, and Siva presented them to Parvati, who treated them as if they were her own sons. They were taken to mount Kailāsa, and employed in preparing toddy for the mysterious and wonderful Sakti worship. Daily they brought the toddy at the moment when it was required for the golden pot. Parvati embraced the boys all at once, and they became one. On a certain day, this boy sent the sacred toddy in charge of a Brāhman, who became curious to know the virtues of the mysterious liquid. As he rested on a river bank thinking about it, he drank a little, and filled the vessel up with water. Then he reached Kailāsa too late for the daily worship. Siva was angry, and ordered the Saunika boy (Parvati's name for him) to be brought before him. But the boy had been told what had happened, and cut off the head of the Brāhman, who had confessed to him. Seeing the boy coming along carrying a Brāhman's head, Siva was astonished, and commanded him to approach nearer. The boy explained that it was not a heinous crime to cut off the head of one who had prevented the Sakti worship. Siva said that the killing of a Brāhman was the worst of crimes, and put the perpetrator out of caste. He would not listen to the boy, who replied that whoever prevented Sakti worship was a Chandāla, and condemned him. The boy asked for death at Siva's hands. The request pleased the God, who forgave him. The boy had to remain out of caste, but was initiated into the mysteries of Sakti worship as the surest means of salvation, and to him was given the exclusive privilege of performing Sakti worship with liquor. He was commanded to follow, and imitate the Brāhmans in everything, except in the matter of repeating the sacred mantrams. By tantrams (signs with the hands) he eventually obtained the merit of making pūja with mantrams. He was the first Tiyan.

It is pretty safe to say that all the ideas of the Tiyans connected with pure Hinduism—the Hinduism of the Vēdas—and of tradition, of which we see very little in Southern India, and which in Malabar is more perverted in confused ideas than perhaps elsewhere, those relating to re-birth, karma, pilgrimages to Benares and distant temples are borrowed from the Brāhmans. In the ceremonies which have been described, notably in those connected with marriage and death, we have seen the expression of many Hindu ideas. Not so is all that relates to offerings to the dead. That is the common property of all the children of men.

A main feature in the religion of the Tiyan is that it is largely connected with Sakti worship. Some Brāhmans indulge therein, but they are unable, like the Tiyans, to use arrack in connection with it, and are obliged to use, instead of this

---

[27] An Indian Olio.

requisite, milk or honey. Siva, not exactly a Vēdic entity, and Sakti, are supposed to be the two primordial and eternal principles in nature. Sakti is, perhaps, more properly the vital energy, and Sakti worship the worship of the life principle in nature. We are not considering the abstract meaning of the term Sakti; nor are we now thinking of the Siva of Monier Williams or Max Müller. We are in Malabar, where the Hinduism of the Vēdas is in almost hopeless confusion, and mingled with animism and nearly every other kind of primitive religious idea. It is not therefore at all an easy task to represent in words anything like a rational conception of what the religion of the Tiyan really is. The poor and ignorant follow, in a blind ignorant way, Hinduism as they know it and feel it. Their Hinduism is very largely imbued with the lower cult, which, with a tinge of Hinduism, varied in extent here and there, is really the religion of the people at large all over Southern India. The Tiyans have a large share of it. To the actions of evil and other spirits are attributable most, if not all of the ills and joys of life. The higher Hinduism is far above them. Nevertheless, we find among them the worship of the obscure and mysterious Sakti, which, unfortunately, is practiced in secret. Nobody seems to be in the least proud of having anything to do with it. In fact, they are rather ashamed to say anything about it. Those who, so to speak, go in for it are obliged to undergo preliminary purificatory ceremonies, before the great mystery can be communicated to them. The mantram, which is whispered by the guru (religious preceptor) in the ear of the devotee is said to be "Brahma aham, Vishnu aham, Bhairavu aham" (I am Brahma, I am Vishnu, I am Bhairavan). It is believed that each individual is a spark of the divinity. Having in him the potentiality of the Supreme Being, he can develop, and attain godhood. There is no distinction of caste in Sakti worship. The devotees may belong to the highest or to the lowest castes, though I doubt very much whether the Nambūtiri Brāhmans indulge in it. The novices, of whatever caste, eat and drink together during the period of pūja. Men and women participate in the secret rites. A solemn oath is taken that the mystery of Sakti will not be revealed, except with the permission of the guru, or on the death-bed. The spirit of the goddess (for Sakti is thought of as the female principle) must be withdrawn from the body of the Sakti worshipper when he is at the point of death. A lamp is lighted beside him. A few leaves of the tulsi plant (*Ocimum sanctum*), a little rice, and a lighted wick are given to the dying man. Holding these things, he makes three passes over his body from head to foot, and, as it were, transfers the spirit to the next man, at the same time communicating his wishes about continuing the worship, and so on. When a man dies before this separation or transfer has been accomplished, a Brāhman must be called in, who, with a silver image representing the deceased, makes symbolic transference of the Sakti spirit. It must be done somehow, or the soul of the deceased cannot attain salvation. It is said that, like many other things in this land, Sakti worship has undergone degeneration, that such lofty ideas and feelings as may have once pervaded it have more or less disappeared, and that the residue is not very edifying. Be this as it may, in every tara there is a Bhagavati temple for Tiyans, where Tiyans officiate as priests. The Komaram (oracle) of the Bhagavati temple is clothed in red, and embellished with red sandal paste mixed with turmeric. Bhagavati is always associated with various jungle spirits or gods, whose Komarams always wear black. There is no daily worship in Tiyan temples, with the exception of a few in the neighbourhood of Cannanore. But there is an annual celebration of pūja during the mannalam (forty day) period, commencing on the first of the month Vrischikam (15th November). Lamps are lighted, and worship is begun on this day, and continued for forty days. At its conclusion, the jungle gods retire to the jungle until the next year. A death in the family of a Komaram involves, I believe, some postponement of the rites. The period is supposed to be first part of the functional activity of the earth, which ends somewhere about the 21st of June. It is during this period that Sakti worship is carried on.

The temple of Subramania at Palni in the Madura district is a favourite objective for Tiyan pilgrims. The subject of pilgrimages to this temple has been touched on in my note on the Nāyars (*see* Nāyar). The Bhagavati temple at Kodungallūr in Cochin territory on the coast is another favourite place of pilgrimage among the Tiyans. All classes of people, with the exception of Brāhmans, undertake this pilgrimage. Everyone under a vow, proceeding to the festival, which takes place in February or March, carries with him a cock, which is beheaded at the shrine. Under the Perumāls, pilgrimage to Kodungallūr was somewhat compulsory. This temple was a fruitful source of revenue to the State, for not only the Tiyans, but the fisherman and artisan castes had their own temple in every tara in the land, and the Mūppan—the Komaram—of each temple was under an obligation to contribute yearly gifts to the temple at Kodungallūr. Rent for the temple lands was set at a nominal figure—a mere pepper-corn rent as acknowledgment of sovereign right. Rent might not be paid in times of trouble, but the gifts eked out of superstition were unfailing. It is not surprising, therefore, that learning and advancement among the inferior castes did not receive much encouragement from the rulers of those days.

The temple of Kotiyūr in North Malabar is also a shrine to which Tiyans make pilgrimage. Indeed, it may be said that they follow Hinduism generally in rather a low form, and that Sakti worship is perhaps more peculiarly theirs than others', owing to their being able to use arrack, a product of the palm, and therefore of their own particular métier. The highest merit in Sakti can be reached only through arrack. The Sakti goddess, Bhagavati, the Tiyans look upon as their own guardian spirit.

As instancing the mixture and confusion of religious ideas in Malabar, it may be mentioned that Māppillas have been known to indulge in Sakti worship, and Tiyans to have made vows, and given offerings at Māppilla mosques and Christian churches. Vows to the well-known mosque at Mambram are made by people of almost every caste. It is not uncommon to present the first fruit of a jāk tree, or the milk of a cow when it brings forth its first calf, to the local Tangal or Māppilla priest.

In many, perhaps in most Tiyan houses, offerings are made annually to a bygone personage named Kunnath Nāyar, and to his friend and disciple Kunhi Rāyan, a Māppilla. It is probable that they excelled in witchcraft and magic, but, according to the story, the Nāyar worshipped the kite until he obtained command and control over all the snakes in the land. The offerings are made in order to prevent accidents from snakes. The snake god will also give children to the family, and promote domestic prosperity. Men without offspring worship him. Leprosy and the death of a child are believed to be the consequence of killing a snake. There are Māppilla devotees of Kunnath Nāyar and Kunhi Rāyan, who exhibit snakes in a box, and collect alms. There is a snake mosque near Manarghāt, at the foot of the Nīlgiri hills, which has its annual festival. The alms are collected ostensibly for this mosque.

An interesting story, which is the legendary account of the exodus of the artisans from Malabar, and their return with the Tiyans, is narrated by the Pānans. There were, in olden times, five recognised classes, which includes the Āsāris (carpenters), Musāris (workers in bell-metal), Thattāns (goldsmiths), and Perin-Kollans (blacksmiths). The fifth class is unknown. When an individual of the artisan classes dies, the Pānan of the tara must bring a death gift to the house, which consists of cocoanuts and jāk fruits or plantains. The Pānan places the gift in the yard and repeats a long formula, which he has learnt by heart. It is very likely that he knows little or nothing of its meaning. But he reels it off, and at its conclusion the gifts are accepted. The same formula is also always repeated among the carpenters, goldsmiths, and blacksmiths during wedding and tāli-tying ceremonies. It relates how the artisans deserted the land of Chēraman Perumāl, and sought an asylum in the country of the Izhuvans with the island king, and how the Perumāl sent the Pānan to bring them back. Every one knows this old story, and believes it firmly. It must be learnt by heart, and the Pānan gives it in the yard when a member of the artisan classes dies. The story is to the following effect. During the four Yugams, Kreta, Treta, Dwapara, and Kāli, many kings reigned over the earth. Parasu Rāman destroyed the Kshatriya kings on twenty-one occasions, and was obliged to make atonement in expiatory ceremonies. He worshipped Varuna, the ocean god, and recovered from the sea a hundred and sixty kāthams of land, consisting of Kōlanād (?), Vēnād (Travancore), Kanya Kumāri (Cape Comorin), Chēranād, and Malayālam up to Changala Vazhi beyond the Anaimalai hills. Chēraman Perūmāl was the ruler of this land, in which were the four castes. His capital was at Tiruvanja Kolam. One day, Veluthēdan[28] Chiraman was washing the Perumāl's cloths in a tank. He beat the cloths on a stone which was flat on the ground, and held one of the cloths in his hand. A girl of the carpenter caste, Ayyesvari by name, was just then going to the tank to bathe after her monthly period. She called out "Ho! Kammal.[29] That is not the way to wash cloths. Put a small stone under one end of your washing stone, so as to make it slope a little. Then hold both ends of the cloth in your hand, and beat the middle of the cloth on the stone." The Veluthēdan did so, and found that he washed better, and the cloths were whiter. The Perumāl asked him "Were you not washing the cloths before? Who washed them to-day?" To which the Veluthēdan replied "Oh! Tamburān (chief or lord), a carpenter girl instructed your slave to-day how to wash cloths properly. May Perumāl be pleased to order the girl to be given to your slave as his wife." Perumāl then said "To whatever caste she may belong, you may take her by force, and will not lose your caste." Having received the king's permission, Veluthēdan Chira-

[28] The washerman of the Nambūtiris and Nāyars is called Veluthēdan.

[29] Nāyars are addressed as Kammal by Tiyans and artisans.

man concealed himself near the carpenter's house, and, when the girl opened the door to sweep the yard at dawn, he seized her, and carried her off to his house. Carpenter Sankaran of Tiruvanja Kalam went to the Perumāl, and complained that Veluthēdan Kammal had carried away his daughter, and disgraced him. He asked the Perumāl whether he would give him an armed guard to rescue her. To which the Perumāl replied "I will not help either party with armed men. You must fight it out among yourselves." Then the five classes of artisans consulted one another, and made common cause. The Pānans, Perin Malayans, and Chēn (red) Koravans joined the artisans. The Ven Thachāns, Vēlans, Paravans, Vēttuvans, Kanisan Panikars, and the Pāndi Pulluvans of Vellālanād joined the other side. There was war for twelve years. In the end, the artisans were defeated. They said among themselves "We have been defeated by the fourteenth caste of Veluthēdan Nāyar, who carried away our daughter. Let us leave this country." So 7,764 families, with the women and children, tied up their mats, and left Chēramān Perumāl's country, and went to Izhuva land, which was beyond it. They went before the Izhuva king (island king), and told him their story. Now Chēramān Perumāl used to be shaved every fifteen days. When the barber (Velakathalavan) was sent for, he came without his knife (razor), as his wife had buried it. He said "Oh! Tamburan, have mercy on your slave. Your slave's knife was given to the blacksmith to be mended, and he took it away with him. He gave me this piece of iron, saying "If you want the knife made ready for use, you must come to the Izhuva land for it, and we will mend it on our return." So Perumāl had to go without shaving, and his hair grew like a Rishi's. As there were neither carpenters nor smiths to make implements, agriculture was almost at a standstill; and, as there were no goldsmiths, the tāli-tying ceremonies could not be performed. Nor could the rice-giving ceremony be done, for want of the "neck-rings." Then Chēramān Perumāl obtained advice, and resolved to send the Mannān (washerman of the Tiyans), who was included in the fourteenth caste, and the Pānan, who belonged to the eleventh caste. The Perumāl gave to each of them a thousand fanams, and told them to go to the Izhuva country, and bring back the Kammālans (artisans). They wandered over various countries, stopping wherever they found a house. The Pānan, being clever, was able to live by his wits, and spent no money of his own. The Mannān, on the contrary, spent all his money. They passed Ramapūri, and reached Trichivampūri. Then the Mannān asked the Pānan for a loan, which was refused. On Friday at noon, the Mannān left the Pānan, saying "The Pānan is no companion for the Mannān." He returned to the Perumāl and reported his failure, and the Pānan's refusal to lend him money. The Pānan went on, crossing rivers, canals, and ferries, and at last reached the Izhuva king's country. He entered the reception hall. At that moment, the king's goldsmith, who had just finished making a golden crown for him, had put it on his own head, to test its suitability for wearing. The Pānan thought he was the king, and made obeisance to him. The Kammālans recognised him. He discovered his mistake too late, for he had addressed the goldsmith as Tamburan. So, to this day, the Pānans, when addressing goldsmiths, say Tamburan. The Pānan told the Kammālans of his mission, but they refused to return unless full reparation was made for the abduction of the carpenter girl, and certain social disabilities were removed. The 7,764 families of Kammālans asked the Izhuva king his advice, and he said that they should not go away. So the Kammālans sent the Pānan back, and gave him the following presents, in order to demonstrate to the Perumāl that they were in comfortable circumstances:—

Gold valam-piri (a sort of string worn over the right shoulder);
Silver edam-piri (a similar sort of string worn on the left shoulder);
Gold netti-pattam (to be tied on the forehead);
Gold bracelet;
Gold ornament for the hair.

The Kammālans sent word to the Perumāl that they would not return, unless they were given a girl in place of the carpenter's daughter, who had been abducted, and certain privileges were granted to them. At the same time, they promised the Pānan that they would share their privileges with him, if he was successful. So the Pānan returned, and appeared before the Perumāl, who asked him where the Kammālans were. The Pānan removed his gold cap, and put it under his arm, and replied that they were prosperous, and not anxious to return. Saying so, he placed before the Perumāl the rich presents given by the Kammālans, and told the king that they would not return, unless they were given a girl and certain concessions. The Perumāl told the Pānan to go back, and invite the Kammālans to return on their own terms. He said they would catch the first girl they met on the way to his palace, and all their demands were granted. The Pānan arrived again in the Izhuva country, and told the Kammālans what the Perumāl had said. They went to the Izhuva king, and obtained his permission to return to their own country. Then they caught an Izhuva boy, and confined him. The king asked them why they did so. They replied that they had lived for twelve years[30] as his subjects, and would never recognise any other king, so they wanted the Izhuva boy to represent him. The king consented. When they started, the boy began to cry. A Nasrāni,[31] by name Thomma (Thomas), was taken to accompany and protect the boy. The Kammālans travelled to their own country, and appeared before Chēramān Perumāl. On the way, they found a girl of the Variar caste plucking flowers, and caught her by the hand. All the five classes claimed her. At last it was resolved to unite her with the Izhuva boy, their Tandān, who represented their king, and treat her as their sister. Chēramān Perumāl confirmed his promise, and granted the following privileges to the Kammālans:—

1. To make ceilings for their houses.

2. To make upstairs houses to live in.

3. To put up single staircases, consisting of one pole, in which notches are cut, or pegs are stuck alternately, for the feet.

4. To have a gate-house.

5. To perform the tāli-tying ceremonies of their girls in a booth having four posts or supports; to place within it, on a stool, a looking-glass with a handle, and the Rāmayana; and to place a silk cloth on the girl's head.

---

[30] The number twelve, so significant in Malabar.
[31] Nasrāni (Nazarene) is a term for Christians on the west coast.

6. To do arpu at the conclusion of the tāli-tying ceremony (Vel! Arpu! is yelled out by the boys).

7. To cook rice in copper vessels on occasions of marriage and other ceremonies, and to serve sugar and pappadams at their feasts.

8. To hold the umbrella and taza (a sort of umbrella), which are carried in front of processions.

9. To clap hands, and dance.

10. To keep milch-cows for their own use.

Permission was further granted for the Kammālans to wear the following ornaments.

1. Netti-pattam, worn on the forehead during the tāli-tying ceremony.

2. Ananthovi, a ear ornament named after Anandan, the endless, the serpent on which Vishnu reposes. The serpent is sometimes represented with its tail in its mouth, forming a circle, an endless figure. Ananthovi is the central pendant of the ear-ring worn by Tiyan women among their kathila (ordinary gold ear-rings). It resembles a serpent in form. It is worn by men of the Tiyan and artisan castes on special occasions.

3. Waist zone or girdle.

4. Bracelets.

5. Anklet with two knobs, formed of two pieces screwed together.

6. Puli-mothiram, or tiger's claws mounted in gold, worn by children.

7. Podippu, a knot of cotton-thread at the end of the string on which coins are hung as ornaments.

8. Kalanchi, a gold knob above the podippu, which represents a flower.

9. Necklace.

10. Edakam and madkam-tāli, neck ornaments, in one of which are set twenty-one stones.

11. Cotton thread above the gold thread on the neck.

The Perumāl conferred like privileges upon the family (Tiruvarankath) of the Pānan who brought back the Kammālans. He wore all his ornaments, and made his obeisance to the Perumāl. He had, however, taken off his gold cap. The Perumāl said "What you have removed, let it be removed." So he lost the privilege of wearing a gold cap. The Perumāl blessed the Kammālans, and they returned to their villages. They made a separate house for the Izhuva boy and the Variar girl, and maintained them. The Izhuva boy, who was the first Tiyan to come to Malabar, brought with him the cocoanut, and retained the right to cultivate and use it. To this day, the people of the serf castes—Cherumans, Kanakans, and the like—use the word Varian when addressing Tiyans, in reference to their descent from the Variar girl.

The orthodox number of classes of Kammālans is five. But the artisans do not admit the workers in leather as of their guild, and say there are only four classes. According to them, the fifth class was composed of the copper-smiths, who did not return to Malabar with the others, but remained in Izhuva land. Nevertheless, they always speak of themselves as the Aiyen kudi or five-house Kammālans.

There is a variant of the legend of the exodus, told by the Āsāris (carpenters), which is worth narrating. Their version of the story is repeated among themselves, and not by the Pānan, at every marriage and tāli-tying ceremony. They identify the village of the Perumāl's washerman as Kanipayyūr. This is the name of a Nambūtiri's illam in the Ponāni tāluk of Malabar. The Nambūtiri is, it may be mentioned, considered to be the highest extant authority in architecture. Disputed points relating to this subject are referred to him, and his decision is final, and accepted by all carpenters and house-builders. The washerman's stone is said to have been lying flat in the water. The girl Ayyesvari was also of Kanipayyūr, and was carried off as in the former story. But there was no request for an armed guard to rescue her. The Perumāl was, instead, asked to make the washerman marry her, and thus avoid disgrace. He consented to do so, and all the 7,764 families of the five classes of Kammālans assembled for the wedding. An immense booth, supported on granite pillars, was erected. The washerman and his party were fed sumptuously. But the booth had been so constructed that it could be made to collapse instantaneously. So the Kammālans went quietly outside, and, at a given signal, the booth collapsed, and crushed to death the washerman and his friends. After this, the Kammālans fled, and remained one year, eight months and eleven days in the Izhuva country. Negotiations were carried on through the Izhuva king, and the Kammālans returned under his guarantee that their demands would be complied with. The Izhuva king sent his own men and the Nasrāni to the capital of the Perumāl. The story of the exodus and the return was inscribed on granite stone with solemn rites, and in the presence of witnesses. This was buried at the northern gate of the Tiruvanchakulam temple on Friday, the eighth of the month of Kanni. It was resolved that, in any case of doubt, the stone should be unearthed. And it was only after all this had been done that the Izhuva king's envoy returned to him. Then the Kammālans came back to Malabar. According to the carpenters, the copper-smiths did not return. They say that eighteen families of Āsāris remained behind. Some of these returned long afterwards, but they were not allowed to rejoin the caste. They are known as Puzhi Tachan, or sand carpenters, and Patinettanmar, or the eighteen people. There are four families of this class now living at or near Parpangadi. They are carpenters, but the Āsāris treat them as outcastes.

There is yet another variant of the story of the exodus, which is obviously of recent manufacture, for a Pattar Brāhman is brought in, and gives cunning advice. We know that the Pattars are comparatively new comers in Malabar.

The Tiyans have recently been summed up as follows.[32] "The Tiyas have always been characterised by their persevering and enterprising habits. A large percentage of them are engaged in various agricultural pursuits, and some of the most profitable industries of Malabar have from time out of mind been in their hands. They are exclusively engaged in making toddy and distilling arrack. Many of them

---

[32] Indian Review, Oct. 1906.

are professional weavers, the Malabar mundu being a common kind of cloth made by them. The various industries connected with cocoanut cultivation are also successfully carried on by the Tiyas. For example, the manufacture of jaggery (crude sugar) is an industry in which a considerable number of the Tiyas are profitably engaged. The preparation of coir from cocoanut fibre is one of their hereditary occupations, and this is done almost wholly by their women at home. They are very skilful in the manufacture of coir matting and allied industries. Commercial pursuits are also common among them. Apart from their agricultural and industrial inclinations, the Tiyas give evidence of a literary taste, which is commendable in a people who are living under conditions which are anything but conducive to literary life. They have among them good Sanskrit scholars, whose contributions have enriched the Malayālam literature; physicians well versed in Hindu systems of medicine; and well-known astrologers, who are also clever mathematicians. In British Malabar, they have made considerable progress in education. In recent years, there has been gaining ground among the Tiyas a movement, which has for its object the social and material improvement of the community. Their leaders have very rightly given a prominent place to industry in their schemes of progress and reform. Organisations for the purpose of educating the members of the community on the importance of increased industrial efforts have been formed. The success which has attended the Industrial Exhibition conducted by the members of the community at Quilon, in 1905, has induced them to make it a permanent annual event. Some of their young men have been sent to Japan to study certain industries, and, on their return, they hope to resuscitate the dying local industries, and to enter into fresh fields of industry awaiting development. Factories for the manufacture of coir matting and allied articles have been established by the Tiyas in some parts of Travancore and Cochin."

In 1906, the foundation stone of a Tiya temple at Tellicherry was laid with great ceremony. In the following year, a very successful Industrial Exhibition was held at Cannanore under the auspices of the Sri Narayan Dharma Paripalana Yogam. Still more recently, it was resolved to collect subscriptions for the establishment of a hostel for the use of Tiya youths who come from other places to Tellicherry for educational purposes.

Tiyōro.—The Tiyōros are described, in the Madras Census Report, 1901, as "Oriya fishermen, who also make lotus-leaf platters. They have four endogamous sections, viz., Torai, Ghodai, Artia, and Kulodondia." It has been suggested that the caste name is a corruption of the Sanskrit tivara, a hunter. (*See* Risley, Tribes and Castes of Bengal, Tiyar.)

Toda.—Quite recently, my friend Dr. W. H. Rivers, as the result of a prolonged stay on the Nīlgiris, has published[33] an exhaustive account of the sociology and religion of this exceptionally interesting tribe, numbering, according to the latest census returns, 807 individuals, which inhabits the Nīlgiri plateau. I shall, therefore, content myself with recording the rambling notes made by myself during occasional visits to Ootacamund and Paikāra, supplemented by extracts from the book just referred to, and the writings of Harkness and other pioneers of the Nīl-

---

[33] The Todas. 1906.

giris.

TODA BUFFALOES IN KRAAL.

The Todas maintain a large-horned race of semi-domesticated buffaloes, on whose milk and its products (butter and ney)[34] they still depend largely, though to a less extent than in bygone days before the establishment of the Ootacamund

[34] Ney = ghi or clarified butter.

bazar, for existence. It has been said that "a Toda's worldly wealth is judged by the number of buffaloes he owns. Witness the story in connection with the recent visit to India of His Royal Highness the Prince of Wales. A clergyman, who has done mission work among the Todas, generally illustrates Bible tales through the medium of a magic-lantern. One chilly afternoon, the Todas declined to come out of their huts. Thinking they required humouring like children, the reverend gentleman threw on the screen a picture of the Prince of Wales, explaining the object of his tour, and, thinking to impress the Todas, added 'The Prince is exceedingly wealthy, and is bringing out a retinue of two hundred people.' 'Yes, yes,' said an old man, wagging his head sagely, 'but how many buffaloes is he bringing?'"

The Todas lead for the most part a simple pastoral life. But I have met with more than one man who had served, or who was still serving Government in the modest capacity of a forest guard, and I have heard of others who had been employed, not with conspicuous success, on planters' estates. The Todas consider it beneath their dignity to cultivate land. A former Collector of the Nīlgiris granted them some acres of land for the cultivation of potatoes, but they leased the land to the Badagas, and the privilege was cancelled. In connection with the Todas' objection to work, it is recorded that when, on one occasion, a mistake about the ownership of some buffaloes committed an old Toda to jail, it was found impossible to induce him to work with the convicts, and the authorities, unwilling to resort to hard remedies, were compelled to save appearances by making him an overseer. The daily life of a Toda woman has been summed up as lounging about the mad or mand (Toda settlement), buttering and curling her hair, and cooking. The women have been described as free from the ungracious and menial-like timidity of the generality of the sex in the plains. When Europeans (who are greeted as swāmi or god) come to a mand, the women crawl out of their huts, and chant a monotonous song, all the time clamouring for tips (inām). Even the children are so trained that they clamour for money till it is forthcoming. As a rule, the Todas have no objection to Europeans entering into their huts, but on more than one occasion I have been politely asked to take my boots off before crawling in on the stomach, so as not to desecrate the dwelling-place. Writing in 1868, Dr. J. Shortt makes a sweeping statement that "most of the women have been debauched by Europeans, who, it is sad to observe, have introduced diseases to which these innocent tribes were once strangers, and which are slowly but no less surely sapping their once hardy and vigorous constitutions. The effects of intemperance and disease (syphilis) combined are becoming more and more apparent in the shaken and decrepit appearance which at the present day these tribes possess." Fact it undoubtedly is, and proved both by hospital and naked-eye evidence, that syphilis has been introduced among the Todas by contact with the outside world, and they attribute the stunted growth of some members of the rising generation, as compared with the splendid physique of the lusty veterans, to the results thereof. It is an oft-repeated statement that the women show an absence of any sense of decency in exposing their naked persons in the presence of strangers. In connection with the question of the morality of the Toda women, Dr. Rivers writes that "the low sexual morality of the Todas is not limited in its scope to the relations within the Toda community. Conflicting views are held by those who know the Nilgiri hills as to the relations of the Todas with the other inhabitants, and especially with the train of natives which the European immigration to the hills has brought in its wake. The general opinion on the hills is that, in this respect, the morality of the Todas is as low as it well could be, but it is a question whether this opinion is not too much based on the behaviour of the inhabitants of one or two villages [*e.g.*, the one commonly known as School or Sylk's mand] near the European settlements, and I think it is probable that the larger part of the Todas remain more uncontaminated than is generally supposed."

I came across one Toda who, with several other members of the tribe, was selected on account of fine physique for exhibition at Barnum's show in Europe, America and Australia some years ago, and still retained a smattering of English, talking fondly of 'Shumbu' (the elephant Jumbo). For some time after his return to his hill abode, a tall white hat was the admiration of his fellow tribesmen. To this man finger-prints came as no novelty, since his impressions were recorded both in England and America.

Writing in 1870,[35] Colonel W. Ross King stated that the Todas had just so much knowledge of the speech of their vassals as is demanded by the most ordinary requirements. At the present day, a few write, and many converse fluently in Tamil. The Nīlgiri C.M.S. Tamil mission has extended its sphere of work to the Todas, and I cannot resist the temptation to narrate a Toda version of the story of Dives and Lazarus. The English say that once upon a time a rich man and a poor man died. At the funeral of the rich man, there was a great tamāsha (spectacle), and many buffaloes were sacrificed. But, for the funeral of the poor man, neither music nor buffaloes were provided. The English believe that in the next world the poor man was as well off as the rich man; so that, when any one dies, it is of no use spending money on the funeral ceremonies. Two mission schools have been established, one at Ootacamund, the other near Paikāra. At the latter I have seen a number of children of both sexes reading elementary Tamil and English, and doing simple arithmetic.

A few years ago a Toda boy was baptised at Tinnevelly, and remained there for instruction. It was hoped that he would return to the hills as an evangelist among his people.[36] In 1907, five young Toda women were baptised at the C.M.S. Mission chapel, Ootacamund. "They were clothed in white, with a white cloth over their heads, such as the Native Christians wear. A number of Christian Badagas had assembled to witness the ceremony, and join in the service."

The typical Toda man is above medium height, well proportioned and stalwart, with leptorhine nose, regular features, and perfect teeth. The nose is, as noted by Dr. Rivers, sometimes distinctly rounded in profile. An attempt has been made to connect the Todas with the lost tribes; and, amid a crowd of them collected together at a funeral, there is no difficulty in picking out individuals, whose features would find for them a ready place as actors on the Ober Ammergau stage, either in leading or subordinate parts. The principal characteristic, which at once

---

[35] Aboriginal Tribes of the Nilgiri Hills.
[36] Madras Diocesan Magazine, November, 1907.

distinguishes the Toda from the other tribes of the Nīlgiris, is the development of the pilous (hairy) system. The following is a typical case, extracted from my notes. Beard luxuriant, hair of head parted in middle, and hanging in curls over forehead and back of neck. Hair thickly developed on chest and abdomen, with median strip of dense hairs on the latter. Hair thick over upper and lower ends of shoulder-blades, thinner over rest of back; well developed on extensor surface of upper arms, and both surfaces of forearms; very thick on extensor surfaces of the latter. Hair abundant on both surfaces of legs; thickest on outer side of thighs and round knee-cap. Dense beard-like mass of hair beneath gluteal region (buttocks). Superciliary brow ridges very prominent. Eyebrows united across middle line by thick tuft of hairs. A dense growth of long straight hairs directed outwards on helix of both ears, bearing a striking resemblance to the hairy development on the helix of the South Indian bonnet monkey (*Macacus sinicus*). The profuse hairy development is by some Todas attributed to their drinking "too much milk."

TODA.

Nearly all the men have one or more raised cicatrices, forming nodulous growths (keloids) on the right shoulder.These scars are produced by burning the skin with red-hot sticks of *Litsæa Wightiana* (the sacred fire-stick). The Todas believe that the branding enables them to milk the buffaloes with perfect ease, or as Dr. Rivers puts it, that it cures the pain caused by the fatigue of milking. "The marks," he says, "are made when a boy is about twelve years old, at which age he begins to milk the buffaloes." About the fifth month of a woman's first pregnancy, on the new-moon day, she goes through a ceremony, in which she brands herself, or is branded by another woman, by means of a rag rolled up, dipped in oil and lighted, with a dot on the carpo-metacarpal joint of each thumb and on each wrist.

The women are lighter in colour than the men, and the colour of the body has been aptly described as of a *café-au-lait* tint. The skin of the female children and young adults is often of a warm copper hue. Some of the young women, with their raven-black hair dressed in glossy ringlets, and bright glistening eyes, are distinctly good-looking, but both good looks and complexion are short-lived, and the women speedily degenerate into uncomely hags. As in Maori land, so in Toda land, one finds a race of superb men coupled to hideous women, and, with the exception of the young girls, the fair sex is the male sex. Both men and women cover their bodies with a white mantle with blue and red lines, called putkūli, which is purchased in the Ootacamund bazar, and is sometimes decorated with embroidery worked by the Toda women. The odour of the person of the Todas, caused by the rancid butter which they apply to the mantle as a preservative reagent, or with which they anoint their bodies, is quite characteristic. With a view to testing his sense of smell, long after our return from Paikara, I blindfolded a friend who had accompanied me thither, and presented before his nose a cloth, which he at once recognised as having something to do with the Todas.

In former times, a Badaga could be at once picked out from the other tribes of the Nīlgiri plateau by his wearing a turban. At the present day, some Toda elders and important members of the community (*e.g.,* monegars or headmen) have adopted this form of head-gear. The men who were engaged as guides by Dr. Rivers and myself donned the turban in honour of their appointment.

TODA WOMAN.

Toda females are tattooed after they have reached puberty. I have seen several multiparæ, in whom the absence of tattoo marks was explained either on the ground that they were too poor to afford the expense of the operation, or that they were always suckling or pregnant—conditions, they said, in which the operation would not be free from danger. The dots and circles, of which the simple devices are made up,[37] are marked out with lamp-black made into a paste with water, and the pattern is pricked in by a Toda woman with the spines of *Berberis aristata*. The system of tattooing and decoration of females with ornaments is summed up in the following cases:—

---

[37] *See* Madras Museum Bull., IV, 1896, pl. XII.

1. Aged 22. Has one child. Tattooed with three dots on back of left hand. Wears silver necklet ornamented with Arcot two-anna pieces; thread and silver armlets ornamented with cowry (*Cypræa moneta*) shells on right upper arm; thread armlet ornamented with cowries on left forearm; brass ring on left ring finger; silver rings on right middle and ring fingers. Lobes of ears pierced. Ear-rings removed owing to grandmother's death.

2. Aged 28. Tattooed with a single dot on chin; rings and dots on chest, outer side of upper arms, back of left hand, below calves, above ankles, and across dorsum of feet. Wears thread armlet ornamented with young cowries on right forearm; thread armlet and two heavy ornamental brass armlets on left upper arm; ornamental brass bangle and glass bead bracelet on left wrist; brass ring on left little finger; two steel rings on left ring finger; bead necklet ornamented with cowries.

3. Aged 35. Tattooed like the preceding, with the addition of an elaborate device of rings and dots on the back.

4. Aged 35. Linen bound round elbow joint, to prevent chafing of heavy brass armlets. Cicatrices of sores in front of elbow joint, produced by armlets.

5. Aged 23. Has one child. Tattooed only below calves, and above ankles.

The following are the more important physical measurements of the Toda men, whom I have examined:—

	Av.	Max.	Min.
	CM.	*CM.*	*CM.*
Stature	169.8	186.8	157.6
Cephalic length	19.4	20.4	18.2
Do. breadth	14.2	15.2	13.3
Do. index	73.3	81.3	68.7
Nasal height	4.7	4.9	4.6
Do. breadth	3.6	3.8	3.4
Do. index	74.9	79.9	70.

Allowing that the cephalic index is a good criterion of racial or tribal purity, the following analysis of the Toda indices is very striking:—

---

[38]   Average 73.

76 ♦♦♦♦♦♦
77 ♦
78 ♦
79 ♦
80
81 ♦

A thing of exceeding joy to the Todas was my Salter's hand-dynamometer, the fame of which spread from mand to mand, and which was circulated among the crowd at funerals. Great was the disgust of the assembled males, on a certain day, when the record of hand-grip for the morning (73 lbs.) was carried off by a big-boned female, who became the unlovely heroine of the moment. The largest English feminine hand-grip, recorded in my laboratory note-book, is only 66 lbs. One Toda man, of fine physique, not satisfied with his grip of 98 lbs., went into training, and fed himself up for a few days. Thus prepared, he returned to accomplish 103 lbs., the result of more skilful manipulation of the machine rather than of a liberal dietary of butter-milk.

The routine Toda dietary is said to be made up of the following articles, to which must be added strong drinks purchased at the toddy shops:—

(*a*) Rice boiled in whey.

(*b*) Rice and jaggery (crude sugar) boiled in water.

(*c*) Broth or curry made of vegetables purchased in the bazar, wild vegetables and pot-herbs, which, together with ground orchids, the Todas may often be seen rooting up with a sharp-pointed digging-stick on the hill-sides. The Todas scornfully deny the use of aphrodisiacs, but both men and women admit that they take sālep misri boiled in milk, to make them strong. Sālep misri is made from the tubers (testicles de chiens) of various species of *Eulophia* and *Habenaria* belonging to the natural order Orchideæ.

The indigenous edible plants and pot-herbs include the following:—

(1) *Cnicus Wallichii* (thistle).—The roots and flower-stalks are stripped of their bark, and made into soup or curry.

(2) *Girardinia heterophylla* (Nīlgiri nettle).—The tender leafy shoots of vigorously growing plants are gathered, crushed by beating with a stick to destroy the stinging hairs, and made into soup or curry. The fibre of this plant, which is cultivated near the mands, is used for stitching the putkuli, with steel needles purchased in the bazar in lieu of the more primitive form. In the preparation of the fibre, the bark is thrown into a pot of boiling water, to which ashes have been added. After a few hours' boiling, the bark is taken out and the fibre extracted.

(3) Tender shoots of bamboos eaten in the form of curry.

(4)   *Alternanthera sessilis.*
      Stellaria media.
      Amarantus spinosus.   } Pot-herbs.
      Amarantus polygonoides.

The following list of plants, of which the fruits are eaten by the Todas, has been brought together by Mr. K. Rangachari:—

Eugenia Arnottiana.—The dark purple juice of the fruit of this tree is used by Toda women for painting beauty spots on their faces.

Rubus ellipticus.
Rubus molucanus.   } Wild raspberry.
Rubus lasiocarpus.

Fragaria nilgerrensis, wild strawberry.

Elæagnus latifolia. Said by Dr. Mason to make excellent tarts and jellies.

Gaultheria fragrantissima.

Rhodomyrtus tomentosa, hill gooseberry.

Loranthus neelgherrensis.
Loranthus loniceroides.   } Parasitic on trees.

Elæocarpus oblongus.

Elæocarpus Munronii.

Berberis aristata.
Berberis nepalensis.   } Barberry.

Solanum nigrum.

Vaccinium Leschenaultii.

Vaccinium nilgherrense.

Toddalia aculeata.

Ceropegia pusilla.

To which may be added mushrooms.

A list containing the botanical and Toda names of trees, shrubs, etc., used by the Todas in their ordinary life, or in their ceremonial, is given by Dr. Rivers.[39]

Fire is, in these advanced days, obtained by the Todas in their dwelling huts for domestic purposes from matches. The men who came to be operated on with my measuring instruments had no hesitation in asking for a match, and lighting the cheroots which were distributed amongst them, before they left the Paikāra bungalow dining-room. Within the precincts of the dairy temple the use of matches is forbidden, and fire is kindled with the aid of two dry sticks of *Litsæa Wightiana.* Of

[39] *Op. cit.*, Appendix IV, 738.

these one, terminating in a blunt convex extremity, is about 2′ 3″ long; the other, with a hemispherical cavity scooped out close to one end, about 2½″ in length. A little nick or slot is cut on the edge of the shorter stick, and connected with the hole in which the spindle stick is made to revolve. "In this slot the dust collects, and, remaining in an undisturbed heap, seemingly acts as a muffle to retain the friction-heat until it reaches a sufficiently high temperature, when the wood-powder becomes incandescent."[40] Into the cavity in the short stick the end of the longer stick fits, so as to allow of easy play. The smaller stick is placed on the ground, and held tight by firm pressure of the great toe, applied to the end furthest from the cavity, into which a little finely powdered charcoal is inserted. The larger stick is then twisted vigorously, "like a chocolate muller" (Tylor) between the palms of the hands by two men, turn and turn about, until the charcoal begins to glow. Fire, thus made, is said to be used at the sacred dairy (ti), the dairy houses of ordinary mands, and at the cremation of males. In an account of a Toda green funeral,[41] Mr. Walhouse notes that "when the pile was completed, fire was obtained by rubbing two dry sticks together. This was done mysteriously and apart, for such a mode of obtaining fire is looked upon as something secret and sacred." At the funeral of a female, I provided a box of tändstickors for lighting the pyre. A firestick, which was in current use in a dairy, was polluted and rendered useless by the touch of my Brāhman assistant! It is recorded by Harkness[42] that a Brāhman was not only refused admission to a Toda dairy, but actually driven away by some boys, who rushed out of it when they heard him approach. It is noted by Dr. Rivers that "several kinds of wood are used for the fire-sticks, the Toda names of these being kiaz or keadj (*Litsæa Wightiana*), mōrs (*Michelia Nilagirica*), parskuti (*Elæagnus latifolia*), and main (*Cinnamomum Wightii*)." He states further that, "whenever fire is made for a sacred purpose, the fire-sticks must be of the wood which the Todas call kiaz or keadj, except in the tesherot ceremony (qualifying ceremony for the office of palol) in which the wood of muli is used. At the niroditi ceremony (ordination ceremony of a dairyman), "the assistant makes fire by friction, and lights a fire of mulli wood, at which the candidate warms himself." It is also recorded by Dr. Rivers that "in some Toda villages, a stone is kept, called tutmûkal, which was used at one time for making fire by striking it with a piece of iron."

---

[40] R. Bache. Royal Magazine, August 1901.

[41] Ind. Ant., III, 1874.

[42] Description of a singular Aboriginal Race inhabiting the summit of the Neilgherry Hills, 1832.

TODA HUT.

The abode of the Todas is called a mad or mand (village or hamlet), which is composed of huts, dairy temple, and cattle-pen, and has been so well described by Dr. Shortt,[43] that I cannot do better than quote his account. "Each mand," he says, "usually comprises about five buildings or huts, three of which are used as dwellings, one as a dairy, and the other for sheltering the calves at night. These huts

____

[43] *Op. cit.*

form a peculiar kind of oval pent-shaped [half-barrel-shaped] construction, usually 10 feet high, 18 feet long, and 9 feet broad. The entrance or doorway measures 32 inches in height and 18 inches in width, and is not provided with any door or gate; but the entrance is closed by means of a solid slab or plank of wood from 4 to 6 inches thick, and of sufficient dimensions to entirely block up the entrance. This sliding door is inside the hut, and so arranged and fixed on two stout stakes buried in the earth, and standing to the height of 2½ to 3 feet, as to be easily moved to and fro. There are no other openings or outlets of any kind, either for the escape of smoke, or for the free ingress and egress of atmospheric air. The doorway itself is of such small dimensions that, to effect an entrance, one has to go down on all fours, and even then much wriggling is necessary before an entrance is effected. The houses are neat in appearance, and are built of bamboos closely laid together, fastened with rattan, and covered with thatch, which renders them water-tight. Each building has an end walling before and behind, composed of solid blocks of wood, and the sides are covered in by the pent-roofing, which slopes down to the ground. The front wall or planking contains the entrance or doorway. The inside of a hut is from 8 to 15 feet square, and is sufficiently high in the middle to admit of a tall man moving about with comfort. On one side there is a raised platform or pial formed of clay, about two feet high, and covered with sāmbar (deer) or buffalo skins, or sometimes with a mat. This platform is used as a sleeping place. On the opposite side is a fire place, and a slight elevation, on which the cooking utensils are placed. In this part of the building, faggots of firewood are seen piled up from floor to roof, and secured in their place by loops of rattan. Here also the rice-pounder or pestle is fixed. The mortar is formed by a hole dug in the ground, 7 to 9 inches deep, and hardened by constant use. The other household goods consist of three or four brass dishes or plates, several bamboo measures, and sometimes a hatchet. Each hut or dwelling is surrounded by an enclosure or wall formed of loose stones piled up two or three feet high [with openings too narrow to permit of a buffalo entering through it]. The dairy is sometimes a building slightly larger than the others, and usually contains two compartments separated by a centre planking. One part of the dairy is a store-house for ghee, milk and curds, contained in separate vessels. The outer apartment forms the dwelling place of the dairy priest. The doorways of the dairy are smaller than those of the dwelling huts. The flooring of the dairy is level, and at one end there is a fire-place. Two or three milk pails or pots are all that it usually contains. The dairy is usually situated at some little distance from the habitations. The huts where the calves are kept are simple buildings, somewhat like the dwelling huts. In the vicinity of the mands are the cattle-pens or tuels[tu], which are circular enclosures surrounded by a loose stone wall, with a single entrance guarded by powerful stakes. In these, the herds of buffaloes are kept at night. Each mand possesses a herd of these animals." It is noted by Dr. Rivers that "in the immediate neighbourhood of a village there are usually well-worn paths, by which the village is approached, and some of these paths or kalvol receive special names. Some may not be traversed by women. Within the village there are also certain recognised paths, of which two are specially important. One, the punetkalvol, is the path by which the dairy man goes from his dairy to milk or tend the buffaloes; the other is the majvatitthkalvol, the path which the women must use when going to the dairy to receive butter-milk (maj) from the dairy man. Women are not allowed to go to the dairy or to other places connected with it, except at appointed times, when they receive buttermilk."

"TODA CATHEDRAL."

In addition to the dairies which in form resemble the dwelling-huts, the Todas keep up as dairy-temples certain curious conical edifices, of which there are said to be four on the Nīlgiri plateau, viz., at the Muttanād mand, near Kotagiri, near

Sholūr, and at Mudimand. The last was out of repair a few years ago, but was, I was informed, going to be rebuilt shortly. It is suggested by Dr. Rivers as probable that in many cases a dairy, originally of the conical form, has been rebuilt in the same form as the dwelling-hut, owing to the difficulty and extra labour of reconstruction in the older shape. The edifice at the Muttanād mand (or Nōdrs), at the top of the Sīgūr ghāt, is known to members of the Ootacamund Hunt as the Toda cathedral. It has a circular stone base and a tall conical thatched roof crowned with a large flat stone, and is surrounded by a circular stone wall. To penetrate within the sacred edifice was forbidden, but we were informed that it contained milking vessels, dairy apparatus, and a swāmi in the guise of a copper bell (mani). The dairyman is known as the varzhal or wursol. In front of the cattle-pen of the neighbouring mand, I noticed a grass-covered mound, which, I was told, is sacred. The mound contains nothing buried within it, but the bodies of the dead are placed near it, and earth from the mound is placed on the corpse before it is removed to the burning-ground. At "dry funerals" the buffalo is said to be slain near the mound. It has been suggested by Colonel Marshall[44] that the "boa or boath [poh.] is not a true Toda building, but may be the bethel of some tribe contemporaneous with, and cognate to the Todas, which, taking refuge, like them, on these hills, died out in their presence."

Despite the hypothesis of Dr. Rivers that the Todas are derived from one or more of the races of Malabar, their origin is buried among the secrets of the past. So too is the history of the ancient builders of cairns and barrows on the Nīlgiri plateau, which were explored by Mr. Breeks when Commissioner of the Nīlgiris.[45] The bulk of the Breeks' collection is now preserved in the Madras Museum, and includes a large series of articles in pottery, quite unlike anything known from other parts of Southern India. Concerning this series, Mr. R. Bruce Foote writes as follows.[46] "The most striking objects are tall jars, many-storied cylinders, of varying diameter with round or conical bases, fashioned to rest upon pottery ring-stands, or to be stuck into soft soil, like the amphoræ of classical times. These jars were surmounted by domed lids. On these lids stood or sat figures of the most varied kind of men, or animals, much more rarely of inanimate objects, but all modelled in the rudest and most grotesque style. Grotesque and downright ugly as are these figures, yet those representing men and women are extremely interesting from the light they throw upon the stage of civilization their makers had attained to, for they illustrate the fashion of the garments as also of the ornaments they wore, and of the arms or implements carried by them. The animals they had domesticated, those they chased, and others that they probably worshipped, are all indicated. Many figures of their domestic animals, especially their buffaloes and sheep, are decorated with garlands and bells, and show much ornamentation, which seems to indicate that they were painted over, a custom which yet prevails in many parts." Among the most interesting figures are those of heavily bearded men riding on horses, and big-horned buffaloes which might have been modelled

---

[44] A Phrenologist among the Todas, 1873.
[45] J. W. Breeks. Account of the Primitive Tribes and Monuments of the Nilgiris, 1873.
[46] Catalogue of the Prehistoric Antiquities, Government Museum, Madras, 1901.

from the Toda buffaloes of to-day, and, like these, at funerals and migration ceremonies, bear a bell round the neck.

Two forms of Toda dairy have so far been noticed. But there remains a third kind, called the ti mand, concerning which Dr. Rivers writes as follows. "The ti is the name of an institution, which comprises a herd of buffaloes, with a number of dairies and grazing districts, tended by a dairy-man priest called palol, with an assistant called kaltmokh. Each dairy, with its accompanying buildings and pasturage, is called a ti mad, or ti village. The buffaloes belonging to a ti are of two kinds, distinguished as persiner and punir. The former are the sacred buffaloes, and the elaborate ceremonial of the ti dairy is concerned with their milk. The punir correspond in some respects to the putiir of the ordinary village dairy, and their milk and its products are largely for the personal use and profit of the palol, and are not treated with any special ceremony. During the whole time he holds office, the palol may not visit his home or any other ordinary village, though he may visit another ti village. Any business with the outside world is done either through the kaltmokh, or with people who come to visit him at the ti. If the palol has to cross a river, he may not pass by a bridge, but must use a ford, and it appears that he may only use certain fords. The palol must be celibate, and, if married, he must leave his wife, who is in most cases also the wife of his brother or brothers." I visited the ti mand near Paikāra by appointment, and, on arrival near the mand, found the two palols, well-built men aged about thirty and fifty, clad in black cloths, and two kaltmokhs, youths aged about eight and ten, naked save for a loin-cloth, seated on the ground, awaiting our arrival. As a mark of respect to the palols, the three Todas who accompanied me arranged their putkūlis so that the right arm was laid bare, and one of them, who was wearing a turban, removed it. A long palaver ensued in consequence of the palols demanding ten rupees to cover the expenses of the purificatory ceremonies, which, they maintained, would be necessary if I desecrated the mand by photographing it. Eventually, however, under promise of a far smaller sum, the dwelling-hut was photographed, with palols, kaltmokhs, and a domestic cat seated in front of it.

In connection with the palol being forbidden to cross a river by a bridge, it may be noted that the river which flows past the Paikāra bungalow is regarded as sacred by the Todas, and, for fear of mishap from arousing the wrath of the river god, a pregnant Toda woman will not venture to cross it. The Todas will not use the river water for any purpose, and they do not touch it unless they have to ford it. They then walk through it, and, on reaching the opposite bank, bow their heads. Even when they walk over the Paikāra bridge, they take their hand out of the putkūli as a mark of respect. Concerning the origin of the Paikāra river, a grotesque legend was narrated to us. Many years ago, the story goes, two Todas, uncle and nephew, went out to gather honey. After walking for a few miles they separated, and proceeded in different directions. The uncle was unsuccessful in the search, but the more fortunate nephew secured two kandis (bamboo measures) of honey. This, with a view to keeping it all for himself, he secreted in a crevice among the rocks, with the exception of a very small quantity, which he made his uncle believe was the entire product of his search. On the following day, the nephew went alone to the spot where the honey was hidden, and found, to his disappointment, that the honey was leaking through the bottom of the bamboo measures, which were transformed into two snakes. Terrified at the sight thereof, he ran away, but the snakes pursued him (may be they were hamadryads, which have the reputation of pursuing human beings). After running a few minutes, he espied a hare (*Lepus nigricollis*) running across his course, and, by a skilful manœuvre, threw his body-cloth over it. Mistaking it for a man, the snakes followed in pursuit of the hare, which, being very fleet of foot, managed to reach the sun, which became obscured by the hoods of the reptiles. This fully accounts for the solar eclipse. The honey, which leaked out of the vessels, became converted into the Paikāra river.

In connection with the migrations of the herds of buffaloes, Dr. Rivers writes as follows. "At certain seasons of the year, it is customary that the buffaloes both of the village and the ti should migrate from one place to another. Sometimes the village buffaloes are accompanied by all the inhabitants of the village; sometimes the buffaloes are only accompanied by their dairy-man and one or more male assistants. There are two chief reasons for these movements of the buffaloes, of which the most urgent is the necessity for new grazing-places.... The other chief reason for the migrations is that certain villages and dairies, formerly important and still sacred, are visited for ceremonial purposes, or out of respect to ancient custom." For the following note on a buffalo migration which he came across, I am indebted to Mr. H. C. Wilson. "During the annual migration of buffaloes to the Kundahs, and when they were approaching the bridle-path leading from Avalanchē to Sispāra, I witnessed an interesting custom. The Toda family had come to a halt on the far side of the path; the females seated themselves on the grass, and awaited the passing of the sacred herd. This herd, which had travelled by a recognised route across country, has to cross the bridle-path some two or three hundred yards above the Avalanchē-Sispāra sign-post. Both the ordinary and sacred herd were on the move together. The former passed up the Sispāra path, while the latter crossed in a line, and proceeded slightly down the hill, eventually crossing the stream and up through the shōlas over the steep hills on the opposite side of the valley. As soon as the sacred herd had crossed the bridle-path, the Toda men, having put down all their household utensils, went to where the women and girls were sitting, and carried them, one by one, over the place where the buffaloes had passed, depositing them on the path above. One of the men told me that the females are not allowed to walk over the track covered by the sacred herd, and have to be carried whenever it is necessary to cross it. This herd has a recognised tract when migrating, and is led by the old buffaloes, who appear to know the exact way."

FIGURES FROM NILGIRI CAIRNS.

The tenure under which lands are held by the Todas is summed up as follows by Mr. R. S. Benson in his report on the revenue settlement of the Nilgiris, 1885. "The earliest settlers, and notably Mr. Sullivan, strongly advocated the claim of the Todas to the absolute proprietary right to the plateau [as lords of the soil]; but another school, led by Mr. Lushington, has strongly combated these views, and apparently regarded the Todas as merely occupiers under the ryotwari system in force generally in the Presidency. From the earliest times the Todas have received from the cultivating Badagas an offering or tribute, called gudu or basket of grain, partly in compensation for the land taken up by the latter for cultivation, and so rendered unfit for grazing purposes, but chiefly as an offering to secure the favour, or avert the displeasure of the Todas, who, like the Kurumbas (*q.v.*), are believed by the Badagas to have necromantic powers over their health and that of their herds. The European settlers also bought land in Ootacamund from them, and to this day the Government pays them the sum of Rs. 150 per mensem, as compensation for interference with the enjoyment of their pastoral rights in and about Ootacamund. Their position was, however, always a matter of dispute, until it was finally laid down in the despatch of the Court of Directors, dated 21st January, 1843. It was then decided that the Todas possessed nothing more than a prescriptive right to enjoy the privilege of pasturing their herds, on payment of a small tax, on the State lands. The Court desired that they should be secured from interference by settlers in the enjoyment of their mands, and of their spots appropriated to religious rites. Accordingly pattas were issued, granting to each mand three bullahs (11.46 acres) of land. In 1863 Mr. Grant obtained permission to make a fresh allotment of nine bullahs (34.38 acres) to each mand on the express condition that the land should be used for pasturage only, and that no right to sell the land or the wood on it should be thereby conveyed. It may be added that the so-called Toda lands are now regarded as the inalienable common property of the Toda community, and unauthorised alienation is checked by the imposition of a penal rate of assessment (G.O., 18th April 1882). Up to the date of this order, however, alienations by sale or lease were of frequent occurrence. It remains to be seen whether the present orders and subordinate staff will be more adequate than those that went before to check the practices referred to." With the view of protecting the Toda lands, Government took up the management of these lands in 1893, and framed rules, under the Forest Act, for their management, the rights of the Todas over them being in no way affected by the rules of which the following is an abstract:—

1. No person shall fell, girdle, mark, lop, uproot, or burn, or strip off the bark or leaves from, or otherwise damage any tree growing on the said lands, or remove the timber, or collect the natural produce of such trees or lands, or quarry or collect stone, lime, gravel, earth or manure upon such lands, or break up such lands for cultivation, or erect buildings of any description, or cattle kraals; and no person or persons, other than the Todas named in the patta concerned, shall graze cattle, sheep, or goats upon such lands, unless he is authorised so to do by the Collector of Nilgiris, or some person empowered by him.

2. The Collector may select any of the said lands to be placed under special fire protection.

3. No person shall hunt, beat for game, or shoot in such lands without a license from the Collector.

4. No person shall at any time set nets, traps, or snares for game on such lands.

5. All Todas in the Nilgiri district shall, in respect of their own patta lands, be exempt from the operation of the above rules, and shall be at liberty to graze their

own buffaloes, to remove fuel and grass for their domestic requirements, and to collect honey or wax upon such lands. They shall likewise be entitled to, and shall receive free permits for building or repairing their mands and temples.

6. The Collector shall have power to issue annual permits for the cultivation of grass land only in Toda pattas by Todas themselves, free of charge, or otherwise as Government may, from time to time, direct; but no Toda shall be at liberty to permit any person, except a Toda, to cultivate, or assist in the cultivation of such lands.

In 1905, the Todas petitioned Government against the prohibition by the local Forest authorities of the burning of grass on the downs, issued on the ground of danger to the shōlas (wooded ravines or groves). This yearly burning of the grass was claimed by the Todas to improve it, and they maintained that their cattle were deteriorating for want of good fodder. Government ruled that the grass on the plateau has been burnt by the inhabitants at pleasure for many years without any appreciable damage to forest growth, and the practice should not be disturbed.

Concerning the social organisation of the Todas, Mr. Breeks states that they are "divided into two classes, which cannot intermarry, viz., Dêvalyâl and Tarser-zhâl. The first class consists of Peiki class, corresponding in some respects to Brāhmans; the second of the four remaining classes the Pekkan, Kuttan, Kenna, and Todi. A Peiki woman may not go to the village of the Tarserzhâl, although the women of the latter may visit Peikis." The class names given by Mr. Breeks were readily recognised by the Todas whom I interviewed, but they gave Tērthāl (comprising superior Peikis) and Tārthāl as the names of the divisions. They told me that, when a Tērthāl woman visits her friends at a Tārthāl mand, she is not allowed to enter the mand, but must stop at a distance from it. Todas as a rule cook their rice in butter-milk, but, when a Tērthāl woman pays a visit to Tarthāl mand, rice is cooked for her in water. When a Tarthāl woman visits at a Tērthāl mand, she is permitted to enter into the mand, and food is cooked for her in buttermilk. The restrictions which are imposed on Tērthāl women are said to be due to the fact that on one occasion a Tērthāl woman, on a visit at a Tarthāl mand, folded up a cloth, and placed it under her putkūli as if it was a baby. When food was served, she asked for some for the child, and on receiving it, exhibited the cloth. The Tarthāls, not appreciating the mild joke, accordingly agreed to degrade all Tērthāl women. According to Dr. Rivers, "the fundamental feature of the social organisation is the division of the community into two perfectly distinct groups, the Tartharol and the Teivaliol [=Dêvalyâl of Breeks]. There is a certain amount of specialisation of function, certain grades of the priesthood being filled only by members of the Teivaliol. The Tartharol and Teivaliol are two endogamous divisions of the Toda people. Each of these primary divisions is sub-divided into a number of secondary divisions [clans]. These are exogamous. Each class possesses a group of villages, and takes its name from the chief of these villages, Etudmad. The Tartharol are divided into twelve clans, the Teivaliol into six clans or madol."

When a girl has reached the age of puberty, she goes through an initiatory ceremony, in which a Toda man of strong physique takes part. One of these splendid specimens of human muscularity was introduced to me on the occasion of a phonograph recital at the Paikāra bungalow.

Concerning the system of polyandry as carried out by the Todas, Dr. Rivers writes as follows. "The Todas have long been noted as a polyandrous people, and the institution of polyandry is still in full working order among them. When the girl becomes the wife of a boy, it is usually understood that she becomes also the wife of his brothers. In nearly every case at the present time, and in recent generations, the husbands of a woman are own brothers. In a few cases, though not brothers, they are of the same clan. Very rarely do they belong to different clans. One of the most interesting features of Toda polyandry is the method by which it is arranged who shall be regarded as the father of a child. For all social and legal purposes, the father of a child is the man who performs a certain ceremony about the seventh month of pregnancy, in which an imitation bow and arrow are given to the woman. When the husbands are own brothers, the eldest brother usually gives the bow and arrow, and is the father of the child, though, so long as the brothers live together, the other brothers are also regarded as fathers. It is in the cases in which the husbands are not own brothers that the ceremony becomes of real social importance. In these cases, it is arranged that one of the husbands shall give the bow and arrow, and this man is the father, not only of the child born shortly afterwards, but also of all succeeding children, till another husband performs the essential ceremony. Fatherhood is determined so essentially by this ceremony that a man who has been dead for several years is regarded as the father of any children born by his widow, if no other man has given the bow and arrow. There is no doubt that, in former times, the polyandry of the Todas was associated with female infanticide, and it is probable that the latter custom still exists to some extent, though strenuously denied. There is reason to believe that women are now more plentiful than formerly, though they are still in a distinct minority. Any increase, however, in the number of women does not appear to have led to any great diminution of polyandrous marriages, but polyandry is often combined with polygyny. Two or more brothers may have two or more wives in common. In such marriages, however, it seems to be a growing custom that one brother should give the bow and arrow to one wife, and another brother to another wife."

The pregnancy ceremony referred to above is called pursutpimi, or bow (and arrow) we touch. According to the account given to me by several independent witnesses, the woman proceeds, accompanied by members of the tribe, on a new moon-day in the fifth or seventh month of her pregnancy, to a shola, where she sits with the man who is to become the father of her child near a kiaz tree (*Eugenia Arnottiana*). The man asks the father of the woman if he may bring the bow, and, on obtaining his consent, goes in search of a shrub (*Sophora glauca*), from a twig of which he makes a mimic bow. The arrow is represented by a blade of grass called nark (*Andropogon Schœnanthus*). Meanwhile a triangular niche has been cut in the kiaz tree, in which a lighted lamp is placed. The woman seats herself in front of the lamp, and, on the return of the man, asks thrice "Whose bow is it?" or "What is it?" meaning to whom, or to which mand does the child belong? The bow and arrow are handed to the woman, who raises them to her head, touches her forehead with them, and places them near the tree. From this moment the lawful father of the child is the man from whom she has received the bow and arrow. He places on the ground at the foot of the tree some rice, various kinds of grain, chillies, jaggery (crude sugar), and salt tied in a cloth. All those present then leave, except the man and woman, who remain near the tree till about six o'clock in the evening, when they return to the mand. The time is determined, in the vicinity of Ootacamund, by the opening of the flowers of *Onothera tetraptera* (evening primrose), a garden escape called by the Todas āru mani pūv (six o'clock flower), which opens towards evening.[47] It may be noted that, at the second funeral of a male, a miniature bow and three arrows are burnt with various other articles within the stone circle (azaram).

A few years ago (1902), the Todas, in a petition to Government, prayed for special legislation to legalise their marriages on the lines of the Malabar Marriage Act. The Government was of opinion that legislation was unnecessary, and that it was open to such of the Todas as were willing to sign the declaration prescribed by section 10 of the Marriage Act III of 1872 to contract legal marriages under the provision of that Act. The Treasury Deputy Collector of the Nīlgiris was appointed Registrar of Toda marriages. No marriage has been registered up to the present time.

The practice of infanticide among the Todas is best summed up in the words of an aged Toda during an interview with Colonel Marshall.[48] "I was a little boy when Mr. Sullivan (the first English pioneer of the Nilgiris) visited these mountains. In those days it was the custom to kill children, but the practice has long died out, and now one never hears of it. I don't know whether it was wrong or not to kill them, but we were very poor, and could not support our children. Now every one has a mantle (putkuli), but formerly there was only one for the whole family. We did not kill them to please any god, but because it was our custom. The mother never nursed the child, and the parents did not kill it. Do you think we could kill it ourselves? Those tell lies who say we laid it down before the opening of the buffalo-pen, so that it might be run over and killed by the animals. We never did such things, and it is all nonsense that we drowned it in buffalo's milk. Boys were never killed—only girls; not those who were sickly and deformed—that would be a sin; but, when we had one girl, or in some families two girls, those that followed were killed. An old woman (kelachi) used to take the child immediately it was born, and close its nostrils, ears, and mouth with a cloth thus—here pantomimic action. It would shortly droop its head, and go to sleep. We then buried it in the ground. The kelachi got a present of four annas for the deed." The old man's remark about the cattle-pen refers to the Malagasy custom of placing a new-born child at the entrance to a cattle-pen, and then driving the cattle over it, to see whether they would trample on it or not.[49] The Missionary Metz[50] bears out the statement that the Toda babies were killed by suffocation.

---

[47] I have seen this plant growing on the grass in front of the Paikāra bungalow.
[48] *Op. cit.*
[49] Ellis. History of Madagascar.
[50] Tribes inhabiting the Neilgherry Hills. By a German missionary, 1856.

TODA AND PHONOGRAPH.

At the census, 1901, 453 male and 354 female Todas were returned. In a note on the proportion of the sexes among the Todas, Mr. R. C. Punnett states[51] that "all who have studied the Todas are agreed upon the frequency of the practice (of infanticide) in earlier times. Marshall, writing in 1872, refers to the large amount of female infanticide in former years, but expresses his conviction that the practice

[51] Proc. Cambridge Philosoph. Soc., XII, 1904.

had by that time died out. Marshall's evidence is that of native assurance only. Dr. Rivers, who received the same assurance, is disinclined to place much confidence in native veracity with reference to this point, and, in view of the lack of encouragement which the practice receives from the Indian Government, this is not altogether surprising. The supposition of female infanticide, by accounting for the great disproportion in the numbers of the sexes, brings the Todas into harmony with what is known of the rest of mankind." In summarising his conclusions, Mr. Punnett notes that:—

(1) Among the Todas, males predominate greatly over females.

(2) This preponderance is doubtless due to the practice of female infanticide, which is probably still to some extent prevalent.

(3) The numerical preponderance of the males has been steadily sinking during recent years, owing probably to the check which foreign intercourse has imposed upon female infanticide.

In connection with the death ceremonies of the Todas, Dr. Rivers notes that "soon after death the body is burnt, and the general name for the ceremony on this occasion is etvainolkedr, the first day funeral. After an interval, which may vary greatly in length, a second ceremony is performed, connected with certain relics of the deceased which have been preserved from the first occasion. The Toda name for this second funeral ceremony is marvainolkedr, the second day funeral, or 'again which day funeral.' The funeral ceremonies are open to all, and visitors are often invited by the Todas. In consequence, the funeral rites are better known, and have been more frequently described than any other features of Toda ceremonial. Like nearly every institution of the Todas, however, they have become known to Europeans under their Badaga names. The first funeral is called by the Badagas hase kedu, the fresh or green funeral, and the term 'green funeral' has not only become the generally recognised name among the European inhabitants of the Nilgiri hills, but has been widely adopted in anthropological literature. The second funeral is called by the Badagas bara kedu, the 'dry funeral,' and this term also has been generally adopted." The various forms of the funeral ceremonies are discussed in detail by Dr. Rivers, and it must suffice to describe those at which we have been present as eye-witnesses.

I had the opportunity of witnessing the second funeral of a woman who had died from smallpox two months previously. On arrival at a mand on the open downs about five miles from Ootacamund, we were conducted by a Toda guide to the margin of a dense shola, where we found two groups seated apart, consisting of (*a*) women, girls, and brown-haired female babies, round a camp fire; (*b*) men, boys, and male babies, carried, with marked signs of paternal affection, by their fathers. In a few minutes a murmuring sound commenced in the centre of the female group. Working themselves up to the necessary pitch, some of the women (near relatives of the deceased) commenced to cry freely, and the wailing and lachrymation gradually spread round the circle, until all, except little girls and babies who were too young to be affected, were weeping and mourning, some for fashion, others from genuine grief. In carrying out the orthodox form of mourning, the women first had a good cry to themselves, and then, as their emotions became more intense, went round the circle, selecting partners with whom to share companionship in grief. Gradually the group resolved itself into couplets of mourners, each pair with their heads in contact, and giving expression to their emotions in unison. Before separating to select a new partner, each couple saluted by bowing the head, and raising thereto the feet of the other, covered by the putkūli. [I have seen women rapidly recover from the outward manifestations of grief, and clamour for money.] From time to time the company of mourners was reinforced by late arrivals from distant mands, and, as each detachment, now of men and now of women, came in view across the open downs, one could not fail to be reminded of the gathering of the clans on some Highland moor. The resemblance was heightened by the distant sound as of pipers, produced by the Kota band (with two police constables in attendance), composed of four Kotas, who made a weird noise with drums and flutes as they drew near the scene of action. The band, on arrival, took up a position close to the mourning women. As each detachment arrived, the women, recognising their relatives, came forward and saluted them in the manner customary among Todas by falling at their feet, and placing first the right and then the left foot on their head. Shortly after the arrival of the band, signals were exchanged, by waving of putkūlis, between the assembled throng and a small detachment of men some distance off. A general move was made, and an *impromptu* procession formed, with men in front, band in the middle, and women bringing up the rear. A halt was made opposite a narrow gap leading into the shola; men and women sat apart as before; and the band walked round, discoursing unsweet music. A party of girls went off to bring fire from the spot just vacated for use in the coming ceremonial, but recourse was finally had to a box of matches lent by one of our party. At this stage we noticed a woman go up to the eldest son of the deceased, who was seated apart from the other men, and would not be comforted in spite of her efforts to console him. On receipt of a summons from within the shola, the assembled Toda men and ourselves swarmed into it by a narrow track leading to a small clear space round a big tree, from a hole cut at the base of which an elderly Toda produced a piece of the skull of the dead woman, wrapped round with long tresses of her hair. It now became the men's turn to exhibit active signs of grief, and all of one accord commenced to weep and mourn. Amid the scene of lamentation, the hair was slowly unwrapt from off the skull, and burned in an iron ladle, from which a smell as of incense arose. A bamboo pot of ghī was produced, with which the skull was reverently anointed, and placed in a cloth spread on the ground. To this relic of the deceased the throng of men, amid a scene of wild excitement, made obeisance by kneeling down before it, and touching it with their foreheads. The females were not permitted to witness this stage of the proceedings, with the exception of one or two near relatives of the departed one, who supported themselves sobbing against the tree. The ceremonial concluded, the fragment of skull, wrapt in the cloth, was carried into the open, where, as men and boys had previously done, women and girls made obeisance to it. A procession was then again formed, and marched on until a place was reached, where were two stone-walled kraals, large and small. Around the former the men, and within the latter the women, took up their position, the men engaging in chit-chat, and the women in mourning, which after a time ceased, and they too engaged in conversation. A party of men, carrying the skull, still in the cloth, set out for a neighbouring shola, where a kēdu of several other dead Todas was being celebrated; and a long pause ensued, broken eventually by the arrival of the other funeral party, the men advancing in several lines, with arms linked, and crying out U, hah! U, hah, hah! in regular time. This party brought with it pieces of the skulls of a woman and two men, which were placed, wrapt in cloths, on the ground, saluted, and mourned over by the assembled multitude. At this stage a small party of Kotas arrived, and took up their position on a neighbouring hill, waiting, vulture-like, for the carcase of the buffalo which was shortly to be slain. Several young men now went off across the hill in search of buffaloes, and speedily re-appeared, driving five buffaloes before them with sticks. As soon as the beasts approached a swampy marsh at the foot of the hill on which the expectant crowd of men was gathered together, two young men of athletic build, throwing off their putkūlis, made a rush down the hill, and tried to seize one of the buffaloes by the horns, with the result that one of them was promptly thrown. The buffalo escaping, one of the remaining four was quickly caught by the horns, and, with arms interlocked, the men brought it down on its knees, amid a general scuffle. In spite of marked objection and strenuous resistance on the part of the animal—a barren cow—it was, by means of sticks freely applied, slowly dragged up the hill, preceded by the Kota band, and with a Toda youth pulling at its tail. Arrived at the open space between the kraals, the buffalo, by this time thoroughly exasperated, and with blood pouring from its nostrils, had a cloth put on its back, and was despatched by a blow on the poll with an axe deftly wielded by a young and muscular man. On this occasion no one was badly hurt by the sacrificial cow, though one man was seen washing his legs in the swamp after the preliminary struggle with the beast. But Colonel Ross-King narrates how he saw a man receive a dangerous wound in the neck from a thrust of the horn, which ripped open a wide gash from the collar-bone to the ear. With the death of the buffalo, the last scene, which terminated the strange rites, commenced; men, women, and children pressing forward and jostling one another in their eagerness to salute the dead beast by placing their hands between its horns, and weeping and mourning in pairs; the facial expression of grief being mimicked when tears refused to flow spontaneously.

The ceremonial connected with the final burning of the relics and burial of the ashes at the stone circle (azaram) are described in detail by Dr. Rivers.

A few days after the ceremony just described, I was invited to be present at the funeral of a young girl who had died of smallpox five days previously. I proceeded accordingly to the scene of the recent ceremony, and there, in company with a small gathering of Todas from the neighbouring mands, awaited the arrival of the funeral cortége, the approach of which was announced by the advancing strains of Kota music. Slowly the procession came over the brow of the hill; the corpse, covered by a cloth, on a rude ladder-like bier, borne on the shoulders of four men, followed by two Kota musicians; the mother carried hidden within a sack; relatives and men carrying bags of rice and jaggery, and bundles of wood of the kiaz tree (*Eugenia Arnottiana*) for the funeral pyre. Arrived opposite a small hut, which had been specially built for the ceremonial, the corpse was removed from the bier, laid on the ground, face upwards, outside the hut, and saluted by men, women, and children, with the same manifestations of grief as on the previous occasion. Soon the men moved away to a short distance, and engaged in quiet conversation, leaving the females to continue mourning round the corpse, interrupted from time to time by the arrival of detachments from distant mands, whose first duty was to salute the dead body. Meanwhile a near female relative of the dead child was busily engaged inside the hut, collecting together in a basket small measures of rice, jaggery, sago, honey-comb, and the girl's simple toys, which were subsequently to be burned with the corpse. The mourning ceasing after a time, the corpse was placed inside the hut, and followed by the near relatives, who there continued to weep over it. A detachment of men and boys, who had set out in search of the buffaloes which were to be sacrificed, now returned driving before them three cows, which escaped from their pursuers to rejoin the main herd. A long pause ensued, and, after a very prolonged drive, three more cows were guided into a marshy swamp, where one of them was caught by the horns, and dragged reluctantly, but with little show of fight, to the strains of Kota drum and flute, in front of the hut, where it was promptly despatched by a blow on the poll. The corpse was now brought from within the hut, and placed, face upwards, with its feet resting on the forehead of the buffalo, whose neck was decorated with a silver chain, such as is worn by Todas round the loins, as no bell was available, and the horns were smeared with butter. Then followed frantic manifestations of grief, amid which the unhappy mother fainted. Mourning over, the corpse was made to go through a form of ceremony, resembling that which is performed during pregnancy with the first child. A small boy, three years old, was selected from among the relatives of the dead girl, and taken by his father in search of a certain grass (*Andropogon Schœnanthus*) and a twig of a shrub (*Sophora glauca*), which were brought to the spot where the corpse was lying. The mother of the dead child then withdrew one of its hands from the putkūli, and the boy placed the grass and twig in the hand, and limes, plantains, rice, jaggery, honey-comb, and butter in the pocket of the putkūli, which was then stitched with needle and thread in a circular pattern. The boy's father then took off his son's putkūli, and replaced it so as to cover him from head to foot. Thus covered, the boy remained outside the hut till the morning of the morrow, watched through the night by near relatives of himself and his dead bride. [On the occasion of the funeral of an unmarried lad, a girl is in like manner selected, covered with her putkūli from head to foot, and a metal vessel filled with jaggery, rice, etc., to be subsequently burnt on the funeral pyre, placed for a short time within the folds of the putkūli. Thus covered, the girl remains till next morning, watched through the dreary hours of the night by relatives. The same ceremony is performed over the corpse of a married woman who has not borne children, the husband acting as such for the last time, in the vain hope that the woman may produce issue in heaven.] The corpse was borne away to the burning-ground within the shola, and, after removal of some of the hair by the mother of the newly wedded boy, burned, with face upwards, amid the music of the Kota band, the groans of the assembled crowd squatting on the ground, and the genuine grief of the nearest relatives. The burning concluded, a portion of the skull was removed from the ashes, and handed over to the recently made mother-in-law of the dead girl, and wrapped up with the hair in the bark of the tūd tree (*Meliosma pungens*). A second buffalo, which, properly speaking, should have been slain before the corpse was burnt, was then sacrificed, and rice and jaggery were distributed among the crowd, which dispersed, leaving behind the youthful widower and his custodians, who, after daybreak, partook of a meal of rice, and returned to their mands; the boy's mother taking with her the skull and hair to her mand, where it would remain until the celebration of the second funeral. No attention is paid to the ashes after cremation, and they are left to be scattered by the winds.

A further opportunity offered itself to be present at the funeral of an elderly woman on the open downs not far from Paikāra, in connection with which certain details possess some interest. The corpse was, at the time of our arrival, laid out on a rude bier within an improvised arbour covered with leaves and open at each end, and tended by some of the female relatives. At some little distance, a conclave of Toda men, who rose of one accord to greet us, was squatting in a circle, among whom were many venerable white-turbaned elders of the tribe, protected from the scorching sun by palm-leaf umbrellas. Amid much joking, and speech-making by the veterans, it was decided that, as the eldest son of the deceased woman was dead, leaving a widow, this daughter-in-law should be united to the second son, and that they should live together as man and wife. On the announcement of the decision, the bridegroom-elect saluted the principal Todas present by placing his head on their feet, which were sometimes concealed within the ample folds of the putkūli. At the funeral of a married woman, three ceremonies must, I was told, be performed, if possible, by a daughter or daughter-in-law, viz.: —

(1) Tying a leafy branch of the tiviri shrub (*Atylosia Candolleana*) in the putkūli of the corpse;

(2) Tying balls of thread and cowry shells on the arm of the corpse, just above the elbow;

(3) Setting fire to the funeral pyre, which was, on the present occasion, done by lighting a rag fed with ghī with a match.

The buffalo capture took place amid the usual excitement, and with freedom from accident; and, later in the day, the stalwart buffalo catchers turned up at the travellers' bungalow for a *pourboire* in return, as they said, for treating us to a good fight. The beasts selected for sacrifice were a full-grown cow and a young calf. As they were dragged near to the corpse, now removed from the arbour, butter was smeared over the horns, and a bell tied round the neck. The bell was subsequently removed by Kotas, in whose custody, it was said, it was to remain till the next day funeral. The death-blow, or rather series of blows, having been delivered with the butt end of an axe, the feet of the corpse were placed at the mouth of the buffalo. In the case of a male corpse, the right hand is made to clasp the horns. [It is recorded by Dr. Rivers that, at the funeral of a male, men dance after the buffalo is killed. In the dancing a tall pole, called tadri or tadrsi, decorated with cowry shells, is used.] The customary mourning in couples concluded, the corpse, clad in four cloths, was carried on the stretcher to a clear space in the neighbouring shola, and placed by the side of the funeral pyre, which had been rapidly piled up. The innermost cloth was black in colour, and similar to that worn by a palol. Next to it came a putkūli decorated with blue and red embroidery, outside which again was a plain white cloth covered over by a red cotton cloth of European manufacture. Seated by the side of the pyre, near to which I was courteously invited to take a seat on the stump of a rhododendron, was an elderly relative of the dead woman, who, while watching the ceremonial, was placidly engaged in the manufacture of a holly walking-stick with the aid of a glass scraper. The proceedings were watched on behalf of Government by a forest guard, and a police constable who, with marked affectation, held his handkerchief to his nose throughout the ceremonial. The corpse was decorated with brass rings, and within the putkūli were stowed jaggery, a scroll of paper adorned with cowry shells, snuff and tobacco, cocoanuts, biscuits, various kinds of grain, ghī, honey, and a tin-framed looking-glass. A long purse, containing a silver Japanese yen and an Arcot rupee of the East India Company, was tied up in the putkūli close to the feet. These preliminaries concluded, the corpse was hoisted up, and swung three times over the now burning pyre, above which a mimic bier, made of slender twigs, was held. The body was then stripped of its jewelry, and a lock of hair cut off by the daughter-in-law for preservation, together with a fragment of the skull. I was told that, when the corpse is swung over the pyre, the dead person goes to amnodr (the world of the dead). In this connection, Dr. Rivers writes that "it would seem as if this ceremony of swinging the body over the fire was directly connected with the removal of the objects of value. The swinging over the fire would be symbolic of its destruction by fire; and this symbolic burning has the great advantage that the objects of value are not consumed, and are available for use another time. This is probably the real explanation of the ceremony, but it is not the explanation given by the Todas themselves. They say that long ago, about 400 years, a man supposed to be dead was put on the funeral pyre, and, revived by the heat, he was found to be alive, and was able to walk away from the funeral place. In consequence of this, the rule was made that the body should always be swung three times over the fire before it is finally placed thereon." [Colonel Marshall narrates the story that a Toda who had revived from what was thought his death-bed, has been observed parading about, very proud and distinguished looking, wearing the finery with which he had been bedecked for his own funeral, and which he would be permitted to carry till he really departed this life.] As soon as the pyre was fairly ablaze, the mourners, with the exception of some of the female relatives, left the shōla, and the men, congregating on the summit of a neighbouring hill, invoked their god. Four men, seized, apparently in imitation of the Kota Dēvādi, with divine frenzy, began to shiver and gesticulate wildly, while running blindly to and fro with closed eyes and shaking fists. They then began to talk in Malayālam, and offer an explanation of an extraordinary phenomenon, which had appeared in the form of a gigantic figure, which disappeared as suddenly as it appeared. At the annual ceremony of walking through fire (hot ashes) in that year, two factions arose owing to some dissension, and two sets of ashes were used. This seems to have annoyed the gods, and those concerned were threatened with speedy ruin. But the whole story was very vague. The possession by some Todas of a smattering of Malayālam is explained by the fact that, when grazing their buffaloes on the northern and western slopes of the Nīlgiris, they come in contact with Malayālam-speaking people from the neighbouring Malabar district.

At the funeral of a man (a leper), the corpse was placed in front of the entrance to a circle of loose stones about a yard and a half in diameter, which had been specially constructed for the occasion. Just before the buffalo sacrifice, a man of the Paiki clan standing near the head of the corpse, dug a hole in the ground with a cane, and asked a Kenna who was standing on the other side, "Puzhut, Kenna,"[52] shall I throw the earth?—three times. To which the Kenna, answering, replied "Puzhut"—throw the earth—thrice. The Paiki then threw some earth three times over the corpse, and three times into the miniature kraal. It is suggested by Dr. Rivers that the circle was made to do duty for a buffalo pen, as the funeral was held at a place where there was no tu (pen), from the entrance of which earth could be dug up.

Several examples of laments relating to the virtues and life of the deceased, which are sung or recited in the course of the funeral ceremonies, are given by Dr. Rivers. On the occasion of the reproduction of a lament in my phonograph, two young women were seen to be crying bitterly. The selection of the particular lament was unfortunate, as it had been sung at their father's funeral. The reproduction of the recitation of a dead person's sins at a Badaga funeral quickly restored them to a state of cheerfulness.

The following petition to the Collector of the Nilgiris on the subject of buffalo sacrifice may be quoted as a sign of the times, when the Todas employ petition-writers to express their grievances:—

"According to our religious custom for the long period, we are bringing forward of our killing buffaloes without any irregular way. But, in last year, when the late Collector came to see the said place, by that he ordered to the Todas first not to keep the buffaloes without feeding in the kraal, and second he ordered to kill each for every day, and to clear away the buffaloes, and not to keep the buffaloes without food. We did our work according to his orders, and this excellent order was an ample one. Now this — —, a chief of the Todas, son of — —, a deceased Toda, the above man joined with the moniagar of — — village, joined together, and, dealing with bribes, now they arose against us, and doing this great troubles on us, and also, by this great trouble, one day Mr. — — came for shooting snapes (snipe) by that side. By chance one grazing buffalo came to him, push him by his horns very forcely, and wounded him on his leg. By the help of another gentleman who came with him he escaped, or he would have die at the moment. Now the said moniagar and — — joined together, want to finish the funeral to his late father on the 18th instant. For this purpose they are going to shut the buffaloes without food in the kraal on the 18th instant at 10 o'clock. They are going to kill the buffaloes on the 19th instant at 4 o'clock in the evening. But this is a great sin against god. But we beg your honour this way. That is, let them leave the buffaloes in the grazing place, and ask them to catch and kill them at the same moment. And also your honour cannot ordered them to keep them in the kraal without food. And, if they will

[52] "Puzhutkina—Shall I throw earth?" Rivers.

desire to kill the buffaloes in this way, these buffaloes will come on us, and also on the other peoples one who, coming to see funs on those day, will kill them all by his anxious. And so we the Todas begs your honour to enquire them before the 18th, the said funeral ceremony commencing, and not to grant the above orders to them."

A Whit Monday at Paikāra was given up to an exhibition of sports and games, whereof the most exciting and interesting was a burlesque representation of a Toda funeral by boys and girls. A Toda, who was fond of his little joke, applied the term pacchai kēdu (green funeral) to the corpses of the flies entrapped by a viscous catch'em-alive-oh on the bungalow table. To the mock funeral rites arrived a party of youths, as from a distant mand, and crying out U, hah, in shrill mimicry of their elders. The lad who was to play the leading part of sacrificial buffalo, stripping off his putkūli, disappeared from sight over the brow of a low hillock. Above this eminence his bent and uplifted upper extremities shortly appeared as representatives of the buffalo horns. At sight thereof, there was a wild rush of small boys to catch him, and a mimic struggle took place, while the buffalo was dragged, amid good-tempered scuffling, kicks, and shouting, to the spot where the corpse should have been. This spot was, in the absence of a pseudo-dead body or stage dummy, indicated by a group of little girls, who had sat chatting together till the boy-beast arrived, when they touched foreheads, and went, with due solemnity, through the orthodox observance of mourning in couples. The buffalo was slain by a smart tap on the back of the head with a cloth, which did duty for an axe. As soon as the convulsive movements and twitchings of the death struggle were over, the buffalo, without waiting for an encore, retired behind the hillock once more, in order that the rough and tumble fight, which was evidently the chief charm of the game, might be repeated. The buffalo boy later on came in second in a flat race, and he was last seen protecting us from a mischievous-looking member of his herd, which was grazing on the main-road. Toda buffaloes, it may be noted, are not at all popular with members of the Ootacamund Hunt, as both horses and riders from time to time receive injuries from their horns, when they come in collision.

While the funeral game was in progress, the men showed off their prowess at a game (eln),[53] corresponding to the English tip-cat, which is epidemic at a certain season in the London bye-streets. It is played with a bat like a broomstick, and a cylindrical piece of wood pointed at both ends. The latter is propped up against a stone, and struck with the bat. As it flies off the stone, it is hit to a distance with the bat, and caught (or missed) by the out fields.

At the Muttanād mand, we were treated to a further exhibition of games. In one of these, called narthpimi, a flat slab of stone is supported horizontally on two other slabs fixed perpendicularly in the ground so as to form a narrow tunnel, through which a man can just manage to wriggle his body with difficulty. Two men take part in the game, one stationing himself at a distance of about thirty yards, the other about sixty yards from the tunnel. The front man, throwing off his mantle, runs as hard as he can to the tunnel, pursued by the 'scratch' man, whose object is to touch the other man's feet before he has squeezed himself through the

---

[53] Called by Breeks ilata, which, Dr. Rivers suggests, is a Badaga name.

tunnel. Another sport, which we witnessed, consists of trial of strength with a heavy globular stone, the object being to raise it up to the shoulder; but a strong, well-built-man—he who was entrusted with slaying the funeral buffalo—failed to raise it higher than the pit of the stomach, though straining his muscles in the attempt. A splendidly made veteran assured me that, when young and lusty, he was able to accomplish the feat, and spoke sadly of degeneration in the physique of the younger members of the tribe.

Mr. Breeks mentions that the Todas play a game resembling puss-in-the-corner, called kāriālapimi, which was not included in the programme of sports got up for our benefit. Dr. Rivers writes that "the Todas, and especially the children, often play with mimic representations of objects from practical life. Near the villages I have seen small artificial buffalo-pens and fireplaces made by the children in sport." I have, on several occasions, come across young children playing with long and short pieces of twigs representing buffaloes and their calves, and going solemnly through the various incidents in the daily life of these animals. Todas, both old and young, may constantly be seen twisting flexible twigs into representations of buffaloes' heads and horns.

Of Toda songs, the following have been collected:—

Sunshine is increasing. Mist is fast gathering. Rain may come.
Thunder roars. Clouds are gathering.
Rain is pouring. Wind and rain have combined.
Oh, powerful god, may everything prosper!
May charity increase!
May the buffaloes become pregnant!
See that the buffaloes have calves.
See that the barren women have children.
Go and tell this to the god of the land.
Keygamor, Eygamor (names of buffaloes).
Evening is approaching. The buffaloes are coming.
The calves also have returned.
The buffaloes are saluted.
The dairy-man beats the calves with his stick.
Milk has been offered to the bell.
It is growing dark.
This is a buffalo with beautiful horns.
A buffalo stupidly given away by the Badaga.
A buffalo brought to the Kāndal mand.
Innerovya (name of buffalo).
Like this buffalo there is no other.
Parkūr (name of a Toda).
Like him there is no man.
The sun is shining. The wind is blowing.
Rain is coming. The trees are in flower.
Tears are falling. The nose is burning.
He is coming, holding up his umbrella.

He is coming, wearing a good body-cloth.
He is coming, wearing a good under-cloth.
He (the palol) is coming, wearing a black cloth.
He is coming, holding his walking-stick of palai wood.
I have a god. What is to become of me?
I am inclined to cry, my heart being heavy.
Oh, my child! Do not cry. It is still crying.
Thuree. Thuree. See. Be quiet.
A robust bull buffalo. Ach! Ach!
A big buffalo not intended for killing. Ach! Ach!
Is leading the cow buffalo. Ah! Ah!
Two or three men are driving it. Ah! Ah!

Song in honour of the arrival of the Maharāni-Regent of Mysore at Ootacamund.

All we Todas go to her house, and dance before her.
She gives us fifteen rupees.
She comes near our women, and talks to them.
She gives cloths to us.
Next day we take milk, eight bottles in the morning, four in the evening.
Month by month she pays us for our milk.
She goes back to Mysore, and, when she goes, we stand in a row before her.
She gives us presents; cloths and three rupees.
The women cut their hair, and stand before her.

Marriage Song.

Boys and girls are singing.
Much money are they spending.
To the girl her father is giving five buffaloes.
The husband tells his wife that she must curl her hair.
If her hair is curled, all the people will rejoice.
The buffalo is slain, and now we must all dance.
Why are not more people here? More should come.
My buffalo is big, very big.
Go quickly and catch it.
The Todas are all there. They are standing in a row.
Who will run, and catch the buffalo first?
To him will a present of five rupees be given.
I will go and catch it first.
The Todas are all fighting.
The Todas are all feasting.
People give them rice.
The buffalo is coming. Two men run to catch it by the neck.
Ten men collect the buffaloes. They pen them in a kraal.
At one o'clock we take our food.

> The buffalo is running, and I hit it on the back with a stick.
> It swerves aside, but I drive it back to the path.
> Night comes, and we all dance.
> Next morning at ten o'clock we bring out the buffalo, and slay it.
> At four in the morning we wrap rice and grain in a white cloth, and burn it.
> At eleven we cut the hair of the boys and girls.
> At four in the morning the priest goes to the temple (dairy).
> He lights the lamp.
> At eight he milks his buffaloes.
> He puts on no cloth.
> He places butter and ghī before the god.
> Then he grazes his buffaloes, and eats his food.
> Then he puts on his cloth.
> At three in the afternoon he goes again to the temple.
> He kindles a fire, and lights the lamp.
> He puts milk in a chatty, and churns it into butter with a cane.
> He mixes water with the butter-milk, and gives it to the women to drink.
> He alone may sleep in the temple.
> At four in the morning he lets out the buffaloes to graze.
> At seven he milks them.
> The woman's house is down the hill.
> The priest must not go in unto the woman.
> He may not marry.
> When he is twenty, he may not enter the temple.
> Another is made priest in his stead.

The religious institutions of the Todas, including the elaborate dairy ritual, and their religion, are described in full detail by Dr. Rivers. The Todas have been to some extent influenced by Hinduism, and some visit the temples at Nanjengōd in Mysore, Karamadai in the Coimbatore district, and other shrines, whereat they worship, present votive offerings, and pray for offspring, etc. Writing in 1872, Mr. Breeks remarked that "about Ootacamund, a few Todas have latterly begun to imitate the religious practices of their native neighbours. Occasionally children's foreheads are marked with the Siva spot, and my particular friend Kinniaven, after an absence of some days, returned with a shaven head from a visit to the temple of Siva at Nanjengudi." A man who came to my laboratory had his hair hanging down in long tails reaching below his shoulders. He had, he said, let it grow long because his wife, though married five years, had borne no child. A child had, however, recently been born, and, as soon as the second funeral of a relation had been performed, he was going to sacrifice his locks as a thank-offering at the Nanjengōd temple. The following extracts from my notes will serve to illustrate the practice of marking (in some instances apparently for beauty's sake) and shaving as carried out at the present day.

(1) Man, aged 28. Has just performed a ceremony at the ti mand. White curved line painted across forehead, and dots below outer ends thereof, on glabella, and

outside orbits. Smeared with white across chest, over outer side of upper arms and left nipple, across knuckles and lower end of left ulna, and on lobes of ears.

(2) Man, aged 21. Painted on forehead as above. Smeared over chest and upper eye lids.

(3) Man, aged 35. White spot painted on forehead.

(4) Man, aged 30. Hair of head and beard cut short owing to death of grandfather.

(5) Boy, aged 12. Shock head of hair, cut very short all over owing to death of grandfather.

(6) Girl, aged 8. Hair shaved on top, back and sides of head, and in median strip from vertex to forehead.

(7) Boy, aged 6. White spot painted between eyebrows. Hair shaved on top and sides of head, and in median strip from vertex to forehead. Hair brought forward in fringe over forehead on either side of median strip, and hanging down back of neck.

(8) Male child, aged 18 months. White spot painted between eyebrows. Shaved on top and sides of head.

Todupuzha Vellāla.—For the following note, I am indebted to Mr. N. Subramani Aiyar. Besides the Nanchinād Vellālas, there are, in Travancore, two sections of the Vellāla caste, inhabiting the mountainous Todupuzha tāluk. These are the Tenkanchi and Kumbakōnam Vellālas. The former are known by the popular name of Anjuttilkar, or the five hundred, and the latter are designated Munnutilkar, or the three hundred, in reference to the number of families which originally settled in the taluk. Like the Nanchinād Vellālas, they take the title of Pillai, and, in special cases, the honorific prefix Kanakku.

The Tenkanchi Vellālas appear to have dwelt originally in the Tenkāsi taluk of the Tinnevelly district, and to have emigrated, as the legend goes, on account of the demand of a Vaduka ruler for the hand of a member of their community in marriage. The Vadakkumkur Rājas were ruling over Todupuzha at the time of their migration, and afforded them a safe asylum. The Kumbakōnam Vellālas believe that they emigrated to Travancore about the commencement of the Malabar era from Kumbakōnam in the Tanjore district. Both divisions speak Malayālam, but there are clear indications in their speech that their mother-tongue was once Tamil, and they always use that language in their ceremonial writings. The Anjuttilkar women have adopted the dress and ornaments of the Nāyars. Both sections wear the tuft of hair in front, but the Munnutilkar women do not tie the hair on the left side like the Nāyars and Anjuttilkars, but behind like the Pāndi Vellālas. Nor do the Anjuttilkar women wear a white dress like the Tenkanchis, but a coloured cloth, sixteen cubits in length, in orthodox Tamil fashion. Again, while the Tenkanchi women largely resort to the todu and other Nāyar ornaments, the Kumbakōnam women are more conservative, and wear only the pampadam and melidu, though they sometimes wear jewels, such as the nāgapata tāli for the neck. Both sections are Saivites, in the sense that they abstain from flesh and fish.

Their principal occupation is agriculture. They worship the two mountain deities Bhadrakāli and Durgā. In the Kirikkot muri of the Karikkod property there is a temple dedicated to Siva or Unnamalanathar, with a large amount of property attached to it. This belongs to the Tenkanchi Vellālas, and a Malayālam Brāhman performs the priestly functions. The Kumbakōnam Vellālas have their own temples, such as the Ankalamma koil, Annamala matam, Vīrabhadran koil, etc., and worship, besides the principal gods of the Hindu pantheon, such minor deities as Vīrabhadran, Karuppan, Bhairavan, Māriamman, and Muttaramman. The priests of both sections are East Coast Brāhmans, who live in the Todupuzha tāluk. As their profession is regarded by other Brāhmans as degrading, they, especially in the case of the Kumbakōnam Vellālas, perform their duties stealthily. The headman of the Kumbakōnam section lives in the Periyakulam tāluk of the Madura district, and, by his order, an image of Siva is worshipped at their homes.

Divorce is not permitted on any ground, and, in ancient days, widow remarriage was forbidden. There is a legend that a woman of this caste, who was a friend of the daughter of a certain Vadakkumkur Rājah, was so aggrieved at the news of her newly married husband's death that, at her intercession, the Rājah issued a proclamation permitting the remarriage of widows. If no husband has been found for a girl before she reaches puberty, certain propitiatory rites have to be performed, at which one of her female relations represents her. On the fourth day of the marriage ceremony, the bride and bridegroom, before they bathe, rub each other's bodies with oil, and, going to a large caldron containing water, throw a gold and silver ring into it, and pick them out three times. Inheritance of both sections is from father to son (makkathāyam). A sambandham alliance does not confer any rite of inheritance.

The names of both sections are such as are unknown among Nāyars, *e.g.*, Sivalingam, Arunāchalam, Chidambaram, Arumukham. The Tenkanchis are considered to be higher in the social scale than the Kumbakōnam section, as they observe only twelve days' death pollution, whereas the latter are under pollution for sixteen days. The Tenkanchis may enter the temple, and, like Nāyars, stand on the left side of the inner shrine, whereas the Kumbakōnam Vellālas may proceed only as far as the balikkalpura, or out-house of the temple, and not enter the nalambalam. Again, butter-milk is freely received by Brāhmans from the Tenkanchis, but not from members of the Kumbakōnam section. While Pāndi Vellālas will not receive food from the Tenkanchis, or give their daughters in marriage to them, the latter will not intermarry with the Nānchinād Vellālas.

Togata.—The Togatas are Telugu weavers, most numerous in the Cuddapah district, who manufacture the coarsest kind of cotton cloths, such as are worn by the poorer classes. They are generally Vaishnavites, wear the sacred thread, and have for their priests Vaishnava Brāhmans or Sātānis. They eat flesh, and their widows are allowed to remarry. Writing concerning the Togatas in 1807, Buchanan states[54] that "widows cannot marry again, but are not expected to kill themselves. The Panchanga, or village astrologer, attends at births, marriages, funerals, at the ceremonies performed in honour of their deceased parents, and at the build-

---

[54] Journey through Mysore, Canara, and Malabar.

ing of a new house, and on each occasion gets a fee of one fanam, or eight pence. On other occasions, when a weaver wants to pray, he calls in a Satanana, who reads something in an unknown language, and gives the votary some holy water, which he consecrates by pouring it on the head of a small image that he carries about for the purpose."

As regards their origin, some Togatas claim to be sons of Chaudēsvari, who threw some rice on to the fire, from which sprang a host of warriors, whose descendants they are. Others give Pūppandaja Rishi as the name of their ancestor. Concerning Chaudēsvari, Mr. Francis writes as follows.[55] "Connected with the margosa tree (*Melia Azadirachta*) is the worship of Chaudēsvari, the goddess of the Togata caste of weavers. She is supposed to reside in margosa trees, and either the tree itself, or a stone representing the goddess and placed at its foot, is worshipped by the Togatas at certain seasons, such as the Telugu New Year Day. Apparently the other weaver castes take no share in the ceremonies. They consist largely of animal sacrifices. Nevertheless, a particular class of Brāhmans, called Nandavarīkula Brāhmans, take a prominent part in the festival. This name Nandavarīkula is derived from the village of Nandavaram in Kurnool, and doubtless many stories are prevalent there about this sub-division. The account given at Tadpatri, where they are fairly numerous, is as follows. Once upon a time, a king from Southern India went on a pilgrimage with his wife to Benares. While there, he unwittingly incurred a nameless but heinous pollution. Horrified, he applied to some Brāhmans there to purify him, promising them half his kingdom in return. They asked for some tangible record of this promise, and the king called upon the goddess Chaudēsvari, who had a temple near by, to witness his oath. The purification was effected, and he departed home. Later on the Brāhmans came south, and asked for the fulfilment of his promise. The king declared that he could not remember having made any such undertaking. The Brāhmans accordingly went to Benares, and asked Chaudēsvari to come south, and bear witness to the king's oaths. She agreed, on the usual condition that they should go in front, and not look back at her as she came. As happens in other stories of the same kind, they are said to have broken the condition. At Nandavaram they looked back, and the goddess instantly stopped, and remained immoveable. A temple was built for her there, and the Brāhmans remained in the south, and still take part in the worship of Chaudēsvari which the Togatas inaugurate, even though she is not one of the Hindu pantheon, and delights in animal sacrifice. At Tadpatri other castes besides the Togatas help at the festival."

Though Chaudēsvari is the patron god of the Togatas, they also worship Poleramma, Ellamma, Kotamma, and other minor deities.

The original occupation of the Togatas is said to have been dyeing, but, at the present day, owing to the depression in the hand-loom weaving industry, a large number have taken to cultivation.

Like many other Telugu castes, they have exogamous septs, of which the following are examples: —

[55] Gazetteer of the Anantapur district.

Pātha, old.	Mékala, goat.
Kambhapu, pillar.	Gōpalam, alms.
Nīli, indigo.	Sāmanthi, *Chrysanthemum indicum*.
Madaka, plough.	Gurram, horse.
Bana, pot.	Perumāl, a god.
Jīlakara, cummin seed.	Bandāri, treasurer?
Annam, food.	Gudditi.

Pūjāris (priests) for temple worship are always elected from the Perumāl sept, and caste messengers from the Bandāri sept, if they are represented in a settlement. Torches are generally carried, at processions, by men of the Gudditi sept. Members of the Gurram sept are not allowed to ride on horseback.

The panchāyat (village council) system is in vogue, but, in some places, a headman is selected, as occasion requires. In their marriage and funeral ceremonies, the Togatas closely follow the Telugu standard Purānic form of ceremonial. The dead are buried in a recumbent posture. On the last day of the death rites, the Sātāni gives arrack (liquor) to the Togatas, as to the Padma Sālēs, in lieu of holy water (thirtham).

Tohala.—Recorded, in the Madras Census Report, 1901, as a small class of Oriya hill cultivators and petty traders in the Ganjam Agency.

Tolagari.—Recorded, in the Madras Census Report, 1901, as a sub-caste of Mutrācha. In the North Arcot Manual the Tolagaris are described as a small cultivating caste, who were formerly hunters, like the Pālayakkārans.

Tolar (Wolf).—An exogamous sept of Halēpaik. The equivalent Tolana occurs as a sept of Mogēr.

Tōlkollan.—The Tōlkollans or Tōlans (skin people) are summed up in the Madras Census Report, 1901, as "leather workers and dyers, and also gymnasts and teachers of gymnastics. They are also called Vatti Kurup, Chāya Kurup, and Vil Kurup. Their title is Kurup." The Tōlkollans are stated[56] to be "blacksmiths by caste, who abandoned their hereditary trade for leather work, and they are chiefly employed by Māppillas. One peculiar custom in this caste is that two or more brothers may have one wife in common. Only those in good circumstances indulge in the luxury of a private wife. The following information furnished by Mr. S. Vaidyanadha Aiyar, the headmaster of the School of Commerce, Calicut, gives some information regarding leather work in Malabar:—

(*a*) Boots and shoes of country make and English pattern.

(*b*) Harness making.

(*c*) Native shoes (ceruppu). These are of the special pattern peculiar to Malabar, and are largely used by all classes of the Hindu and Māppilla communities. The Arabs who visit this coast once a year purchase a considerable number to take back with them. The price of a pair varies from Rs. 1–8–0 to Rs. 5. Those with orna-

[56] A. Chatterton. Monograph on Tanning and Working in Leather. Madras, 1904.

mental gold lace work cost from Rs. 10 to Rs. 50. These shoes are generally used by well-to-do Māppillas. White of egg is used to give a creaking sound to the shoes. This work is mainly done by Thōlperunkollans and Māppillas, and the latter show more skill in finish and ornamental work.

(*d*) Knife sheaths. Almost every Nāyar, Tiyan and Māppilla carries a knife about a foot in length, and there is a demand for leather sheaths. These are made by Pānans as well as by Thōlperunkollans and Māppillas.

(*e*) Leather baskets are also made, and are largely used as receptacles for carrying pepper, paddy (rice), and other grain.

(*f*) Winnowing fans are made of leather, and are used in pepper and paddy yards, etc.

(*g*) Muttu ceruppu (clogs) are leather shoes with wooden soles. These are largely used during the rainy season."

Tollakkādan (one with a big hole in the lobes of his ears).—Taken, at the census, 1901, as a sub-caste of Shānān, as those returning the name, who are vendors of husked rice in Madras, used the Shānān title Nādān. The equivalent Tollakādu was returned as a sub-division of Konga Vellāla.

Tōl Mēstri.—A sub-division of Semmān.

Tondamān.—It is stated, in the Madras Census Report, 1901, that the Tondamāns are "also called Sunnāmbukkāran (*q.v.*), a Tamil caste of lime (chunam) burners found only in the Tinnevelly district. They are said to be a branch of the Kallans who migrated to Tinnevelly from Pudukkōttai, or the Tondamān's country. Its members are now drummers and pipers as well as lime-burners. Brāhmans are their purōhits, but they are not allowed to go into Hindu temples. They will eat in the houses of Maravans. Their title is Sōlagan." It is noted, in the same report, that the Semmān caste "has two sub-divisions, Tondamān and Tōl-mēstri, and men of the former take wives from the latter, but men of the latter may not marry girls of the former." Tondamān is the family name of the Rāja of Pudukkōttai, a Native State surrounded by the British districts of Tanjore, Madura, and Trichinopoly. The Rāja is the head of the Kallan caste. Copper coins, called amman kāsu, are current only within the State, and their greatest distribution is during Navarātri or Dusserah, when they are issued to the people with a dole of rice every day during the nine days of the festival. They bear on one side the word "Vijaya," meaning victory, or more probably having reference to our faithful ally Vijaya Ragunātha Tondamān, in whose reign they were first struck, it is said in 1761, after the surrender of Pondicherry to the British.

Tondamandalam.—The name of a sub-division of Vellāla, derived from Tondanādu, the ancient Pallava country.

Tonti.—The Tontis are said to be cotton-weavers of Bengal, who have settled in Ganjam.[57] The name denotes threadmen, and the weaving of rough white cloths is the traditional occupation of the caste. All Tontis belong to a single gōtra named after Kāsyapa, one of the seven important rishis, and the priest of Para-

[57] *Cf.* Tanti. Risley, *Tribes and Castes of Bengal*.

surāma. Various bamsams or exogamous septs, the names of some of which occur also as titles, exist, *e.g.*, Biswālo, Dasso, Pālo, Bono, Chondo, Parimaniko, Korono, Bēhara, and Mahāpātro. The marriage and death ceremonies conform to the standard Oriya type. On the fourth day of the marriage rites, a Bhondāri (barber) is presented with some beaten rice and sugar-candy in a new earthen pot. These are sold to those who have assembled, and the proceeds go to the Bhondāri. The corpse of a dead person is washed at the burning ground, instead of, in accordance with the common custom among other castes, at the house.

Toppa Tāli.—A name applied to certain Vāniyans in the North Arcot district, owing to the peculiar tāli (marriage badge) which married women wear.

Torai.—A title of various Oriya castes.

Toreya.—The Toreyas are a Canarese class, living chiefly in the Tamil districts of Coimbatore and Salem. They are said to have been originally fishermen and palanquin bearers, and the name is derived from turai, a river ghāt. Most of them are now cultivators, especially of the betel vine (*Piper betle*). Those whom I examined at Coimbatore were earning their living as betel and sugar-cane cultivators, vendors of tobacco, bakers, cloth merchants, contractors, petty traders, and police constables.

By the Coimbatore Toreyas, the following endogamous divisions were returned:—

Elai, leaf. Betel cultivators.

Chunam, lime. Lime burners.

Gāzul, glass bangle. The Toreya caste is said to have originated from the bangles of Machyagandhi or Gandhavati, the daughter of a fisherman on the Jumna. She was married to king Shantanu of Hastinapūr, who was one of the ancestors of the heroes of the Mahābhārata.

Many exogamous septs exist among the Toreyas, of which the following are examples:—

Belli, silver. May not wear silver toe-rings.
Nāga, snake. The members of the sept, at times of marriage, worship ant-hills, which are the home of snakes.
Alwar or Garuda.
Chinnam, gold.
Kansugaje, small bronze bells, tied to the legs when dancing.
Urukathi, a kind of knife.
Vajjira, diamond.
Vasishta, a Hindu saint.
Mogila, clouds.

Onne (*Pterocarpus Marsupium*). Do not mark their foreheads with the juice from the trunk of this tree.

Kuzhal, the flute played by shepherd boys and snake charmers. If the sound thereof is heard during a meal, what remains of the food should be thrown away.

Rākshasa, a giant. Do not celebrate the Dīpāvali festival in honour of the victory over, and death of, a rākshasa.

Erumai, buffalo.

The headman of the caste is called Ejaman, who has under him an officer entitled Dalavayi. The caste messenger bears the name of Kondikar. These three offices are hereditary. The Ejaman presides at council meetings which are held at the temple of the caste. The eldest member of each family is entitled to a seat on the council. Those who come late to a meeting thereof prostrate themselves before the assembly. Witnesses before the council have to take an oath, which is administered by the Kondikar. He makes the witness stand within a circle drawn on the ground, and makes him repeat the formula "Before God and the elders assembled, with the sky above and the earth beneath, I will state only the truth." The Kondikar then takes up a pinch of earth, and puts it on the head of the witness. For merely threatening to beat a person with shoes, the offender has to feed twenty-five castemen. If he takes the shoes in his hands he must feed fifty, and, if he actually resorts to beating with them, he has to feed a hundred men. In addition, the culprit has to pay a small fine, and both parties have to be purified at the temple. A similar punishment is enforced for beating, or threatening to beat with a broom. For adultery the guilty person is excommunicated, and is admitted back into the caste only after the death of one of the parties concerned. He then has to feed a large number of castemen, or pay a money fine, and, prostrating himself before the assembly, he is beaten with a tamarind switch. He further makes obeisance to the Ejaman, and washes his feet. The Ejaman then purifies him by a small piece of burning camphor in his mouth.

When a married girl reaches puberty, she is taken to her father's house, and her husband constructs a hut with branches of *Ficus glomerata*. On the last day of her confinement therein, the hut is pulled down, and the girl sets fire to it. The house is purified, and the female relations go to the houses of the Ejaman and caste people, and invite them to be present at a ceremonial. A small quantity of turmeric paste is stuck on the doors of the houses of all who are invited. The relations and members of the caste carry betel, and other articles, on trays in procession through the streets. The girl is seated on a plank, and the trays are placed in front of her. Rice flour, fruits, betel, etc., are tied in her cloth, and she is taken into the house. In the case of an unmarried girl, the hut is built by her maternal uncle.

Marriage is always celebrated at the house of the bridegroom, as there is a legend that a Rājah belonging to the Toreya caste had a son, who was taken to the house of his bride elect, and there murdered. The bridegroom's father and relations go to the house of the bride, and make presents of money, cloths, ornaments, etc. They also have to make obeisance to, and feed five married women sumptuously. Pandals (booths) are constructed at the houses of both the bride and bridegroom. Five married women go, on behalf of each of the contracting parties, to their houses, and pound rice there. On the second day, five such women fetch water from a tank, and bathe the bride and bridegroom respectively. The ten women then go to the potter's house, and bring five decorated pots. Three of these are taken to a tank, and filled with water. On the following day, the bridegroom and his sister take the two remaining pots to the tank, and fill them with water. The five pots are placed in the pandal, and represent the household gods. The relations of the bridegroom take twelve kinds of ornaments, a new cloth, flowers, etc., to the house of the Ejaman, and go with him to the bride's house. She is then bathed, and decked with finery. A Brāhman does pūja (worship) and ties on her forehead a mandaikettu or bashingham (chaplet) made of gold leaf or tinsel. She is then carried in procession to the house of the bridegroom. Meanwhile, the Brāhman ties a mandaikettu on the forehead of the bridegroom, who puts on the sacred thread, and sits within the pandal, holding a katar (dagger) in his hand, and closed in by a screen. The bride goes thrice round this screen, and the Brāhman does pūja and gives advice (upadēsam) to the couple. The screen is then lowered slightly, and the bride and bridegroom garland each other. The bride's parents place a few gingelly (*Sesamum*) seeds in the hand of the bridegroom, and pour water thereon, saying that their daughter belongs to him, and telling him to take care of her. The tāli, after being blessed by those assembled, is given by the Brāhman to the bridegroom, who ties it on the bride's neck. The screen is then removed, and the couple sit side by side. The sacred fire is lighted, their hands are linked together, and the ends of their cloths tied together. They then leave the pandal, and, placing their feet on a grindstone, look at the pole-star (Arundati). Entering the pandal once more, they sit therein, and the elders bless them by throwing rice coloured with turmeric over their heads. On the fourth day, they again sit within the pandal, and cooked rice, coloured white, red, yellow, green, and black, on five trays, and nine lighted wicks on a tray are waved before them. Five married men and women, holding a string, stand round them in a circle, within which is the bride's brother with a twig of pīpal (*Ficus religiosa*). The bridegroom places his hands together, and small rice cakes are placed on the head, shoulders, bend of the elbows and knees, and between the fingers of the couple. They are then bathed, and, taking betel in their hands, bow to the four corners of the earth. The bridegroom makes a nāmam (Vaishnavite sect mark), or places vibhūti (sacred ashes) on the twelve posts of the pandal, and the bride places a little cooked rice and water before each post, to which camphor is burnt, and pūja done. They then start for the bride's house, but the bride's sister meets them at the entrance thereto, and will not allow them to go in until she has extracted a promise that their child shall marry hers. The bride proceeds to a tank, sowing some paddy (rice) on the way thither, and brings back a pot of water, with which she washes her husband's hands and feet. Husband and wife then feed each other with a small quantity of rice and milk. Their hands are then cleaned, and the bride's brother puts a gold ring on the finger of the bridegroom. A tray with betel leaves and areca nuts is brought, and the bridegroom ties three handfuls thereof in his cloth. The newly married couple then worship at the temple. On the fifth day, they carry the earthen pots to a river, and, on their return, five married women are worshipped and fed. Five men have to come forward as sureties for the good behaviour of the couple, and declare before those assembled that they will hold themselves responsible for it. In the evening the pair go to the bride's house, and rub oil over each other's head before bathing in turmeric water.

On the following day they repair to the house of the bridegroom.

The corpse of a dead Toreya is placed in a pandal constructed of cocoanut leaves and stems of the milk-hedge (*Euphorbia Tirucalli*). Sect marks are placed on the foreheads of the corpse and the widow. The son of the deceased dons the sacred thread. The funeral ceremonies resemble, in many particulars, those of the Oddēs. A mound is piled up over the grave. A Paraiyan places a small twig of the arka plant (*Calotropis gigantea*) in three corners of the grave, leaving out the northeast corner, and the son puts a small coin on each twig. As he goes round the grave with a water-pot and fire-brand, his maternal uncle, who stands at the head of the grave, makes holes in the pot. On the third, fifth, seventh, or ninth day, the widow, dressed in new cloths, and bedecked with ornaments and flowers, is taken to the burial-ground, with offerings of milk, ghī (clarified butter), tender cocoanut, sandal, camphor, etc. Five small stones, smeared with turmeric and lime, are set up at the head of the grave, and worshipped. The widow goes thrice round the grave, and seats herself near the head thereof. Her brother holds up her arms, and one of her husband's male relations breaks her bangles. She breaks, and throws her tāli on the grave, with the flowers which adorn her. Her ornaments are removed, and she is covered with a cloth, and taken to a river, where she is rubbed with cowdung and bathed. The son and other relatives go to the temple with butter and other articles. A Brāhman does pūja, and shuts the doors of the temple. The son, with his back to the temple, throws a little butter on the doors, which are then opened by the Brāhman. This is done thrice. On the seventh day, pollution is removed by sprinkling holy water, and the caste people are fed. A widow remains in seclusion (gōsha) for three months. Srādh (memorial ceremony) is performed.

The Toreyas worship both Siva and Vishnu, but consider Ayodhya Rāman as their special deity, and sacrifice sheep and fowls to Koriamma.

Toreya.—A sub-division of the Badagas of the Nīlgiris.

Tōta (garden).—Recorded as a sub-division of cultivating Balijas, and an exogamous sept of Bōya, Chenchu, Vāda Balija (or Mila), Mutrācha and Bonthuk Savara. The equivalent Tōta occurs as an exogamous sept of Kāpu and Yānādi. Tōta Dēvaru, or garden god, is the name of an exogamous sept of the Tigala gardeners and cultivators.

Tōtakūra (*Amarantus gangeticus*).—An exogamous sept of Kamma.

Toththala or Tottadi.—A sub-division of Velama.

Tōti.—The Tōti or Totti is one of the village communal servants. The name has been derived from tondu, to dig, or tott, to go round, as the Tōti is the purveyor of news, and has to summon people to appear before the village council. The functions of this useful person to the community have been summed up as follows by a district official.[58] "This individual has all the dirty work of the village allotted to him. He is of the lowest caste, and hence makes no scruple of doing any manner of work that he may be called upon to perform. The removal and sepulture of unclaimed dead bodies, the cleansing of choultries, rest-houses and the like, where travellers carrying infectious diseases might have halted, and oth-

[58] Madras Mail, 1906.

er gruesome duties are entrusted to him. In spite of all this, the Tōti is one of the most trusted of the humbler servants of the village community. Considering his humble status and emoluments, which average between Rs. 3 and Rs. 4 a month, his honesty with regard to pecuniary matters is wonderful. He may be trusted with untold wealth, as is often done when he is the sole custodian of the revenue collections of his village to the tune of several thousands at a time, when on their way from the collecting officers to the Government Treasury." Testimony is borne to the industry of the Tōti in the proverb that if you work like a Tōti, you can enjoy the comforts of a king.

In the Madras Census Report, 1891, Tōti is returned as a sub-division of Chakkiliyan. The Tōti of Mysore is defined by Mr. L. Rice[59] as a menial among the village servants, a deputy talāri, who is employed to watch the crops from the growing crop to the granary.

Odiya Tōti is a Tamil synonym for Oriya Haddis employed as scavengers in municipalities in the Tamil country.

Tottiyan.—In the Census Report, 1901, Mr. W. Francis writes that the Tottiyans are "Telugu cultivators. The Tottiyans or Kambalattāns of the Tanjore district are, however, said to be vagrants, and to live by pig-breeding, snake-charming, and begging. So are the sub-division called Kāttu Tottiyans in Tinnevelly. The headman among the Tinnevelly Tottiyans is called the Mandai Periadanakkāran or Sērvaikāran. Their marriages are not celebrated in their houses, but in pandals (booths) of green leaves erected for the purpose on the village common. However wealthy the couple may be, the only grain which they may eat at the wedding festivities is either cumbu (*Pennisetum typhoideum*) or horse-gram (*Dolichos biflorus*). The patron deities of the caste are Jakkamma and Bommakka, two women who committed sati. The morality of their women is loose. The custom of marrying boys to their paternal aunt's or maternal uncle's daughter, however old she may be, also obtains, and in such cases the bridegroom's father is said to take upon himself the duty of begetting children to his own son. Divorce is easy, and remarriage is freely allowed. They offer rice and arrack (alcoholic liquor) to their ancestors. The Kāttu Tottiyans will eat jackals, rats, and the leavings of other people. Tottiya women will not eat in the houses of Brāhmans, but no explanation of this is forthcoming. The men wear silver anklets on both legs, and also a bracelet upon one of the upper arms, both of which practices are uncommon, while the women wear bangles only on the left arm, instead of on both as usual. Some of the Zamindars in Madura belong to this caste. The caste title is Nāyakkan." At the census, 1901, Kudulukkāran was returned as a sub-caste of the Tottiyans in Madura and Tinnevelly. The Urumikkāran, meaning those who play on the drum called urumi, are said to be Tottiyans in Madura and Paraiyans elsewhere.

"The Tottiyans or Kambalattāns," Mr. H. A. Stuart writes,[60] "are a caste of Telugu cultivators settled in the districts of Madura, Tinnevelly, Coimbatore and Salem. They are probably the descendants of poligars and soldiers of the Nāyak-

[59] Mysore and Coorg Gazetteer.
[60] Madras Census Report, 1891.

kan kings of Vijayanagar, who conquered the Madura country about the beginning of the sixteenth century. As regards the origin of their caste, the Tottiyans say with pride that they are the descendants of the eight thousand gōpastris (milkmaids) of Krishna — a tradition which seems to indicate that their original occupation was connected with the rearing and keeping of cattle. The most important sub-divisions are Kollar and Erkollar, the Tamil form of the Telugu Golla and Yerragolla, which are now shepherd castes, though probably they formerly had as much to do with cattle as sheep. Another large sub-division is Kille or Killavar, which I take to be a corruption of the Telugu kilāri, a herdman. The bride and bridegroom, too, are always seated on bullock saddles. They do not wear the sacred thread. Most of them are Vaishnavites, some of whom employ Brāhman priests, but the majority of them are guided by gurus of their own, called Kodāngi Nāyakkan. [It is noted, in the Gazetteer of the Madura district, that caste matters used to be settled by the Mēttu Nāyakkan or headman, and a Kodāngi Nāyakkan, or priest, so called because he carried a drum.] Each family has its own household deity, which appears to be a sort of representation of departed relations, chiefly women who have burned themselves on the funeral pile of their husbands, or have led a chaste and continent life, or died vestals. Their girls are married after they have attained maturity. Adultery is no crime when committed within the family circle, but a *liaison* with an outsider involves expulsion from the caste. It is said that their newly married girls are even compelled to cohabit with their husband's near relatives. [It is further said to be believed that ill-luck will attend any refusal to do so, and that, so far from any disgrace attaching to them in consequence, their priests compel them to keep up the custom, if by any chance they are unwilling.[61]] The pongu tree (*Pongamia glabra*) is the sacred tree of the caste. Suttee was formerly very common, and the remarriage of widows is discouraged, if not actually forbidden. The dead are generally burned. Both men and women are supposed to practice magic, and are on that account much dreaded by the people generally. They are especially noted for their power of curing snake-bites by means of mystical incantations, and the original inventor of this mode of treatment has been deified under the name Pāmbalamman. They are allowed to eat flesh. The majority speak Telugu in their houses."

The traditional story of the migration of the Tottiyans to the Madura district is given in several of the Mackenzie manuscripts, and is still repeated by the people of the caste. "Centuries ago, says this legend, the Tottiyans lived to the north of the Tungabhadra river. The Muhammadans there tried to marry their women, and make them eat beef. So one fine night they fled southwards in a body. The Muhammadans pursued them, and their path was blocked by a deep and rapid river. They had just given themselves up for lost when a pongu (*Pongamia glabra*) tree on either side of the stream leant forward, and, meeting in the middle, made a bridge across it. Over this they hurried, and, as soon as they had passed, the trees stood erect once more, before the Mussulmans could similarly cross by them. The Tottiyans in consequence still reverence the pongu tree, and their marriage pandals (booths) are always made from its wood. They travelled on until they came to the city of Vijayanagar, under whose king they took service, and it was in the train of

[61] Manual of the Madura district.

the Vijayanagar armies that they came to Madura."[62]

The Tottiyans are most numerous in the Madura and Tinnevelly districts, and include two grades in the social scale. Of these, one consists of those who are engaged in cultivation, and petty Zamindars. The other is made up of those who wander about begging, and doing menial work. Between the two classes there is neither interdining nor intermarriage. In districts other than Madura and Tinnevelly, the name Tottiyan is applied by Tamil-speaking castes to the Jōgis, who are beggars and pig breeders, and, like the Tottiyans, speak Telugu. The following legend is current, to account for the division of the Tottiyans into two sections. They once gave a girl in marriage to a Muhammadan ruler, and all the Tottiyans followed him. A large number went to sleep on one side of a river, while the rest crossed, and went away. The latter are represented today by the respectable section, and the begging class is descended from the former. To this day the Muhammadans and Tottiyans of the Trichinopoly district are said to address each other as if they were relations, and to be on terms of unusual intimacy.

In the Madura district, the Tottiyans are apparently divided into three endogamous sections, viz., Vēkkili, Thokala, and Yerrakolla, of which the last is considered inferior to the other two. Other names for the Vēkkili section are Kambalattar, or Rāja Kambalattar. In some places, *e.g.*, in Tinnevelly, there seem to be six divisions, Thokala, Chilla or Silla, Kolla, Narasilla, Kānthikolla and Pāla. Of these, Pāla may intermarry with Chilla, but the other four are endogamous. As examples of exogamous septs occurring among the Yerrakollas may be noted Chīkala (broom), and Udama (lizard, *Varanus*), of which the latter also occurs as an exogamous sept of the Kāpus.

In the neighbourhood of Nellakota in the Madura district, the Yerrakollas have a group of seven septs called Rēvala, Gollavīrappa, Kambli-nayudi, Karadi (bear), Uduma, Chīla, and Gelipithi. Intermarriage between these is forbidden, as they are all considered as blood-relations, and they must marry into a group of seven other septs called Gundagala, Būsala, Manni, Sukka, Alivīrappa, Sikka, and Mādha. The names of these septs are remembered by a system of mnemonics.

In a note on the Tottiyans of the Trichinopoly district, Mr. F. R. Hemingway writes as follows. "Three endogamous sub-divisions exist in the caste, namely, the Erra (red) Gollas or Pedda Inti (big family), the Nalla (black) Gollas or Chinna Inti (small family), and the Vālus, who are also called Kudukuduppai Tottiyans. The Vālus are said to be a restless class of beggars and sorcerers. The red Gollas are, as a rule, fairer than the blacks (whence perhaps the names). The women of the former wear white cloths, while those of the latter do not. Again, they tie their hair in different ways, and their ornaments differ a good deal. The red women carry no emblem of marriage at all, while the black women wear the pottu. The reds allow their widows to remarry, but the blacks do not. Both sections have exogamous sections, called Kambalams—the reds fourteen, and the blacks nine. The reds are divided, for purposes of caste discipline, into nine nādus and the blacks into fourteen mandais. Each village is under a headman called the Ūr-Nāyakan, and each nādu or mandai under a Pattakāran. The former decide petty disputes, and the

[62] Gazetteer of the Madura district.

latter the more serious cases. The Pattakāran is treated with great deference. He is always saluted with clasped hands, ought never to look on a corpse, and is said to be allowed to consort with any married woman of the caste."

The Tottiyans are supposed to be one of the nine Kambalam (blanket) castes, which, according to one version, are made up of Kāppiliyans, Anappans, Tottiyans, Kurubas, Kummaras, Parivārams, Urumikkārans, Mangalas, and Chakkiliyans. According to another version, the nine castes are Kāppiliyan, Anappan, Tottiyan, Kolla Tottiyan, Kuruba, Kummara, Mēdara, Oddē, and Chakkiliyan. At tribal council-meetings, representatives of each of the nine Kambalams should be present. But, for the nine castes, some have substituted nine septs. The Vekkiliyans seem to have three headmen, called Mettu Nāyakan, Kodia Nāyakan, and Kambli Nāyakan, of whom the first mentioned is the most important, and acts as priest on various ceremonial occasions, such as puberty and marriage rites, and the worship of Jakkamma and Bommakka. The Kambli Nāyakan attends to the purification of peccant or erring members of the community, in connection with which the head of a sheep or goat is taken into the house by the Kambli Nāyakan. It is noted, in the Gazetteer of the Madura district, that "persons charged with offences are invited to prove their innocence by undergoing ordeals. These are now harmless enough, such as attempting to cook rice in a pot which has not been fired, but Turnbull says that he saw the boiling oil ordeal in 1813 in Pudukkōttai territory. Perhaps the most serious caste offence is adultery with a man of another community. Turnbull says that women convicted of this used to be sentenced to be killed by Chakkiliyans, but nowadays rigid excommunication is the penalty."

The Kambalam caste is so called because, at caste council meetings, a kambli (blanket) is spread, on which is placed a kalasam (brass vessel) filled with water, and containing margosa (*Melia Azadirachta*) leaves, and decorated with flowers. Its mouth is closed by mango leaves and a cocoanut.

A correspondent writes to me that "the Zamindars in the western parts of Madura, and parts of Tinnevelly, are known as Kambala Palayapat. If a man belongs to a Zamindar's family, he is said to be of the Rāja Kambala caste. The marriage ceremony is carried out in two temporary huts erected outside the village, one for the bridegroom, the other for the bride. The tāli is tied round the bride's neck by an elderly female or male belonging to the family. If the marriage is contracted with a woman of an inferior class, the bridegroom's hut is not made use of, and he does not personally take part in the ceremony. A dagger (kattar), or rude sword, is sent to represent him, and the tali is tied in the presence thereof."

In a zamindari suit, details of which are published in the Madras Law Reports, Vol. XVII, 1894, the Judge found that the plaintiff's mother was married to the plaintiff's father in the dagger form; that a dagger is used by the Saptūr Zamindars, who are called Kattari Kamaya, in the case of inequality in the caste or social position of the bride; that, though the customary rites of the Kambala caste were also performed, yet the use of the dagger was an essential addition; and that, though she was of a different and inferior caste to that of the plaintiff's father, yet that did not invalidate the marriage. The defendant's argument was that the dagger was used to represent the Zamindar bridegroom as he did not attend in person, and that, by his non-attendance, there could have been no joining of hands, or other essential for constituting a valid marriage. The plaintiff argued that the nuptial rites were duly performed, the Zamindar being present; that the dagger was there merely as an ornament; and that it was customary for people of the Zamindar's caste to have a dagger paraded on the occasion of marriages. The Judge found that the dagger was there for the purpose of indicating that the two ladies, whom the Zamindar married, were of an inferior caste and rank.

It is recorded, in the Gazetteer of the Madura district, that, when a Tottiyan girl attains maturity, "she is kept in a separate hut, which is watched by a Chakkili-yan. Marriage is either infant or adult. A man has the usual claim to his paternal aunt's daughter, and so rigorously is this rule followed that boys of tender years are frequently married to grown women. These latter are allowed to consort with their husband's near relations, and the boy is held to be the father of any children which may be born. Weddings last three days, and involve very numerous ceremonies. They take place in a special pandal erected in the village, on either side of which are smaller pandals for the bride and bridegroom. Two uncommon rites are the slaughtering of a red ram without blemish, and marking the foreheads of the couple with its blood, and the pursuit by the bridegroom, with a bow and arrow, of a man who pretends to flee, but is at length captured and bound. The ram is first sprinkled with water, and, if it shivers, this, as usual, is held to be a good omen. The bride-price is seven kalams of kumbu (*Pennisetum typhoideum*), and the couple may eat only this grain and horse-gram until the wedding is over. A bottu (marriage badge) is tied round the bride's neck by the bridegroom's sister."

Concerning the marriage ceremonies of the Yerrakollas, I gather that, on the betrothal day, kumbu must be cooked. Food is given to seven people belonging to seven different septs. They are then presented with betel leaves and areca nuts and four annas tied in a cloth, and the approaching marriage is announced. On the wedding day, the bride and bridegroom are seated on planks on the marriage dais, and milk is sprinkled over them by people of their own sex. A few hours later, the bridegroom takes his seat in the pandal, whither the bride is brought in the arms of her maternal uncle. She sits by the side of the bridegroom, and the Mettu Nāyakan links together the little fingers of the contracting couple, and tells them to exchange rings. This is the binding portion of the ceremony, and no bottu is tied round the bride's neck. At a marriage among the Vekkiliyans, two huts are constructed in an open space outside the village, in front of which a pandal is erected, supported by twelve posts, and roofed with leafy twigs of the pongu tree and *Mimusops hexandra*. On the following day, the bride and bridegroom are conducted to the huts, the bride being sometimes carried in the arms of her maternal uncle. They worship the ancestral heroes, who are represented by new cloths folded, and placed on a tray. The bridegroom's sister ties the bottu on the bride's neck inside her hut, in front of which kumbu grain is scattered. Betel and a fanam (coin) are placed in the bride's lap. On the third day the bridegroom is dressed up, and, mounting a horse, goes, accompanied by the marriage pots, three times round the huts. He then enters the bride's hut, and she is carried in the arms of the cousins of the bridegroom thrice round the huts. The contracting couple then sit on planks, and the cousins, by order of the Mettu Nāyakan, link their little fingers together. They then enter the bridegroom's hut, and a mock ploughing ceremony is performed. Coming out from the hut, they take up a child, and carry it three times round the huts. This is, it is said, done because, in former days, the Tottiyan bride and bridegroom had to remain in the marriage huts till a child was born, because the Mettu Nāyakan was so busy that he had no time to complete the marriage ceremony until nearly a year had elapsed.

At a wedding among the nomad Tottiyans, a fowl is killed near the marriage (aravēni) pots, and with its blood a mark is made on the foreheads of the bride and bridegroom on their entry into the booths. The Vekkiliyans sacrifice a goat or sheep instead of a fowl, and the more advanced among them substitute the breaking of a cocoanut for the animal sacrifice.

In connection with marriage, Mr. Hemingway writes that "the Tottiyans very commonly marry a young boy to a grown woman, and, as among the Konga Vellālas, the boy's father takes the duties of a husband upon himself until the boy is grown up. Married women are allowed to bestow their favours upon their husbands' relations, and it is said to be an understood thing that a man should not enter his dwelling, if he sees another's slippers placed outside as a sign that the owner of them is with the mistress of the house. Intercourse with men of another caste is, however, punished by expulsion, and widows and unmarried girls who go astray are severely dealt with. Formerly, it is said, they were killed."

At a Tottiyan funeral, fire is carried to the burning-ground by a Chakkiliyan, and the pyre is lighted, not by the sons, but by the sammandhis (relations by marriage).

The Tottiyans of the Madura district observe the worship of ancestors, who are represented by a number of stones set up somewhere within the village boundaries. Such places are called mālē. According to Mr. Hemingway, when a member of the caste dies, some of the bones are buried in this shed, along with a coin, and a stone is planted on the spot. The stones are arranged in an irregular circle. The circles of the Yerrakollas are exceedingly simple, and recall to mind those of the Nāyādis of Malabar, but without the tree. The stones are set up in an open space close to the burning-ground. When a death occurs, a stone is erected among the ashes of the deceased on the last day of the funeral ceremonies (karmāndhiram), and worshipped. It is immediately transferred to the ancestral circle. The mālē of the Vekkiliyan section of the Tottiyans consists of a massive central wooden pillar, carved with male and female human figures, set up in a cavity in a round boulder, and covered over by a conical canopy supported on pillars. When this canopy is set in motion, the central pillar appears to be shaking. This illusion, it is claimed, is due to the power of the ancestral gods. All round the central pillar, which is about ten feet high, a number of stones of different sizes are set up. The central pillar represents Jakkamma and other remote ancestors. The surrounding stones are the representatives of those who have died in recent times. Like the Yerrakollas, the Vekkiliyans erect a stone on the karmāndhiram day at the spot where the body was cremated, but, instead of transferring it at once to the ancestral circle, they wait till the day of periodical mālē worship, which, being an expensive ceremonial, may take place only once in twelve years. If the interval is long, the number of stones representing those who have died meanwhile may be very large. News of the approaching mālē worship is sent to the neighbouring villages, and, on the appointed day, people of all castes pour in, bringing with them several hundred bulls. The hosts supply their guests with fodder, pots, and a liberal allowance of sugar-cane. Refusal to bestow sugar-cane freely would involve failure of the object of the ceremonial. After the completion of the worship, the bulls are let loose, and the animal which reaches the mālē first is decorated, and held in reverence. Its owner is presented with cloths, money, etc. The ceremony may be compared with that of selecting the king bull among the Kāppiliyans.

TOTTIYAN MĀLĒ.

Self-cremation is said[63] to have been "habitually practiced by Tottiya widows in the times anterior to British domination; and great respect was always shown to the memory of such as observed the custom. Small tombs termed thipanjankōvil (fire-torch temple) were erected in their honour on the high-roads, and at these oblations were once a year offered to the manes of the deceased heroines. Sati was not, however, compulsory among them, and, if a widow lived at all times a perfectly chaste and religious life, she was honoured equally with such as performed the rite." It is noted, in the Gazetteer of the Madura district, that "sati was formerly very common in the caste, and the two caste goddesses, Jakkamma and Bommayya, are deifications of women who thus sacrificed themselves. Every four years a festival is held in their honour, one of the chief events in which is a bullock race. The owner of the winning animal receives a prize, and gets the first betel and nut during the feast. The caste god is Perumāl, who is worshipped in the form of a curry-grinding stone. The story goes that, when the Tottiyans were fleeing to the south, one of their women found her grinding-stone so intolerably heavy that she threw it away. It, however, re-appeared in her basket. Thrown away again, it once more re-appeared, and she then realised that the caste god must be accompanying them."

"The Tottiyans," Mr. Hemingway writes, "do not recognise the superiority of Brāhmans, or employ them as priests at marriages or funerals. They are deeply devoted to their own caste deities. Some of these are Bommaka and Mallamma (the spirits of women who committed sati long ago), Vīrakāran or Vīramāti (a bridegroom who was killed in a fight with a tiger), Pattālamma (who helped them in their flight from the north), and Mālai Tambirān, the god of ancestors. Mutta-lamma and Jakkamma are also found. Mālai Tambirān is worshipped in the mālē. The Tottiyans are known for their uncanny devotion to sorcery and witchcraft. All of them are supposed to possess unholy powers, especially the Nalla Gollas, and they are much dreaded by their neighbours. They do not allow any stranger to enter their villages with shoes on, or on horseback, or holding up an umbrella, lest their god should be offended. It is generally believed that, if any one breaks this rule, he will be visited with illness or some other punishment."

The Tottiyans have attached to them a class of beggars called Pichiga vādu, concerning whose origin the following legend is narrated. There were, once upon a time, seven brothers and a sister belonging to the Irrivāru exogamous sept. The brothers went on a pilgrimage to Benares, leaving their sister behind. One day, while she was bathing, a sacred bull (Nandi) left its sperm on her cloth, and she conceived. Her condition was noticed by her brothers on their return, and, suspecting her of immorality, they were about to excommunicate her. But they discovered some cows in calf as the result of parthenogenesis, and six of the brothers were satisfied as to the girl's innocence. The seventh, however, required further proof. After the child was born, it was tied to a branch of a dead chilla tree (*Strychnos potatorum*), which at once burst into leaf and flower. The doubting brother became a cripple, and his descendants are called Pichiga vāru, and those of the baby Chilla vāru.

---

[63] Manual of the Madura district.

TOTTIYAN MĀLĒ.

Traivarnika (third caste men).—Recorded, in the Madras Census Report, 1901, as a section of Kōmatis (who claim to be Vaisyas, or members of the third caste of Manu), who follow the details of Brāhmanical customs more scrupulously than the others. They are described, in the Vizagapatam Manual, as followers of the Rāmānuja faith, who deal chiefly in gold and silver, and ornaments made thereof.

Triputa (*Ipomæa Turpethum*, Indian jalap).—A sept of Vīramushti.

Tsākala.—The Tsākalas, Sākalas, or Chākalas, who derive their name from chāku (to wash), are the washermen of the Telugu country, and also act as torch and palanquin bearers. In the Census Report, 1901, Tellakula (the white class) is given as a synonym. The Rev. J. Cain writes[64] that the "Tellakulavandlu are really washermen who, in consequence of having obtained employment as peons (order-lies) in Government offices, feel themselves to be superior to their old caste people. In their own towns or villages they acknowledge themselves to be washermen, but in other places they disclaim all such connection." It is noted in the Kurnool Manual (1886) that, in the Cumbum division, "they serve as palanquin-bearers, and are always at the mercy of Government officials, and are compelled to carry baggage for little or no wage. Some are Inamdars (landholders), while others work for wages."

The ordinary Tsākalas are called Bāna Tsākala, in contradistinction to the Gūna or Velama Tsākāla. Bāna is the Telugu name for the large pot, which the washermen use for boiling the clothes.[65] The Gūna Tsākalas are dyers. In a note on the Velamas, Mr. H. A. Stuart writes[66] that "some say they form a sub-division of the Balijas, but this they themselves most vehemently deny, and the Balijas de-risively call them Gūni Sākalavāndlu (hunchbacked washermen). The pride and jealousy of Hindu castes was amusingly illustrated by the Velamas of Kālahasti. The Deputy Tahsildar of that town was desired to ascertain the origin of the name Gūni Sākalavāndlu, but, as soon as he asked the question, a member of the caste lodged a complaint of defamation against him before the District Magistrate. The nickname appears to have been applied to them because in the northern districts some print chintz, and, carrying their goods in a bundle on their backs, walk stooping like a laden washerman. This derivation is more than doubtful, for, in the Godāvari district, the name is Gūna Sākalavāndlu, gūna being the large pot in which they dye the chintzes."

Like other Telugu castes, the Tsākalas have exogamous septs or intipēru, among which chīmala (ant) is of common occurrence. Members of the gummadi sept do not cultivate, or eat the fruit of *Cucurbita maxima* (gummadi), and those of the magili pula gōtra avoid the fruit of *Pandanus fascicularis*. In like manner, sword beans (*Canavalia ensiformis*) may not be eaten by those who belong to the thamballa gōtra.

Among the sub-divisions of the caste are Reddi Bhūmi (Reddi earth), Mu-rikināti, Pākanāti (eastern country), Dēsa, and Golkonda. Of these, some are also sub-divisions of other Telugu classes, as follows:—

Dēsa or Dēsūr Balija—Kāpu.

Murikināti or Murikinādu—Kamsala, Mangala, Māla and Rāzu.

Pākanāti—Balija, Golla, Kamsala, Kāpu, and Māla.

---

[64] Ind. Ant., VIII, 1879.
[65] *Ibid.*
[66] Manual of the North Arcot district.

Reddi Bhūmi—Māla, Mangala.

At the census, 1891, Odde was recorded as a sub-division of the Tsākalas, and it is noted in the Vizagapatam Manual (1869) that the Vadde or Odde Cakali wash clothes, and carry torches in that district. The name Odde Tsākala refers to Oriya-speaking washermen. Telugus call the Oriya country Ōdra or Odde dēsam and Oriyas Ōdra or Odde Vāndlu.

Like the Tamil Vannāns, the Tsākalas prepare for various castes torches for processional or other ceremonial occasions, and the face cloth, and paddy piled up at the head of a corpse, are their perquisite. The Reddi Bhūmi and other sub-divisions wash the clothes of all classes, except Mālas and Mādigās, while the Dēsa and Golkonda sub-divisions will wash for both Mālas and Mādigās, provided that the clothes are steeped in water, and not handed to them, but left therein, to be taken by the washerman. Every village has its families of washermen, who, in return for their services, receive an allowance of grain once a year, and may have land allotted to them. Whenever a goat or fowl has to be sacrificed to a deity, it is the privilege of the Tsākala to cut off the head, or wring the neck of the animal. When Kāpu women go on a visit to a distant village, they are accompanied by a Tsākala. At a Kāpu wedding, a small party of Kāpus, taking with them some food and gingelly (*Sesamum*) oil, proceed in procession to the house of a Tsākala, in order to obtain from him a framework made of bamboo or sticks, over which cotton threads (dhornam) are wound, and the Ganga idol, which is kept in his custody. The food is presented to him, and some rice poured into his cloth. Receiving these things, he says that he cannot find the dhornam and idol without a torch-light, and demands gingelly oil. This is given to him, and the Kāpus return with the Tsākala carrying the dhornam and idol to the marriage house. The Tsākala is asked to tie the dhornam to the pandal (marriage booth) or roof of the house, and he demands some paddy (unhusked rice) which is heaped up on the ground. Standing thereon, he ties the dhornam. At a Panta Kāpu wedding, the Ganga idol, together with a goat and kāvadi (bamboo pole), with baskets of rice, cakes, betel leaves and areca nuts, is carried in procession to a pond or temple. The washerman, dressed up as a woman, heads the procession, and keeps on dancing and singing till the destination is reached. At the conclusion of the ceremonial, he takes charge of the idol, and goes his way. Among the Panta Reddis of the Tamil country, the idol is taken in procession by the washerman, who goes to every Reddi house, and receives a present of money. At a wedding among the Idigas (Telugu toddy-drawers), the brother of the bride is fantastically dressed, with margosa (*Melia Azadirachta*) leaves in his turban, and carries a bow and arrow. This kodangi (buffoon) is conducted in procession to the temple by a few married women, and made to walk over cloths spread on the ground by the village washerman. The cloth worn by a Kāpu girl at the time of her first menstrual ceremony is the perquisite of the washerwoman.

The tribal deity of the Tsākalas is Madivālayya, in whose honour a feast, called Mailar or Mailar Pandaga, is held in January immediately after the Pongal festival. Small models of pots, slabs of stone such as are used for beating the wet clothes on, and other articles used in their work, are made in rice and flour paste. After they have been worshipped, fruits, cooked vegetables, etc., are offered, and a sheep or goat is sacrificed. Some of its blood is mixed with the food, of which a little is sprinkled over the pots, stones, etc., used during washing operations. If this ceremonial was not observed, it is believed that the clothes, when boiling in the water pot, would catch fire, and be ruined. The festival, which is not observed by the Dēsa and Golkonda Tsākalas, lasts for five or seven days, and is a time of holiday.

At the first menstrual ceremony, the maternal uncle of the girl has to erect a hut made of seven different kinds of sticks, of which one must be from a *Strychnos Nux-vomica* tree. The details of the marriage ceremony are very similar to those of the Balijas and Kammas. The distribution of pān-supāri, and the tying of the dhornam to the pandal must be carried out by an assistant headman called Gatamdar. On the last day, a goat or sheep is sacrificed to the marriage pots. Liberal potations of toddy are given to those who attend the wedding.

The Tsākalas have a caste beggar called Mailāri, or Patam, because he carries a brass plate (patam) with the figure of a deity engraved on it. He is said to be a Lingāyat.

Tsalla or Challa (butter-milk).—An exogamous sept of Māla.

Tsanda or Chanda (tax or subscription).—An exogamous sept of Kamma and Mēdara.

Tulabhāram.—In his description[67] of the Tulabhāram or Tulapurushadānam ceremony performed by the Mahārājas of Travancore, Mr. Shungoony Menon explains that the latter word is a compound of three Sanskrit words, tula (scales), purusha (man), and dānam (gift, particularly of a religious character). And he gives the following description of the ceremonial, for the performance of which a Tulamandapam is erected, wherein the scales are set up, and the weighing and other rites performed. On the eighth day "after worshipping and making offerings, the Mahārāja proceeds to the Tulamandapam, where, in the south-east corner, he is sprinkled with punyāham water. Then he goes to the side room, where the 'nine grains' are sown in silver flower pots, where the achārya anoints him with nine fresh-water kalasas. Thence the Mahārāja retires to the palace, changes clothes, wears certain jewels specially made for the occasion, and, holding the State sword in his right hand and the State shield in his left, he proceeds to the pagoda; and, having presented a bull elephant at the foot of the great golden flagstaff, and silks, gold coins, jewels and other rich offerings in the interior, he walks round by the Sevaimandapam, and re-enters the Tulamandapam. He walks thrice round the scales, prostrates himself before it, bows before the priests and elderly relatives, and obtains their sanction to perform the Tulapurushadānam. He then mounts the western scale, holding Yama's and Surya's pratimās in his right and left hand respectively. He sits facing to the east on a circular heavy plank cut out of fresh jackwood (*Artocarpus integrifolia*), and covered with silk. He repeats mantras (prayers) in this position. The opposite or eastern scale then receives the gold, both coined and in ingots, till it not only attains equality but touches the ground, and the scale occupied by the Mahārāja rises high. The Mahārāja then comes down, and, sitting facing to the east, places the gold, the Tulupurusha pratimā and other pratimās,

____

[67] History of Travancore, 1878.

with flowers, sandal paste, etc., in a basin of water, and, meditating on Brahma or the Supreme Being, he offers the contents to Brāhmans generically." Of the gold placed in the scale, one-fourth is divided among the priests who conduct the ceremony, and the remaining three-fourths are distributed among Brāhmans. For use in connection with the ceremony, gold coins, called tulabhāra kāsu, are specially struck. They bear on one side the Malayālam legend Srī Padmanābha, and on the other a chank shell.

In connection with the tulabhāram ceremony as performed at the temple of Kāli, the goddess of cholera and small-pox at Cranganore in the Cochin State, Mr. T. K. Gopal Panikkar writes as follows.[68] "When a man is taken ill of any infectious disease, his relations generally pray to this goddess for his recovery, solemnly covenanting to perform what goes by the name of a thulabhāram ceremony. The process consists in placing the patient in one of the scale-pans of a huge balance, and weighing him against gold or more generally pepper (and sometimes other substances as well) deposited in the other scale-pan. Then this weight of the substance is offered to the goddess. This is to be performed right in front of the goddess in the temple yard."

In connection with weighing ceremonies, it may be noted that, at Mulki in South Canara, there is a temple of Venkatēswara, which is maintained by Konkani Brāhmans. A Konkani Brāhman, who is attached to the temple, becomes inspired almost daily between 10 and 11 A.M. immediately after pūja (worship), and people consult him. Some time ago, a rich merchant (a Baniya from Gujarat) consulted the inspired man (Darsana) as to what steps should be taken to enable his wife to be safely delivered. The Darsana told him to take a vow that he would present to the god of the temple silver, sugar-candy, and date fruits, equal in weight to that of his wife. This he did, and his wife was delivered of a male child. The cost of the ceremonial is said to have been five thousand rupees.

Tulabīna.—The Tulabīnas are a class of cotton-cleaners, who are scattered over the Ganjam district, and said to be more numerous in Cuttack. It is suggested that the name is derived from tula, the beam of a balance, and bīna (or vīna) a stringed musical instrument. The apparatus used by them in cleaning cotton, which bears a fanciful resemblance to a vīna, is suspended by a rope so that it is properly balanced, and the gut-string thereof struck with a dumb-bell shaped implement, to set it vibrating.

Tulasi (*Ocimum sanctum*, sacred basil).—A sub-division of Velama, and gōtra of Kōmati. The tulsi plant is planted in Hindu houses and worshipped by women, and the wood is made into beads for rosaries.

Tulukkar (Turks).—A Tamil name sometimes applied to Muhammadans.

Tuluva.—Tulu, Tuluva, or Tuluvan occurs as the name of a sub-division of the Tamil Vellālas, and of the Agasas, Billavas, Gaudas, Kumbāras, and other classes in South Canara. The equivalent Tulumar is recorded as a sub-caste of Māvilan, which speaks Tulu.

---

[68] Malabar and its Folk, Madras, 1900.

Concerning the Tuluva Vellālas, Mr. H. A. Stuart writes[69] that these are immigrants from the Tulu country, a part of the modern district of South Canara. Mr. Nelson is of opinion that these are the original Vellālas, who were invited to Tondamandalam after its conquest by the Chola king Adondai Chakravarti.[70]

Tunnaran (tailor).—An occupational sub-division of Nāyar.

Tupākala.—Tupākala or Tupāki (gun) has been recorded as an exogamous sept of Balija, Kavarai, and Yānādi.

Turaka.—Recorded as a sept of Kuruba. It is further a Telugu name sometimes applied to Muhammadans. There is also a thief class, known as Bhattu Turaka. (*See* Bhatrāzu.)

Turuvalar.—Recorded in the Salem Manual as a caste name, by which some of the Vēdans call themselves. "The Turuvalar are distinguished as the Kattukudugirajāti, a name derived from a custom among them which authorizes informal temporary matrimonial arrangements."

---

[69] Madras Census Report, 1891.
[70] Manual of the Madura district.

U

Udāsi.—A few members of this Central India sect of religious mendicants and devotees have been returned at times of census. It is said to have been founded three hundred years ago by one Gopāldas.

Udaiya.—Udaiya, meaning lord, is the title of many well-to-do Lingāyats and of some Jains, and Udaiya or Wodeiyar occurs as the name of a Lingāyat sub-division of the Badagas of the Nīligiri hills. The Mahārājas of Mysore belong to the Wodeiyar dynasty, which was restored after the Muhammadan usurpation of Haidar Āli and Tīpu Sultan. The name of the present Maharāja is Srī Krishna Rāja Wodeiyar Bahādur.

Udaiyān.—It is noted in the Madras Census Report, 1891, that "the four Tamil castes Nattamān, Malaimān, Sudarmān (or Suruthimān), and Udaiyān are closely connected. The last is probably a title rather than a caste, and is the usual agnomen of the Nattamāns, Malaimāns, and Sudarmāns, as also of the potter caste (Kusavan). Nattamān means a man of the plains, Malaimān a man of the hills, and Sudarmān one who does good, a hero. Nattampadi is another form of Nattamān. Tradition traces the descent of the three castes from a certain Dēva Rāja, a Chēra king, who had three wives, by each of whom he had a son, and these were the ancestors of the three castes. There are other stories, but all agree in ascribing the origin of the castes to a single progenitor of the Chēra dynasty. It seems probable that they are descendants of the Vēdar soldiers of the Kongu country, who were induced to settle in the eastern districts of the Chēra kingdom. Additional evidence of the important position they once held is afforded by the titles Pandariyār, Pandārāttār (custodians of the treasury), which some of them still use. Some of them again are locally styled Poligars (Pālayakkāran) by the ordinary ryots, and the title Kāvalgar is not infrequent."

In a note on the Udaiyāns, Malaiyamāns, Nattamāns, and Sudarmāns of the Trichinopoly district, Mr. F. R. Hemingway writes as follows. "Though, in the Census Report, 1901, they are shown as separate castes, in this district they are endogamous sub-divisions of one and the same caste, namely the Udaiyāns. The three sub-divisions are unanimous in saying that they are the descendants of the three Paraiyan foster-daughters of the poetess Auvaiyar, all of whom became the wives of the king of Tirukkoyilūr in South Arcot, a certain Daivika, who was warned that only by marrying these women could he save his family from disaster. The Chōla, Pāndya, and Chēra kings were present at the wedding, and, on their blessing the bridegroom and his brides, they were themselves blessed by the poetess, to whom the Chēra kingdom owes its unfailing rain, the Chōla country its rice fields, and the Pāndyan realm its cotton. The poorness of the last blessing is due to the fact that the Pāndya king was slow to offer his good wishes. The three sub-divisions eat together, and recognise the tie of a common descent, but do not intermarry. The section called Arisakkāra Nattamān is looked down upon by the rest, and may not intermarry with any of them. All have well-defined exogamous sub-divisions, called kānis, derived from places where their different ancestors are supposed to have lived, *e.g.*, Kolattūr, Kannanūr, Ariyalūr. The Udaiyāns put on sacred threads at marriages and funerals, and some of them have recently begun to wear them always. They are generally cultivators, and, with the exception of the Sudarmāns, who are supposed to have a turn for crime, are law-abiding citizens. One section of the Sudarmāns, the Mūppans of Kapistalam in Tanjore, have a bad reputation for criminality. A curious practice is that, before arranging a marriage, it is customary for the bride's party to go to the bridegroom's house, to dine with him, and test his health by seeing how much he can eat. They allow a boy, whose suit for the hand of a girl within certain degrees of relationship is refused by her parents, to marry the girl, notwithstanding, by tying a tāli (marriage emblem) round her neck. They also permit the betrothal of infants, the form observed being to present the child with a new cloth and a mat, and to apply sacred ashes to its forehead. At their funerals, the mourning party has to chew some rice and spit it out on the return from the burning-ground, and, on the sixteenth day, the widow is made to worship a light, and to touch a salt pot. The Nattamān women do not, as a rule, cover their breasts. The lobes of their ears are very distended, and they tattoo their chins and cheeks in the Paraiyan fashion. This is supposed to be in recollection of their origin. The Malaiyamān women wear their tāli on a golden wire instead of on a thread."

"The Udaiyāns," Mr. Francis writes,[71] are a caste, which is specially numerous in South Arcot. Most of them are cultivators, and in Kallakurchi many are also money-lenders on a large scale. They adopt numerous different titles in an indiscriminate way, and four brothers have been known to call themselves respectively Nāyak, Pillai, Mudali, and Udaiyān. They have three sub-divisions—Malaiyamān, Nattamān, and Sudarmān—which all admit that they are descended from one common stock, will usually dine together, but do not intermarry. Some of the caste, however, are now turning vegetarians, and these will not only not eat with the others, but will not let their girls marry them. They do not, nevertheless, object to their sons taking brides from the meat-eating classes, and thus provide an interesting, if small, instance of the (on this coast) uncommon practice of hypergamy. In all general matters the ways of the three sub-divisions are similar. Sudarmāns are uncommon in this district, and are stated to be chiefly found in Trichinopoly and Tanjore. The Udaiyāns say that the three groups are the descendants of a king who once ruled at Tirukkōyilūr, the first of whom took the hilly part of his father's country, and so was called Malaiyamān; the second the level tracts, whence his name Nattamān, and the third was the scholar of the family, and learned in the holy books (srutas), and so was called Sudarmān. These Udaiyāns are the caste from which were drawn some of the kāvalgārs (watchmen) who, in pre-British days, were appointed to perform police duties, and keep the country

[71] Gazetteer of the South Arcot district.

clear of thieves; and some of the descendants of these men, who are known to their neighbours as poligars, and still have considerable local influence, are even now to be met with. The connection of the members of the caste with the Vēpūr (criminal) Paraiyans, which is of course confined to the less reputable sections among them, seems to have had its origin in the days when they were still head kāvalgārs, and these Paraiyans were their talaiyāris, entrusted, under their orders, with police duties in the different villages. It now consists in acting as receivers of the property these people steal, and in protecting them in diverse ways—finding and feeing a vakil (law pleader) for their defence, for instance—when they are in trouble with the police. It is commonly declared that their relations are sometimes of a closer nature, and that the wives of Vēppūr Paraiyans who are in enforced retirement are cared for by the Udaiyāns. To this is popularly attributed the undoubted fact that these Paraiyans are often much fairer in complexion than other members of that caste."

The village of Mangalam in the South Arcot district is "chiefly interesting on account of its being the only village in the district where buffalo sacrifices on any scale are still regularly made. Buffaloes are dedicated to the Kāli shrine in Mangalam even by persons in the Salem, Tanjore and Trichinopoly districts, and the village is commonly known as Māduvetti Mangalam, or buffalo-sacrificing Mangalam. When a man or any of his belongings gets seriously sick, he consecrates an animal to this shrine, and, if the illness ends favourably, it is sent to its fate at the temple on the date of the annual sacrifice (May-June). When the buffalo is dedicated, a piece of saffron-coloured cloth, in which is placed some small coin and a cadjan (palm) leaf containing an announcement of the dedication, is tied to its horns, and it is allowed to roam wherever it likes through the fields. On the day of the sacrifice, fourteen of the best of the animals which have been dedicated and brought to the temple are selected, and seven of them are tied to an equal number of stone posts in front of the goddess' shrine. The pūjāri (priest), who is an Udaiyān by caste, then walks down the line, and beheads them one after the other. The goddess is next taken round on a car, and, on her return to the temple, the other seven buffaloes are similarly killed. The animals which are not selected are sold, and the proceeds paid into the temple treasury. There are two images in the temple, one of Kāli, and the other, which is placed at the back of the shrine, of Mangalayāchi. The latter goddess does not approve of animal sacrifices, and, while the above ceremonies are proceeding, a blanket is hung in front of her so that she may not see them."[72]

It is noted by Bishop Whitehead that, a few years ago, an untoward event occurred in connection with a Pidāri festival at a village in the Trichinopoly district. "The festival had commenced, and the pūjāri had tied the kapu (cord dyed with turmeric) on his wrist, when a dispute arose between the trustees of the shrine, which caused the festival to be stopped. The dispute could not be settled, and the festival was suspended for three years, and, during all that time, there could be no marriages among the Udaya caste, while the poor pūjāri, with the kapu on his wrist, had to remain the whole of the three years in the temple, not daring to go

---

[72] Gazetteer of the South Arcot district.

out lest Pidāri in her wrath should slay him."

It is recorded, in the Madras Census Report, 1901, that "the Nattamāns say they originally settled in South Arcot, and then spread to Tanjore and Trichinopoly, and finally to Madura, and this theory is supported by the fact that they have fifteen exogamous sub-divisions called kānis or fields, which are all named after villages (*e.g.*, Ariyalūr, Puththūr) in the first three of these districts. A man has a right to marry the daughter of his father's sister, and, if she is given to another man, the father's sister has to return to her father or brother the dowry which she received at the time of her marriage, and this is given to the man who had the claim upon the girl. The same custom occurs among the Kuravans and the Kallans. The eldest son in each family has to be named after the god of the village which gives its name to the kāni or sept to which the family belongs, and the child is usually taken to that village to be named. Marriage is infant or adult. Widow marriage is forbidden. Brāhmans are employed for ceremonies, but these are not received on terms of equality by other Brāhmans. Both cremation and burial are practised. Vellālas will eat with Nattamāns. The caste title is Udaiyān." Another title is Nayinar, which is also used by Pallis and Jains. There is a proverb "Nattumuththinal Nayinar", *i.e.*, when the Nattamān ripens, he is a Nayinar. At the census, 1901, some Nattamāns returned themselves as Natramiludaiyān, meaning the repository of chaste Tamil; and Ūr-Udaiyān (lord of a village) was given as their caste name. Nattamān also occurs as a sub-division of the Pallis.

Under the name Nattamādi, the Nattamāns are described in the Tanjore Manual as "peasant population. Some are ryotwari land-holders in their own right and possess large estates. The word is derived from nattam, village, and is used in three forms, Nattamakkal, Nattamar, and Nattamādi. A considerable proportion are converts to the Roman Catholic religion, and, in the neighbourhood of Vallam, there are very few who profess any other faith." In the Madura Manual, the Nattambādiyans are further described as being "usually respectable cultivators. They are said to have emigrated into the Madura country not more than about eight years ago. They are an interesting class of Tamils, inasmuch as very many of them have adopted the Roman Catholic faith under the leadership of the Jesuit missionaries. They are said to be a fine race physically; finer even than the Vellālans. They are also called Udaiyans, and tradition says that they came from the Toreiyur nādu or district in Tanjore, from a village called Udeiyāpāleiyam. They are chiefly resident in the great zamindāris, and contrast favourably with the Maravans, being very orderly, frugal, and industrious."

I am informed that Nattamān women will do cooly work and carry food for their husbands when at work in the fields, but that Malaimān women will not do so.

The Sudarmāns are described, in the Madras Census Report, 1901, as "cultivators chiefly found in the districts of Tanjore and Trichinopoly. They are imitating the Brāhmans and Vellālas in their social customs, and some of them have left off eating meat, with the idea of raising themselves in general estimation; but they nevertheless eat in the houses of Kallans and Idaiyans. Their title is Mūppan." Some Sudarmāns, I am told, have become Agamudaiyans.

Uddāri.—A synonym for the village Taliyāri.

Uddu (*Phaseolus Mungo*).—An exogamous sept of Kāppiliyan.

Udhdhandra.—A title conferred by Zamindars on some Kurumos.

Uduma.—Uduma or Udumala, meaning the lizard *Varanus*, has been recorded as an exogamous sept of Bōya, Kāpu, Tottiyan, and Yānādi.

Ugrāni.—A village servant in South Canara, appointed to watch the store-rooms (ugrāna), *e.g.*, the village granary, treasury, or bhūta-sthāna. In 1907, the powers of village policeman were conferred on the Ugrāni, who now wears a brass badge on his arm, with the words Village Police in the vernacular engraved on it. It is the duty of the Ugrāni to report the following to the village magistrate:—

1. The commission of grave crimes, such as theft, house-breaking, robbery, dacoity, accidental deaths, suicides, etc.

2. The existence of disputes in connection with landed property, likely to give occasion to any fight or rioting.

3. The arrival of Fakirs, Bairāgis, or other strangers in the village.

4. The arrival or residence in the village of any person whom the villagers suspect to be a bad character.

5. The commission of mischief in respect of any public property, such as roads, road avenues, bridges, cattle pounds, Government trees on unreserved lands, etc.

Ūliyakāran.—A synonym, denoting menial servant, of Parivāram.

Ullādan.—It is recorded, in the Travancore Census Report, 1901, that "the Ullātans and Nāyātis are found in the low country, as well as on the hills. At a remote period, certain Ullāta families from the plains settled themselves at Tal-purakkōtta near Sabarimala, and even to-day pilgrims to Sabarimala consider this place as sacred. In the low country, the offerings to the same deities as the Ullātans worship are offered by the Vālans. Hence the Ullātans were called by them Koch-chuvālans. The place near Sabarimala where they once dwelt is known as Kochu-vālakkuti, or the cottage of the Kochchuvālan. Most of these Ullātans have left this place for fear of wild beasts, and are now straying in the woods with no fixed abode. It is said that they are the descendants from a Nambūtiri woman, who, on being proclaimed an outcast, said Ullatāna, meaning that (the offence for which she was ostracised) is true. [According to another derivation, the name is derived from ull, within, and otunnu, runs, and means one who runs away into the forest at the sight of a member of any of the higher castes.] They are good hunters, and experts in the collection of wax and other forest produce. A curious marriage cus-tom, prevalent among them, is thus related by Dr. Day. 'A large round building is made of leaves, and inside this the bride is ensconced. All the eligible young men of the village then assemble, and form a ring round this hut. At a short distance sits the girl's father or the nearest male relative with tom-tom in his hands, and a few more musical instruments complete the scene. Presently the music begins. The young men, each armed with a bamboo, commence dancing round the hut, into which each of them thrusts his stick. This continues about an hour, when the owner of whichever bamboo she seizes becomes the fortunate husband of the concealed bride. A feast then follows.'[73] They subsist chiefly on fruits, wild yams, and other forest products, and eke out a wretched existence. When armed with guns, they make excellent sportsmen."

It is noted by the Rev. S. Mateer[74] that the Ullādans "subsist chiefly on wild yams, arrowroot, and other esculents, which they find in the jungle, and for the grubbing up of which they are generally armed with a long pointed staff. They also further enjoy the fruits of the chase, and are adepts in the use of the bow and arrow. The arrow they use has an iron spear-head, and an Ullādan has been known to cut a wriggling cobra in half at the first shot. They were claimed as the property of celebrated hill temples, or great proprietors, who exacted service of them, and sometimes sold their services to Nairs, Syrians, and others. A few Ullādans in the low country say they or their fathers were stolen in childhood, and brought down as slaves."

At Kottayam in Travancore, I came across a party of Ullādans carrying cross-bows. These were said to be used for catching fish in rivers, lagoons, and tanks. The arrow is between two and three feet in length, and has an iron hook at one end. Attached to it is a thin but strong string, one end of which is tied to the hook, while the other end passes through a small hole in the wooden part of the arrow, and is fastened to the cross-bar of the bow. This string is about thirty feet in length, and serves not only to drag the captured fish out of the water, and land it, but also to prevent the arrow from being lost. The origin of the cross-bow, which I have not found in the possession of any other tribe, puzzled me until the word Firingi was mentioned in connection with it. The use of this word would seem to indicate that the cross-bow is a survival from the days of the Portuguese on the west coast, Firingi (a Frank) or Parangi being used by Natives for European or Portuguese.

For the following note on the Ullādans of the Cochin State, I am indebted to Mr. L. K. Anantha Krishna Iyer.[75] "Their huts are situated in the forest of the plains, by the side of paddy (rice) flats, or in cocoanut gardens remote from those of the members of the higher castes. Only Christian Moplahs are found in the neighbourhood. Their huts are erected on short bamboo posts, the roof and four sides of which are covered with plaited cocoanut leaves. A bamboo framework, of the same leaves, serves the purpose of a door. A few plaited cocoanut leaves, and a mat of their own weaving, form the only furniture, and serve as beds for them at night. Their vessels in domestic use consist of a few earthen pots for cooking and keeping water in, and a few shallow earthen dishes, from which they drink water, and take their food. Some large pieces of the bark of the areca palm, containing salt, chillies, etc., were also seen by me. What little they possess as food and clothing is placed in small baskets suspended from the framework of the roof by means of wooden hooks.

"The caste assembly consists of the elderly members of the caste. There is a

---

[73] *Cf.* Nāyādi.
[74] Native Life in Travancore, 1883.
[75] Monograph, Eth. Survey, Cochin, No. 9, 1906.

headman, who is called Mūppan, and he has an assistant who is known as Ponamban. The headman has to preside at all marriage and funeral ceremonies, and to decide all disputes connected with the caste. The caste assembly meets chiefly to deal with cases of immorality. The guilty parties are summoned before the assembly. The headman, who presides, inquires into the matter, and, in the event of the accused parties confessing their guilt, they are taken before His Highness the Rāja, who is informed of the circumstances. The male culprit is sometimes beaten or fined. The woman is given some water or the milk of a green cocoanut, and this is supposed to set her free from all sin. When a fine is imposed, it is sometimes spent on the purchase of toddy, which is shared among the castemen present. The headman gets a few puthans (Cochin coins) for his trouble.

"In religion, the Ullādans are pure animists or demon worshippers. All cases of sickness, and other calamities, are attributed to the malignant influence of demons, whom it is necessary to propitiate. They worship Kappiri, Thikutti, and Chāthan, all of whom are represented by a few stones placed under a thatched roof called kottil. Offerings of rice flour, sheep, fowls, toddy, rice, cocoanuts and plantains, are given on Fridays in the month of Kanni (September-October). One of the castemen acts as Velichapād (oracle), and speaks as if by inspiration. He also casts out demons from the bodies of women who are believed to be influenced by them. When he resumes his former self, he takes half the offerings to himself, allowing the other half for distribution among the bystanders. They also worship the spirits of the departed members of their families, who, they think, sometimes appear to them in dreams, and ask them for whatever they want. They believe that, in the event of their neglecting to give what is asked, these spirits will cause serious calamity to their family.

"The Ullādans generally bury their dead in special places called chotala, but some of them bury the corpse a few yards away from their huts. The young are buried deep in the ground, while the old ones are buried not so deep. The dead body is placed on a new piece of cloth spread on a bamboo bier, which is carried by the relatives to the grave-yard. The castemen of the neighbourhood, including the relations and friends of the deceased, accompany the bier to the burial-ground, and return home after bathing. The members of the family fast for the night. They observe pollution for fifteen days, and, on the morning of the sixteenth day, the Thalippan (barber priest) comes and cleans the huts and its surrounding, and sprinkles cow-dung mixed with water on the members of the family as they return from bathing, in order that they may be freed from pollution. They entertain their castemen on that day. It is a custom among the Ullādans, Pulayas, and other low classes, that, when they are invited to a feast, they bring with them some rice, curry stuffs, toddy, or a few annas to meet the expenses of the feast. Very often the above articles are obtained as a gift from the charitably disposed members of the higher castes. At the end of the year, a similar feast is given to the castemen. Among the Ullādans, the nephew is the chief mourner, for he usually succeeds to the property of the dead, and proves his right of ownership by acting as the chief mourner.

"The Ullādans on the sea-coast make boats, and cut timber. Their brethren in the interior gather honey, and collect minor forest produce, and sell it to contractors. During the agricultural season, they engage in every kind of agricultural work, such as ploughing, sowing, transplanting, reaping, etc. They also graze the cattle of the farmers. They get a few annas worth of paddy (unhusked rice) for their labour. For most of the months in the year they are in a half-starving condition, and resort to eating wild roots, and animals, which they can get hold of (*e.g.,* rats, tortoises, fish, or crocodiles). They know where rats are to be found. They thrust a long stick into their holes, moving it so violently as to kill them there, or forcing them to come out, when they catch and kill them. Very often in the rural parts, both men and women are found with long poles ready to be thrust into any holes there may be by the side of a fence, or where bamboos are growing luxuriantly. They also catch crocodiles. They place the carcase of a fowl, sheep, or other animal, on the bank of a canal, or by the side of a tank where crocodiles are to be found. Into it is thrust a pointed piece of iron, fastened to a long cord. When a crocodile comes out of the water to eat it, or tries to get away with it, the piece of iron is fixed firmly into its mouth, upon which the Ullādans, who are watching, approach and kill it with their clubs and knives. They catch fish by means of bait, and by poisoning the water. They are also very skilful in spearing fish swimming near the surface. They are more trackers of game than hunters, and very often accompany Moplahs, who go out hunting to provide themselves with meat of all kinds for feasts during their weddings. The Ullādans are engaged only as beaters. For this service, they are given meals during the wedding, in addition to three annas worth of paddy for each beater. They are armed with clubs, and seldom go with dogs, fearing that they may drive away the game. When any animal is killed in hunting, the right side of the back of the animal goes to the Government. It is given to the Forest Officer, who auctions it, and the money obtained is sent to the tāluk treasury. The left side of the back goes to the member of the party who shoots the animal. He also gets the face with the tongue. The headman among the Ullādans also gets a share. The remainder of the carcase is equally divided among the members who have formed the party. Should any dispute arise regarding the division of the game, the man who shoots the animal is entrusted with the settlement of the dispute, and his decision is final. In cases where the hunting party is organised by the Moplahs, the Ullādans get wages and meals for their trouble. In places where elephant pits are dug, hunting is forbidden.

"As regards their social status, the Ullādans, like the Nāyādis, form the Chandālas of the plains. Their approach to within a radius of sixty-four feet pollutes Brāhmans, and all higher castes, including the Sūdras (Nāyars). The Ullādans cannot walk along the public roads, or come to the bazaars. Nor can they approach the precincts of any town or locality where the members of higher castes reside. The Pulayas and Parayas profess to be polluted by them. It is curious to note that the Ullāda women consider it degrading to go to work like the Pulaya woman. They say that their husbands have to provide for them."

Ulli (onions or garlic).— A sub-division of the Tigala market-gardeners. The equivalent Ullipōyala occurs as an exogamous sept of Golla, and Ulligadda as a sept of Bōya and Korava.

Ulumban.—It is recorded in the Gazetteer of Malabar that "an endogamous sub-caste (of Nāyars) of foreign origin are the Ulumbans or cowherds. According to one tradition, they were originally immigrants from Dvāraka (Guzerat). Their original occupation still survives in the privileges of supplying ghee (clarified butter) for the abhishēgam or libation at the great annual festival at the jungle shrine of Kōttiyur, and of supplying butter-milk to the Tiruvangād temple at Tellicherry, which are exercised by families of this caste; and in the general privilege of offering milk in any temple without previous ablution."

Uluvala (seeds of horse-gram: *Dolichos biflorus*).—An exogamous sept of Bōya and Jōgi.

Ungara.—Ungara and Ungarāla, meaning rings, have been recorded as exogamous septs of Balija and Kuruba.

Unittiri.—Unittiri, or Unyātiri, meaning, it is said, venerable boy, has been recorded as a sub-division of Sāmantam. Unnittān appears, in the Travancore Census Report, 1901, as a title of Nāyars, and is said to be derived from unni, small, tān, a title of dignity.

Unnekankana.—A sub-division of Kurubas, who tie a woollen thread (unne kankana) round the wrist at times of marriage.

Unni.—For the following note on the Unnis of Travancore, I am indebted to Mr. N. Subramani Aiyar. The word Unni, whatever its significance may have been of old, at present forms the common title of four castes of the Ambalavāsi group, whose manners and custom differ considerably in their details. They are known, respectively, as Pushpakans, Brāhmanis, Tiyattunnis, and Nattu Pattars, their social precedence being in this order. Pushpakan comes from pushpa, which in Sanskrit means either a flower or menses. Brāhmanis, more vulgarly known as Pappinis, are so named because they perform some of the priestly functions of the Brāhmans for the Sūdra population of Travancore. Tīyattunnis, also known as Taiyampatis in British Malabar, are so called from the peculiar religious service they perform in some Hindu temples. Nattu Pattars are also known as Pattar Unnis and Karappuram Unnis. Unni means a child, and is used as an honorific term to denote the male children of a Nambūtiri's household. The reason why these Ambalavāsi castes came to be so called was that they were looked upon as more respectable than the Nāyars, by whom the term must doubtless have been made use of at first. The Pushpakans are said to be divided into three classes, namely Pushpakans, Nambiassans, and Puppallis. The first section live only as far south as Evūr in Central Travancore, and are called Nambiyars in the north. The Nambiyassans live in Cochin and North Travancore, while the Puppallis are found only towards the south. There are no sub-divisions among the Brāhmanis and Karappuramunnis. But the Tīyattunnis are divided into two classes, namely the Tīyatinambiyans of the north, who are generally employed in the temples of Sastha, and Tīyattunnis proper, who perform a similar function in the shrines of Bhadrakāli. Women are also known as Atovarammamar and Kōvillammamar.

Pushpakans are said to have arisen out of the union of a Brāhman woman in her menses with her husband. Parasurāma set them apart, and gave them the occupation of making garlands in the temples of Malabar. Though this derivation is given in the Kēralamahatmya, it may be more easily believed that Pushpakan is derived from the occupation of working in flowers. Puppalli, at any rate, is thus derived, and, as Palli signifies anything sacred, the caste name arose from the occupation of preparing garlands for deities. Nambiyassans, called also Nambiyars and Nambis, must have been, as also the Puppallis and Brāhmanis, one with the Pushpakans. In some places, Nambiyassans are known to have kept gymnasia and military training schools. The Brāhmanis must have undergone some degree of degradation because of the religious songs which they sang during the marriages of the Nāyars, while those who did not take part therein became, as it were, a separate sept. Another tradition, accounting for the origin of the caste, is that, as in primitive ages early marriages prevailed among the Malayāla Brāhmans, the family of the Nambūtiri who first married his daughter after puberty was excommunicated, and gave origin to the Pushpakas. This is untrue, as, in Vēdic times, adult marriage was the rule, and the Nambūtiris in this respect have been known to follow a more primitive custom than the Brāhmans of the east coast. The Tīyattunnis are said to be the descendants of a Bhūta or demon directed by Siva to sing songs in praise of Bhadrakāli, and appease her anger after the murder of Darika. They must from the first have formed a distinct section of the Ambalavāsis. The Karappuram Unnis are supposed to have been elevated to their present status by Cheraman Perumāl, one of the rulers of ancient Kērala, as, though belonging to the Sūdra caste, they were obliged on one occasion to perform Brāhmanical service for him. Perumāl is believed to have permitted them to take the title of Unni, and call themselves Pattar, by which name East Coast Brāhmans are known in Malabar. Thus they came to own the three names Nattu Pattar, Pattar Unni, and Karappuram Unni, Karappuram or Shertallay being the territory where the sept received the above-mentioned social elevation from their sovereign. Even now, many of them reside in the tāluks of Ambalapuzha and Shertallay.

The house of a Pushpaka is variously known as pushpakam, pumatum, or padodakam, the last signifying a place where the water falls from the feet of the deity, on account of its close proximity to the temple, where the daily avocation of the Pushpaka lies. The houses of the Tīyattunnis and Nattu Pattars are only known by the name of bhavanam. As in the case of the Brāhmans, the Pushpanis and Brāhmanis cover their bodies with a piece of cloth, carry an umbrella, and are accompanied by Nāyar servant-maids when they go out in public. The women have one more fold in their dress than the Nambūtiris. The neck ornament of women is the cherutāli-kuttam, and the ear ornament the katila. Bell-metal bangles are worn round the wrists. Female Tīyattunnis and Nattu Pattars do not wear the last, and are generally unaccompanied by Nāyar servant-maids when they go out.

Pushpakans are believed to be the most fitting caste for the preparation of flower garlands to be used in temples. They also assist in the preparation of the materials for the daily offering. Nambiyassans were instructors in arms in days of old, and kalari or gymnasia are owned by them even at the present day. Their punyaha, or purificatory ceremony after pollution, is performed by Pushpakans. Brāhmani women sing religious songs on the occasion of marriage among all castes from Kshatriyas to Nāyars. In Kumaranallūr and other Bhagavati shrines, women are employed to sing propitiatory songs, while the men make garlands, sweep the floor of the inner court-yard and plinth, clean the temple vessels, and carry the lamp when images are taken round in procession. It is only the first of these temple services that the Pushpakas do, and their women never go out to sing on marriage occasions. The word Tīyattu or Teyyatu is said to be a corruption of Daivamattu, or dancing to please the deity. According to one tradition, they were degraded from Pushpakas for undertaking service in the temples. In more orthodox times, tīyattu could be performed only in temples and Brāhman houses, but now Sūdras also share the privilege of inviting the Tīyattunnis to their homes for this purpose, though the ceremony cannot be performed in their houses without a previous punyaha. The rite is extremely popular when epidemic disease prevails. Ganapati and Bhadrakāli are, as a preliminary measure, worshipped, to the accompaniment of musical instruments. As this has to be done in the noon, it is called uchchappattu, or noon-day song. In the evening, an image of Bhadrakāli is drawn on the ground with powders of five colours, white, yellow, black, green and red. At night, songs are sung in praise of that deity by the Tīyattunni and his followers. A member of the troupe then plays the part of Bhadrakāli in the act of murdering the demon Darika, and, in conclusion, waves a torch before the inmates of the house, to ward off the evil eye, which is the most important item in the whole ceremony. The torch is believed to be given by Siva, who is worshipped before the light is waved.

The Karappuram Unnis, unlike the other septs of their class, are mostly agriculturists. The Unnis are all Smartas, but a partiality for Bhadrakāli is manifested by the Tīyattunnis and Brāhmanis. All social matters among the Unnis are superintended by Nambūtiri Brāhmans, but, in all that directly touches the social well-being, their own headmen are the judges. Before entering a Pushpaka's house for the observation of any ceremony, the Nambūtiris insist upon the performance of punyaha. Though the superiority of Ilayatus is acknowledged, they are never employed by the Pushpakas for priestly functions. The Ilayatus are believed to have once been the priests of the Nattu Pattars, though at the present time learned men from their own sept are employed for this purpose. The punyaha is, however, performed through the agency of Nambūtiris. The priests of the Nambiyassans, Tīyattunnis, and Brāhmanis are Ilayatus.

Adult marriage prevails, twelve being the earliest age of a girl when she ceases to be single. On the evening of the day before the wedding, the bride has a ceremonial bath, and performs the ceremony of growing a jasmine shoot, the flowers of which she should cull and present as an offering to the deity. On the marriage day, the bridegroom's party arrives in procession at the house of the bride, who awaits them with her face covered, and holding a brass mirror and garland of flowers in her hands. Her veil is removed, and the contracting couple gaze at each other. At the auspicious hour their hands are joined, and other items of the marriage rites carried out. In connection with a Pushpaka marriage, ammana āttam or tossing of metal balls, kaikottikali or the circular dance, and yātrakali are among the amusements indulged in. Divorce was common among the Pushpakas in bygone days, but, at the present time, the marriage tie is usually permanent, and it is only after the first husband's death that cloths may be received from a Malayāla Brāhman in token of sambandham (alliance). The Brāhmanis, however, have not given up the practice of divorce. Nambiyassans, Puppallis, Pattar Unnis, and Brāhmanis follow the marumakkattāyam system of inheritance (through the female line), while the Pushpakas and Tīyattunnis are makkattāyis, and follow the law of inheritance from father to son. The offspring of a Brāhmani by a Pushpaka woman are regarded as issue in a makkattāyam family. As is the custom among the Nambūtiris, only the eldest son marries, the other sons remaining as snātakas, and contracting alliances with Nāyar women. The Illam Nāyars, however, do not give their daughters to the Unnis.

The jatakarma, though not strictly proper, is observed in modern days. The namakarana takes place, along with the annaprasana, in the sixth month after birth. The chaula is performed in the third year, though, among the Nattu Pattars, it is a preliminary ceremony before upanayana. The proper time for the performance of the upanayana is between the eighth and sixteenth year. Samāvartana takes place on the fourteenth day after upanayana. Pollution lasts for only ten days among the Tīyattunnis, whereas the Brāhmanis observe twelve, and the Nattu Pattars thirteen days' pollution. Ten gayatris (hymns) are allowed to be recited thrice daily.

The Pushpakas are the highest of the thread-wearing sections of the Ambalavāsis, according to their traditional origin as well as their religious and social practices. The Pattar Unnis are the lowest, and are only a step higher than the Kurukkals. Consecrated water and flowers are not given to them directly by the temple priest, but they may stand on the right side of the stone steps leading to the inner shrine. This is the rule with all Ambalavāsi divisions. Other Ambalavāsis do not receive food from the Unnis. These sections of the Unnis which have Ilayatus for their priests accept food from them. As the Pushpakas proper employ only Nambūtiris for purificatory purposes, the latter freely cook food in their houses, as in those of the Mūttatus.

It is recorded by Mr. Logan[76] that the Tīyattunnis or Tīyādis (ti, fire; āttam, play) are "a class of pseudo-Brāhmans in Malabar, who derive their name from the ceremony of jumping through fire before temples." Mr. Subramani Aiyar writes, in this connection, that "I do not think Mr. Logan is quite right when he describes the service of the Tīyattunnis as jumping through fire. It is dancing with lighted wicks in the hands, to exorcise the genius representing the evil eye, or as a propitiatory service in temples. It answers to the pallippanna and kolantullal of the Kaniyans. A figure of Bhadrakāli is drawn on the ground with powders of different colours, and the chief incidents in the incarnate life of the deity are recited by the Tīyattunnis. After this, some cocoanuts are broken in two, and lighted wicks are then placed before the presiding deity if done in a temple as a propitiatory service, or before any particular individual or individuals, if the object is to free him or them from the effect of the evil eye."

Uppalavar (salt workers).—A synonym of Alavan.

---

[76] Manual of the Malabar district.

Uppara.—For the following note, I am mainly indebted to Mr. C. Hayavadana Rao. Uppiliyan, Uppara, Uppāra or Uppaliga, are different names for a class of people, who followed the same professional occupation, the manufacture of salt (uppu), in various parts of Southern India. The Uppiliyans live in the Tamil country, and speak Tamil; the Upparas in the Telugu country, and speak Telugu; while the Uppāras inhabit the Mysore province and the districts bordering thereon, and speak Canarese. The Upparas are described by Mr. H. A. Stuart[77] as "a caste of tank-diggers and earth-workers, corresponding to the Uppiliyans of the Tamil districts. They resemble greatly the Oddes (Voddas or Wudders) in appearance, customs, and manner of earning a living. Their traditional occupation is, as the name implies, manufacturing earth-salt. They profess to be Saivites and Vaishnavites, but practically worship village deities, *e.g.,* Sunkalamma, Timmappa, and Jambulamma." It is possible that the Uppiliyans, Upparas, and Uppāras were originally a homogeneous caste, the members of which, in course of time, migrated to different parts of the country, and adopted the language of the locality in which they settled. The causes, which may have led to the breaking up of the caste, are not far to seek. The original occupation thereof, according to the legendary story of its origin, was tank, channel, and well digging. Southern India depended in days gone by, as at the present time, mainly on its agricultural produce, and people were required, then as now, to secure, conserve, and distribute the water, which was essential for agricultural prosperity. Inscriptions, such as those quoted by Mr. V. Venkayya,[78] bear testimony to the energy displayed by former rulers in Southern India in having tanks, wells, and irrigation channels constructed. Uppiliyans, Upparas or Uppāras, are, at the present day, found all over the Madras Presidency, from Ganjam in the north to Tinnevelley in the south. From early times they seem to have, in addition to the work already indicated, been engaged in bricklaying, house-building, the construction of forts, and every kind of earth-work.

Writing concerning the Telugu Upparas at the beginning of the nineteenth century, Buchanan states[79] that "their proper occupation is the building of mud walls, especially those of forts." A very important occupation of these people was the manufacture of earth-salt and saltpetre, of which the latter was an important ingredient in the manufacture of gunpowder. "Throughout India," Dr. G. Oppert writes,[80] "saltpetre is found, and the Hindus are well acquainted with all its properties; it is even commonly prescribed as a medicine. India was famous for the exportation of saltpetre, and is so. The Dutch, when in India, traded especially in this article."

The Uppiliyans say that they are descended from a man who was created to provide salt for the table of their god, but lost the favour of the deity because his wife bartered the salt for some glass bangles. In his wrath he put his wife into the oven to kill her, but she escaped through a hole in the back. As evidence of

[77] Manual of the North Arcot district.

[78] Archæolog. Survey of India. Annual Report, 1902–1903.

[79] Journey through Mysore, Canara and Malabar. Ed., 1807.

[80] On the Weapons, Army Organization, and Political Maxims of the Ancient Hindus, with special reference to gunpowder and fire-arms, Madras, 1880.

the truth of the story, they point to the facts that their women wear no glass bangles, and that their ovens always have a hole in them. The caste further traces its descent from a mythical individual, named Sagara, to whom is ascribed the digging of the Bay of Bengal. His story is narrated in the Vishnu Purāna,[81] and is briefly as follows. Sagara was son of Bāhu, who was overrun by the Haihayas and Tālajanghas, and consequently retired to the forest, where, near the hermitage of Muni Aurva, one of his queens conceived. A rival queen poisoned her, so as to prevent her from being delivered of the child. Meanwhile, Bāhu waxed old, and his pregnant wife prepared to ascend the funeral pyre with him. But the Muni forbade her, saying that she was going to be the mother of an universal emperor. She accordingly desisted from the desperate act, and a splendid boy was born, and the poison expelled along with him. The Muni, on this account, gave him the name of Sagara, meaning with poison. As he grew up, the boy came to know of the troubles of his father, and resolved to recover his kingdom. He put to death nearly the whole of the Haihayas, and made the others acknowledge his suzerainty. He had two wives, by one of whom he had a son named Asamanja, and by the other sixty thousand sons. He subsequently performed the asvamēdha or sacrifice of a horse, which was guarded by his sons. The animal was, however, carried off by some one into a chasm in the earth. Sagara commanded his sons to search for the steed, and they traced him by the impressions of the hoofs to the chasm, which he had entered. They proceeded to enlarge it, and dug downwards, each for a league. Coming to Pātālā, they saw the horse wandering freely about, and at no great distance from it was Kapila Rishi, sitting in meditation. Exclaiming "This is the villain who has maliciously interrupted our sacrifice, and stolen the horse, kill him, kill him," they ran towards him with uplifted weapons. The Rishi raised his eyes, and for an instant looked upon them, and they became reduced to ashes by the sacred flame that darted from him. On learning of the death of his sons, Sagara sent Amsumat, the son of Asamanja, to secure the animal. He went by the deep path which his father and uncles had dug, and, arriving at the place where Kapila was, propitiated him with an obeisance. The Rishi gave him the horse, to be delivered to his father, and in conferring the boon which Amsumat prayed for, said that his grandson would bring down the divine Ganges, whose "waters shall wash the bones and ashes of thy grandfather's sons," and raise them to swarga. Sagara then completed his sacrifice, and, in affectionate memory of his sons, called the chasm which they had dug Sagara. This is still the name of the ocean, and especially of the Bay of Bengal at the mouth of the Ganges, which, in accordance with the boon of Kapila, was brought down to earth by Amsumat's grandson Bhagīratha, from whom it received the name of Bhāgirathi, which it retains to this day. Such is the story of the origin of the caste, members of which often call it Sagara kula, or the family of Sagara. As his sons excavated the ocean, so they dig tanks, channels, wells, etc. In the Mysore Census Reports, the Upparas are said to be called "Uppara in the eastern, Uppaliga in the southern, and Mēlu (west) Sakkre in the western districts. [Some explain that they work in salt, which is more essential than sugar, and that Mēl Sakkare means superior sugar.] This caste is divided into the Telugu and Karnataka sub-divisions. The latter make earth-salt, while the former work

[81] *Vide* F. Hall's edition of H. H. Wilson's Vishnu Purana, 1864. III. 289–303.

as bricklayers and builders. The well-to-do section of the caste further undertake public works on contract, and some of them are good architects of ordinary Hindu houses, which do not call for much scientific precision. There are also agriculturists and labourers among them." In the Madras Presidency, at the present day, some members of the caste are well and tank diggers, house-builders or bricklayers; others are agricultural labourers, or village servants. A few are earth-work contractors, or, as at Muthialpet near Conjeeveram, yarn dyers. Some are in the service of Government as police constables. The women are very hard-working, and help their husbands at their work. To this fact is said to be due the high rate at which the bride-price is fixed. The well-kept roads of the city of Madras are the work of a colony of Upparas, who have settled there. The following curious custom is recorded by the Rev. J. Cain in a note[82] on the tank-diggers of the Godāvari district. "A disturbance in a little camp of tank-diggers confirmed a statement which I heard at Masulipatam as to the manner in which the tank-diggers divide their wages. They had been repairing the bank of a tank, and been paid for their work, and, in apportioning the shares of each labourer, a bitter dispute arose because one of the women had not received what she deemed her fair amount. On enquiry, it turned out that she was in an interesting condition, and therefore could claim not only her own, but also a share for the expected child. This had been overlooked, and, when she asserted her right to a double portion, those who had already received their money objected to part with any, although they acknowledged that the claim was fair and just."

By the Madras Salt Act, 1889, it is enacted that any person who—

(*a*) removes any salt without or in excess of the permits necessary by this Act; or

(*b*) except for agricultural or building purposes, excavates, collects or possesses salt-earth in any local area where it is contraband salt; or

(*c*) manufactures contraband salt in any other way than by excavating or collecting salt-earth; or

(*d*) purchases, obtains, possesses, sells or weighs contraband salt other than salt-earth, knowing or having reason to believe it to be contraband; or

(*e*) refines saltpetre without such license as is prescribed by the Act; or

(*f*) attempts to commit, or within the meaning of the Indian Penal Code abets the commission of any of the above acts,

shall on conviction be punishable for every such offence with imprisonment for a term not exceeding six months, or with fine not exceeding five hundred rupees, or with both.

It is noted, in the Gazetteer of the Bellary district, that "at the time when the Company came into possession of the district, the salt consumed in it was of two kinds, namely, the earth-salt manufactured from saline soils by men of the Uppara caste, and the marine salt made on the west coast. The latter was imported by the Lambādis and Korachas, who brought it up the ghāts by means of large

[82] Ind. Ant., VIII, 1879.

droves of pack-bullocks. The earth-salt was made in what were known as modas, which were peculiar to the Ceded Districts, and were especially common in Bellary. A heap of earth was piled up, and on the top of it were hollowed out one or more circular basins, some five feet in diameter and two feet deep. From the bottom of these basins, channels lined with chunam (lime) ran down to one or more reservoirs similarly lined. Salt-earth was collected in the places where it effloresced naturally in the dry months, and taken to the moda on pack-buffaloes. It was thrown into the basins, and then a quantity of water was poured upon it. The brine so obtained flowed through the channels at the bottom of the basins into the reservoirs. From these it was baled with chatties (pots) into a set of masonry evaporating pans, carefully levelled and plastered with chunam, where it was left to be converted into salt by solar evaporation. Each lot of salt-earth, which was thus lixiviated, was taken from the basins and thrown outside them, and this process constantly repeated gradually raised the level of the moda and the basins, which were perpetually being re-made on the top of it. Some of the modas gradually grew to be as much as twenty feet in height. When they became too high for the buffaloes to carry the salt-earth up to their summits with comfort, they were abandoned, and others started elsewhere. The earth-salt made in this manner was neither so good nor so strong as marine salt, but it was much used by the poorer classes and for cattle, and thus interfered with the profits of the Government salt monopoly, which was established in 1805. As early as 1806, therefore, it was proposed to prohibit its manufacture. The chief arguments against any such step were that it would inflict hardship upon the Upparas who made the salt, and upon the poorer classes who consumed it, and, for the next three quarters of a century, a wearisome correspondence dragged on regarding the course which it would be proper to pursue. In 1873, Mr. G. Thornhill, Member of the Board of Revenue, visited the Ceded Districts, to see how matters stood. He reported that it was not possible to check the competition of the earth-salt with the Government marine salt by imposing an excise duty, as the modas were numerous and scattered. For similar reasons, and also because all the Upparas were very poor, a license-tax was out of the question. At the same time he calculated that the loss to Government due to the system was from eight to ten lakhs annually, and, seeing that Government salt was obtainable in Bellary as cheaply as in other inland districts, he recommended that the industry should be gradually suppressed. Government agreed, and ordered that the opening of new modas should be prohibited, and that those in existence should be licensed, with reference to their productive capacity, at rates to increase by annual increments until 1879, when the full duty leviable on sea-salt should be imposed on their entire produce. These measures, though they checked the manufacture, failed to entirely protect the revenue, and, in 1876, the Madras Salt Commission and Board of Revenue concurred in recommending that the manufacture of earth-salt should be at once and entirely suppressed. The Government of India agreed, and in 1880 orders were given that the modas should all be destroyed, reasonable compensation being paid to their owners. The manufacture of earth-salt in the district is now entirely a thing of the past, though in many places the remains of the old modas may still be seen. Some of the Upparas, however, still go annually to the Nizam's Dominions in the dry season, and make earth-salt by the old methods for sale there. Apparently they agree with the Nizam's Government to pay a certain fee, one-fourth of which is paid in advance, for the privilege. If the season is sufficiently dry, they make a small profit, but if, on the other hand, it is wet, manufacture is impossible, and they lose the amount of the fee, and their labour as well." A good deal of saltpetre is still made by members of the caste in various parts of the Madras Presidency by lixiviating the alkaline efflorescence of the earth. For this purpose, licenses are obtained annually from the Salt Department. Crude saltpetre is sold for manure on coffee estates, and also used in the manufacture of fireworks.

Speaking different languages, and living in different parts of the country, the Uppiliyans, Upparas, and Uppāras do not intermarry, though, where they are found close together, they interdine.

The caste recognises the authority of its headmen, who are called Periyathanakāran, Ejamān, etc., and are assisted in some places, for example Madras, by a Jātibidda (son of the caste), who does the duties of caste peon or messenger, summoning members to a caste council-meeting, and so on. The usual punishments inflicted by a caste council are excommunication, fine, and the giving of a caste dinner. I am informed that, among the Canarese Uppāras, a woman found guilty of adultery is punished as follows. A lock of her hair is cut off, and she is bathed in cold water, and made to drink a little cow-dung water. She is then taken to the temple, where the pūjāri (priest) sprinkles holy water over her head. A fine is paid by her family. A man, who is proved guilty of a similar offence, has one side of his moustache and one of his eyebrows shaved off, and the hair of his head is removed in three parallel lines. Seven small booths are constructed of straw, and set on fire. Through this the man has to pass. He is then plunged into a tank, and, after bathing therein, he is sprinkled with holy water. I am told that a woman has also to go through the fire ordeal.

Girls are married either before or after puberty, but usually after. Among the Uppiliyans and Upparas, it is customary for a man to claim his paternal aunt's daughter in marriage. The ceremonies in connection with marriage vary in accordance with the locality. Amongst the Uppiliyans of Madura, the tāli (marriage badge) is usually tied to the bride's neck by a special woman, resident in her village, called Sīrkāri. In some places it is tied, as among some other Tamil castes, by the bridegroom's sister. Among the Telugu and Canarese sections, it is tied by the bridegroom himself. By the Uppāras of South Canara, the dhāre marriage rite is performed, in which the father of the bride pours water from a vessel over the united hands of the contracting couple. I am told that, among some Canarese Uppāras, the bridegroom's head is shaved, and, after bathing, he puts on a double brass wire corresponding to the sacred thread of the Brāhmans, which he wears for five days. Among the Telugu Upparas there are two sub-divisions, which are called, according to the amount of the bride-price, Yēdu (seven) Mādala and Padahāru (sixteen) Mādala, a māda being equal to two rupees. Some say that māda refers to the modas (heaps of earth) used in former times. At a marriage among some Uppiliyans, it is customary for the bride and bridegroom to sit inside a wall made of piled up water pots, with the ends of their cloths tied together, while some of the women present pour water from the pots over their heads. The remarriage of widows is permitted, and I gather that, among the Uppāras, a widow may only marry a widower, and *vice versâ*.

In a note on the Uppiliyans of the Trichinopoly district, Mr. F. R. Hemingway states that "some of the marriage ceremonies are peculiar. They allow an unborn boy to be betrothed to his unborn cousin. The bride has to be asked in marriage a number of times, before consent is given, lest it be thought that she is yielding too easily. The marriage is performed at her house, lest it should be thought that her parents are forcing her on the bridegroom. The caste does not use the marriage pole or pāligai pots. Instead of the usual turmeric threads, the wrists of the contracting couple are tied together with wool. A curious custom among the Tamil section is that, at the beginning of the ceremonies, both on the first and second day, three matrons wash their faces in turmeric water, and the bride and bridegroom are bathed with the water used by them. They also have unusual observances connected with a girl's attainment of maturity. A husband may not look into his bride's eyes until this occurs. When she has at length attained maturity, the husband comes to his bride's house with a sheep and some vegetables, and kills the former. His brother-in-law then marks his forehead with the sheep's blood. The husband eats some plantain and milk, and spits it out at his bride, who is made to stand behind a screen. If the girl has attained maturity before her marriage, the Tamil section of the caste make her walk over seven wooden hoops on the wedding day. The husband has to give his formal consent to the ceremony, and a washerman has to be present. The Telugus perform this rite on the last day of the girl's first menstrual period, and her maternal uncle has to be present. The Uppiliyans allow the remarriage of widows and divorced women. A man may not shave until he marries a virgin, and, if he does not do so, he has to remain unshaved all his life."

The dead are, as a rule, buried. Among the Uppiliyans, who occupy a higher social position than the Canarese and Telugu sections, death pollution is observed for seven days. Among the Uppāras, the period of pollution is sixteen days.

Concerning the death ceremonies, Mr. Hemingway writes as follows. "Widows of the Tamil section never remove their tāli, but leave it till it drops off of itself. When a man dies, his widow is made to pretend he is still alive, and bathes him with oil, and puts garlands on him. If a man is to be buried, the chief mourner pretends to dig the grave. The karumāntaram, or final death ceremony, of the Tamil section consists merely in taking some milk to an erukka (*Calotropis gigantea*) shrub on the sixteenth evening, just before the jackals begin to howl. They pour it over the shrub with the help of a barber, saying 'Go to Swarga (the abode of Indra), and make your way to Kailāsam (heaven).'"

Some members of the caste are Vaishnavites, and others Saivites. In some places, the former are branded by their gurus, who are Vaishnava Brāhmans. They also worship various village deities, which vary according to the place of residence. In the Census Report, 1891, the worship of Sunkalamma, Jambulamma, and Timmappa is noted.

It is stated by Mr. Hemingway that "the Uppiliyans have a caste god, named

Karuvandarāya Bommadēva. He has no temple, but all the Uppiliyans in a village join in offering him an annual sacrifice in Tai (January-February), before the earth is scraped for the first time in the season for making saltpetre. They use āvaram (*Cassia auriculata*) flowers and river sand in this worship. They also have three special caste goddesses, called Tīppanjāl, who are supposed to be women who committed sati. They have also Brāhman gurus, who visit them every year, and bless their salt pits."

Concerning the caste organisation of the Uppiliyans, Mr. Hemingway writes that "when a complaint of a caste offence is made, notice is sent to the Pattakkāran (headman), and to the whole Uppiliyan community in the neighbourhood, notifying the accusation and the provisional expulsion of the accused. A second notice summons the community to a panchāyat (council), which is presided over by at least two or three Pattakkārans, the caste god being represented by some āvaram flowers, a pot of water, and margosa (*Melia Azadirachta*) leaves. If acquitted, the accused is made to touch the water pot in token of his innocence. If he is convicted, both he and the complainant are fined, the latter for the purification of his house, if it has been polluted by the offence. The purification is performed by a man of the Marudūr Nādu called Rettai Vilakkukāran (man of two lights), who eats a meal in the polluted house, with his hands held behind his back."

It was recently noted that the Uppāras are, as a rule, uneducated, and their ignorance of the three R's often leads to bitter disputes among themselves and with their employers in disbursing their wages. Some years ago, one of the Madras Missions opened a school for the benefit of this backward caste. In 1906, the Hindu Educational Mission of Madras started a night and day school, Upparapālaiyam Ārya Pāthasāla, in the Upparapālaiyam quarter of Madras.

There is a Telugu proverb to the effect that one is ruined both ways, like an Uppāra who has turned Sanyāsi (ascetic), in reference to the fact that he neither follows his ancestral occupation, nor is tolerated in his new calling. The usual caste title is Chetti.

Uppāra occurs as a synonym of Kūsa Holeya.

Uppu (salt).—A sub-division of Balijas and Koravas, who trade in salt, which they carry about the country in panniers on donkeys or bullocks. It is also an occupational sub-division of Kōmati. The equivalent Uppa is an exogamous sept of Kēlasi. Uppukōttei occurs as a division of Maravan, Upputholuvāru (salt-carriers) as an exogamous sept of Oddē, and Uppiri (salt-earth) as a sept of Kuruba.

Urāli.—In the Madras Census Report, 1891, the Urālis are described as "a caste of agricultural labourers found chiefly in the districts of Madura and Trichinopoly. The word Urāli means a ruler of a village. Like the Ambalakkārans, they trace their descent from one Mutturāja, and the only sub-division returned by any number is Mutrācha. They also assert that they were formerly employed as soldiers. In the Wynād there is a section of Kurumbas called Urāli Kurumbas, and it is not improbable that these Urālis of the Tamil country are an offshoot of the great Kurumba race." The Urālis are further summed up in the same report, as "agricultural labourers in Coimbatore, Trichinopoly, and Madura. There seems to be some connection between the Urālis and the Ambalakkārans or Muttiriyans. Muttiriyan is a sub-division of both Urāli and Ambalakkāran, and both of these are found in the same districts. Perhaps the Urālis are an offshoot of the Tamil Valaiyans, which by change of occupation has transformed itself into a distinct caste (*see* Ambalak-kāran). The caste is split up into a number of sub-divisions, called after the name of the tract or nādu in Trichinopoly which each inhabits. To get back into the caste, an excommunicated man has to kill a sheep or goat before the elders, and mark his forehead with the blood. He then gives a feast to the assembly, and puts part of the food on the roof of his house. If the crows eat this, he is received back into the caste. [Brāhmans always put out portions of the srāddha offerings in the same way, and judge whether they are acceptable or not by noting if the crows eat them or not.] Marriage is infant or adult. A man detected in an intrigue with an unmarried woman is fined, and has to marry her, and at the wedding his waist string is tied round her neck instead of a tāli. The well-to-do people of the caste employ Brāhmans as priests, but others content themselves with their own elders. Widows and divorced women may marry again. The dead are either burned or buried. The richer members of the caste perform srāddha (memorial service for the dead). They drink alcohol, and eat fowls, mutton, pork, fish, rats, etc. In social position they come below the Idaiyans, Tottiyans, and Kallans. Their title is Kavandan."

For the following note on the Urālis of the Trichinopoly district, I am indebted to Mr. F. R. Hemingway. "They say that they were originally Kshatriyas living in 'Alipuram near Oudh,' and left that place in search of adventure, or in consequence of disputes at home, leaving their wives behind them, and finally settled in the south, where they married serving women (pulukkachis). They say that they belong to the Mutturāja Kuttam, a phrase they cannot explain, and protest that the Ambalakkārans, who make a similar claim, have no ground for so doing. They seem to eat with no other caste on equal terms, but will, of course, accept separate meals from Vellālans. They are split into seven nādus, which are in effect endogamous sub-divisions. These are called after villages in the country inhabited by the caste, namely, Vadasēri, Pillūru, Sēngudi, Kadavangudi or Virāli, Talakka, Paluvinji or Magali, and Marungi. The members of the first three of these nādus are called Vadasēri Urālis, and those of the other four Nāttu-sīmai Urālis, Kundu-va-nāttu-tokkādus, or Nandutindis. All of them will mess together. They say that the nādus were originally intended to facilitate the decision of caste disputes, and they are still the unit of self-government. Each nādu has a headman, who exercises supreme control over the villages included within it. The Urālis also have a number of exogamous septs called karais by the Vadasēris and kāniyacchis by the Nāttu-sīmais, which are called after the names of places. They are generally cultivators, but are said sometimes to be given to crime. They wear the sacred thread on occasions of marriages and funerals. The women can be recognised by their dress, the kusavam being spread out behind, and a characteristic pencil-shaped ornament (kuchu) being suspended from the neck. Some of their marriage and funeral customs are peculiar. Among the Nāttu-sīmais, the betrothal is ratified by the maternal uncle of each of the pair solemnly measuring out three measures of paddy (rice) in the presence of the other party at their house. At their funerals, the bier is not brought into the village, but left outside, and the corpse is carried to it.

Among the Vadasēris, while preparations are being made for the removal of the body, a Paraiyan woman performs a dance. Among the Nāttu-sīmais this is done on the Ettu day. On the second day after the funeral, the relatives of the deceased dip their toes in a mortar full of cow-dung water placed in front of his house, and put sacred ashes on the head. The karumāntaram, or final death ceremony, is only performed by the rich. It can take place at any time after the third day. The Ettu ceremony is similarly performed at any time after the third day, and is attended with a curious ritual. Both sections of the caste erect a booth, in which three plantain trees are planted, and the chief mourner and his cousins stand there all day to receive the condolences of their friends. From this point the practice of the two sections differs in small points of detail. Among the Vadasēris, the friends come one by one, and are asked by the chief mourner, "Will you embrace, or will you strike your forehead?" In reply, the friend either closes the open hand of the chief mourner with his own as a form of embrace, or flings himself on the ground in the booth, and weeps. Each visitor then goes to a meeting of the nādu which is being held outside the village, and a Paraiyan and three Urālis inform the headman who have visited the booth and who have not, and ask if it may be removed. Permission being given, the plantains are cut down, and the woman-folk wail round a chembu (vessel) placed there. All then proceed to the nādu meeting, where a turban is put on a Paraiyan, a dancing-girl and a Pandāram, and the Paraiyan (called Nāttu Sāmban) beats his drum, and pronounces a blessing on the nādu. Finally all repair to the house of the deceased, where the headman puts three handfuls of kambu (millet) into the cloth of his wife or some other member of the family, and throws a mortar on the ground. Punishments for caste offences take some curious forms. A margosa (*Melia Azadirachta*) leaf is put on the house of anyone who is excommunicated. If a man seduces a girl of the caste, an enquiry is held, and the pair are married. The waist-string of the man is tied round the neck of the woman, and a Tottiyan is called in to take away the pollution which they and their relatives have incurred. They are taken to a tank (pond), where 108 holes have been made by the Tottiyan, and are made to bathe in every hole, sprinkling the water over their heads. A sheep is then killed by a Tottiyan and a Chakkiliyan, its head is buried, and the couple and their relatives are made to walk over the spot. The blood of the animal is then smeared on their foreheads, and they all have to bathe again. They are next given cow's urine to drink, and then once more bathe. After that they are given milk, and are made to prostrate themselves before the panchāyat (council). Finally they have to give a feast to the panchāyat, at which a part of the food is offered to the crows, and the purification is not complete till the birds have partaken thereof. The Urālis are fond of shikār (hunting). On the Sivarātri night, sacrifices are offered to their family gods, and, on the following day, all the men of the village go out hunting. They have a head shikāri (huntsman), called Kāvēt-taikāran, who receives every animal which is killed, cuts off its head, and breaks its legs. The head is given to the man who killed the animal, and the rest is shared among the castemen."

Of the Urālis who inhabit the hill country of Travancore, the following account is given in the Travancore Census report, 1901. "The Urālis are a class of hill tribes resident in the Cardamom Hills. They are chiefly found in the tracts known as

Kunnanāt, Velampan, Kurakkanāt, Mannukāt, Kalanāt, and Periyūr. The headman of the Urālis in each of these areas is called a Kānikkāran. Tradition tells us that they were the dependents of the kings of Madura, and that their duty was to hold umbrellas in times of State processions. In ancient times, many of the parts now included in the Todupuzha tāluk belonged to the kingdom of Madura. Once, when the king came to Nēriyamangalam, the ancestors of these Urālis are said to have accompanied him, and to have been left there to rule (āli) that locally (ūr). The males dress like the low-country people, with cloths about four cubits long extending from the hip to the knee. Another cloth, about one or two cubits in length, is put over the back, one end of which passes under their right arm and the other over the shoulder, both meeting in front over the chest, where they are tied together in a peculiar knot by folding the extremities, thus forming a bag wherein to contain their wayside necessaries. Females wear two pieces of cloth, nine and two and a half cubits in length respectively, and folded in the middle. The larger is the lower garment, and the smaller upper garment is worn with two ends tied around the neck. Males wear brass finger and toe-rings, sometimes of silver. Some adorn their necks with wreaths of beads, from fifteen to thirty in number. Females wear ear-ornaments known as kātumani, which are rings of metal wire, four or five in number. Males generally allow their hair to grow, the face alone being now and then shaven. The Urālis eat rice for six months of the year, and subsist on roots, fruits, and other forest produce during the remaining half. A large portion of the paddy (rice) that the Urālis gather by cultivation goes to the low country in exchange for clothing and salt. The flesh of most animals is eaten, but the elephant and buffalo are held in such great respect that no Urāli ever ventures to hurt them. Even the approach of the buffalo is religiously avoided. They begin to fell forest trees in Dhanu (December-January), and seeds are sown by the end of Mētam (April-May). They have only a katti, which is a kind of chopping knife, for purposes of ploughing. After cultivation they change their abodes. They put up huts in the vicinity of the cultivated areas, and use bamboo and reeds as materials. After leaving the old, and before putting up the new hut, they live for several days in caves or under trees. They are very good watchmen, and take great care in putting up fences, weeding, and protecting cultivation from wild animals. They make excellent mats of reed. They are clever huntsmen, and are passionately attached to their hunting dogs. They hoard their grains in wicker baskets called virivallam. They possess copper and brass vessels, mortar, chopping knives, sickles, spades, flint and steel. A man after marriage lives with his wife, apart from his parents. Pollution of a very aggravated kind is observed during the menstrual and puerperal periods. On these occasions a separate mātam (hut), called the pāttu-pandal, is put up at a distance from the dwelling hut. Here the woman stays for three days. After bathing on the fourth day, she shifts to another mātam still nearer, and stays there for one or two days. On the seventh day she rejoins the family. In cases of confinement, twelve days are spent in the remotest hut, and five days in the nearer one. But for another period of twenty days the woman is not permitted to touch any one in the house, or even the roofing of the hut. During these days food is prepared by others, and given to her. The water in which those who are confined, and those who are in their menses bathe, is considered to be defiled beyond remedy. Hence, for bathing purposes some secluded and out-of-the-way pool, called pāttuvellam, is selected. Urālis coming to the low country hesitate to drink water, on the score that it might be thus polluted. When the woman delivers herself of her first child, her husband observes three days' pollution, but none for subsequent confinements. On all such occasions, the maternal relations of the woman have to observe five days' pollution. On the eighteenth day after birth, the eldest member of the family names the child, and bores the ear. The head of the child is shaved as soon as it is able to walk, and a tuft of hair is left in front. The corpses of the Urālis are not burnt, but buried at a sufficient distance from the house. A new cloth is put into the grave by each relative. After filling in the grave, they erect a shed over it, within which the chopping knife of the deceased, a quantity of boiled rice, and some chewing materials (betel and nuts) are placed. After the lapse of seven years, an offering of food and drink is made to the departed soul. Death pollution lasts for sixteen days. The Urālis address their father as appan, and maternal uncle as achchan. Marumakkathāyam is the prevailing form of inheritance (in the female line). Marriage is settled by the parents. There is no tāli symbol to indicate the wedded state. After the marriage is settled, the girl is merely sent to the pandal or hut of the husband. The Urālis intermarry with the Ullādans, and in rare cases with Muduvans. Remarriage is permitted. An Urāli, wishing to get married into a particular family, has to wed into the family a girl belonging to his own. The Urālis have a fine ear for music, and sing many songs in the night before going to bed. Like the Kānis (Kānikars), they resort to enchantments called cheppuka and chāttuka for the cure of diseases. Their would-be sorcerers have to leave the community, and wander alone in the forest for a number of months. They are said to then get into a trance, when their forefathers appear before them as maidens, and teach them the mystic arts. The Urālis bear their loads only on the back, and never on the head. They never go to distant places without their chopping knife. They are good forest guides." The Urālis are stated by the Rev. S. Mateer[83] to practice polyandry like the Todas.

Urāli is further a synonym of the Tandans of Travancore, in reference, it is said, to their having been guardians of villages (ur) in former times. It is also the title of the headman of the Kuravas of Travancore and a synonym of the Kōlāyans of Malabar.

Urāli.—The Urālis, who form the subject of the present note, dwell at an altitude of 1,800 feet in the jungles of Dimbhum in the Coimbatore district, where a forest bungalow, situated on a breezy ridge overlooking the plains, formed a convenient centre from which to study both Urālis and the more primitive Shōlagas.

The Urālis are familiar with the Badagas, who have a settlement not many miles distant; the Todas, who occasionally migrate across the adjacent Nīlgiri frontier in search of grazing land for their buffaloes; and the Kurumbas and Irulas, who inhabit the lower slopes of the Nīlgiris, which run down to Coimbatore. With the civilised world they are acquainted, as they carry loads to the plains, and run down to market at the town of Sathyamangalam, which is only seventeen miles distant from Dimbhum. Like the Nīlgiri Badagas, they are clad in turban, and long

---

[83] Native Life in Travancore.

flowing body-cloth, white (when new), or striped with red and blue. The hair is worn long and unkempt, or shaved *á la* Hindu with kudimi in mimicry of the more civilised classes. A man was introduced to us as an expert mimic of the note of the paroquet, peacock, jungle-fowl and other forest birds; and a small party improvised, in front of the bungalow, a bird trap cleverly constructed out of stones, an iron plate from the camp kitchen, bamboo, and rope made on the spot from the bark of *Ficus Tsiela*. The making of fire with flint and steel is fast disappearing in favour of safety matches.

The Urālis say that they are men of seven kulams (*i.e.*, having seven posts to the marriage booth), and are children of Billayya, while they describe the Shōlagas as men of five kulams and children of Karayya. They call themselves Urālis or Irulas, and, when questioned, say that, as Billayya and Karayya are brothers, they may also be called Shōlagas. But there is no intermarriage between Urālis and Shōlagas, though members of the two tribes sometimes interdine. According to another legend, the Urālis and Shōlagas are both descended from Karayan, and the Sivachāris (Lingāyats) from Billaya or Mādhēswaram (*see* Shōlaga). They speak a patois of mixed Tamil and Canarese, and have a number of exogamous septs, the meaning of the names of which is not clear. They indulge in a large repertoire of nicknames, for the most part of a personal nature, such as donkey-legged, big-navelled, pot-bellied, hare-lipped, hairy like a bear or the tail of a mungoose, toothless, lying, brought up on butter-milk. One man was named Kothē Kallan (kotha, a stone), because he was born on a rock near Kotagiri.

The majority of the tribe earn a modest livelihood by collecting minor forest produce, such as myrabolams, wax and honey, and poles for use as primitive breaks for country carts during the ascent of the ghāt road. These poles are tied to the carts by ropes, and trail behind on the ground, so that, when the cart stops, the backward course of the wheels is arrested. Some till the soil, and cultivate various kinds of food-grains. Others are sheep and cattle owners. A few families possess land, which is given free of rent by the Forest Department, on condition that they work for the department whenever their services are required. As a class they are not inclined to do hard work, and they appear to get into the clutches of money-lending Chettis. Their staple food is rāgi (*Eleusine Coracana*). But they eat also sheep, fowls, goat, deer, pigeons and doves, black monkeys, wild boar, hare, hedgehogs, paroquets, quails and partridges, jungle-fowl, woodcock, woodpeckers, and other denizens of the jungle. A man who was asked whether they eat beef, cats, toads, bears, or white monkeys, expectorated violently at the mention of each, and the suggestion of the first three produced the most explosive oral demonstration.

Tribal disputes are referred to a headman, called Yejamana, who must belong to the exogamous sept called Sambē, and whose appointment is an hereditary one. To assist him, three others, belonging to the Kalkatti, Kolkara and Kurinanga septs, whose hereditary titles are Pattagara, Gouda and Kolkara, are appointed. The Kolkara has to invite people to the panchāyat (tribal council), collect the fines inflicted, and be present on the occasion of marriages. A woman who, after marriage, refuses to live with her husband, is punished thus. She is tied to a tree, and the Kolkaran empties the contents of a hornet or wasp's nest at her feet. After a few minutes the woman is questioned, and, if she agrees to live with her husband, she must, in token of assent, lick a mark made on his back by the Kolkara with fowl's excrement, saying "You are my husband. In future I shall not quarrel with you, and will obey you." Even after this ordeal has been gone through, a woman may, on payment of a fine, leave her husband in favour of another man of the tribe.

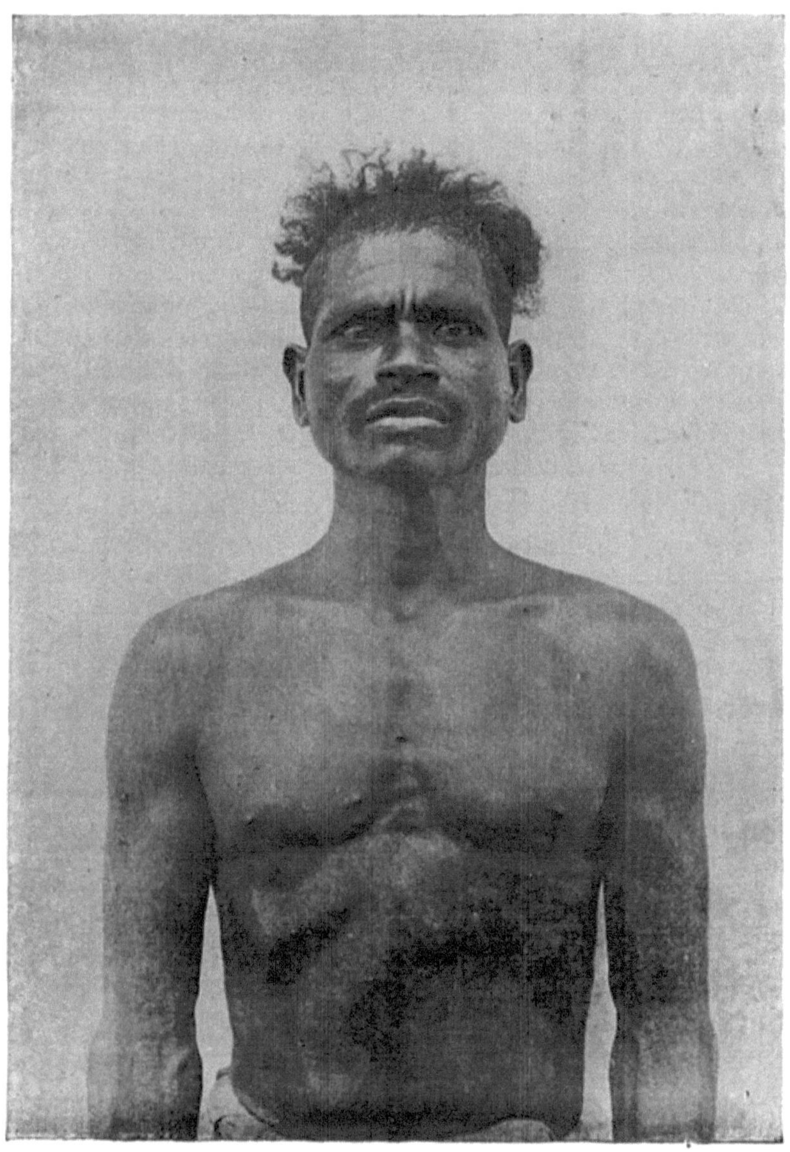

URĀLI.

When a girl reaches puberty, she is anointed, decorated with jewelry, and made to occupy a separate hut for seven days, during which time two young girls keep her company. On the eighth day, all three bathe in a pond or stream, and return in their wet clothes to the girl's home, where they sit on a pestle placed in front of the door. A plantain leaf is then placed in front of them, on which cooked rice and curry are spread. A child, aged about eight or nine months, is set in the girl's lap, and she feeds the infant with a small quantity of rice, of which she herself swallows a few mouthfuls. Those assembled then sit down to a meal, at the conclusion of which they wash their hands in a dish, and the girl throws the water away. The feast concluded, the spot is sprinkled with cowdung water, and cleaned up by the girl.

Marriage is either infant or adult, but, as a rule, the latter. The match-making is carried out by the boy's parents, who, with his other relations, pay two visits, one with and one without the boy, to the parents of the girl. At the first visit a present of rāgi, and at the second of plantains, rice, and millet pudding is made. The party must be received with due respect, which is shown by taking hold of the walking-sticks of the guests on arrival, and receiving them on a mat spread inside the house. The customary form of salute is touching the feet with both hands, and raising them, with palms opposed, to the forehead. Before taking their seats, the guests salute a vessel of water, which is placed on the mat, surrounded by betel leaves and nuts. A flower is placed on the top of the stone or figure which represents the tribal goddess, and, after pūja (worship) has been done to it, it is addressed in the words "Oh, Swāmi! drop the flower to the right if the marriage is going to be propitious, and to the left if otherwise." Should the flower remain on the image, without falling either way, it is greeted as a very happy omen. On the occasion of the betrothal ceremony, if the bridegroom's party, on their way to the bride's village, have to cross a stream, running or dry, the bridegroom is not allowed to walk across it, but must be carried over on the back of his maternal uncle. As they approach the bride's home, they are met by the Kolkara and two other men, to whom the Kolkara, after receiving the walking-sticks of the guests, hands them over. Failure to do so would be an act of discourtesy, and regarded as an insult to be wiped out by a heavy fine. When the procession arrives at the house, entrance into the marriage booth is prevented by a stick held across it by people of the bride's village. A mock struggle takes place, during which turmeric water is thrown by both sides, and an entrance into the house is finally effected. After a meal has been partaken of, the bridal party proceed to the village of the bridegroom, where the bride and bridegroom are lodged in separate houses. In front of the bridegroom's house a booth, supported by twelve posts arranged in four rows, has been erected. The two pillars nearest the entrance to the house are called murthi kamba. Into the holes made for the reception of these, after a cocoanut has been broken, ghī (clarified butter), milk, and a few copper coins are placed. The bridal pair, after an oil bath, are led to the booth, decorated with jewels and wearing new cloths, and made to sit on a plank. A cocoanut is broken, and they salute a vessel placed on a plate. The bridal party then adjourn to a pond or stream, and do pūja to their god. On the return thence the bridal couple must be accompanied by their maternal uncles, who should keep on dancing, while cocoanuts are broken in front of them till the house is reached. The contracting parties then again sit on the plank with their little fingers linked, while the bride money (theravu) is paid to the father-in-law, and the milk money (pāl kuli) to the mother-in-law. The tāli (a golden disc) is then tied on to the bride's neck by some female relation of the bridegroom, and the bride and bridegroom, after saluting those assembled, enter the house, where the young wife is at once told to cook some rice, of which she and her husband partake from the same leaf plate.

There exists, among the Urālis, a kind of informal union called kuduvali. A man and woman will, by mutual agreement, elope into the jungle, and live there together, till they are discovered and brought back by their relations. A panchāyat (council) is held, and they are recognised as man and wife if the bride money and fine inflicted are paid. Failure to pay up would render them liable to excommunication. To celebrate the event, a feast must be given by the man; and, if he should die without having fed the community, any children born to him are considered as illegitimate. In such a case, the widow or her near relatives are asked to give food to at least a few before the corpse is removed, so as to legitimatise the children.

The Urālis bury their dead, and the death ceremonies are, to a certain extent, copied from those of the Badagas. As soon as a member of the tribe dies, the corpse is anointed, washed, and dressed in new clothes and turban. On the face three silver coins are stuck, viz.:—a rupee on the forehead, and a quarter rupee outside each eye. When all have assembled for the funeral, the corpse is brought out and placed under a car (tēru) of six storeys, made of bamboo and sticks, covered with coloured cloths and flags, and having at the top a kalasa (brass vessel) and umbrella. To the accompaniment of a band a dance takes place around the car, and the procession then moves on to the burial-ground, where a cow buffalo is brought near the car, and a little milk drawn and poured three times into the mouth of the corpse. A cow and one or two calves are taken round the car, and the calves presented to the sister of the deceased. The car is then broken up, after the decorations have been stripped off. The corpse is buried either on the spot, or taken away to distant Nīrgundi, and buried there. On the eighth day after the funeral or return from Nīrgundi, the eldest son of the deceased has his head shaved, and, together with his brother's wife, fasts. If the funeral has been at Nīrgundi, the son, accompanied by his relations, proceeds thither after tying some cooked rice in a cloth. On arrival, he offers this to all the memorial stones in the burial-ground (goppamane), and erects a stone, which he has brought with him, in memory of the deceased. He then anoints all the stones with ghī, which is contained in a green bamboo measure. He collects the rice, which has been offered, and one of the party, becoming inspired, gives vent to oracular declarations as to the season's prospects, the future of the bereaved family, etc. The collected rice is regarded as sacred, and is partaken of by all. Each sept has its own goppamane, which is a rectangular space with mud walls on three sides. In cases in which the corpse has been buried close to the village, the grave is marked by a file of stones. Two or three years afterwards, the body is exhumed, and the bones are collected, and placed in front of the house of the deceased. All the relations weep, and the son conveys the bones to Nīrgundi, where he buries them. On the eighth day he revisits the spot, and erects a stone with the ceremonial already described.

The Urālis worship a variety of minor deities, and sacrifice sheep and goats to Pālrayan. They observe two annual festivals, viz.:—(*a*) Thai nombu, when the whole house is cleaned, and margosa (*Melia Azadirachta*) twigs and spikes of *Achyranthes aspera* are tied together, and placed in front of the house over the roof, or stuck into the roof overhanging the entrance. A sumptuous repast is partaken of. This ceremonial takes place in the month Thai (December-January). (*b*) In the month Vyāsi (March-April) a large trough is placed close to a well, and filled with a mixture of salt and water. The cattle, decorated with leaves and flowers, are brought, one by one, to the trough, and made to drink the salt water.

Uril Parisha.—A class of Mūssad.

Urū.—Ur, Urū, meaning village, is the name of a division of Bēdar, Bōya, Golla, Korava, Kuruba, Mādiga, and Oddē. The Bēdars and Bōyas are divided into two main divisions, Urū or those who dwell in villages, and Myāsa (grass-land or forest people) who live away from villages. In like manner, the Urū Oddes are those who have abandoned a nomad life, and settled in villages. Among some of the Tamil cultivating classes, the headman is known as the Ur Goundan.

Ur-Udaiyān (lord of a village).—A synonym of Nattamān.

Urukathi (a kind of knife).—An exogamous sept of Toreva.

Urukkāran, a class of Muhammadan pilots and sailors in the Laccadive islands. (*See* Māppilla.)

Urumikkāran.—The Urumikkārans, or those who play on the drum (urumi), are said[84] to be "Tottiyans in Madura, and Parayans elsewhere." The Kāppiliyans say that they migrated with the Urumikkārans from the banks of the Tungabadra river, because the Tottiyans tried to ravish their women. At a Kāppiliyan wedding, a Urumikkāran must be present at the distribution of betel on the second day, and at the final death ceremonies a Urumikkāran must also be present.

Usira (usirika, *Phyllanthus Emblica*).—A sept of Kōmati.

Utla.—Utla or Utlavādu has been recorded as an occupational sub-caste of Yerukala, and an exogamous sept of Bōya and Padma Sālē. The name is derived from utlam, a hanging receptacle for pots, made of palmyra fibre, which some Yerukalas make and sell.[85]

Uttarēni (*Achyranthes aspera*).—An exogamous sept of Bōya.

Uyyāla (a swing).—An exogamous sept of Māla, Mutrācha, and Yerukala. During the marriage ceremonies of Brāhmans and some non-Brāhman castes, the bride and bridegroom are seated in a swing within the marriage booth, and songs called uyyāla patalu (swing songs) are sung by women to the accompaniment of music.

---

[84] Madras Census Report, 1901.
[85] Madras Census Report, 1901.

V

Vāda.—On the coast of Ganjam and Vizagapatam, the sea fishermen are either Vādas or Jālāris, both of which are Telugu castes. The fishing operations are carried on by the men, and the fish are sold by the women in markets and villages. Various Oriya castes, *e.g.*, Kevuto, Kondra, Tiyoro, etc., are employed as fishermen, but only in fresh-water. The Vādas seem to be a section of the Palles, with whom they will interdine and intermarry. They call themselves Vāda Balijas, though they have no claim to be regarded as Balijas. Sometimes they are called Kalāsis by Oriya people.

Socially the Vādas occupy a low position. Their language is a corrupt and vulgar form of Telugu. The men wear a conical palm leaf cap, such as is worn by the Pattanavan fishermen in the Tamil country. In the presence of a superior, they remove their loin-cloth and place it round their neck and shoulders as a mark of respect. Among many other castes, this would, on the contrary, be regarded as an act of impertinence.

Like other Telugu castes, the Vādas have exogamous intipērus, some of which seem to be peculiar to them, *e.g.*, Mailapilli, Ganupilli, Sodupilli, Davulupilli. Other intipērus are such as are common to many Telugu castes. The caste headmen are entitled Kularāju and Pilla, and the appointments are apparently held by members of particular septs. At Chatrapūr, for example, they belong to the Mailapilli and Vanka septs. There is also a caste servant styled Samayanōdu. The headmen seem to have more power among the Vādas than among other Telugu castes, and all kinds of caste matters are referred to them for disposal. They receive a fee for every marriage, and arrange various details in connection with the wedding ceremonial. This is based on the Telugu type, with a few variations. When a young man's relations proceed to the house of the girl whom it is proposed that he should marry, the elders of her family offer water in a brass vessel to their guests, if they approve of the match. During the marriage rites, the bride and bridegroom sit within a pandal (booth), and the men of the bridegroom's party exhibit to those assembled betel leaf, areca nuts, oil, turmeric paste, etc., in which no foreign matter, such as fragments of paper, rags, etc., must be found. If they are discovered, a fine is inflicted.

VĀDA GODS.

There is exhibited in the Madras Museum a collection of clay figures, such as are worshipped by fishermen on the Ganjam coast, concerning which Mr. H. D'A. C. Reilly writes to me as follows. "I am sending you specimens of the chief gods worshipped by the fishermen. The Tahsildar of Berhampūr got them made by the potter and carpenter, who usually make such figures for the Gopalpūr fishermen. I have found fishermen's shrines at several places. Separate families appear to have separate shrines, some consisting of large chatties (earthen pots), occasionally ornamented, and turned upside down, with an opening on one side. Others are made of brick and chunam (lime). All that I have seen had their opening towards the sea. Two classes of figures are placed in these shrines, viz., clay figures of gods, which are worshipped before fishing expeditions, and when there is danger from a particular disease which they prevent; and wooden figures of deceased relations, which are quite as imaginative as the clay figures. Figures of gods and relations are placed in the same family shrine. There are hundreds of gods to choose from, and the selection appears to be a matter of family taste and tradition. The figures, which I have sent, were made by a potter at Venkatarayapalle, and painted by a carpenter at Uppulapathi, both villages near Gopalpūr. The Tahsildar tells me that, when he was inspecting them at the Gopalpūr travellers' bungalow, sixty or seventy fisher people came and worshipped them, and at first objected to their gods being taken away. He pacified them by telling them that it was because the Government had heard of their devotion to their gods that they wanted to have some of them in Madras." The collection of clay figures includes the following:—

Bengali Bābu wears a hat, and rides on a black horse. He blesses the fishermen, secures large hauls of fish for them, and guards them against danger when out fishing. It has been observed that "this affinity between the Ganjam fishermen and the Bengali Bābu, resulting in the apotheosis of the latter, is certainly a striking manifestation of the catholicity of hero-worship, and it would be interesting to have the origin of this particular form of it, to know how long, and for what reasons the conception of protection has appealed to the followers of the piscatory industry. It was Sir George Campbell, the Lieutenant-Governor of Bengal, who compelled his Bengali officials, much against their inclination, to cultivate the art of equitation."

Sāmalamma wears a red skirt and green coat, and protects the fishermen from fever.

Rājamma, a female figure, with a sword in her right hand, riding on a black elephant. She blesses barren women with children, and favours her devotees with big catches when they go out fishing.

Yerenamma, riding on a white horse, with a sword in her right hand. She protects fishermen from drowning, and from being caught by big fish.

Bhāgirathamma, riding on an elephant, and having eight or twelve hands. She helps fishermen when fishing at night, and protects them against cholera, dysentery, and other intestinal disorders.

Nūkalamma wears a red jacket and green skirt, and protects the fishing community against small-pox.

Orusandi Ammavaru prevents the boats from being sunk or damaged.

Bhāgadēvi rides on a tiger, and protects the community from cholera.

VĀDA POT SHRINES.

Veyyi Kannula Ammavaru, or goddess of a thousand eyes, represented by a pot pierced with holes, in which a gingelly (*Sesamum*) oil light is burnt. She attends to the general welfare of the fisher folk.

The chief sea goddess of the Vādas seems to be Orusandiamma, whose image must be made out of the wood of the nīm (*Melia Azadirachta*) tree. She is supposed to have four arms. Many of the pot temples set up on the sea-shore are her shrines. On no account should she be provoked, lest the fishing boat should be upset. She is regarded as constantly roaming over the sea in a boat at night. Associated with her is a male deity, named Ramasondi, who is her brother. His vāhanam (vehicle) is an elephant. Orusandi is worshipped separately by each family. At the time of worship, flowers, two cloths, a fowl, a goat, and a bottle of toddy or arrack, are carried in procession to the sea-shore. Before the procession starts, people collect in front of the house of the person who is doing the pūja (worship), and tie him and the goat to a long post set up in front thereof. A toy boat is placed before the post, and Ramasondi is invoked by a person called Mannāru, who becomes inspired by the entrance of the deity into him. A fowl is sacrificed, and, with the boat on his head, the Mannāru proceeds towards the shore. Orusandi is then invoked, but does not come so easily as Ramasondi. Repeated invocations are necessary before some one becomes inspired. The goat, post, and a pot shrine for the goddess are taken to the shore. A small platform is erected there, on which the shrine, smeared with chunam (lime), is placed, and in it the image is deposited. Worship is then performed, and the goat sacrificed if it crawls along on all fours and shivers. If it does not do so, another goat is substituted for it. As every family sets up its own pot shrine, the number of these is considerable, and they extend over several furlongs.

The sea goddess Marulupōlamma is housed in a small shed made of date palm leaves. A goddess who is very much feared, and worshipped at the burial-ground, is Būlokamma. Her worship is carried out at noon or midnight. She is represented by a pot, of which the neck is removed. In the sides of the pot four holes are made, into each of which a twig is inserted. The ends of the twigs are tied together with thread, so that they represent a miniature pandal (booth). The pot is carried by a Mannāru, dressed up like a woman in black and white cloths, together with another pot representing Enuga Sakthi. The former is carried in the bend of the left elbow, and the latter on the head. The pots are accompanied in procession to the burial-ground, and on the way thither some one becomes inspired, and narrates the following legend:—"I am Būlokasakthi. Ages ago I was in an egg, of which the upper half became the sky and the lower half the earth, and was released. The moon was the mark on my forehead, and the sun was my mirror. Seven gadhis (a measure of time) after my birth, a west wind arose. By that time I had grown into an adult woman, and so I embraced the wind, which impregnated me, and, after nine gadhis, Brahma was born. He grew into a young man, and I asked him to embrace me, but he refused, and, as a curse, I caused him to become a stone. Vishnu underwent the same fate, but Siva promised to satisfy me, if I gave him my third eye, shoulder-bag, and cane. This I did, and lost my power. Then all the water disappeared, and I was covered with mud. Siva again caused water to appear, and of it I took three handfuls, and threw them over my body. The third handful consumed me, and reduced me to ashes. From these were created Sarasvati, Parvati, and Būlokamma. I am that Būlokamma. I asked a favour of Siva. He made me remain within this earth, and, drawing three lines, said that I should not come out, and should receive offerings of fowls and goats." At this stage, a chicken is given to the Mannāru, who bites, and kills it. At the burial-ground worship is performed, and a goat sacrificed. The goddess being confined within the earth, no shrine is erected to her, and she is not represented by an image. A small pandal is erected, and the pot placed near it.

The goddess Kalimukkamma is represented by a paper or wooden mask painted black, with protruding tongue. With her is associated her brother Bāithari. She is believed to be one of the sisters created by Brahma from his face at the request of Iswara, the others being Polamma, Maridipoli, Kothapoli, Jungapoli, Nukapoli, Runjamma, and Kundamma. The shrine of Kalimukkamma is a low hut made of straw. At the time of worship to her, a Mannāru, dressed up as a woman, puts on the mask, and thus represents her. A stone slab, containing a figure of Kalimukkamma, is carried by a woman. She is the only goddess who may be represented by a stone. To her pigs are offered.

Peddamma or Polamma is represented by a wooden effigy. Along with her, Maridiamma is also worshipped. The offerings to Peddamma consist of a goat or sheep, and a pot of milk. A pig is sacrificed to Maridiamma. When the people proceed in procession to the place of worship, a toy cart is tied to the person representing Maridiamma, and some one must carry a toy boat. At a distance from the house, the cart is detached, and a pig is killed by an abdominal incision.

Samalamma is a mild goddess, with vegetarian propensities, to whom animal food must not be offered. She is associated with the aforesaid Bengali Bābu riding on a horse. Her image may only be carried by young girls, and grown-up women may not touch it.

Of the Sakthis worshipped by the Vādas, the chief is Koralu Sakthi. The man who performs the worship is tied to a country cart, to which a central stake, and a stake at each corner are attached. Dressed up in female attire, he drags the cart, with which he makes three rounds. A chicken is then impaled on each of the corner stakes, and a pig on the central stake.

In former times, the images of the deities were made in clay, but it has been found by experience that wooden images are more durable, and do not require to be replaced so often. Along with the images of gods and goddesses, the Vādas place figures representing deceased relatives, after the peddadinam (final death ceremony).

The Mannārus are very important individuals, for not only do they perform worship, but are consulted on many points. If a man does not secure good catches of fish, he goes to the Mannāru, to ascertain the cause of his bad luck. The Mannāru holds in his hand a string, to which a stone is tied, and invokes various gods and goddesses by name. Every time a name is mentioned, the stone either swings to and fro like a pendulum, or performs a circular movement. If the former occurs, it is a sign that the deity whose name has been pronounced is the cause of the misfortune, and must be propitiated in a suitable manner.

Vadakkupurattu.—A synonym, meaning belonging to the north side of the temple, of Mārāns in Travancore.

VĀDA SHRINES.

Vadra.—Vadra, Vadrangi, or Vadla is a name of a sub-division of Telugu Kam-salas, the professional calling of which is carpentering. It is noted, in the Gazetteer of Tanjore, that "wood-carving of a very fair quality is done at several places in the Tanjore district by a class of workmen called car carpenters, from the fact that their skill is generally exercised in carving images on temple cars. They are found at Tanjore, Mannargudi, Tiruvādaturai and Tiruvadi, and perhaps elsewhere. The workmen at the last-named place are Vaddis. The Vaddis of the Godavari district are also found to do wood-carving, sometimes with great skill."

Vadugan.—At the census, 1891, 180,884 individuals were returned as Vadugan, which is described as meaning "a native of the northern or Telugu country, but in ordinary usage it refers to the Balijas." I find, however, that 56,380 Vadugars have returned their sub-division as Kammavar or Kammas, and that the term has been used to denote many Telugu castes. At the census, 1901, the number of people returning themselves as Vadugan dropped to 95,924, and the name is defined by the Census Superintendent as a "linguistic term meaning a Telugu man, wrongly returned as a caste name by Kammas, Kāpus and Balijas in the Tamil districts." In the Salem Manual, Vaduga is noted as including all who speak Telugu in the Tamil districts, *e.g.*, Oddē, Bestha, etc.

It is recorded, in the Gazetteer of Malabar, that "of the same social standing as the Kammālans are the Vadugans (northerners), a makkattāyam caste of foreigners found in Palghat and the adjoining part of Waluvanad. They are divided into two exogamous classes, one of which is regarded as inferior to the other, and performs purificatory ceremonies for the caste. They cut their hair close all over the head, and have no kudumis (hair knot)."

It is noted by Mr. L. Moore[86] that "Xavier, writing in 1542 to 1544, makes frequent references to men whom he calls Badages, who are said to have been collectors of royal taxes, and to have grievously oppressed Xavier's converts among the fishermen of Travancore."[87] Dr. Caldwell, alluding to Xavier's letters, says[88] that these Badages were no doubt Vadages or men from the North, and is of opinion that a Jesuit writer of the time who called them Nayars was mistaken, and that they were really Nayakans from Madura. I believe, however, that the Jesuit rightly called them Nayars, for I find that Father Organtino, writing in 1568, speaks of these Badages as people from Narasinga, a kingdom north of Madura, lying close to Bishnaghur. Bishnaghur is, of course, Vijayanagar, and the kingdom of Narasinga was the name frequently given by the Portuguese to Vijayanagar. There is a considerable amount of evidence to show that the Nayars of Malabar are closely connected by origin with the Nayakans of Vijayanagar." (*See* Nāyar.)

Vadugāyan (Telugu shepherd).—A Tamil synonym for Golla.

Vagiri or Vāgirivāla.—*See* Kuruvikkāran.

Vāgiti (doorway or court-yard).—An exogamous sept of Jōgi.

Vaguniyan.—*See* Vayani.

Vaidyan.—Vaidyon or Baidya, meaning physician or medicine-man, occurs as a title of Kshaurakas, Billavas, and Pulluvans, and, at times of census, has been returned as an occupational sub-division of Paraiyans.

Village physicians are known as Vaidyans, and may belong to any caste, high or low. The Vaidyan diagnoses all diseases by feeling the pulse, and, after doing

[86] Malabar Law and Custom, 3rd ed., 1905.
[87] Father Coleridge's Life and Letters of St. Francis Xavier.
[88] History of Tinnevelly.

this for a sufficiently long time, remarks that there is an excess of vātham, pitham, ushnam, and so on. His stock phrases are vātham, pitham, ushnam, slēshmam, kārakam, mēgham or mēham, saithyam, etc. Orthodox men and women do not allow the Vaidyan to feel the pulse by direct contact of the fingers, and a silk cloth is placed on the patient's wrist. The pulse of males is felt with the right hand, and that of females with the left. Some Vaidyans crack the finger and wrist-joints before they proceed to feel the pulse. Some are general practitioners, and others specialists in the treatment of fever, piles, jaundice, syphilis, rheumatism, and other diseases. The specialists are generally hereditary practitioners. In the treatment of cases, the Vaidyan prescribes powders and pills, and a decoction or infusion (kashayam) of various drugs which can easily be obtained at the village drug-shop, or with the help of the village herbalist. Among these are ginger, pepper, *Abies Webbiana*, *Acorus calamus*, nīm (*Melia Azadirachta*), or *Andrographis paniculata* sticks, *Alpinia Galanga*, etc. If the medicine has to be taken for a long time, the drugs are compounded together in the form of a lēhyam, *e.g.*, bilvadi, kūshpanda, and purnadi lēhyam. Some Vaidyans prepare powders (basmam), such as swarna (gold) basmam, pavala (coral powder) basmam, or sānkha (chank shell powder) basmam. Special pills (māthre), prepared at considerable cost, are sometimes kept by Vaidyans, and passed on from generation to generation as heirlooms. Such pills are usually intended for well-known specific diseases. These pills are used in very minute quantities, and consequently last for a long time. A drop of honey or butter is placed on a slab of sandstone, on which the pill is rubbed. The honey or butter is then administered to the patient. A standing rule of the Vaidyan is to keep his patient on a very low diet, such as rice gruel without salt. His usual saying is "Langanam paramoushadam," *i.e.*, fasting is an excellent medicine. A well-known treatment in cases of jaundice is the drinking of curds, in which twigs of *Phyllanthus Niruri* have been well mashed.

In a very interesting note[89] on couching of the lens as practiced by native practitioners, Major R. H. Elliot, I.M.S., writes as follows. "The ignorance and stupidity of the ryot (villager) is so great that he will not very infrequently try one eye in an English hospital, and one in a Vaithyan's hands. It is a very common thing for a native patient to deny ever having visited a native doctor, when he first comes to hospital. After the other eye has been successfully operated on, he will sometimes own up to the fact.... Here in the south, there appear to be two classes of operators, the resident men who live for long periods in one bazaar, and the travellers who move continuously from place to place. Both are Mahomedans. The former appear to get somewhat better results than the latter, and are spoken of as 'men of experience.' The latter seem never to stop long in one place. They collect a number of victims, operate on them, and then move on before their sins can find them out. Both kinds of operators seem to be innocent of any attempt at securing asepsis or antisepsis; they use a dirty needle or a sharp wooden skewer; no anæsthetic is employed; a bandage is kept on for ten days, and counter-irritation is freely resorted to, to combat iritis, etc. Many of the victims are ashamed to come to a European hospital after the failure of their hopes. It has been said that, if the Vaithyan did <u>not get good re</u>sults, he would be dropped, and the practice would die out. This

[89] Indian Medical Gazette, XLI, 8, 1906.

remark can only have come from one who knew nothing of the Indian character, or the crass ignorance of the lower classes of the people. It is hard for those who have not lived and worked among them to realise how easily the ryot falls a dupe to impudent self-advertisement. He is a simple kindly person, whose implicit trust in confident self-assertion will bring him to grief for many another generation. The vision of these poor unfortunate people sitting down in a dusty bazaar to let an ignorant charlatan thrust a dirty needle into their blind eyes has evoked the indignation of the English surgeon from the time of our first occupation of the country. Side by side with a well-equipped English hospital, which turns out its ninety odd per cent. of useful vision, there sits in the neighbouring bazaar even to-day the charlatan, whose fee is fixed at anything from 3*d.* to 8 shillings, *plus*, in every case, a fowl or other animal. The latter is ostensibly for sacrificial purposes, but I understand ends uniformly in the Vaithyan's curry-pot. Weirdest, perhaps, of all the Vaithyan's methods is the use of the saffron-coloured rag, with which pus is wiped away from the patient's inflamed eye. On this colour, the pus, etc., cannot be seen, and therefore all is well. It is the fabled ostrich again, only this time in real life, with vital interests at stake."

It is noted[90] in connection with the various classes of Nambūtiri Brāhmans that "the Vaidyans or physicians, known as Mūssads, are to study the medical science, and to practice the same. As the profession of a doctor necessitates the performance of surgical operations entailing the shedding of blood, the Mūssads are considered as slightly degraded."

Further information concerning native medicine-men will be found in the articles on Kusavans and Mandulas.

Vaikhānasa.—Followers of the Rishi Vaikhānasa. They are Archaka Brāhman priests in the Telugu country.

Vairavan Kōvil.—An exogamous section or kōvil (temple) of Nāttukōttai Chetti.

Vairāvi.—The equivalent of Bairāgi or Vairāgi. Recorded, in the Madras Census Report, 1901, as "a sub-caste of Pandāram. They are found only in the Tinnevelly district, where they are measurers of grain, and pūjāris in village temples." In the Madura district, Vairāvis are members of the Mēlakkāran caste, who officiate as servants at the temples of the Nāttukōttai Chettis.

Vaisya.—Vaisya is the third of the traditional castes of Manu. "It is," Mr. Francis writes,[91] "doubtful whether there are any true Dravidian Vaisyas, but some of the Dravidian trading castes (with the title Chetti), notably the Kōmatis, are treated as Vaisyas by the Brāhmans, though the latter do not admit their right to perform the religious ceremonies which are restricted by the Vēdas to the twice-born, and require them to follow only the Purānic rites. The Mūttāns (trading caste in Malabar) formerly claimed to be Nāyars, but recently they have gone further, and some of them have returned themselves as Vaisyas, and added the Vaisya title of Gupta to their names. They do not, however, wear the sacred thread or perform

[90] Cochin Census Report, 1901.
[91] Madras Census Report, 1901.

any Vēdic rites, and Nāyars consider themselves polluted by their touch." Some Vellālas and Nāttukōttai Chettis describe themselves as being Bhū (earth) Vaisyas, and some Gollas claim to be regarded as Gō(cow) Vaisyas.[92] Some Gānigas and Nagartas call themselves Dharmasivāchar Vaisyas,[93] and, like the Canarese Gānigas (oil-pressers), the Tamil oil-pressers (Vāniyan) claim to rank as Vaisyas. Vaisya Brāhman is noted[94] as being a curious hybrid name, by which the Konkani Vānis (traders) style themselves. A small colony of "Baniyans," who call themselves Jain Vaisyas, is said[95] to have settled in Native Cochin. Vaisya is recorded as the caste of various title-holders, whose title is Chetti or Chettiyar, in the Madras Quarterly Civil List.

Vajjira (diamond).—An exogamous sept of Toreya.

Vakkaliga.—*See* Okkiliyan.

Vālagadava.—An occupational name for various classes in South Canara, *e.g.*, Sappaligas, Mogilis, and Patramelas, who are engaged as musicians.

Valai (net).—The name, said to indicate those who hunt with nets, of a section of Paraiyans. The Ambalakkārans, who are also called Valaiyans, claim that, when Siva's ring was swallowed by a fish in the Ganges, one of their ancestors invented the first net made in the world.

Valaiyal.—A sub-division of Kavarai, *i.e.*, the Tamil equivalent of Gāzula (glass bangle) Balija.

Valaiyan.—The Valaiyans are described, in the Manual of Madura district (1868), as "a low and debased class. Their name is supposed to be derived from valai, a net, and to have been given to them from their being constantly employed in netting game in the jungles. Many of them still live by the net; some catch fish; some smelt iron. Many are engaged in cultivation, as bearers of burdens, and in ordinary cooly work. The tradition that a Valaiya woman was the mother of the Vallambans seems to show that the Valaiyans must be one of the most ancient castes in the country." In the Tanjore Manual they are described as "inhabitants of the country inland who live by snaring birds, and fishing in fresh waters. They engage also in agricultural labour and cooly work, such as carrying loads, husking paddy (rice), and cutting and selling fire-wood. They are a poor and degraded class." The Valaiyans are expert at making cunningly devised traps for catching rats and jungle fowl. They have "a comical fairy-tale of the origin of the war, which still goes on between them and the rat tribe. It relates how the chiefs of the rats met in conclave, and devised the various means for arranging and harassing the enemy, which they still practice with such effect."[96] The Valaiyans say that they were once the friends of Siva, but were degraded for the sin of eating rats and frogs.

---

[92] Madras Census Report, 1901.
[93] Mysore Census Report, 1891.
[94] Madras Census Report, 1901.
[95] N. Sankuni Wariar, Ind. Ant. XXI, 1892.
[96] Gazetteer of the Madura district.

VALAYAN HUNTING FESTIVAL.

In the Census Report, 1901, the Valaiyans are described as "a shikāri (hunting) caste in Madura and Tanjore. In the latter the names Ambalakāran, Sērvaikāran, Vēdan, Siviyān, and Kuruvikkāran are indiscriminately applied to the caste." There is some connection between Ambalakārans, Muttiriyans, Mutrāchas, Urālis, Vēdans, Valaiyans, and Vēttuvans, but in what it exactly consists remains to be ascertained. It seems likely that all of them are descended from one common parent stock. Ambalakārans claim to be descended from Kannappa Nāyanar, one of the sixty-three Saivite saints, who was a Vēdan or hunter by caste. In Tanjore the Valaiyans declare themselves to have a similar origin, and in that district Ambalakāran and Muttiriyan seem to be synonymous with Valaiyan. Moreover, the statistics of the distribution of the Valaiyans show that they are numerous in the districts where Ambalakārans are few, and *vice versâ*, which looks as though certain sections had taken to calling themselves Ambalakārans. The upper sections of the Ambalakārans style themselves Pillai, which is a title properly belonging to Vellālas, but the others are usually called Mūppan in Tanjore, and Ambalakāran, Muttiriyan, and Sērvaikāran in Trichinopoly. The usual title of the Valaiyans, so far as I can gather, is Mūppan, but some style themselves Sērvai and Ambalakāran."

The Madura Valaiyans are said[97] to be "less brāhmanised than those in Tanjore, the latter employing Brāhmans as priests, forbidding the marriage of widows, occasionally burning their dead, and being particular what they eat. But they still cling to the worship of all the usual village gods and goddesses." In some places, it is said,[98] the Valaiyans will eat almost anything, including rats, cats, frogs and squirrels.

Like the Pallans and Paraiyans, the Valaiyans, in some places, live in streets of their own, or in settlements outside the villages. At times of census, they have returned a large number of sub-divisions, of which the following may be cited as examples:—

> Monathinni. Those who eat the vermin of the soil.
> Pāsikatti (pāsi, glass bead).
> Saragu, withered leaves.
> Vanniyan. Synonym of the Palli caste.
> Vellāmputtu, white-ant hill.

In some places the Saruku or Saragu Valaiyans have exogamous kīlais or septs, which, as among the Maravans and Kallans, run in the female line. Brothers and sisters belong to the same kīlai as that of their mother and maternal uncle, and not of their father.

It is stated, in the Gazetteer of the Madura district, that "the Valaiyans are grouped into four endogamous sub-divisions, namely, Vahni, Valattu, Karadi, and Kangu. The last of these is again divided into Pāsikatti, those who use a bead necklet instead of a tāli (as a marriage badge), and Kāraikatti, those whose women wear horsehair necklaces like the Kallans. The caste title is Mūppan. Caste matters are settled by a headman called the Kambliyan (blanket man), who lives at Aruppukōttai, and comes round in state to any village which requires his services, seated on a horse, and accompanied by servants who hold an umbrella over his head and fan him. He holds his court seated on a blanket. The fines imposed go in equal shares to the aramanai (literally palace, *i.e.*, to the headman himself), and to the oramanai, that is, the caste people.

It is noted by Mr. F. R. Hemingway that "the Valaiyans of the Trichinopoly

[97] Madras Census Report, 1901.
[98] *Ibid.*, 1891.

district say that they have eight endogamous sub-divisions, namely, Sarahu (or Saragu), Ettarai Kōppu, Tānambanādu or Valuvādi, Nadunāttu or Asal, Kurumba, Vanniya, Ambunādu, and Punal. Some of these are similar to those of the Kallans and Ambalakārans."

In the Gazetteer of the Tanjore district, it is recorded that the Valaiyans are said to possess "endogamous sub-divisions called Vēdan, Sulundukkāran and Ambalakkāran. The members of the first are said to be hunters, those of the second torch-bearers, and those of the last cultivators. They are a low caste, are refused admittance into the temples, and pollute a Vellālan by touch. Their occupations are chiefly cultivation of a low order, cooly work, and hunting. They are also said to be addicted to crime, being employed by Kallans as their tools."

Adult marriage is the rule, and the consent of the maternal uncle is necessary. Remarriage of widows is freely permitted. At the marriage ceremony, the bridegroom's sister takes up the tāli (marriage badge), and, after showing it to those assembled, ties it tightly round the neck of the bride. To tie it loosely so that the tāli string touches the collar-bone would be considered a breach of custom, and the woman who tied it would be fined. The tāli-tying ceremony always takes place at night, and the bridegroom's sister performs it, as, if it was tied by the bridegroom, it could not be removed on his death, and replaced if his widow wished to marry again. Marriages generally take place from January to May, and consummation should not be effected till the end of the month Ādi, lest the first child should be born in the month of Chithre, which would be very inauspicious. There are two Tamil proverbs to the effect that "the girl should remain in her mother's house during Ādi," and "if a child is born in Chithre, it is ruinous to the house of the mother-in-law."

In the Gazetteer of the Madura district, it is stated that "at weddings, the bridegroom's sister ties the tāli, and then hurries the bride off to her brother's house, where he is waiting. When a girl attains maturity, she is made to live for a fortnight in a temporary hut, which she afterwards burns down. While she is there, the little girls of the caste meet outside it, and sing a song illustrative of the charms of womanhood, and its power of alleviating the unhappy lot of the bachelor. Two of the verses say: —

> What of the hair of a man?
> It is twisted, and matted, and a burden.
> What of the tresses of a woman?
> They are as flowers in a garland, and a glory.
> What of the life of a man?
> It is that of the dog at the palace gate.
> What of the days of a woman?
> They are like the gently waving leaves in a festoon.

"Divorce is readily permitted on the usual payments, and divorcées and widows may remarry. A married woman who goes astray is brought before the Kambliyan, who delivers a homily, and then orders the man's waist-string to be tied round her neck. This legitimatises any children they may have." The Valaiyans of

Pattukkōttai in the Tanjore district say that intimacy between a man and woman before marriage is tolerated, and that the children of such a union are regarded as members of the caste, and permitted to intermarry with others, provided the parents pay a nominal penalty imposed by the caste council.

In connection with the Valaiyans of the Trichinopoly district, Mr. Hemingway writes that "they recognise three forms of marriage, the most usual of which consists in the bridegroom's party going to the girl's house with three marakkāls of rice and a cock on an auspicious day, and in both parties having a feast there. Sometimes the young man's sister goes to the girl's house, ties a tāli round her neck, and takes her away. The ordinary form of marriage, called big marriage, is sometimes used with variations, but the Valaiyans do not like it, and say that the two other forms result in more prolific unions. They tolerate unchastity before marriage, and allow parties to marry even after several children have been born, the marriage legitimatising them. They permit remarriage of widows and divorced women. Women convicted of immorality are garlanded with erukku (*Calotropis gigantea*) flowers, and made to carry a basket of mud round the village. Men who too frequently offend in this respect are made to sit with their toes tied to the neck by a creeper. When a woman is divorced, her male children go to the husband, and she is allowed to keep the girls."

The tribal gods of the Valaiyans are Singa Pidāri (Aiyanar) and Padinettāmpadi Karuppan. Once a year, on the day after the new-moon in the month Māsi (February to March), the Valaiyans assemble to worship the deity. Early in the morning they proceed to the Aiyanar temple, and, after doing homage to the god, go off to the forest to hunt hares and other small game. On their return they are met by the Valaiyan matrons carrying coloured water or rice (ālām), garlands of flowers, betel leaves and areca nuts. The ālām is waved over the men, some of whom become inspired and are garlanded. While they are under inspiration, the mothers appeal to them to name their babies. The products of the chase are taken to the house of the headman and distributed. At a festival, at which Mr. K. Rangachari was present, at about ten o'clock in the morning all the Valaiya men, women, and children, dressed up in holiday attire, swarmed out of their huts, and proceeded to a neighbouring grove. The men and boys each carried a throwing stick, or a digging stick tipped with iron. On arrival at the grove, they stood in a row, facing east, and, throwing down their sticks, saluted them, and prostrated themselves before them. Then all took up their sticks, and some played on reed pipes. Some of the women brought garlands of flowers, and placed them round the necks of four men, who for a time stood holding in their hands their sticks, of which the ends were stuck in the ground. After a time they began to shiver, move quickly about, and kick those around them. Under the influence of their inspiration, they exhibited remarkable physical strength, and five or six men could not hold them. Calling various people by name, they expressed a hope that they would respect the gods, worship them, and offer to them pongal (boiled rice) and animal sacrifices. The women brought their babies to them to be named. In some places, the naming of infants is performed at the Aiyanar temple by any one who is under the influence of inspiration. Failing such a one, several flowers, each with a name attached to it, are thrown in front of the idol. A boy, or the pūjāri (priest) picks up one of the flowers, and the infant receives the name which is connected with it.

The Valaiyans are devoted to devil worship, and, at Orattanādu in the Tanjore district, every Valaiyan backyard is said to contain an odiyan (*Odina Wodier*) tree, in which the devil is supposed to live.[99] It is noted by Mr. W. Francis[100] that "certain of the Valaiyans who live at Ammayanāyakkanūr are the hereditary pūjāris to the gods of the Sirumalai hills. Some of these deities are uncommon, and one of them, Pāppārayan, is said to be the spirit of a Brāhman astrologer whose monsoon forecast was falsified by events, and who, filled with a shame rare in unsuccessful weather prophets, threw himself off a high point on the range."

According to Mr. Hemingway, the Valaiyans have a special caste god, named Muttāl Rāvuttan, who is the spirit of a dead Muhammadan, about whom nothing seems to be known.

The dead are as a rule buried with rites similar to those of the Kallans and Agamudaiyans. The final death ceremonies (karmāndhiram) are performed on the sixteenth day. On the night of the previous day, a vessel filled with water is placed on the spot where the deceased breathed his last, and two cocoanuts, with the pores ('eyes') open, are deposited near it. On the following morning, all proceed to a grove or tank (pond). The eldest son, or other celebrant, after shaving and bathing, marks out a square space on the ground, and, placing a few dry twigs of *Ficus religiosa* and *Ficus bengalensis* therein, sets fire to them. Presents of rice and other food-stuffs are given to beggars and others. The ceremony closes with the son and sapindas, who have to observe pollution, placing new cloths on their heads. Mr. Francis records that, at the funeral ceremonies, "the relations go three times round a basket of grain placed under a pandal (booth), beating their breasts and singing:—

> For us the kanji (rice gruel): kailāsam (the abode of Siva) for thee;
> Rice for us; for thee Svargalōkam,

and then wind turbans round the head of the deceased's heir, in recognition of his new position as chief of the family. When a woman loses her husband, she goes three times round the village mandai (common), with a pot of water on her shoulder. After each of the first two journeys, the barber makes a hole in the pot, and at the end of the third he hurls down the vessel, and cries out an adjuration to the departed spirit to leave the widow and children in peace." It is noted, in the Gazetteer of the Tanjore district, that "one of the funeral ceremonies is peculiar, though it is paralleled by practices among the Paraiyans and Karaiyāns. When the heir departs to the burning-ground on the second day, a mortar is placed near the outer door of his house, and a lamp is lit inside. On his return, he has to upset the mortar, and worship the light."

Vālan.—For the following note on the Vālan and Katal Arayan fishing castes of the Cochin State, I am indebted to Mr. L. K. Anantha Krishna Aiyar.

The name Vālan is derived from vala, meaning fish in a tank. Some consider

[99] Gazetteer of the Tanjore district.
[100] Gazetteer of the Madura district.

the word to be another form of Valayan, which signifies a person who throws a net for fishing. According to the tradition and current belief of these people, they were brought to Kērala by Parasurāma for plying boats and conveying passengers across the rivers and backwaters on the west coast. Another tradition is that the Vālans were Arayans, and they became a separate caste only after one of the Perumāls had selected some of their families for boat service, and conferred on them special privileges. They even now pride themselves that their caste is one of remote antiquity, and that Vedavyasa, the author of the Purānas, and Guha, who rendered the boat service to the divine Rāma, Sita, and Lakshmana, across the Ganges in the course of their exile to the forest, were among the caste-men.

There are no sub-divisions in the caste, but the members thereof are said to belong to four exogamous illams (houses of Nambūtiris), namely, Alayakad, Ennalu, Vaisyagiriam, and Vazhapally, which correspond to the gōtras of the Brāhmans, or to four clans, the members of each of which are perhaps descended from a common ancestor. According to a tradition current among them, they were once attached to the four Nambūtiri illams above mentioned for service of some kind, and were even the descendants of the members of the illams, but were doomed to the present state of degradation on account of some misconduct. Evidently, the story is looked up to to elevate themselves in social status. I am inclined to believe that they must have been the Atiyars (slaves) of the four aforesaid Brāhman families, owing a kind of allegiance (nambikooru) like the Kanakkans to the Chittur Manakkal Nambūtripād in Perumanam of the Trichur tāluk. Even now, these Brāhman families are held in great respect by the Vālans, who, when afflicted with family calamities, visit the respective illams with presents of a few packets of betel leaves and a few annas, to receive the blessings of their Brāhman masters, which, according to their belief, may tend to avert them.

The low sandy tract of land on each side of the backwater is the abode of these fishermen. In some places, more especially south of Cranganore, their houses are dotted along the banks of the backwater, often nearly hidden by cocoanut trees, while at intervals the white picturesque fronts of numerous Roman Catholic and Romo-Syrian churches are perceived. These houses are in fact mere flimsy huts, a few of which, occupied by the members of several families, may be seen huddled together in the same compound abounding in a growth of cocoanut trees, with hardly enough space to dry their fish and nets. In the majority of cases, the compounds belong to jenmis (landlords), who lease them out either rent-free or on nominal rent, and who often are so kind as to allow them some cocoanuts for their consumption, and leaves sufficient to thatch their houses. About ten per cent. of their houses are built of wood and stones, while a large majority of them are made of mud or bamboo framework, and hardly spacious enough to accommodate the members of the family during the summer months. Cooking is done outside the house, and very few take rest inside after hard work, for their compounds are shady and breezy, and they may be seen basking in the sun after midnight toil, or drying the nets or fish. Their utensils are few, consisting of earthen vessels and enamel dishes, and their furniture of a few wooden planks and coarse mats to serve as beds.

The girls of the Vālans are married both before and after puberty, but the tā-li-kettu kalyānam (tāli-tying marriage) is indispensable before they come of age, as otherwise they and their parents are put out of caste. Both for the tāli-tying ceremony and for the real marriage, the bride and bridegroom must be of different illams or gōtras. In regard to the former, as soon as an auspicious day is fixed, the girl's party visit the Aravan with a present of six annas and eight pies, and a few packets of betel leaves, when he gives his permission, and issues an order to the Ponamban, his subordinate of the kadavu (village), to see that the ceremony is properly conducted. The Ponamban, the bridegroom and his party, go to the house of the bride. At the appointed hour, the Ponambans and the castemen of the two kadavus assemble after depositing six annas and eight pies in recognition of the presence of the Aravan, and the tāli is handed over by the priest to the bridegroom, who ties it round the neck of the bride amidst the joyous shouts of the multitude assembled. The ceremony always takes place at night, and the festivities generally last for two days. It must be understood that the tāli tier is not necessarily the husband of the girl, but is merely the pseudo-bridegroom or pseudo-husband, who is sent away with two pieces of cloth and a few annas at the termination of the ceremony. Should he, however, wish to have the girl as his wife, he should, at his own expense, provide her with a tāli, a wedding dress, and a few rupees as the price of the bride. Generally it is the maternal uncle of the girl who provides her with the first two at the time of the ceremony.

The actual marriage is more ceremonial in its nature. The maternal uncle, or the father of a young Vālan who wishes to marry, first visits the girl, and, if he approves of the match for his nephew or son, the astrologer is consulted so as to ensure that the horoscopes agree. If astrology does not stand in the way, they forthwith proceed to the girl's house, where they are well entertained. The bride's parents and relatives return the visit at the bridegroom's house, where they are likewise treated to a feast. The two parties then decide on a day for the formal declaration of the proposed union. On that day, a Vālan from the bridegroom's village, seven to nine elders, and the Ponamban under whom the bride is, meet, and, in the presence of those assembled, a Vālan from each party deposits on a plank four annas and a few betel leaves in token of enangu māttam or exchange of co-castemen from each party for the due fulfilment of the contract thus publicly entered into. Then they fix the date of the marriage, and retire from the bride's house. On the appointed day, the bridegroom's party proceed to the bride's house with two pieces of cloth, a rupee or a rupee and a half, rice, packets of betel leaves, etc. The bride is already dressed and adorned in her best, and one piece of cloth, rice and money, are paid to her mother as the price of the bride. After a feast, the bridal party go to the bridegroom's house, which is entered at an auspicious hour. They are received at the gate with a lamp and a vessel of water, a small quantity of which is sprinkled on the married couple. They are welcomed by the seniors of the house and seated together, when sweets are given, and the bride is formally declared to be a member of the bridegroom's family. The ceremony closes with a feast, the expenses in connection with which are the same on both sides.

A man may marry more than one wife, but no woman may enter into conjugal relations with more than one man. A widow may, with the consent of her parents, enter into wedlock with any member of her caste except her brothers-in-law, in which case her children by her first husband will be looked after by the members of his family. Divorce is effected by either party making an application to the Aravan, who has to be presented with from twelve annas to six rupees and a half according to the means of the applicant. The Aravan, in token of dissolution, issues a letter to the members of the particular village to which the applicant belongs, and, on the declaration of the same, he or she has to pay to his or her village castemen four annas.

When a Vālan girl comes of age, she is lodged in a room of the house, and is under pollution for four days. She is bathed on the fourth day, and the castemen and women of the neighbourhood, with the relatives and friends, are treated to a sumptuous dinner. There is a curious custom called theralikka, *i.e.*, causing the girl to attain maturity, which consists in placing her in seclusion in a separate room, and proclaiming that she has come of age. Under such circumstances, the caste-women of the neighbourhood, with the washerwoman, assemble at the house of the girl, when the latter pours a small quantity of gingelly (*Sesamum*) oil on her head, and rubs her body with turmeric powder, after which she is proclaimed as having attained puberty. She is bathed, and lodged in a separate room as before, and the four days' pollution is observed. This custom, which exists also among other castes, is now being abandoned by a large majority of the community.

In respect of inheritance, the Vālans follow a system, which partakes of the character of succession from father to son, and from maternal uncle to nephew. The self-acquired property is generally divided equally between brothers and sons, while the ancestral property, if any, goes to the brothers. The great majority of the Vālans are mere day-labourers, and the property usually consists of a few tools, implements, or other equipments of their calling.

The Vālans, like other castes, have their tribal organisation, and their headman (Aravan or Aravar) is appointed by thītturam or writ issued by His Highness the Rāja. The Aravan appoints other social heads, called Ponamban, one, two, or three of whom are stationed at each dēsam (village) or kadavu. Before the development of the Government authority and the establishment of administrative departments, the Aravans wielded great influence and authority, as they still do to a limited extent, not only in matters social, but also in civil and criminal disputes between members of the community. For all social functions, matrimonial, funeral, etc., their permission has to be obtained and paid for. The members of the community have to visit their headman, with presents of betel leaves, money, and sometimes rice and paddy (unhusked rice). The headman generally directs the proper conduct of all ceremonies by writs issued to the Ponambans under him. The Ponambans also are entitled to small perquisites on ceremonial occasions. The appointment of Aravan, though not virtually hereditary, passes at his death to the next qualified senior member of his family, who may be his brother, son, or nephew, but this rule has been violated by the appointment of a person from a different family. The Aravan has the honour of receiving from His Highness the Rāja a present of two cloths at the Ōnam festival, six annas and eight pies on the

Athachamayam day, and a similar sum for the Vishu. At his death, the ruler of the State sends a piece of silk cloth, a piece of sandal-wood, and about ten rupees, for defraying the expenses of the funeral ceremonies.

The Vālans profess Hinduism, and Siva, Vishnu, and the heroes of the Hindu Purānas are all worshipped. Like other castes, they entertain special reverence for Bhagavathi, who is propitiated with offerings of rice-flour, toddy, green cocoanuts, plantain fruits, and fowls, on Tuesdays and Fridays. A grand festival, called Kumbhom Bharani (cock festival), is held in the middle of March, when Nāyars and low caste men offer up cocks to Bhagavathi, beseeching immunity from diseases during the ensuing year. In fact, people from all parts of Malabar, Cochin, and Travancore, attend the festival, and the whole country near the line of march rings with shouts of "Nada, nada" (walk or march) of the pilgrims to Cranganore, the holy residence of the goddess. In their passage up to the shrine, the cry of "Nada, nada" is varied by unmeasured abuse of the goddess. The abusive language, it is believed, is acceptable to her, and, on arrival at the shrine, they desecrate it in every conceivable manner, in the belief that this too is acceptable. They throw stones and filth, howling volleys of abuse at the shrine. The chief of the Arayan caste, Koolimuttah Arayan, has the privilege of being the first to be present on the occasion. The image in the temple is said to have been recently introduced. There is a door in the temple which is apparently of stone, fixed in a half-opened position. A tradition, believed by Hindus and Christians, is attached to this, which asserts that St. Thomas and Bhagavathi held a discussion at Palliport about the respective merits of the Christian and Hindu religions. The argument became heated, and Bhagavathi, considering it best to cease further discussion, decamped, and, jumping across the Cranganore river, made straight for the temple. St. Thomas, not to be outdone, rapidly gave chase, and, just as the deity got inside the door, the saint reached its outside, and, setting his foot between it and the door-post, prevented its closure. There they both stood until the door turned to stone, one not allowing its being opened, and the other its being shut.

Another important festival, which is held at Cranganore, is the Makara Vilakku, which falls on the first of Makaram (about the 15th January), during the night of which there is a good deal of illumination both in and round the temple. A procession of ten or twelve elephants, all fully decorated, goes round it several times, accompanied by drums and instrumental music.

Chourimala Iyappan or Sāstha, a sylvan deity, whose abode is Chourimala in Travancore, is a favourite deity of the Vālans. In addition, they worship the demigods or demons Kallachan Muri and Kochu Mallan, who are ever disposed to do them harm, and who are therefore propitiated with offerings of fowls. They have a patron, who is also worshipped at Cranganore. The spirits of their ancestors are also held in great veneration by these people, and are propitiated with offerings on the new moon and Sankranthi days of Karkadakam, Thulam, and Makaram.

The most important festivals observed by the Vālans in common with other castes are Mandalam Vilakku, Sivarāthri, Vishu, Ōnam, and Desara.

Mandalam Vilakku takes place during the last seven days of Mandalam (November to December). During this festival the Vālans enjoy themselves with music and drum-beating during the day. At night, some of them, developing hysterical fits, profess to be oracles, with demons such as Gandharva, Yakshi, or Bhagavathi, dwelling in their bodies in their incorporeal forms. Consultations are held as to future events, and their advice is thankfully received and acted upon. Sacrifices of sheep, fowls, green cocoanuts, and plantain fruits are offered to the demons believed to be residing within, and are afterwards liberally distributed among the castemen and others present.

The Sivarāthri festival comes on the last day of Magha. The whole day and night are devoted to the worship of Siva, and the Vālans, like other castes, go to Alvai, bathe in the river, and keep awake during the night, reading the Siva Purāna and reciting his names. Early on the following morning, they bathe, and make offerings of rice balls to the spirits of the ancestors before returning home.

The Vālans have no temples of their own, but, on all important occasions, worship the deities of the temples of the higher castes, standing at a long distance from the outer walls of the sacred edifice. On important religious occasions, Embrans are invited to perform the Kalasam ceremony, for which they are liberally rewarded. A kalasam is a pot, which is filled with water. Mango leaves and dharba grass are placed in it. Vēdic hymns are repeated, with one end of the grass in the water, and the other in the hand. Water thus sanctified is used for bathing the image. From a comparison of the religion of the Vālans with that of allied castes, it may be safely said that they were animists, but have rapidly imbibed the higher forms of worship. They are becoming more and more literate, and this helps the study of the religious works. There are some among them, who compose Vanchipāttu (songs sung while rowing) with plots from their Purānic studies.

The Vālans either burn or bury their dead. The chief mourner is either the son or nephew of the dead person, and he performs the death ceremonies as directed by the priest (Chithayan), who attends wearing a new cloth, turban, and the sacred thread. The ceremonies commence on the second, fifth, or seventh day, when the chief mourner, bathing early in the morning, offers pinda bali (offerings of rice balls) to the spirit of the deceased. This is continued till the thirteenth day, when the nearest relatives get shaved. On the fifteenth day, the castemen of the locality, the friends and relatives, are treated to a grand dinner, and, on the sixteenth day, another offering (mana pindam) is made to the spirit of the departed, and thrown into the backwater close by. Every day during the ceremonies, a vessel full of rice is given to the priest, who also receives ten rupees for his services. If the death ceremonies are not properly performed, the ghost of the deceased is believed to haunt the house. An astrologer is then consulted, and his advice is invariably followed. What is called Samhara Hōmam (sacred fire) is kept up, and an image of the dead man in silver or gold is purified by the recitation of holy mantrams. Another purificatory ceremony is performed, after which the image is handed over to a priest at the temple, with a rupee or two. This done, the death ceremonies are performed.

The ears of Vālan girls are, as among some other castes, pierced when they are a year old, or even less, and a small quill, a piece of cotton thread, or a bit of wood, is inserted into the hole. The wound is gradually healed by the application of cocoanut oil. A piece of lead is then inserted in the hole, which is gradually enlarged by means of a piece of plantain, cocoanut, or palmyra leaf rolled up.

The Vālans are expert rowers, and possess the special privilege of rowing from Thripunathura the boat of His Highness the Rāja for his installation at the Cochin palace, when the Aravan, with sword in hand, has to stand in front of him in the boat. Further, on the occasion of any journey of the Rāja along the backwaters on occasions of State functions, such as a visit of the Governor of Madras, or other dignitary, the headman leads the way as an escort in a snake-boat rowed with paddles, and has to supply the requisite number of men for rowing the boats of the high official and his retinue.

The Katal Arayans, or sea Arayans, who are also called Katakkoti, are lower in status than the Vālans, and, like them, live along the coast. They were of great service to the Portuguese and the Dutch in their palmy days, acting as boatmen in transhipping their commodities and supplying them with fish. The Katal Arayans were, in former times, owing to their social degradation, precluded from travelling along the public roads. This disability was, during the days of the Portuguese supremacy, taken advantage of by the Roman Catholic missionaries, who turned their attention to the conversion of these poor fishermen, a large number of whom were thus elevated in the social scale. The Katal Arayans are sea fishermen. On the death of a prince of Malabar, all fishing is temporarily prohibited, and only renewed after three days, when the spirit of the departed is supposed to have had time enough to choose its abode without molestation.

Among their own community, the Katal Arayans distinguish themselves by four distinct appellations, viz., Sankhan, Bharatan, Amukkuvan, and Mukkuvan. Of these, Amukkuvans do priestly functions. The castemen belong to four septs or illams, namely, Kattotillam, Karotillam, Chempotillam, and Ponnotillam.

Katal Arayan girls are married both before and after puberty. The tāli-tying ceremony, which is compulsory in the case of Vālan girls before they come of age, is put off, and takes place along with the real marriage. The preliminary negotiations and settlements thereof are substantially the same as those prevailing among the Vālans. The auspicious hour for marriage is between three and eight in the morning, and, on the previous evening, the bridegroom and his party arrive at the house of the bride, where they are welcomed and treated to a grand feast, after which the guests, along with the bride and bridegroom seated somewhat apart, in a pandal tastefully decorated and brightly illuminated, are entertained with songs of the Vēlan (washerman) and his wife alluding to the marriage of Sīta or Parvathi, in the belief that they will bring about a happy conjugal union. These are continued till sunrise, when the priest hands over the marriage badge to the bridegroom, who ties it round the neck of the bride. The songs are again continued for an hour or two, after which poli begins. The guests who have assembled contribute a rupee, eight annas, or four annas, according to their means, which go towards the remuneration of the priest, songsters, and drummers. The guests are again sumptuously entertained at twelve o'clock, after which the bridegroom and his party return with the bride to his house. At the time of departure, or nearly an hour before it, the bridegroom ties a few rupees or a sovereign to a corner of the bride's body-cloth, probably to induce her to accompany him. Just then, the bride-price, which is 101 puthans, or Rs. 5–12–4, is paid to her parents. The bridal party is entertained at the bridegroom's house, where, at an auspicious hour, the newly married couple are seated together, and served with a few pieces of plantain fruits and some milk, when the bride is formally declared to be a member of her husband's family. If a girl attains maturity after her marriage, she is secluded for a period of eleven days. She bathes on the first, fourth, seventh, and eleventh days, and, on the last day the caste people are entertained with a grand feast, the expenses connected with which are met by the husband. The Katal Arayans rarely have more than one wife. A widow may, a year after the death of her husband, enter into conjugal relations with any member of the caste, except her brother-in-law. Succession is in the male line.

The Katal Arayans have headmen (Aravans), whose duties are the same as those of the headmen of the Vālans. When the senior male or female member of the ruling family dies, the Aravan has the special privilege of being the first successor to the masnad with his tirumul kazcha (nuzzer), which consists of a small quantity of salt packed in a plantain leaf with rope and a Venetian ducat or other gold coin. During the period of mourning, visits of condolence from durbar officials and sthanis or noblemen are received only after the Aravan's visit. When the Bhagavathi temple of Cranganore is defiled during the cock festival, Koolimutteth Aravan has the special privilege of entering the temple in preference to other castemen.

The Katal Arayans profess Hinduism, and their modes of worship, and other religious observances, are the same as those of the Vēlans. The dead are either burnt or buried. The period of death pollution is eleven days, and the agnates are freed from it by a bath on the eleventh day. On the twelfth day, the castemen of the village, including the relatives and friends, are treated to a grand feast. The son, who is the chief mourner, observes the dīksha, or vow by which he does not shave, for a year. He performs the srādha (memorial service) every year in honour of the dead.

Some of the methods of catching fish at Cochin are thus described by Dr. Francis Day.[101] "Cast nets are employed from the shore, by a number of fishermen, who station themselves either in the early morning or in the afternoon, along the coast from 50 to 100 yards apart. They keep a careful watch on the water, and, on perceiving a fish rise sufficiently near the land, rush down and attempt to throw their nets over it. This is not done as in Europe by twisting the net round and round the head until it has acquired the necessary impetus, and then throwing it; but by the person twirling himself and the net round and round at the same time, and then casting it. He not infrequently gets knocked over by a wave. When fish are caught, they are buried in the sand, to prevent their tainting. In the wide inland rivers, fishermen employ cast nets in the following manner. Each man is in a boat, which is propelled by a boy with a bamboo. The fisherman has a cast net, and a small empty cocoanut shell. This last he throws into the river, about twenty yards before the boat, and it comes down with a splash, said to be done to scare away the

[101] The land of the Permauls, or Cochin, its past and its present, 1863.

crocodiles. As the boat approaches the place where the cocoanut shell was thrown, the man casts his net around the spot. This method is only for obtaining small fish, and as many as fifteen boats at a time are to be seen thus employed in one place, one following the other in rapid succession, some trying the centre, others the sides of the river.

"Double rows of long bamboos, firmly fixed in the mud, are placed at intervals across the backwater, and on these nets are fixed at the flood tide, so that fish which have entered are unable to return to the sea. Numbers of very large ones are occasionally captured in this way. A species of Chinese nets is also used along the river's banks. They are about 16 feet square, suspended by bamboos from each corner, and let down like buckets into the water, and then after a few minutes drawn up again. A piece of string, to which are attached portions of the white leaves of the cocoanut tree, is tied at short intervals along the ebb side of the net, which effectually prevents fish from going that way. A plan somewhat analogous is employed on a small scale for catching crabs. A net three feet square is supported at the four corners by two pieces of stick fastened crosswise. From the centre of these sticks where they cross is a string to pull it up by or let it down, and a piece of meat is tied to the middle of the net inside. This is let down from a wharf, left under water for a few minutes, and then pulled up. Crabs coming to feed are thus caught.

"Fishing with a line is seldom attempted in the deep sea, excepting for sharks, rays, and other large fish. The hooks employed are of two descriptions, the roughest, although perhaps the strongest, being of native manufacture; the others are of English make, denominated China hooks. The hook is fastened to a species of fibre called thumboo, said to be derived from a seaweed, but more probably from one of the species of palms. The lines are either hemp, cotton, or the fibre of the talipot palm (*Caryota urens*), which is obtained by maceration. In Europe they are called Indian gut.

"Trolling from the shore at the river's mouth is only carried on of a morning or evening, during the winter months of the year, when the sea is smooth. The line is from 80 to 100 yards in length, and held wound round the left hand; the hook is fastened to the line by a brass wire, and the bait is a live fish. The fisherman, after giving the line an impetus by twirling it round and round his head, throws it with great precision from 50 to 60 yards. A man is always close by with a cast net, catching baits, which he sells for one quarter of an anna each. This mode of fishing is very exciting sport, but is very uncertain in its results, and therefore usually carried on by coolies either before their day's work has commenced, or after its termination.

"Fishing with a bait continues all day long in Cochin during the monsoon months, when work is almost at a standstill, and five or six persons may be perceived at each jetty, busily engaged in this occupation. The *Bagrus* tribe is then plentiful, and, as it bites readily, large numbers are captured.

"Fishing in small boats appears at times to be a dangerous occupation; the small canoe only steadied by the paddle of one man seated in it looks as if it must every minute be swamped. Very large fish are sometimes caught in this way. Should one be hooked too large for the fisherman to manage, the man in the next boat comes to his assistance, and receives a quarter of the fish for his trouble. This is carried on all through the year, and the size of some of the Bagri is enormous.

"Fish are shot in various ways, by a Chittagong bamboo, which is a hollow tube, down which the arrow is propelled by the marksman's mouth. This mode is sometimes very remunerative, and is followed by persons who quietly sneak along the shores, either of sluggish streams or of the backwater. Sometimes they climb up into trees, and there await a good shot. Or, during the monsoon, the sportsman quietly seats himself near some narrow channel that passes from one wide piece of water into another, and watches for his prey. Other fishermen shoot with bows and arrows, and again others with cross-bows, the iron arrow or bolt of which is attached by a line to the bow, to prevent its being lost. But netting fish, catching them with hooks, or shooting them with arrows, are not the only means employed for their capture. Bamboo labyrinths, bamboo baskets, and even men's hands alone, are called into use.

"Persons fish for crabs in shallow brackish water, provided with baskets like those employed in Europe for catching eels, but open at both ends. The fishermen walk about in the mud, and, when they feel a fish move, endeavour to cover it with the larger end of the basket, which is forced down some distance into the mud, and the hand is then passed downward through the upper extremity, and the fish taken out. Another plan of catching them by the hand is by having two lines to which white cocoanut leaves are attached tied to the fisherman's two great toes, from which they diverge; the other end of each being held by another man a good way off, and some distance apart. On these lines being shaken, the fish become frightened, and, strange as it may appear, cluster for protection around the man's feet, who is able to stoop down, and catch them with his hands, by watching his opportunity.

"Bamboo labyrinths are common all along the backwater, in which a good many fish, especially eels and crabs, are captured. These labyrinths are formed of a screen of split bamboos, passing perpendicularly out of the water, and leading into a larger baited chamber. A dead cat is often employed as a bait for crabs. A string is attached to its body, and, after it has been in the water some days, it is pulled up with these crustacea adherent to it. Persons are often surprised at crabs being considered unwholesome, but their astonishment would cease, if they were aware what extremely unclean feeders they are.

"Fish are obtained from the inland rivers by poisoning them, but this can only be done when the water is low. A dam is thrown across a certain portion, and the poison placed within it. It generally consists of *Cocculus indicus* (berries) pounded with rice; croton oil seeds, etc."

Valangai.—Valangai, Valangan, Valangamattān, or Balagai, meaning those who belong to the right-hand faction, has, at times of census, been returned as a sub-division, synonym or title of Dēva-dāsis, Holeyas, Nōkkans, Panisavans, Paraiyans, and Sāliyans. Some Dēva-dāsis have returned themselves as belonging to the left-hand (idangai) faction.

Valayakāra Chetti.—A Tamil synonym of Gāzula Balijas who sell glass bangles. The equivalent Vala Chetti is also recorded.

Vālēkāra.—A Badaga form of Billēkāra or belted peon. The word frequently occurs in Badaga ballads. Tāluk peons on the Nīlgiris are called Vālēkāras.

Vāli Sugrīva.—A synonym of the Lambādis, who claim descent from Vāli and Sugrīva, the two monkey chiefs of the Rāmāyana.

Valinchiyan.—*See* Velakkattalavan.

Valiyatān (valiya, great, tān, a title of dignity).—Recorded, in the Travancore Census Report, 1901, as a title of Nāyar.

Vallabarayan.—A title of Ōcchan.

Vallamban.—The Vallambans are a small Tamil cultivating class living in the Tanjore, Trichinopoly, and Madura districts. They are said[102] to be "the offspring of a Vellālan and a Valaiya woman, now a small and insignificant caste of cultivators. Some of them assert that their ancestors were the lords of the soil, for whose sole benefit the Vellālans used to carry on cultivation. Tradition makes the Vellambans to have joined the Kallans in attacking and driving away the Vellālans. It is customary among the Vallambans, when demising land, to refer to the fact of their being descendants of the Vallambans who lost Vallam, *i.e.*, the Vallama nādu in Tanjore, their proper country." Some Vallambans claim to be flesh-eating Vellālas, or to be superior to Kallans and Maravans by reason of their Vellāla ancestry. They call themselves Vallamtōtta Vellālas, or the Vellālas who lost Vallam, and say that they were Vellālas of Vallam in the Tanjore district, who left their native place in a time of famine.

Portions of the Madura and Tanjore districts are divided into areas known as nādus, in each of which a certain caste, called the Nāttar, is the predominant factor. For example, the Vallambans and Kallans are called the Nāttars of the Pālaya nādu in the Sivaganga zemindari of the Madura district. In dealing with the tribal affairs of the various castes inhabiting a particular nādu, the lead is taken by the Nāttars, by whom certain privileges are enjoyed, as for example in the distribution to them, after the Brāhman and zamindar, of the flowers and sacred ashes used in temple worship. For the purposes of caste council meetings the Vallambans collect together representatives from fourteen nādus, as they consider that the council should be composed of delegates from a head village and its branches, generally thirteen in number.

It is noted by Mr. F. R. Hemingway that the Vallambans "speak of five sub-divisions, namely, Chenjinādu, Amaravatinādu, Palayanādu, Mēlnādu, and Kilnādu. The Mēl and Kilnādu people intermarry, but are distinguishable by the fact that the former have moustaches, and the latter have not. The women dress like the Nāttukōttai Chettis. Tattooing is not allowed, and those who practice it are expelled from the caste. The men generally have no title, but some who enjoy State service inams call themselves Ambalakāran. The Mēlnādu people have no exoga-

[102] Manual of the Madura district.

mous divisions, though they observe the rule about Kōvil Pangōlis. The Kilnādus have exogamous kilais, karais, and pattams." As examples of exogamous septs, the following may be cited:—Sōlangal (Chōla), Pāndiangal (Pāndyan), Nariangal (jackal), and Piliyangal (tiger).

The headman of the Vallambans is referred to generally as the Servaikāran. The headman of a group of nādus is entitled Nāttuservai, while the headman of a village is known as Ūr Servai, or simply Servai.

Marriage is celebrated between adults, and the remarriage of widows is not objected to. It is stated[103] that "the maternal uncle's or paternal aunt's daughter is claimed as a matter of right by a boy, so that a boy of ten may be wedded to a mature woman of twenty or twenty-five years, if she happens to be unmarried and without issue. Any elderly male member of the boy's family—his elder brother, uncle, or even his father—will have intercourse with her, and beget children, which the boy, when he comes of age, will accept as his own, and legitimatise." This system of marriage, in which there is a marked disparity in the ages of the contracting couple, is referred to in the proverb: "The tāli should be tied at least by a log of wood." The marriage rites are as a rule non-Brāhmanical, but in some well-to-do families the services of a Brāhman purōhit are enlisted. The presence of the Umbalakāran or caste headman at a marriage is essential. On the wedding day the contracting couple offer, at their homes, manaipongal (boiled rice), and the alangu ceremony is performed by waving coloured rice round them, or touching the knees, shoulders, and head with cakes, and throwing them over the head. The wrist-threads, consisting of a piece of old cloth dyed with turmeric, are tied on by the maternal uncle. Cooked rice and vegetables are placed in front of the marriage dais, and offered to the gods. Four betel leaves are given to the bridegroom, who goes round the dais, and salutes the four cardinal points of the compass by pouring water from a leaf. He then sits down on a plank on the dais, and hands the tāli (marriage badge) to his sister. Taking the tāli, she proceeds to the bride's house, where the bride, after performing the alangu ceremony, is awaiting her arrival. On reaching the house, she asks for the bride's presents, and one of her brothers replies that such a piece of land, naming one, is given as a dowry. The bridegroom's sister then removes the string of black and gold beads, such as is worn before marriage, from the bride's neck, and replaces it by the tāli. The conch shell should be blown by women or children during the performance of manaipongal, and when the tāli is tied. The bride is conveyed to the house of the bridegroom, and sits with him on the dais while the relations make presents to them.

The messenger who conveys the news of a death in the community is a Paraiyan. The corpse is placed within a pandal (booth) supported on four posts, which is erected in front of the house. Some paddy (unhusked rice) is poured from a winnow on to the ground, and rice is thrown over the face of the corpse. On the second day rice, and other articles of food, are carried by a barber to the spot where the corpse has been buried or burnt. If the latter course has been adopted, the barber picks out some of the remains of the bones, and hands them to the son of the deceased. On the third day, the widow goes round the pandal three times,

[103] Manual of the Madura district.

and, entering within it, removes her tāli string, and new clothes are thrown over her neck. On the sixteenth day the final death ceremonies (karmāndhiram) are performed. A feast is given, and new cloths are tied on the heads of those under pollution. Pollution lasts for thirty days.

The Vallambans profess to be Saivaites, but they consider Periya Nāyaki of Vēlangkudi as their tribal goddess, and each nādu has its own special deity, such as Vēmbu Aiyanar, Nelliyandi Aiyanar, etc. In some places the tribal deity is worshipped on a Tuesday at a festival called Sevvai (Tuesday). On this day pots containing fermented rice liquor, which must have been made by the caste people and not purchased, are taken to the place of worship. On a Friday, those families which are to take part in the festival allow a quantity of paddy (rice) to germinate by soaking it in water, and on the following Tuesday flower spikes of the palmyra palm are added to the malted rice liquor in the pots. The pots of ordinary families may be placed in their houses, but those of the Umbalakārans and Servaikārans must be taken to the temple as representing the deity. Into these pots the flower spikes should be placed by some respected elder of the community. A week later, a small quantity of rice liquor is poured into other pots, which are carried by women to the temple car, round which they go three times. They then throw the liquor into a tank or pond. The pots of the Umbalakāran and Servaikāran must be carried by young virgins, or grown-up women who are not under menstrual pollution. One of the women who carries these pots usually becomes possessed by the village deity. At the time of the festival, cradles, horses, human figures, elephants, etc., made by the potter, are brought to the temple as votive offerings to the god.

Valli Ammai Kuttam.—A synonym of the Koravas, meaning followers of Valli Ammai, the wife of the God Subrahmanya, whom they claim to have been a Korava woman.

Vallōdi.—The name denotes a settlement in the Valluvanād tāluk of Malabar, and has been returned as a sub-division of Nāyar and Sāmantan, to which the Rāja of Valluvanād belongs.

Valluvan.—The Valluvans are summed up by Mr. H. A. Stuart[104] as being "the priests of the Paraiyans and Pallans. Tiruvalluvar, the famous Tamil poet, author of the Kurāl, belonged to this caste, which is usually regarded as a sub-division of Paraiyans. It appears that the Valluvans were priests to the Pallava kings before the introduction of the Brāhmans, and even for some time after it.[105] In an unpublished Vatteluttu inscription, believed to be of the ninth century, the following sentence occurs 'Sri Velluvam Pūvanavan, the Uvac'chan (Ōc'chan) of this temple, will employ daily six men for doing the temple service.' Again, the Valluvans must have formerly held a position at least equal to that of the Vellālas, if the story that Tiruvalluva Nāyanar married a Vellāla girl is true.[106] He is said to have "refused to acknowledge the distinctions of caste, and succeeded in obtaining a Vellāla woman as his wife, from whom a section of the Valluvans say it has its

---

[104] Madras Census Report, 1891, and Manual of the North Arcot district.
[105] *See* Divakaram and Chudamani Nikhandu.
[106] *See* Life of Tiruvalluvar, in Lazarus' edition of the Kural.

descent. As their ancestor amused himself in the intervals between his studies by weaving, they employ themselves in mending torn linen, but chiefly live by astrology, and by acting as priests of Paraiyans, and officiating at their funerals and marriages, though some refuse to take part in the former inauspicious ceremony, and leave the duty to those whom they consider impure Valluvans called Paraiya Tādas. Another section of the Valluvans is called Ālvar Dāsari or Tāvadadhāri (those who wear the necklace of tulsi beads). Both Saivites and Vaishnavites eat together, but do not intermarry. Unlike Paraiyans, they forbid remarriage of widows and even polygamy, and all males above twelve wear the sacred thread." According to one account, the Valluvans are the descendants of an alliance between a Brāhman sage and a Paraiyan woman, whose children complained to their father of their lowly position. He blessed them, and told them that they would become very clever astrologers, and, in consequence, much respected. At the Travancore census, 1901, the Valluvans were defined as a sub-division of the Pulayas, for whom they perform priestly functions.

"Both men and women are employed as astrologers and doctors, and are often consulted by all classes of people. In many villages they have the privilege of receiving from each ryot a handful of grain during the harvest time."[107] Of three Valluvans, whom I interviewed at Coimbatore, one, with a flowing white beard, had a lingam wrapped up in a pink cloth round the neck, and a charm tied in a pink cloth round the right upper arm. Another, with a black beard, had a salmon-coloured turban. The third was wearing a discarded British soldier's tunic. All wore necklaces of rūdrāksha (*Elæocarpus Ganitrus*) beads, and their foreheads were smeared with oblong patches of sandal paste. Each of them had a collection of panchangams, or calendars for determining auspicious dates, and a bundle of palm leaf strips (ulla mudyan) inscribed with slōkas for astrological purposes. Their professional duties included writing charms for sick people, preparing horoscopes, and making forecasts of good or evil by means of cabalistic squares marked on the ground. Some Valluvans would have us believe that those who officiate as priests are not true Valluvans, and that the true Valluvan, who carries out the duties of an astrologer, will not perform priestly functions for the Paraiyans.

The most important sub-divisions of the Valluvans, returned at times of census, are Paraiyan, Tāvidadāri, and Tiruvalluvan. From information supplied to me, I gather that there are two main divisions, called Arupathu Katchi (sixty house section) and Narpathu Katchi (forty house section). The former are supposed to be descendants of Nandi Gurukkal, and take his name as their gōtra. The gōtra of the latter is Sidambara Sayichya Ayyamgar. Sidambara, or Chidambaram, is the site of one of the most sacred Siva temples. The sub-division Ālvār claims descent from Tiruppān Ālvār, one of the twelve Vaishnava saints. In the Tanjore district, the Valluvans have exogamous septs or pattaperu, named after persons, *e.g.*, Marulipichan, Govindazhvan, etc.

The Valluvans include in their ranks both Vaishnavites and Saivites. The majority of the latter, both males and females, wear the lingam. The affairs of the community are adjusted by a caste council and there are, in most places, two hereditary officers called Kōlkaran and Kanakkan.

VALLUVAN DRESSED UP AS SIVA AT MALAYANŪR FESTIVAL.

At the betrothal ceremony the bride's money (pariyam), betel, jewels, flowers, and fruit, are placed in the future bride's lap. The money ranges from seven to ten rupees if the bridegroom's village is on the same side of a river as the bride's, and from ten to twenty rupees if it is on the other side. A small sum of money, called uramurai kattu (money paid to relations) and panda varisai (money paid in the pandal), is also paid by the bridegroom's party for a feast of toddy to the relations. This is the proper time for settling caste disputes by the village council. On the wedding day, the milk-post, consisting of a green bamboo pole, is set up, and a number of pots, brought from the potter's house, are placed near it. On the dais are set four lamps, viz., an ordinary brass lamp, kudavilakku (pot light), alankāra vilakku (ornamental light), and pāligai vilakku (seedling light). The bride and bridegroom bring some sand, spread it on the floor near the dais, and place seven leaves on it. Cotton threads, dyed with turmeric, are tied to the pots and the milk-post. On the leaves are set cakes and rice, and the contracting couple worship the pots and the family gods. The Valluvan priest repeats a jumble of corrupt Sanskrit, and ties the kankanams (threads) on their wrists. They are then led into the house, and garlanded with jasmine or *Nerium* flowers. The pots are arranged on the dais, and the sand is spread thereon close to the milk-post. Into one of the pots the female relations put grain seedlings, and four other pots are filled with water by the bridegroom's party. A small quantity of the seedlings is usually wrapped up in a cloth, and placed over the seedling pot. Next morning the bundle is untied, and examined, to see if the seedlings are in good condition. If they are so, the bride is considered a worthy one; if not, the bride is either bad, or will die prematurely. The usual nalagu ceremony is next performed, bride and bridegroom being anointed with oil, and smeared with *Phaseolus Mungo* paste. This is followed by the offering of food on eleven leaves to the ancestors and house gods. Towards evening, the dais is got ready for its occupation by the bridal couple, two planks being placed on it, and covered with cloths lent by a washerman. The couple, sitting on the planks, exchange betel and paddy nine or twelve times, and rice twenty-seven times. The priest kindles the sacred fire (hōmam), and pours some ghī (clarified butter) into it from a mango leaf. The bridegroom is asked whether he sees Arundati (the pole-star) thrice, and replies in the affirmative. The tāli is shown the sky, smoked over burning camphor, and placed on a tray together with a rupee. After being blessed by those present, it is tied round the neck of the bride by the bridegroom, who has his right leg on her lap. On the second day there is a procession through the village, and, on the following day, the wrist-threads are removed.

In some places, the Valluvans, at their marriages, like the Pallis and some other castes, use the pandamutti, or pile of pots reaching to the top of the pandal.

The Saivite lingam wearers bury their dead in a sitting posture in a niche excavated in the side of the grave. After death has set in, a cocoanut is broken, and camphor burnt. The corpse is washed by relations, who bring nine pots of water for the purpose. The lingam is tied on to the head, and a cloth bundle, containing a rupee, seven bilva (*Ægle Marmelos*) leaves, nine twigs of the tulsi (*Ocimum sanctum*), and nine *Leucas aspera* flowers, to the right arm. The corpse is carried to the grave on a car surmounted by five brass vessels. The grave is purified by the sprinkling of cow's urine and cow-dung water before the corpse is lowered into it. On the way to the burial-ground, the priest keeps on chanting various songs, such as "This is Kailāsa. This is Kailāsa thillai (Chidambaram). Our request is this. Nallia

Mutthan of the Nandidarma gōtra died on Thursday in the month Thai in the year Subakruthu. He must enter the fourth stage (sayichyam), passing through Sālokam, Sāmīpa, and Sārupa. He crosses the rivers of stones, of thorns, of fire, and of snakes, holding the tail of the bull Nandi. To enable him to reach heaven safely, we pound rice, and put lights of rice." The priest receives a fee for his services, which he places before an image made on the grave after it has been filled in. The money is usually spent in making a sacred bull, lingam, or stone slab, to place on the grave. On the third day after death, the female relatives of the deceased pour milk within the house into a vessel, which is taken by the male relatives to the burial-ground, and offered at the grave, which is cleaned. A small platform, made of mud, and composed of several tiers, decreasing in size from below upwards, is erected thereon, and surmounted by a lingam. At the north and south corners of this platform, a bull and paradēsi (mendicant) made of mud are placed, and at each corner leaves are laid, on which the offerings in the form of rice, fruits, vegetables, etc., are laid. The final death ceremonies are celebrated on the seventeenth day. A pandal (booth) is set up, and closed in with cloths. Within it are placed a pot and five pestles and mortars, to which threads are tied. Five married women, taking hold of the pestles, pound some rice contained in the pot, and with the flour make a lamp, which is placed on a tray. The eldest son of the deceased goes, with the lamp on his head, to an enclosure having an entrance at the four cardinal points. The enclosure is either a permanent one with mud walls, or temporary one made out of mats. Within the enclosure, five pots are set up in the centre, and four at each side. The pots are cleansed by washing them with the urine of cows of five different colours, red, white, black, grey, and spotted. Near the pots the articles required for pūja (worship) are placed, and the officiating priest sits near them. The enclosure is supposed to represent heaven, and the entrances are the gates leading thereto, before which food is placed on leaves. The eldest son, with the lamp, stands at the eastern entrance, while Siva is worshipped. The priest then repeats certain stanzas, of which the following is the substance. "You who come like Siddars (attendants in the abode of Siva) at midnight, muttering Siva's name, why do you come near Sivapadam? I will pierce you with my trident. Get away. Let these be taken to yamapuri, or hell." Then Siva and Parvati, hearing the noise, ask "Oh! sons, who are you that keep on saying Hara, Hara? Give out truly your names and nativity." To which the reply is given "Oh! Lord, I am a devotee of that Being who graced Markandeya, and am a Vīrasaiva by faith. I have come to enter heaven. We have all led pure lives, and have performed acts of charity. So it is not just that we should be prevented from entering. Men who ill-treat their parents, or superiors, those addicted to all kinds of vice, blasphemers, murderers, perverts from their own faith and priests, and other such people, are driven to hell by the southern gate." At this stage, a thread is passed round the enclosure. The son, still bearing the lamp, goes from the eastern entrance past the south and western entrances, and, breaking the thread, goes into the enclosure through the northern entrance. The Nandikōl (hereditary village official) then ties a cloth first round the head of the eldest son, and afterwards round the heads of the other sons and agnates.

The Valluvans abstain from eating beef. Though they mix freely with the Paraiyans, they will not eat with them, and never live in the Paraiyan quarter.

The Valluvans are sometimes called Pandāram or Valluva Pandāram. In some places, the priests of the Valluvans are Vellāla Pandārams.

Valluvan.—A small inferior caste of fishermen and boatmen in Malabar.[108]

Vālmika.—Vālmīka or Vālmīki is a name assumed by the Bōyas and Paidis, who claim to be descended from Vālmīki, the author of the Rāmāyana, who did penance for so long in one spot that a white-ant hill (vālmīkam) grew up round him. In a note before me, Vālmīki is referred to as the Spenser of India. In the North Arcot Manual, Vālmīkulu, as a synonym of the Vēdans, is made to mean those who live on the products of ant-hills.

Vāl Nambi.—Recorded, in the Madras Census Report, 1901, as "a synonym for Mūssad. Nambi is a title of Brāhmans, and vāl means a sword. The tradition is that the name arose from the ancestors of the caste having lost some of the privileges of the Vēdic Brāhmans owing to their having served as soldiers when Malabar was ruled by the Brāhmans prior to the days of the Perumāls."

Valuvādi.—The Valuvādis are returned, in the Madras Census Report, 1901, as cultivators in the Pudukōttai State. I am informed that the Valuvādis are a section of the Valaiyan caste, to which the Zamindar of Nagaram belongs. The name Valuvādi was originally a title of respect, appended to the name of the Nagaram Zamindars. The name of the present Zamindar is Balasubramanya Valuvādiar. Thirty years ago there is said to have been no Valuvādi caste. Some Valaiyans in prosperous circumstances, and others who became relatives of the Nagaram Zamindar by marriage, have changed their caste name, to show that they are superior in social status to the rest of the community.

Vamme.—A gōtra of Janappans, the members of which abstain from eating the fish called bombadai, because, when some of their ancestors went to fetch water in the marriage pot, they found a number of this fish in the water contained in the pot.

Vana Palli.—A name, meaning forest Palli, assumed by some Irulas in South Arcot.

Vandikkāran.—An occupational name for Nāyars who work as cartmen (vandi, cart) for carrying fuel.

Vandula or Vandi Rāja.—A sub-division of Bhatrāzu, named after one Vandi, who is said to have been a herald at the marriage of Siva.

Vangu (cave).—A sub-division of Irula.

Vāni.—"The Vānis or Bāndēkars," Mr. H. A. Stuart writes,[109] "have been wrongly classified in the census returns (1891) as oil-pressers; they are in reality traders. They are said to have come from Goa, and they speak Konkani. Their spiritual guru is the head of the Kumbakōnam math." In the Census Report, 1901, it is noted that Vāni, meaning literally a trader, is a Konkani-speaking trading caste, of which Bāndēkara is a synonym. "They ape the Brāhmanical customs, and call

[108] Gazetteer of Malabar.
[109] Manual of the South Canara District.

themselves by the curious hybrid name of Vaisya Brāhmans." Hari Chetti has been returned as a further synonym.

Vāniyan.—The Vāniyans are, Mr. Francis writes,[110] "oil-pressers among the Tamils, corresponding to the Telugu Gāndlas, Canarese Gānigas, Malabar Chakkāns, and Oriya Tellis. For some obscure reason, Manu classed oil-pressing as a base occupation, and all followers of the calling are held in small esteem, and, in Tinnevelly, they are not allowed to enter the temples. In consequence, however, of their services in lighting the temples (in token of which all of them, except the Malabar Vāniyans and Chakkāns, wear the sacred thread), they are earning a high position, and some of them use the sonorous title of Jōti Nagarattār (dwellers in the city of light) and Tiru-vilakku Nagarattār (dwellers in the city of holy lamps). They employ Brāhmans as priests, practice infant marriage, and prohibit widow marriage, usually burn their dead, and decline to eat in the houses of any caste below Brāhmans. However, even the washermen decline to eat with them. Like the Gāndlas they have two sub-divisions, Ottai-sekkān and Irattai-sekkān, who use respectively one bullock and two bullocks in their mills. Oddly enough, the former belong to the right-hand faction, and the latter to the left. Their usual title is Chetti. The name Vānuvan has been assumed by Vāniyans, who have left their traditional occupation, and taken to the grain and other trades."

"The word Vānijyam," Mr. H. A. Stuart informs us,[111] "signifies trade, and trade in oil, as well as its manufacture, is the usual employment of this caste, who assert that they are Vaisyas, and claim the Vaisya-Apurānam as their holy book. They are said to have assumed the thread only within the last fifty or sixty years, and are reputed to be the result of a yāgam (sacrifice by fire) performed by a saint called Vakkuna Mahārishi. The caste contains four sub-divisions called Kāmākshiamma, Visālākshiamma, Ac'chu-tāli, and Toppa-tāli, the two first referring to the goddesses principally worshipped by each, and the two last to the peculiar kinds of tālis, or marriage tokens, worn by their women. They have the same customs as the Bēri Chettis, but are not particular in observing the rule which forbids the eating of flesh. A bastard branch of the Vāniyas is called the Pillai Kūttam, which is said to have sprung from the concubine of a Vāniyan, who lived many years ago. The members of this class are never found except where Vāniyans live, and are supposed to have a right to be fed and clothed by them. Should this be refused, they utter the most terrible curse, and, in this manner, eventually intimidate the uncharitable into giving them alms." In the Census Report, 1891, Mr. Stuart writes further that the Vāniyans "were formerly called Sekkān (oil-mill man), and it is curious that the oil-mongers alone came to be called Vāniyan or trader. They have returned 126 sub-divisions, of which only one, Ilai Vāniyan, is numerically important. One sub-division is Iranderudu, or two bullocks, which refers to the use of two bullocks in working the mill. This separation of those who use two bullocks from those who employ only one is found in nearly every oil-pressing caste in India. The Vāniyans of Malabar resemble the Nāyars in their customs and habits, and neither wear the sacred thread, nor employ Brāhmans as priests.

[110] Madras Census Report, 1901.
[111] Manual of the North Arcot district.

In North Malabar, Nāyars are polluted by their touch, but in the south, where they are called Vattakādans, they have succeeded in forcing themselves into the ranks of the Nāyar community. A large number of them returned Nāyar as their main caste." In this connection, Mr. Francis states[112] that followers of the calling of oil-pressers (Chakkāns) are "known as Vattakādans in South Malabar, and as Vāniyans in North Malabar; but the former are the higher in social status, the Nāyars being polluted by the touch of the Vāniyans and Chakkāns but not by that of the Vattakādans. Chakkāns and Vāniyans may not enter Brāhman temples. Their customs and manners are similar to those of the Nāyars, who will not, however, marry their women."

Of the Vāniyans of Cochin, it is stated in the Cochin Census Report, 1901, that "they are Vaisyas, and wear the sacred thread. In regard to marriage, inheritance, ceremonies, dress, ornaments, etc., there is practically no difference between them and the Konkanis. But, as they do not altogether abstain from meat and spirituous liquors, they are not allowed free access to the houses of Konkanis, nor are they permitted to touch their tanks and wells. They are Saivites. They have their own priests, who are called Panditars. They observe birth and death pollution for ten days, and are like Brāhmans in this respect. They are mostly petty merchants and shop-keepers. Some can read and write Malayālam, but they are very backward in English education."

The oils expressed by the Vāniyans are said to be "gingelly (*Sesamum indicum*), cocoanut, iluppei (*Bassia longifolia*), pinnei (*Calophyllum inophyllum*), and ground-nut (*Arachis hypogæa*). According to the sāstras the crushing of gingelly seeds, and the sale of gingelly oil, are sinful acts, and no one, who does not belong to the Vāniyan class, will either express or sell gingelly oil."[113]

When a Vāniyan dies a bachelor, a *post-mortem* mock ceremony is performed as by the Gānigas, and the corpse is married to the arka plant (*Calotropis gigantea*), and decorated with a wreath made of the flowers thereof.

Vankāyala (brinjal or egg plant: *Solanum Melongena*).—An exogamous sept of Golla. The fruit is eaten by Natives, and, stuffed with minced meat, is a common article of Anglo-Indian dietary.

Vanki (armlet).—A gōtra of Kurni.

Vannān.—The Vannāns are washermen in the Tamil and Malayalām countries. The name Vannān is, Mr. H. A. Stuart writes,[114] "derived from vannam, beauty. There is a tradition that they are descendants of the mythological hero Vīrabadra, who was ordered by Siva to wash the clothes of all men, as an expiation of the sin of putting many people to death in Daksha's Yāga. Hence the Tamil washermen are frequently called Vīrabadran. Having to purify all the filthy linen of the villagers, they are naturally regarded as a low, unclean class of Sūdras, and are always poor. They add to their income by hiring out the clothes of their customers to funeral parties, who lay them on the ground before the pall-bearers,

[112] Madras Census Report, 1901.
[113] Manual of the Tanjore district.
[114] Manual of the North Arcot district; Madras Census Report, 1891.

so that these may not step upon the ground, and by letting them out on the sly to persons wishing to use them without having to purchase for themselves. In social standing the Vannāns are placed next below the barbers. They profess to be Saivites in the southern districts, and Vaishnavites in the north. The marriage of girls generally takes place after puberty. Widow remarriage is permitted among some, if not all, sub-divisions. Divorce may be obtained by either party at pleasure on payment of double the bride-price, which is usually Rs. 10–8–0. They are flesh-eaters, and drink liquor. The dead are either burned or buried. The Pothara (or Podora) Vannāns are of inferior status, because they wash only for Paraiyans, Pallans, and other inferior castes."

It is noted, in the Madura Manual, that those who have seen the abominable substances, which it is the lot of the Vannāns to make clean, cannot feel any surprise at the contempt with which their occupation is regarded. In the Tanjore Manual, it is recorded that, in the rural parts of the district, the Vannāns are not allowed to enter the house of a Brāhman or a Vellāla; clothes washed by them not being worn or mixed up with other clothes in the house until they have undergone another wash by a caste man.

It is on record that, on one occasion, a party of Europeans, when out shooting, met a funeral procession on its way to the burial-ground. The bier was draped in many folds of clean cloth, which one of the party recognised by the initials as one of his bed-sheets. Another identified as his sheet the cloth on which the corpse was lying. He cut off the corner with the initials, and a few days later the sheet was returned by the washerman, who pretended ignorance of the mutilation, and gave as an explanation that it must have been done, in his absence, by one of his assistants. On another occasion, a European met an Eurasian, in a village not far from his bungalow, wearing a suit of clothes exactly similar to his own, and, on close examination, found they were his. They had been newly washed and dressed.

The most important divisions numerically returned by Vannāns at times of census are Pāndiyan, Peru (big), Tamil, and Vaduga (northerner). It is recorded, in the Gazetteer of the Madura district, that Vannān "is rather an occupational term than a caste title, and, besides the Pāndya Vannāns or Vannāns proper, includes the Vaduga Vannāns or Tsākalas of the Telugu country, and the Palla, Pudara, and Tulukka Vannāns, who wash for the Pallans, Paraiyans, and Musalmans respectively. The Pāndya Vannāns have a headman called the Periya Manishan (big man). A man can claim the hand of his paternal aunt's daughter. At weddings, the bridegroom's sister ties the tāli (marriage badge). Nambis officiate. Divorce is freely allowed to either party on payment of twice the bride-price, and divorcées may marry again. The caste god is Gurunāthan, in whose temples the pūjāri (priest) is usually a Vannān. The dead are generally burnt, and, on the sixteenth day, the house is purified from pollution by a Nambi."

Some Vannāns have assumed the name Irkuli Vellāla, and Rājakan and Kāttavarāya vamsam have also been recorded as synonyms of the caste name.

The Vannāns of Malabar are also called Mannān or Bannān. They are, Mr.

Francis writes,[115] "a low class of Malabar washermen, who wash only for the polluting castes, and for the higher castes when they are under pollution following births, deaths, etc. It is believed by the higher castes that such pollution can only be removed by wearing clothes washed by Mannāns, though at other times these cause pollution to them. The washing is generally done by the women, and the men are exorcists, devil-dancers and physicians, even to the higher castes. Their women are midwives, like those of the Velakkatalavan and Vēlan castes. This caste should not be confused with the Mannān hill tribe of Travancore."

It is recorded, in the Gazetteer of Malabar, that "the Mannāns, a makkattāyam caste of South Malabar, apparently identical with the marumakkattāyam Vannāns of the north, are a caste of washermen; and their services are indispensable to the higher castes in certain purificatory ceremonies when they have to present clean cloths (māttu). They are also devil-dancers and tailors. They practice fraternal polyandry in the south. Mannāns are divided into two endogamous classes, Peru-mannāns (peru, great), and Tinda-mannāns (tinda, pollution); and, in Walavanād, into four endogamous classes called Chōppan, Peru-mannān, Punnekādan, and Puliyakkōdam. The Tinda-mannān and Puliyakkōdam divisions perform the purificatory sprinklings for the others."

The services of the Mannān, Mr. T. K. Gopal Panikkar writes,[116] "are in requisition at the Nāyar Thirandukaliānam ceremonies on the attainment of puberty by a girl, when they sing ballads, and have to bring, for the girl's use, the māttu or sacred dress. Then, on occasions of death pollution, they have a similar duty to perform. Among the Nāyars, on the fourth, or rarely the third day after the menses, the woman has to use, during her bath, clothes supplied by Mannān females. The same duty they have to perform during the confinement of Nāyar females. All the dirty cloths and bed sheets used, these Mannān females have to wash." Mr. S. Appadorai Iyer informs us that those Mannāns who are employed by the Kammālan, or artisan class, as barbers, are not admitted into the Mannān caste, which follows the more honourable profession of washing clothes. The Mannāns perform certain ceremonies in connection with Mundian, the deity who is responsible for the weal or woe of cattle; and, at Pūram festivals, carry the vengida koda or prosperity umbrella, composed of many tiers of red, green, orange, black and white cloth, supported on a long bamboo pole, before the goddess.

It is recorded by Bishop Whitehead[117] that, in various places in Malabar, there are temples in honour of Bhagavati, at which the pūjāris (priests) are of the Vannān caste. "There is an annual feast called gurusi tarpanam (giving to the guru) about March, when the hot weather begins, and the people are at leisure. Its object is to appease the wrath of the goddess. During the festival, the pūjāri sits in the courtyard outside the temple, thickly garlanded with red flowers, and with red kunkuma marks on his forehead. Goats and fowls are then brought to him by the devotees, and he kills them with one blow of the large sacrificial sword or chopper. It is thought auspicious for the head to be severed at one blow, and, apparent-

[115] Madras Census Report, 1901.
[116] Malabar and its Folk, 1900.
[117] Madras Dioc: Magazine, 1906.

ly, pūjāris who are skilful in decapitation are much in request. When the head is cut off, the pūjāri takes the carcase, and holds it over a large copper vessel partly filled with water, turmeric, kunkuma, and a little rice, and lets the blood flow into it. When all the animals are killed, the pūjāri bails out the blood and water on the ground, uttering mantrams (sacred lines or verses) the while. The people stand a little way off. When the vessel is nearly empty, the pūjāri turns it upside down as a sign that the ceremony is ended. During these proceedings, a number of Vannāns, dressed in fantastic costumes, dance three times round the temple. During the festival, processions are held round the various houses, and special swords with a curved hook at the end, called palli val (great or honourable sword), are carried by the worshippers. These swords are worshipped during the Dusserah festival in October, and, in some shrines, they form the only emblem of the deity. The Tiyans have small shrines in their own gardens sacred to the family deity, which may be Bhagavati, or some demon, or the spirit of an ancestor. Once a year, Vannāns come dressed in fancy costume, with crowns on their heads, and dance round the courtyard to the sound of music and tom-toms, while a Tiyan priest presents the family offerings, uncooked rice and young cocoanuts, with camphor and incense, and then rice fried with sugar and ghī (clarified butter)."

In an account of the Tiyans, Mr. Logan writes[118] that "this caste is much given to devil-charming, or devil-driving as it is often called. The washermen (Vannān) are the high priests of this superstition, and with chants, ringing cymbals, magic figures, and waving lights, they drive out evil spirits from their votaries of this caste at certain epochs in their married lives. One ceremony in particular, called teyyāttam—a corrupt form of Dēva and āttam, that is, playing at gods—takes place occasionally in the fifth month of pregnancy. A leafy arbour is constructed, and in front of it is placed a terrible figure of Chāmundi, the queen of the demons, made of rice flour, turmeric powder, and charcoal powder. A party of not less than eighteen washermen is organized to represent the demons and furies—Kuttichāttan (a mischievous imp), and many others. On being invoked, these demons bound on to the stage in pairs, dance, caper, jump, roar, fight, and drench each other with saffron (turmeric) water. Their capers and exertions gradually work up their excitement, until they are veritably possessed of the devil. At this juncture, fowls and animals are sometimes thrown to them, to appease their fury. These they attack with their teeth, and kill and tear as a tiger does his prey. After about twenty minutes the convulsions cease, the demon or spirit declares its pleasure, and, much fatigued, retires to give place to others; and thus the whole night is spent, with much tom-tomming and noise and shouting, making it impossible, for Europeans at least, to sleep within earshot of the din."

Vannattān.—A synonym of Veluttēdan, the caste of washermen, who wash for Nāyars and higher castes.

Vanni Kula Kshatriya.—A synonym of the Pallis, who claim to belong to the fire race of Kshatriyas.

Vanniyan.—A synonym of Palli. The name further occurs as a sub-division of Ambalakāran and Valaiyan. Some Maravans also are known as Vanniyan or

[118] Manual of Malabar.

Vannikutti. Tēn (honey) Vanniyan is the name adopted by some Irulas in the South Arcot district.

Vantari.—*See* Telaga.

Vanuvan.—A name assumed by Vāniyans who have abandoned their hereditary occupation of oil-pressing, and taken to trade in grain and other articles.

Vārakurup.—Recorded, in the Madras Census Report, 1901, as a title of Malayālam Paravans.

Varige (millet).—An exogamous sept of Kāpu.

Vāriyar.—For the following note on the Vāriyar section of the Ambalavāsis, I am indebted to Mr. N. Subramani Aiyar. The name is believed to be derived from Parasava, which, according to Yajnavalkya and other law-givers, is the name given to the son of a Brāhman begotten on a Sūdra woman, and suggests the fact that the Vāriyar is no Brāhman, though the blood of the latter may course through his veins, and though such marriages were regarded as sacraments in early days. This is the derivation given by Pachumuttalu in his Kēralaviseshamāhātmya, who adds that the chief occupation of the Vāriyars is to sweep the floor of the temples. In some of the Asauchavidhis (works on pollution) of Kērala, the commentator explains the word Parasava as Vāriya. Many Vāriyars add the title Parasava to their name, when writing in Sanskrit. Some derive the word from varija or one born of water, in accordance with a tradition that Parasurāma created from water a class of persons for special service in temples, and to take the place of Sūdras, who, being meat-eaters, were ineligible for the same. Others again, like the late Professor Sundaram Pillay, would take Vāriyar as being derived from varuka, to sweep. Recently, some ingenuity has been displayed in splitting the word into two words, giving it a meaning equivalent to pseudo-Aryan. The title Asan, or teacher, is possessed by certain families, whose members have held the hereditary position of tutors in noblemen's houses. In mediæval times, many Vāriyar families received royal edicts, conferring upon them the privileges of being tutors and astrologers. These special rights are even now possessed by them.

The following legend is narrated concerning the origin of the Vāriyars. A Sūdra woman removed a bone from within a temple in obedience to the wish of certain Brāhman priests, and was excommunicated from her caste. The priests, on hearing this, were anxious to better her condition, and made her the progenitor of a class of Ambalavāsis or temple servants, who were afterwards known as Vāriyars. According to another legend, the corpse of a Mārān, which was found inside a Nambūtiri's house, was promptly removed by certain Nāyars, who on that account were raised in the social scale, and organised into a separate caste called Vāriyar. There is a still further tradition that, in the Treta Yuga, a Sūdra woman had five sons, the first of whom became the progenitor of the Tiyatunnis, and the second that of Vāriyars. A fourth account is given in the Kēralamahātmya. A young Brāhman girl was married to an aged man. Not confident in unaided human effort, under circumstances such as hers, she devoted a portion of her time daily to preparing flower garlands for the deity of the nearest temple, and conceived. But the Brāhman welcomed the little stranger by getting the mother thrown out of caste.

Her garlands could no longer be accepted, but, nothing daunted, she worked as usual, and made a mental offering of the garlands she prepared, which, through an unseen agency, became visible on the person of the deity. Though the people were struck with shame at their unkind treatment of the innocent girl, they were not prepared to take her back. The Variyan caste was accordingly constituted, and her child was brought up by the Azhancheri Tambrakkal, and accommodated in the padippura or out-house at the entrance gate. In the Pāsupata Tantra, the Vāriyars are called Kailāsavāsins, or those who live in Kailās, as they are supposed to be specially devoted to the worship of Siva. Kailāsa is the abode of Siva, whither the blessed go after death.

The Vāriyars of Travancore are divided into four groups, called Onattukara, Venattukara, Ilayetattunad (or Ilayathu), and Tekkumkur. The Venattukaras have the privilege of interdining with the Onattukaras, and having their ceremonies performed by priests from that group. But the ceremonies of the Onattukaras appear to be performed without the Venattukaras being admitted into their midst. The third and fourth groups take food in the houses of the first and second, though the reverse seldom happens. The Vāriyars in British Malabar are divided into several other groups.

The Vāriyars are generally well-read, especially in Sanskrit, make excellent astrologers, and are also medical practitioners. A Vāriyar's house is called variyam, as the Pishārati's is known as pishāram.

Married women have the hair-knot on the left side of the head, like Nāyar ladies. They cover the breast with a folded cloth, and never wear a bodice or other innovations in the matter of dress. The marriage ornament is called mātra, and is in the shape of a maddalam or drum. Other neck ornaments are called entram and kuzhal. The todu, or ornament of Nāyar women, is worn in the ear-lobes. Women mark their foreheads, like Nambūtiri ladies, with sandal paste.

The Vāriyars, Pushpakans, and Pishāratis, are said to constitute the three original garland-making castes of Malabar, appointed by Parasurāma. At the present day, in all the important temples, except in South Travancore, where Kurukkals perform that function, garlands can only be prepared by one of these castes. The technical occupation of a Vāriyar in a temple is called kazhakam, which is probably derived from the Dravidian root kazhaku, to cleanse. Kazhakam is of two kinds, viz., malakkazhakam or garland-making service, and talikkazhakam or sweeping service, of which the former is more dignified than the latter. Under the generic term kazhakar are included making flower garlands for the temple, preparing materials for the offering of food, sweeping the beli offering, carrying lights and holding umbrellas when the god is carried in procession, having the custody of the temple jewels, etc. The Vāriyar is at the beck and call of the temple priest, and has to do sundry little services from morning till evening. He is remunerated with some of the cooked food, after it has been offered to the deity. The Vāriyars are to Saivite temples what the Pishāratis are to Vaishnavite temples. Their prayers are prominently addressed only to Siva, but they also worship Vishnu, Subramanya, Sasta, Ganēsa, and Bhadrakāli. Their chief amusement is the farce called Kūttappāthakam, the hero of which is one Vankāla Nikkan, and the heroine

Naityar. An Ilayatu is the stage-manager, and a Pishārati the actor. Parangotan is the buffoon, and Māppa his wife. In the eighteenth century, a grand festival lasting over twenty-eight days, called mamangam, was celebrated in British Malabar. The above characters are represented as proceeding to this festival, which came off once in twelve years on the Magha asterism in the month of Magha, and is hence popularly called Mahāmagha.

The Vāriyar caste is governed in all matters by the Nambūtiri Brahmans, but they have their own priests. The Ilayatus believe that they were the preceptors of all the Ambalavāsi castes in former times, but were dislodged from that position owing to most of them employing priests from among their own caste men. Even at the present day, Ilayatus are known to express their displeasure when they are asked to drink water from a Vāriyar's well. As, however, consecrated water from the Nambūtiris is taken to a Vāriyar for its purification, they entertain no scruples about cooking their food there, provided they carry with them the aupasana fire.

Inheritance among the Vāriyars of Cochin and British Malabar is in the female line (marumakkathāyam). Among the Vāriyars of Travancore, chiefly these belonging to the Onattukara section, a kind of qualified makkathāyam prevails, in accordance with which both sons and daughters have an equal right to inherit ancestral property. The eldest male member is entitled to the management of the estate in all undivided families. Partition, however, is largely followed in practice.

The tāli-kettu ceremony of the Vāriyars generally takes place before a girl reaches puberty, and, in the case of boys, after the ceremony of Sivadiksha has been performed, that is between the twelfth and sixteenth years. If the marriage is in the kudi-vaippu form, or, in other words, if there is an intention on the part of both parties to treat the marital alliance as permanent, no separate sambandham need be celebrated afterwards; and, in all cases where marriages are celebrated between members of the same section, the kudi-vaippu form is in vogue. If a girl is unmarried when she reaches puberty, she is not permitted to take part in any religious ceremonies, or enter any temple until she is married. The first item of a Vāriyar's marriage is ayani-unu, when the bridegroom, decked in new clothes and ornaments, dines sumptuously with his relations. He then goes in procession to the bride's house, and, after bathing, puts on clothes touched by the bride. After this some prayers are recited, and a sacrifice is offered. The bride is then brought to the marriage hall, and, all the Brāhmanical rites are strictly observed. After sunset, some grass and a leopard's skin are placed on the floor on which white cloth is spread. The bridegroom, who is seated on the northern side, worships Ganapati, after which the couple take their seats on the cloth bed spread on the floor. Lights are then waved in front of them. This ceremony is known as diksha-virikkuka. In the kudi-vaippu form of marriage, the bride is taken to the house of the bridegroom, where the dikshavirippu is observed. Otherwise the marital rite becomes a mere tāli-kattu ceremony, and the girl, when she comes of age, may receive clothes in token of conjugal connection with another person. When the first husband dies, clothes may be received from another Vāriyar, or a Brāhman, whose wife the woman becomes.

Most of the ceremonies observed by Malayāli Brāhmans are also performed by the Vāriyars, the vratas and upanayana being among those which are omitted. Sivadiksha, as already indicated, is observed between the twelfth and sixteenth years. The festival lasts for four days, though the religious rites are over on the first day. At an auspicious hour, the priest and the Vāriyar youth put on the tattu dress, or dress worn for ceremonial purposes, and worship a pot full of water with incense and flowers, the contents of which are then poured by the priest over the youth. The priest and a Mārān then perform the tonsure, and the youth bathes. Some Nambūtiris are then engaged to perform the purificatory rite, after which the Vāriyar wears the tattu as well as an upper cloth, marks his forehead with ashes and sandal paste, and decorates himself with jewels, rudrāksha (*Elæocarpus Ganitrus*) beads, and flowers. Alms are received by the young Vāriyar from his mother, and he takes seven steps in a northerly direction which symbolise his pilgrimage to Benares. It is only after the performance of this rite that the Vāriyar is believed to become a grihastha (married person, as opposed to a bachelor). The funeral rites of the caste have been elaborated in many places. Death pollution lasts for twelve days, and the sanchayana (milk ceremony) is observed on the seventh or ninth day. Anniversary ceremonies are celebrated in memory of close relations, and others are propitiated by the performance of srādh, and the feeding of a Vāriyar on a new-moon day.

In an account of a royal wedding in Travancore in 1906, I read that "a number of Vāriyars left the thēvarathu koikal, or palace where worship is performed, for a compound (garden) close by to bring an areca palm. It is supposed that they do this task under divine inspiration and guidance. One man is given a small rod by the Potti or priest in the palace, and, after receiving this, he dances forward, followed by his comrades, and all wend their way to a compound about a furlong away. On reaching the spot, they uproot a big areca palm without the use of any implement of iron, and take it away to the thēvarathu koikal without its touching the ground, to the accompaniment of music. They then plant it in front of the portico, and do some pūja (worship) after the manner of Brāhmans. The function is comparable to the dhwajarohanam, or hoisting of the flag during temple utsavams. The Vāriyars dance round the tree, singing songs, and performing pūja. A piece of white cloth is tied to the top of the tree, to serve as a flag, and a lamp is lighted, and placed at the foot of the tree."

The Vāriyars are described, in the Gazetteer of Malabar, as "a caste whose traditional duty is to sweep the temple precincts (vāruga). At the present day, some members of the caste are important land-owners or petty chieftains, occupying a very high social position. They generally follow the marumakkatāyam principle, but they have also a form of marriage called Kudivekkal similar to the Brahman Sarvasvadhānam, by which the wife is adopted as a member of the family into which she marries, and her children also belong to it. The Vāriyar's names and ceremonies indicate Sivaite proclivities, just as those of the Pishārodi are tinged with Vishnavism. The Vāriyar's house is called a Vāriyam, and his woman-folk Varassiars. This class is perhaps the most progressive among the Ambalavāsis, some of its members having received a Western education and entered the learned professions."

Varugu Bhatta.—A mendicant class, which begs from Perikes.

Varuna.—Some Pattanavan fishermen have adopted the name of Varunakula Vellāla or Varunakula Mudali after Varuna the god of the waters.

Vasa (new).—A sub-division of Kurubas, who are said to weave only white blankets.

Vasishta.—A Brāhmanical gōtra adopted by Khatris and Toreyas. Vasishta, one of the seven great Rishis, was the son of Mitra and Varuna, whose quarrels with Viswamitra are narrated in the Rāmayana.

Vastra.—One division of the Koragas is called Vastra, meaning cloths such as are used as a shroud for a corpse, which were given to them as an act of charity, the wearing of new cloths by them being prohibited. Vastrala (cloth) further occurs as an exogamous sept of the Karna Sālē and Dēvānga weavers.

Vattakādan.—Recorded as a sub-division of Nāyar, the occupation of which is expressing oil, chiefly for use in temples. Mr. F. Fawcett writes[119] that, in North Malabar, he has frequently been told by Nāyars of the superior classes that they do not admit the Vattakādans to be Nāyars. According to them, the Vattakādans have adopted the honorary affix Nāyar to their names quite recently. In the Madras Census Report, 1891, Vattakādan is stated to be a synonym of Vāniyan; and in the report, 1901, this name is said to mean a Native of Vattakād, and to be given to the Chakkāns.

Vattē (camel).—A gōtra of Kurni.

Vātti.—Vātti or Vāttikurup has been recorded at times of census as a sub-division of Nāyar, and a synonym of Kāvutiyan and Tōlkollan. Vātti is said to mean one who prays for happiness.

Vayani.—The Vayanis, Vayinis, Vaguniyans, or Pavinis, are a section of Mādigas, the members of which play on a single-stringed mandoline, and go about from village to village, singing the praises of the village goddesses. Each Vayani has his recognised beat. He plays a prominent part in the celebration of the annual festival of the village goddess, and receives a sacred thread (kappu), which is usually tied to his mandoline, before the commencement of the festival. He regards himself as superior in social position to ordinary Mādigas, with whom he will not marry. The name Vayani is said to be a corruption of varnane, meaning to describe. In some localities, *e.g.*, the Chingleput district, the Vayani enjoys mirāsi rights in connection with land.

Vēdan.—The Vēdans are described by Mr. H. A. Stuart, in the North Arcot Manual, as having been "formerly hunters and soldiers, and it is this caste which furnished a considerable and valuable contingent to the early Hindu kings, and later to the armies of Hyder and Tippoo. They are supposed by some to be the remnants of the earliest inhabitants of the peninsula, and identical with the Veddahs of Ceylon. They are also called Vālmīkulu, which means those who live on the products of ant-hills (vālmīkum)." It is noted, in the Census Report, 1891, that the two castes Bēdar (or Bōya) and Vēdan were, "through a misapprehension of

[119] Madras Museum Bull. III, 3. 1901.

instructions, treated as identical in the tabulation papers. The two words are, no doubt, etymologically identical, the one being Canarese and the other Tamil, but the castes are quite distinct." It may be noted that the name Vālmīka or Vālmī-ki is assumed by the Bōyas, who claim descent from Vālmīki, the author of the Rāmayana, who did penance for so long in one spot that a white-ant hill grew up round him.

In the Madras Census Report, 1901, the Vēdans are described as "a Tam-il-speaking labouring and hunting caste, the members of which were formerly sol-diers, and subsequently dacoits. The name means a hunter, and is loosely applied to the Irulas in some places (*e.g.*, Chingleput). There is some connection between the Vēdans and Tamil Vēttuvans, but its precise nature is not clear. The Vēttu-vans now consider themselves superior to the Vēdans, and are even taking to call-ing themselves Vēttuva Vellālas. Marriage (among the Vēdans) is either infant or adult. Widows may marry their late husband's brother or agnates. Some employ Brāhmans as priests. They either burn or bury their dead. They claim descent from Kannappa Nāyanar, one of the sixty-three Saivite saints. Ambalakārans also claim to be descended from Kannappa Nāyanār. In Tanjore, the Valaiyans declare them-selves to have a similar origin. The title of the Vēdans is Nāyakkan." In the Madura Manual, the Vēdans are described as a very low caste, who get their living in the jungles. They are not numerous now. They appear to have been naked savages not very long ago, and their civilisation is far from complete. They are held in the greatest contempt by men of all classes. They are described further, in the Coim-batore Manual, as "a very degraded, poor tribe, living by basket-making, snaring small game, and so on. They speak a low Canarese, and are as simple as savage. The delight of a party at the gift of a rupee is something curious." In the Salem district some Vēdans are said[120] to be "known by the caste name Tiruvalar, who are distinguished as the Kattukudugirajāti, a name derived from a custom among them, which authorises temporary matrimonial arrangements."

The following story in connection with bears and Vēdans is worthy of being placed on record. The bears are said to collect ripe wood-apples (*Feronia elephan-tum*) during the season, and store them in the forest. After a small quantity has been collected, they remove the rind of the fruits, and heap together all the pulp. They then bring honey and petals of sweet-smelling flowers, put them on the heap of pulp, and thresh them with their feet and with sticks in their hands. When the whole has become a consistent mass, they feed on it. The Vēdan, who knows the season, is said to drive off the bears by shooting at them, and rob them of their feast, which is sold as karadi panchamritham, or bear delicacy made of five ingre-dients.

The Vēdars of Travancore are summed up by the Rev. S. Mateer[121] as "living in jungle clearings or working in the rice fields, and formerly sold and bought as slaves. They have to wander about in seasons of scarcity in search of wild yams, which they boil and eat on the spot, and are thorough gluttons, eating all they can get at any time, then suffering want for days. Polygamy is common, as men are not

[120] Manual of the Salem district.
[121] Native Life in Travancore.

required to provide for the support of their wives. Some, who have been converted to Christianity, show wonderful and rapid improvement in moral character, civilisation and diligence."

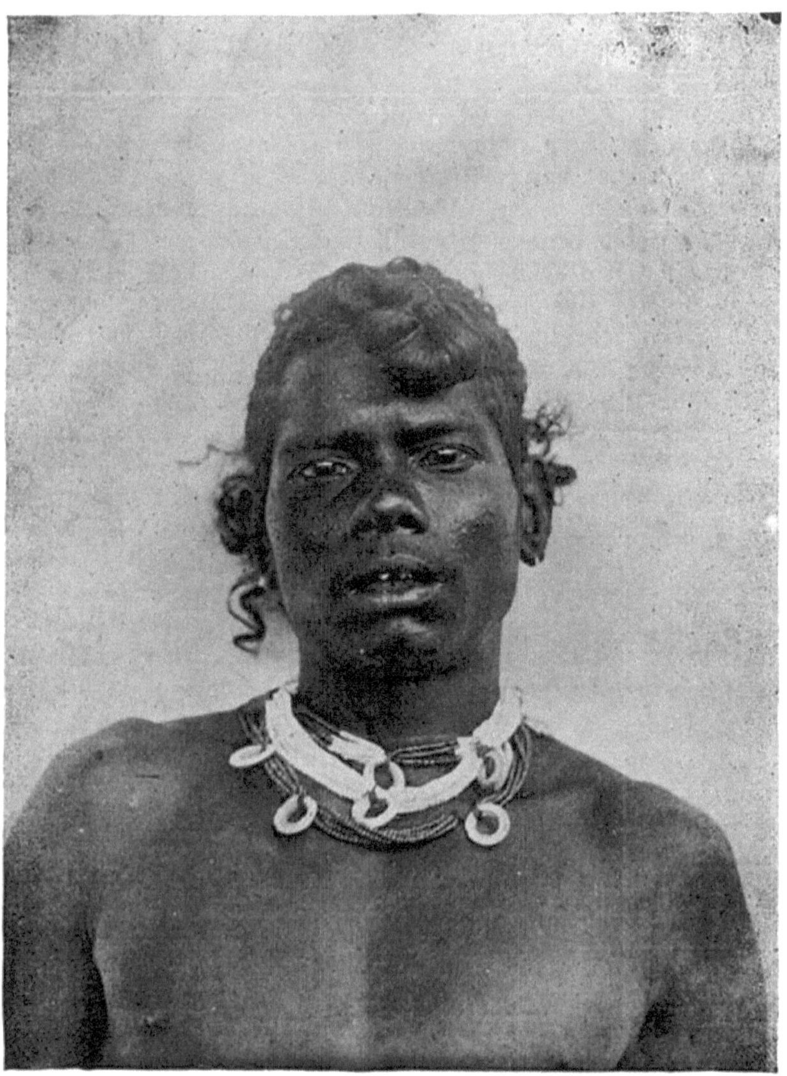

MALA VĒDAN WITH FILED TEETH.

For the following note on the Mala (hill) Vēdans of Travancore, I am indebted to Mrs. J. W. Evans.[122] "They live in wretched huts amid the rice-flats at the foot of the hills, and are employed by farmers to guard the crops from the ravages of wild beasts. The upper incisor teeth of both men and women are filed to a sharp point, like crocodile's fangs. One ugly old man, Tiruvātiran by name (the name of

[122] Madras Museum, Bull. III, I, 1900.

a star), had the four teeth very slightly filed. On being pressed for the reason why he had not conformed to Mala Vēdar fashion, he grinned, and said 'What beauty I was born with is enough for me.' Probably the operation had been more painful than he could bear, or, may be, he could not afford to pay the five betel leaves and areca nuts, which are the customary fee of the filer. Any man may perform the operation. A curved bill-hook, with serrated edge, is the instrument used. On being asked whether they had any tradition about the custom of tooth-filing, they replied that it was to distinguish their caste, and the god Chāttan would be angry if they neglected the custom. It may be noted that tooth-filing is also practiced by the jungle Kādirs (*q.v.*). Both males and females wore a cotton loin-cloth, mellowed by wear and weather to a subtle greenish hue. Red and blue necklaces, interstrung with sections of the chank shell (*Turbinella rapa*) adorned the necks and chests. One woman was of special interest. Her neck and breasts were literally concealed by a medley of beads, shells, brass bells, and two common iron keys — these last, she said, for ornament. Around her hips, over her cloth, hung several rows of small bones of pig and sāmbar (*Cervus unicolor*). The Mala Vēdans find these bones in the jungle. An aged priest said that he used to perform devil-dancing, but was now too stiff to dance, and had to labour like the younger men. The Mala Vēdans apparently possess no temples or shrines, but Hindus permit them to offer money at the Hindu shrines from a distance, at times of sudden sickness or during other seasons of panic. Their god Chāttan, or Sāttan, has no fixed abode, but, where the Mala Vēdans are, there is he in the midst of them. They bury their dead in a recumbent posture, near the hut of the deceased. The Mala Vēdans practice the primitive method of kindling fire by the friction of wood (also practiced by the Kānakars), and, like the Kānakars, they eat the black monkey. Their implements are bill-hooks, and bows and arrows. They weave grass baskets, which are slung to their girdles, and contain betel, etc."

The more important measurements of twenty-five Mala Vēdans examined by myself were —

	Max.	Min.	Average.
Stature (cm.)	163.8	140.8	154.2
Cephalic index	80.9	68.8	73.4
Nasal index	102.6	71.1	85.0

The figures show that, like other primitive jungle tribes in Southern India, the Mala Vēdans are short of stature, dolichocephalic, and platyrhine.

The following menstrual ceremony has been described[123] as occurring among the Vēdans of Travancore. "The wife at menstruation is secluded for five days in a hut a quarter of a mile from her home, which is also used by her at childbirth. The next five days are passed in a second hut, half way between the first and her house. On the ninth day her husband holds a feast, sprinkles his floor with wine, and invites his friends to a spread of rice and palm wine. Until this evening, he has not dared to eat anything but roots, for fear of being killed by the devil. On the tenth day he must leave his house, to which he may not return until the women,

[123] Crawley. The Mystic Rose. Fide Jagor. Zeitsch: Ethnol. XI, 164.

his and her sister have bathed his wife, escorted her home, and eaten rice together. For four days after his return, however, he may not eat rice in his own house, or have connection with his wife."

MALA VĒDAN.

Vēdunollu.—A gōtra of Gānigas, members of which may not cut *Nyctanthes Arbor-tristis*. The flowers thereof are much used in Hindu worship, as the plant is supposed to have been brought from heaven by Krishna for his wife Satyābhāma.

Vēginādu.—A sub-division of Kōmatis, who belong to the Vēgi or Vengi country, the former name of part of the modern Kistna district. The Vēgina Kōmatis are said to have entered the fire-pits with the caste goddess Kanyakamma.

Vekkāli Puli (cruel-legged tiger).—An exogamous section of Kallan.

Vēl (lance).—A sub-division of Malayālam Paraiyans, and an exogamous sept or sub-division of Kānikars in Travancore. Vēlanmar (spearmen) occurs as a name for the hill tribes of Travancore.

Velakkattalavan.—Velakkattalavan or Vilakkattalavan is stated in the Travancore Census Report, 1901, to indicate chieftains among barbers, and to be the name for members of families, from which persons are selected to shave kings or nobles. In the Madras Census Report, 1891, Velakkattalavan is said to be "the name in South Malabar of the caste that shaves Nāyars and higher castes. The same man is called in North Malabar Valinchiyan, Nāvidan, or Nāsiyan. In dress and habits the caste resembles Nāyars, and they call themselves Nāyars in the south. Many returned their main caste as Nāyar. The females of this caste frequently act as mid-wives to Nāyars. In North Malabar, the Valinchiyan and Nāsiyan follow the Nāyar system of inheritance, whereas the Nāvidan has inheritance in the male line; but, even amongst the latter, tāli-kettu and sambandham are performed separately by different bridegrooms. In South Malabar the caste generally follows descent in the male line, but in some places the other system is also found." Sūdra Kāvutiyan is recorded, in the Madras Census Report, 1901, as a synonym of Velakkatalavan.

Velama.—The Velamas, or, as they are sometimes called, Yelamas, are a caste of agriculturists, who dwell in the Telugu country and Ganjam. Concerning them Mr. H. A. Stuart writes as follows.[124] "Who the Velamas were it seems difficult to decide. Some say they form a sub-division of the Balijas, but this they themselves most vehemently deny, and the Balijas derisively call them Gūna Sākala (or Tsākala) vāndlu (hunch-backed washermen). The pride and jealousy of Hindu castes was amusingly illustrated by the Velamas of Kālahasti. The Deputy Tahsildar of that town was desired to ascertain the origin of the name Gūni Sākalavāndlu, but, as soon as he asked the question, a member of the caste lodged a complaint of defamation against him before the District Magistrate. The nickname appears to have been applied to them, because, in the northern districts, some print chintzes, and, carrying their goods in a bundle on their backs, walk stooping like a laden washerman. This derivation is more than doubtful, for, in the Godāvari district, the name is Gūna Sākalavāndlu, gūna being the big pot in which they dye the chintzes. Some Velamas say that they belong to the Kammas, but divided from them in consequence of a difference of opinion on the subject of gōsha, most Velama females being now kept in seclusion. [In the Kurnool Manual it is noted that the Velama women are supposed to be gōsha, but, owing to poverty, the rule is not strictly observed.] Both Kammas and Velamas, before they divided, are said to have adopted gōsha from the Muhammadans, but, finding that they were thus handicapped in their competition with other cultivating castes, it was proposed that the original custom of their ancestors should be reverted to. Those who agreed signed a bond, which, being upon palm leaf, was called kamma, and from it they took this name. The dissentients retained gōsha, and were therefore called outsiders or Velamas. This does not, however, explain what the original name of the caste was, and the

[124] Manual of the North Arcot district.

truth of the story is doubtful. Since this dispute, the Velamas have themselves had a split on the subject of gōsha, those who have thrown it off being called Adi or original Velamas, and the others Padma Velamas. The Velamas seem to have come south with the Vijayanagara kings, and to have been made Menkāvalgars, from which position some rose to be Poligars. Now they are chiefly the hangers-on of poligars or cultivators. To distinguish them from the Vellālas in the southern tāluks, they call themselves Telugu Vellālas, but it seems very improbable that the Velamas and Vellālas ever had any connection with one another. They are styled Naidus." [The Velamas style themselves Telugu Vellālas, not because of any connection between the two castes, but because they are at the top of the Telugu castes as the Vellālas are of the Tamil castes. For the same reason, Vellālas are sometimes called Arava (Tamil) Velamalu.]

The most important sub-divisions returned by the Velamas at the census, 1891, were Kāpu, Koppala, Padma, Ponnēti, and Yānādi. "It is," the Census Superintendent writes, "curious to find the Yānādi sub-division so strongly represented, for there is at the present day a wide gulf between Velamas and Yānādis" (a Telugu forest tribe). In the Vizagapatam Manual, a class of cultivators called Yānādulu is referred to; and, in the Madras Census Report, 1901, it is recorded that entries under the name Yānāti "were clubbed with Yānādi; but it has since been reported that, in Bissam-Acuttack tāluk of the Vizagapatam Agency, there is a separate caste called Yānāti or Yēnēti Dora which is distinct from Yānādi." It would appear that, as in the south, the Velamas call themselves Telugu Vellālas, so in the north they call themselves Yānātis.

Concerning the Gūna Velamas, the Rev. J. Cain writes[125] that "in years gone by, members of this class, who were desirous of getting married, had to arrange and pay the expenses of two of the Palli (fisherman) caste, but now it is regarded as sufficient to hang up a net in the house during the time of the marriage ceremony." The custom had its origin in a legend that, generations ago, when all the members of the caste were in danger of being swept off the face of the earth by some of their enemies, the Pallis came to the rescue with their boats, and carried all the Gūna Velamas to a place of safety. The Gūna Velamas, Mr. Cain continues, were "formerly regarded as quite an inferior caste, but, as many members of it have been educated in Anglo-Vernacular schools, they have found their way into almost every department and risen in the social scale. Their caste occupation is that of dyeing cloth, which they dip into large pots (gūnas). The term Gūna Tsākala is one of reproach, and they much prefer being called Velamalu to the great disgust of the Rāca (Rāja) Velamalu." To the Rāca Velama section belong, among other wealthy land-owners, the Rājas of Bobbili, Venkatagiri, Pittapūr, and Nuzvīd. At the annual Samasthānam meeting, in 1906, the Mahārāja of Bobbili announced that "none of the Velamavāru were working in any of the offices at the time when I first came to Bobbili. There were then a small number acting as mere supervisors without clerical work. Only from the commencement of my administration these people have been gradually taken into the office, and induced to read at the High School."

For the following note on the Velamas who have settled in the Vizagapatam

---

[125] Ind. Ant. VIII, 1879.

district, I am indebted to Mr. C. Hayavadana Rao. The following sub-divisions of the caste may be noted:—

(1) Pedda or Padma found chiefly in the Bobbili tāluk. Those composing it are said to be the descendants of the military followers and dependents of Pedda Rāju-du, the founder of the Bobbili family, who received a territorial grant in 1652 from Shēr Muhammad Khān, the Moghul Fauzdar of Chicacole. It is to this sub-division that Orme refers, when he says[126] that they "esteem themselves the highest blood of Native Indians, next to the Brāhmans, equal to the Rajpoots, and support their pre-eminence by the haughtiest observances, insomuch that the breath of a different religion, and even of the meaner Indians, requires ablution; their women never transfer themselves to a second, but burn with the husband of their virginity." The remarriage of widows is forbidden, and women remain gōsha (in seclusion), and wear gold or silver bangles on both wrists, unlike those of the Koppala section. The title of members of this sub-division is Dora.

(2) Kamma Velama found chiefly in the Kistna district, from which some families are said to have emigrated in company with the early Rājas of Vizianāgram. They are met with almost solely in the town of Vizianāgram. The remarriage of widows is permitted, but females are gōsha. The title is Nāyudu.

(3) Koppala, or Toththala, who do not shave their heads, but tie the hair in a knot (koppu) on the top of the head. They are divided into sections, *e.g.*, Nāga (cobra), Sankha (chank shell, *Turbinella rapa*), Tulasi (*Ocimum sanctum*), and Tābēlu (tortoise). These have no significance so far as marriage is concerned. They are further divided into exogamous septs, or intipērulu, of which the following are examples:—Nalla (black), Doddi (court-yard, cattle-pen or sheep-fold), Reddi (synonym of Kāpu). The custom of mēnarikam, by which a man marries his maternal uncle's daughter, is observed. A Brāhman officiates at marriages. Widows are permitted to remarry seven times, and, by an unusual custom, an elder brother is allowed to marry the widow of his younger brother. Women wear on the right wrist a solid silver bangle called ghatti kadiyam, and on the left wrist two bangles called sandēlu, between which are black glass bangles, which are broken when a woman becomes a widow. The titles of members of this sub-division are Anna, Ayya, and, when they become prosperous, Nāyudu.

In a note on the Velamas of the Godāvari district, Mr. F. R. Hemingway writes that they "admit that they always arrange for a Māla couple to marry, before they have a marriage in their own houses, and that they provide the necessary funds for the Māla marriage. They explain the custom by a story to the effect that a Māla once allowed a Velama to sacrifice him in order to obtain a hidden treasure, and they say that this custom is observed out of gratitude for the discovery of the treasure which resulted. The Rev. J. Cain gives[127] a similar custom among the Velamas of Bhadrāchalam in the Godāvari district, only in this case it is a Palli (fisherman) who has to be married."

There is, a correspondent informs me, a regular gradation in the social scale

---

[126] History of the Military Transactions in Indostan.
[127] Ind. Ant. VIII, 1879.

among the Velamas, Kammas, and Kāpus, as follows: —

> Velama Dora = Velama Esquire.
> Kamma Vāru = Mr. Kamma.
> Kāpu.

A complaint was once made on the ground that, in a pattah (title-deed), a man was called Kamma, and not Kamma Vāru.

It is noted by Mr. H. G. Prendergast[128] that the custom of sending a sword to represent an unavoidably absent bridegroom at a wedding is not uncommon among the Telugu Rāzus and Velamas.

Vēlampan (rope-dancer).—Possibly a name for the Koravas of Malabar, who perform feats on the tight-rope.

Vēlan.—As a diminutive form of Vellāla, Vēlan occurs as a title assumed by some Kusavans. Vēlan is also recorded as a title of Paraiyans in Travancore. (*See* Pānan.)

For the following note on the Vēlans of the Cochin State, I am indebted to Mr. L. K. Anantha Krishna Iyer.[129]

The Vēlans, like the Pānans, are a caste of devil-dancers, sorcerers and quack doctors, and are, in the northern parts of the State, called Perumannāns or Mannāns (washermen). My informant, a Perumannān at Trichūr, told me that their castemen south of the Karuvannūr bridge, about ten miles south of Trichūr, are called Vēlans, and that they neither interdine nor intermarry, because they give māttu (a washed cloth) to carpenters to free them from pollution. The Mannāns, who give the māttu to Izhuvans, do not give it to Kammālans (artisan classes), who are superior to them in social status. The Vēlans at Ernakulam, Cochin, and other places, are said to belong to eight illams. A similar division into illams exists among the Perumannāns of the Trichūr tāluk. The Perumannāns of the Chittūr tāluk have no knowledge of this illam division existing among them.

The following story was given regarding the origin of the Vēlans and Mannāns. Once upon a time, when Paramēswara and his wife Parvati were amusing themselves, the latter chanced to make an elephant with earth, which was accidentally trodden on by the former, whence arose a man who stood bowing before them. He was called the Mannān because he came out of man (earth), and to him was assigned his present occupation. This tradition is referred to in the songs which are sung on the fourth day of a girl's first menses, when she takes a ceremonial bath to free her from pollution.

The Vēlans are found all over the southern parts of the State, as their brethren are in the northern parts. They live in thatched huts in cocoanut gardens, while the Mannāns occupy similar dwellings in small compounds either of their own, or of some landlord whose tenant they may be.

When a girl attains puberty, she is at once bathed, and located in a room in the

[128] Ind. Ant. XX, 1891.
[129] Monograph Eth. Survey of Cochin, No. 12, 1907.

hut. Her period of seclusion is four days. On the morning of the fourth day, she is seated in a pandal (booth) put up in front of the hut, and made to hold in her hand a leafy vessel filled with rice, a few annas and a lighted wick, when a few of the castemen sing songs connected with puberty till so late as one or two o'clock, when the girl is bathed. After this, the castemen and women who are invited are feasted along with the girl, who is neatly dressed and adorned in her best. Again the girl takes her seat in the pandal and the tunes begin, and are continued till seven or eight o'clock next morning, when the ceremony comes to an end. The songsters are remunerated with three paras of paddy (unhusked rice), twenty-eight cocoanuts, thirteen annas and four pies, and two pieces of cloth. The songs are in some families postponed till the sixteenth day, or to the day of the girl's marriage. Very poor people dispense with them altogether. The following is a translation of one of the songs.

One day a girl and her friends were playing merrily on the banks of a river, when one of them noticed some blood on her dress. They took her home, and her parents believed it to have been caused by some wound, but on enquiry knew that their daughter was in her menses. The daughter asked her mother as to what she did with the cloth she wore during her menses, when she was told that she bathed and came home, leaving it on a branch of a mango tree. On further enquiry, she knew that the goddess Ganga purified herself by a bath, leaving her cloth in the river; that the goddess earth buried it in earth; and that Panchali returned home after a bath, leaving her dress on a branch of a banyan tree. Unwilling to lose her dress, the girl went to the god Parameśwara, and implored his aid to get somebody to have her cloth washed. When muttering a mantram (prayer), he sprinkled some water, a few drops of which went up and became stars, and from a few more, which fell on the leaves of a banyan tree, there came out a man, to whom was assigned the task of washing the cloths of the women in their courses, wearing which alone the women are purified by a bath.

When a young man of the Vēlan caste has attained the marriageable age, his father and maternal uncle select a suitable girl as a wife, after a proper examination and agreement of their horoscopes. The preliminaries are arranged in the hut of the girl, and a portion of the bride's price, fifteen fanams, is paid. The auspicious day for the wedding is fixed, and the number of guests that should attend it is determined. The wedding is celebrated at the girl's hut, in front of which a shed is put up. The ceremony generally takes place at night. A few hours before it, the bridegroom and his party arrive at the bride's hut, where they are welcomed, and seated on mats spread on the floor in the pandal (shed). At the auspicious hour, when the relatives on both sides and the castemen are assembled, the bridegroom's enangan (relation by marriage) hands over a metal plate containing the wedding suit, the bride's price, and a few packets of betel leaves and nuts to the bride's enangan, who takes everything except the cloth to be given to the bride's mother, and returns the plate to the same man. The bridegroom's sister dresses the bride in the new cloth, and takes her to the pandal, to seat her along with the bridegroom, and to serve one or two spoonfuls of milk and a few pieces of plantain fruit, when the bride is formally declared to be the wife of the young man and a member of his family. The guests assembled are treated to a feast, after which they are served with betel leaves, nuts, and tobacco. The rest of the night is spent in merry songs and dancing. The songs refer to the marriage of Sīta, the wife of Rāma, of Subhadra, wife of Arjuna, and of Panchali, wife of the Pāndavas. Next morning, the bride's party is treated to rice kanji (gruel) at eight o'clock, and to a sumptuous meal at twelve o'clock, after which they repair to the bridegroom's hut, accompanied by the bride, her parents and relations, all of whom receive a welcome. The formalities are gone through here also, and the bride's party is feasted. On the fourth morning, the newly married couple bathe and dress themselves neatly, to worship the deity at the local temple. After dinner they go to the bride's hut, where they spend a week or two, after which the bridegroom returns to his hut with his wife. It is now that the bride receives a few ornaments, a metal dish for taking meals, a lamp, and a few metal utensils, which vary according to the circumstances of her parents. Henceforward, the husband and wife live with the parents of the former in their family.

Among the Mannāns of the northern parts of the State, the following marriage customs are found to prevail. The bridegroom's father, his maternal uncle, enangan, and the third or middle man, conjointly select the girl after due examination and agreement of horoscopes. The preliminaries are arranged as before, and the day for the wedding is determined. At the auspicious moment on the wedding day, when the relatives on both sides and the castemen are assembled at the shed in front of the bride's hut, the bridegroom's father takes up a metal plate containing the wedding dress, the bride's price (twelve fanams), and a few bundles of betel leaves, nuts and tobacco, and repeats a formula, of which the substance runs thus. "A lighted lamp is placed in the shed. Four mats are spread round it in the direction of east, west, north and south. A metal plate, containing rice, flowers and betel leaves, is placed in front of the lamp, and the elderly members of the caste and the relatives on both sides are assembled. According to the traditional custom of the caste, the young man's father, maternal uncle, enangan, and the middle man conjointly selected the girl after satisfying themselves with due agreement of horoscopes, and ascertaining the illams and kriyams on both sides. They have negotiated for the girl, and settled the day on which the marriage is to take place. In token of this, they have taken meals in the bride's family. The claims of the girl for two pieces of cloth for the Ōnam festival, two fanams or nine annas for Thiruwatira (a festival in Dhanu, *i.e.*, December-January), and Vishu, are satisfied, and she is by the young man taken to the village festival. They have now come for the celebration of the wedding. There have been times when he has heard of 101 fanams as the price of the bride, and has seen 51 fanams as the price of the same, but it is now 21 fanams. It thus varies, and may be increased or diminished according to the will, pleasure, and means of the parties. With four fanams as the price of the bride and eight fanams for ornaments, and with the bundles of betel leaves, nuts, and the wedding dress in a metal plate, may I, ye elderly members, give it to the girl's parents?" "Shall I," answers the girl's father, "accept it?" Receiving it, he gives it to his brother-in-law, who gives it to the enangan, and he takes everything in it except the wedding suit, which he hands over to the bridegroom's enangan, who gives it to the bridegroom's sister, to have the bride dressed in it. The other portions of the ceremony are the same as those described above. In Palghat and the Chittūr tāluk, the following declaration is made. "According to the customary traditions of the caste, when a young man of one locality comes to tame a girl of another locality, and takes her as his wife, ye elderly members assembled here, may these four bundles of betel leaves, four measures of rice, two pieces of cloth, and ten fanams be given to the bride's parents?" "Shall these be accepted?" says the bride's enangan. When the bride accompanies the bridegroom to his hut, the following formal statement is made. "Thrash thou mayst, but not with a stick. Thou mayst not accuse her of bad conduct. Thou mayst not cut off her ears, breasts, nose and tufts of hair. Thou mayst not take her to a tank (to bathe), or to a temple (for swearing). Thou mayst keep and protect her as long as thou wantest. When thou dost not want her, give her maintenance, and take back the children, for they are thine own."

Polygamy is not prohibited, but is rarely practiced by the Vēlans and Mannāns. They are very poor, and find it difficult to support their wives and children born in a single married life. Want of children, bodily defect or incurable disease, or want of additional hands for work, may sometimes induce them to take more than one wife. Polyandry does not prevail among the Vēlans, but is common among the Mannāns of the northern parts of the State. A Vēlan woman who loses her husband may marry another of her caste, if she likes, a year after her husband's death. The formalities of the wedding consist in the husband giving two pieces of cloth to the woman who wishes to enter into wedlock with him. After this she forfeits all claim on the property of her former husband. Among the Mannāns, a widow may marry any one of her brothers-in-law. A woman committing adultery with a member of her own caste is well thrashed. One who disposes of herself to a member of a lower caste is sent out of caste. She may then become a Christian or Muhammadan convert. If an unmarried young woman becomes pregnant, and this is known to her castemen, they convene a meeting, and find out the secret lover, whom they compel to take her as his wife. Very often they are both fined, and the fine is spent on toddy. Both among the Vēlans and Mannāns, divorce is easy. A man who does not like his wife has only to take her to her original home and give charge of her to her parents, informing them of the circumstances which have induced him to adopt such a course. A woman who does not like her husband may relinquish him, and join her parents. In both cases, the woman is at liberty to marry again.

When a woman is pregnant, the ceremony of pulikuti (drinking of tamarind juice) is performed for her during the ninth month at the hut of her husband. The juice is extracted from tamarind (*Tamarindus indica*), kotapuli (*Garcinia Cambogia*), nerinjampuli (*Hibiscus surattensis*) and the leaves of ambazhampuli (*Spondias mangifera*). A large branch of ambazhampuli is stuck in the ground in the central courtyard, near which the pregnant woman is seated. The husband gives her three small spoonfuls, and then seven times with her cherutāli (neck ornament) dipped in the juice. Among the washermen, the woman's brother gives it three times to her. Should her sister-in-law give it in a small vessel, she has a claim to two pieces of cloth. After this, a quarter measure of gingelly (*Sesamum*) oil is poured upon her head, to be rubbed all over her body, and she bathes, using *Acacia Intsia* as soap. Those of her relatives and the castemen who are invited are sumptuously fed. Some of them crack jokes by asking the pregnant woman to promise her baby son or daughter to theirs when grown up. All bless her for a safe delivery and healthy child.

A woman who is about to become a mother is lodged in a separate room for her delivery, attended by her mother and one or two grown-up women, who act as midwives. The period of pollution is fifteen days. For the first three days the woman is given a dose of dried ginger mixed with palmyra (*Borassus flabellifer*) jaggery (crude sugar), and for the next three days a mixture of garlic and jaggery. Her diet during the first three days is rice kanji with scrapings of cocoanut, which are believed to help the formation of the mother's milk. For the next three days, the juice of kotapuli (*Garcinia Cambogia*), cumin seeds, and kotal urikki (*Achyranthes aspera*), and of the leaves of muringa (*Moringa pterygosperma*) is given, after which, for a few more days, a dose of the flesh of fowl mixed with mustard, cumin seeds and uluva (*Trigonella fœnum-græcum*) boiled in gingelly oil is taken. She bathes in water boiled with medicinal herbs on the fourth, seventh, ninth, eleventh, and sixteenth days. On the morning of the sixteenth day, her enangathi (enangan's wife) cleans her room with water mixed with cow-dung, and sweeps the compound. Wearing a māttu (washed cloth) brought by a washerman, she bathes to be freed from pollution. She may now enter the hut, and mingle with the rest of the family.

Among Vēlans and Mannāns, the sons inherit the property of their fathers, but they are very poor, and have little or nothing to inherit.

Vēlans and Mannāns practice magic and sorcery. All diseases that flesh is heir to are, in the opinion of these people, caused by malignant demons, and they profess to cure, with the aid of their mantrams and amulets, people suffering from maladies. The muttering of the following mantram, and throwing of bhasmam (holy ashes), in propitiation of the small-pox demon is believed to effect a cure.

(1) Ōm, Oh! thou, Pallyamma, mother with tusk-like teeth, that in demoniacal form appearest on the burning ground called omkara, with burning piles flaming around, with one breast on one of thy shoulders, and playing with the other as with a ball, with thy tongue stretched out and wound round thy head, with grass, beans, and pepper in thy left hand, with gingelly seeds and chama grains in thy right hand, that scatterest and sowest broadcast the seeds of small-pox; Oh! let the seeds that thou hast sown, and those that thou hast not sown, dry up inside, and get charred outside. Be thou as if intoxicated with joy! Protect thou, protect thou!

(2) Malign influence of birds on children.

Oh! thou round-eyed, short Karinkali with big ears, born from the third incessantly burning eye of Siva, come, come and be in possession.

If this mantram be muttered sixteen times, and bhasmam thrown over the body of a child, the operator breathing violently the while, a cure will be effected. If the mantram be muttered in a vessel of water the same number of times, and the child bathed in it, the cure will be equally effective.

(3) To cure fits and fever.

Oh! thou swine-faced mother, thou catchest hold of my enemy, coming charging me, by the neck with thy tusks thrust into his body; draggest him on the ground, and standest slowly chewing and eating, thrusting thy tusks, rubbing again, and wearing down his body, chewing once more and again; thou, mother that controllest 41,448 demons presiding over all kinds of maladies, seventy-two Bhiravans, eighteen kinds of epileptic fits (korka), twelve kinds of muyalis and all other kinds of illness, as also Kandakaranans (demons with bell-shaped ears), be under my possession so long as I serve thee.

This mantram should be repeated sixteen times, with bhasmam thrown on the body of the patient.

(4) Oh! Bhadrakali, thou hast drunk the full cup. Oh! thou that holdest the sword of royalty in thy right hand, and that half sittest on a high seat. Place under control, as I am piously uttering the mantrams to serve thee, all demons, namely Yakshi, Gandharvan, Poomalagandharvan, Chutali, Nīrali, Nīlankari, Chuzali, and many others who cause all kinds of illness that flesh is heir to. Oh! holy mother, Bhadrakali, I vow by my preceptor.

(5) For devil driving.

Oh! thou, Karinkutti (black dwarf) of Vedapuram in Vellanad, that pluckest the fruits of the right hand branch of the strychnine tree (*Strychnos Nux-vomica*), and keepest toddy in its shell, drinking the blood of the black domestic fowl, drumming and keeping time on the rind of the fruit, filling and blowing thy pipe or horn through the nose. Oh! thou primeval black dwarf, so long as I utter the proper mantrams, I beg thee to cause such demons as would not dance to dance, and others to jump and drive them out. Oh! thou, Karinkutti, come, come, and enable me to succeed in my attempts.

(6) Oh! thou goddess with face. Oh! thou with face like that of a bear, and thou, a hunter. I utter thy mantrams and meditate upon thee, and therefore request thee to tread upon my enemies, burst open their bodies to drink their blood, and yawn to take complete rest; drive out such demons as cause convulsions of the body both from within and without, and all kinds of fever. Scatter them as dust. I swear by thee and my preceptor. Swahah.

(7) For the evil eye.

Salutations to thee, Oh! God. Even as the moon wanes in its brightness at the sight of the sun, even as the bird chakora (Eraya) disappears at the sight of the moon; even as the great Vasuki (king of serpents) vanishes at the sight of chakora; even as the poison vanishes from his head; so may the potency of his evil eye with thy aid vanish.

(8) To cause delay in the occurrence of menses.

Salutation to thee, Oh! Mars (the son of the goddess Earth).

If this mantram is muttered on a thread dyed yellow with turmeric, and if the thread be placed on both the palms joined together, and if the number of days to which the occurrence of the menses should be delayed be thought of, the post-ponement will be procured by wearing it either round the neck or the loins. The thread with a ring attached to it, and worn round the neck is equally effective.

(9) To prevent cows from giving milk.

Ōm, Koss, dry up the liquid, kindly present me with thy gracious aspect. Oh! thou with the great sword in thy hands, the great trident, dry up the cow's udder even as a tiger, I swear by thee and my preceptor.

(10) To cause cows to give milk.

Even as the swelling on the holy feet of Mahādēva due to the bite of a crocodile has subsided and gone down, so go down. I swear by my preceptor.

(11) To remove a thorn from the sole of the foot.

When Paramēswara and Parvathi started on their hunting expedition, a thorn entered the foot of her lady-ship. It was doubted whether it was the thorn of a bamboo, an ant, or a strychnine tree. Even so may this poison cease to hurt, Oh! Lord. I swear by my preceptor.

(12) To effect metamorphosis.

Take the head of a dog and burn it, and plant on it vellakutti plant. Burn camphor and frankincense, and adore it. Then pluck the root. Mix it with the milk of a dog and the bones of a cat. A mark made with the mixture on the forehead will enable any person to assume the figure of any animal he thinks of.

(13) Before a stick of the Malankara plant, worship with a lighted wick and incense. Then chant the Sakti mantram 101 times, and mutter the mantram to give life at the bottom. Watch carefully which way the stick inclines. Proceed to the south of the stick, and pluck the whiskers of a live tiger, and make with them a ball of the veerali silk, string it with silk, and enclose it within the ear. Stand on the palms of the hand to attain the disguise of a tiger, and, with the stick in hand, think of a cat, white bull, or other animal. Then you will, in the eyes of others, appear as such.

(14) Take the nest of a crow from a margosa tree, and bury it at the cremation ground. Then throw it into the house of your enemy. The house will soon take fire.

(15) Take the ashes of the burial-ground on which an ass has been rolling on a Saturday or Sunday, and put it in the house of your enemy. The members of the family will soon quit the house, or a severe illness will attack them.

The Vēlans and Mannāns are animists, and worship demoniacal gods, such as Chandan, Mundian, Kandakaranan, Karinkutti, and Chāthan. All of them are separately represented by stones located underneath a tree in the corners of their compounds. Offerings of sheep, fowls, plantain fruits, cocoanuts, parched rice and beaten rice, are made to them on the tenth of Dhanu (last week in December), on a Tuesday in Makaram (January-February), and on Kumbham Bharani (second asterism in March-April). They also adore the goddess Bhagavathi and the spirits of their departed ancestors, who are believed to exercise their influence in their families for good or evil. Sometimes, when they go to Cranganore to worship the goddess there, they visit the senior male members of the local Nāyar, Kammālan and Izhuvan families to take leave of them, when they are given a few annas with which they purchase fowls, etc., to be given as offerings to the local goddess. Wooden or metal images, representing the spirits of their ancestors, are located in a room of their huts, and worshipped with offerings on New Moon and Sankranti nights.

The Vēlans and Mannāns either burn or bury the dead. The son is the chief mourner who performs the funeral rites, and the nephews and brothers take part in them. Their priests are known as Kurup, and they preside at the ceremonies. Death pollution lasts for sixteen days, and on the morning of the sixteenth day the hut of the dead person is well swept and cleansed by sprinkling water mixed with cowdung. The members of the family, dressed in the māttu (a washed cloth worn before bathing) brought by the washerman, bathe to be free from pollution. The castemen, including their friends and relations, are invited and feasted. A similar funeral feast is also held at the end of the year.

The chief occupation of the Vēlans and Mannāns is the giving of māttu to Brāhmans, Kshatriyas, Anthalarajātis, Nāyars, Kammālans and Izhuvans, for wearing before going to bathe on the day on which they are freed from pollution. A girl or woman in her courses on the morning of the fourth day, a woman in confinement on the fifth, ninth, eleventh and sixteenth days, and all the members of a family under death pollution on the sixteenth day, have to use it. They bathe wearing the washed cloth, and return it as soon as the bath is over. It may either belong to the washerman, or have been previously given to him by the members of the family. He gets an anna or a measure of paddy for his service to a woman in her menses, and a para of paddy or six annas for birth and death pollutions. The Vēlans give the māttu to all the castes above mentioned, while the Mannāns refuse to give it to the Kammālans, and thereby profess themselves to be superior in status to them. They wash clothes to dress the idols in some of the high caste temples. Their washing consists in first plunging the dirty cloths in water mixed with cowdung, and beating them on a stone by the side of a tank (pond), canal or river, and again immersing them in water mixed with wood ashes or charamannu, after which they are exposed to steam for a few hours, and again beaten on the stone, slightly moistening in water now and then, until they are quite clean. They are then dried in the sun, and again moistened with a solution of starch and indigo, when they are exposed to the air to dry. When dry, they are folded, and beaten with a heavy club, so as to be like those ironed. The Vēlans of the Cranganore, Cochin, and Kanayannūr tāluks, climb cocoanut trees to pluck cocoanuts, and get about eight to ten annas for every hundred trees they go up. They make umbrellas. Some among them practice magic and sorcery, and some are quack doctors, who treat sickly children. Some are now engaged in agricultural operations, while a few make beds, pillows, and coats. There are also a few of them in every village who are songsters, and whose services are availed of on certain ceremonial occasions, namely, on the bathing day of a girl in her first menses, on the wedding night, and when religious ceremonies are performed, and sacrifices offered to their gods. Some are experts in drum-beating, and are invited by low caste people of the rural parts. The Mannāns also follow the same occupations.

The Vēlans and Mannāns eat at the hands of all castes above them, namely, Brāhmans, Kshatriyas, Nāyars, and Izhuvans. The former take food from Kammālans, while the latter abstain from so doing. They do not eat the food prepared by Kaniyans, Pānans, Vilkurups, or other castes of equal or inferior status. They have to stand at a distance of twenty-four feet from Brāhmans. They have their own barbers, and are their own washermen. They stand far away from the outer wall of the temples of high castes. They are not allowed to take water from the wells of high caste Sūdras, nor are they allowed to live in their midst.

The following note on the Vēlans of Travancore has been furnished by Mr. N. Subramani Iyer.

The word Vēlan has been derived from vel a spear, and also from vela work. The usual title of the Vēlans is Panikkan. They are believed to be divided into four classes, viz., Bharata Vēlan, Vaha Vēlan, Pana Vēlan, and Manna Vēlan. While the last of these sections, in addition to their traditional occupation, are washermen and climbers of areca palm trees, the Pana Vēlans take sawing as a supplementary employment. Some of the members of the first and second classes are also physicians. This classification is gradually going out of vogue.

The Vēlans are said traditionally to have been descended from Siva, who, on one occasion, is believed to have removed the evil effects of the sorcery of demons upon Vishnu by means of exorcism. As this kind of injury began to increase among men, a man and woman were created by this deity, to prevent its dire consequences. In the Kēralolpatti, this caste is mentioned as Velakkuruppu. But at present the Puranadis, who are the barbers and priests of this class, are known by this name. A Puranadi means one who stands outside, and is not admitted as of equal rank with the Vēlans proper. The Puranadis are not washermen. Commensal relations exist only between the male members of the Vēlans and Puranitis (Puranadi females).

The Vēlans perform a number of useful services in the body politic of Malabar. In the Kēralolpatti their duty is said to be the nursing of women in their confinement. In the Kērala-Visesha-Mahatmya, exorcism, climbing of trees, and washing clothes, are mentioned as their occupations. There are various kinds of exorcism, the chief being Vēlan Tullal and Vēlan Pravarti. The former is a kind of masque performed by the Vēlans for warding off the effects of the evil eye, and preventing the injurious influences of demons and spirits. Atavi is a peculiar female divinity worshipped by the caste, by whose help these feats are believed to be performed in the main. She, and a host of minor gods and goddesses, are represented by them, and a dance commences. After it is over, all the characters receive presents. Vēlan Pravarti, or Otuka, may either last for eleven days, or may be finished on a minor scale within three days, and in emergent cases even in one day. A Puranadi acts as buffoon, and serves the purpose of a domestic servant on the occasion. This is called Pallipana when performed in temples, Pallipperu when in palaces, and Vēlan Pravarti or Satru-eduppu in the case of ordinary people. This is also done with a view to prevent the effect of the evil eye. On the first day, a person representing the enchanted man or woman is placed in a temporary shed built for the purpose, and lights are waved before him. On the third day, a pit is dug, and a cock sacrificed. On the fourth day, the Pattata Bali, or human sacrifice, takes place. A person is thrown into a pit which is covered with a plank of wood, upon which sacrifices are offered. The buried person soon resuscitates himself, and, advancing as if possessed, explains the cause of the disease or calamity. On the eighth day, figures of snakes, in gold or silver, are enclosed in small copper vessels, and milk and fruit are offered to them. On the ninth day, the Vēlans worship the lords of the eight directions, with Brahma or the creator in the midst of them. On the tenth day, there is much festivity and amusement, and the Mahābhārata is sung in a condensed form. The chief of the Vēlans becomes possessed, and prays that, as the Pāndavas emerged safely from the sorcery of the Kauravas, the person affected by the calamity may escape unhurt. On the last day, animals are sacrificed at the four corners of the compound surrounding the house. No special rite is performed on the first day, but the Ituvanabali, Kuzhibali, Pattatabali, Kitangubali, Patalabali, Sarakutabali, Pithabali, Azhibali, Digbali, and Kumpubali, are respectively observed during the remaining ten days. The Pana, of which rite the breaking of cocoanuts is the most important item, completes this long ceremony. It was once supposed that the Bharata Vēlans exorcised spirits in the homes of high caste Hindus, the same work being done among the middle classes by the Vaha Vēlans, and among the low by the Manna Vēlans. This rule does not hold good at the present day. The Vēlans are also engaged in the event of bad crops.

Besides standing thirty-two feet apart from Hindu temples, and worshipping the divinities therein, the Vēlans erect small sanctuaries for Siva within their own compounds, called Kuriyala. They worship this deity in preference to others, and offer tender cocoanuts, fried rice, sugar, and plantain fruits to him on the Uttradam day in the month of August.

Velanāti (foreign).—A sub-division of Kāpus, and other Telugu castes, and of Telugu Brāhmans.

Velanga (wood apple: *Feronia elephantum*).—An exogamous sept of Mūka Dora.

Velichchapād.—Of the Velichchapāds, or oracles, of Malabar, the following account is given by Mr. F. Fawcett.[130] "Far away in rural Malabar, I witnessed the ceremony in which the Velichchapād exhibited his quality. It was in the neighbourhood of a Nāyar house, to which thronged all the neighbours (Nāyars), men and women, boys and girls. The ceremony lasts about an hour. The Nāyar said it was the custom in his family to have it done once a year, but could give no account of how the custom originated; most probably in a vow, some ancestor having vowed that, if such or such benefit be received, he would for ever after have an annual performance of this ceremony in his house. It involved some expenditure, as the Velichchapād had to be paid, and the neighbours had to be fed. Somewhere about the middle of the little courtyard, always as clean as a dinner table, the Velichchapād placed a lamp (of the Malabar pattern) having a lighted wick, a kalasam (brass vessel), some flowers, camphor, saffron (turmeric) and other paraphernalia. Bhagavati was the deity invoked, and the business involved offering flowers, and

[130] Madras Museum Bull. III, 3, 1901.

waving a lighted wick round the kalasam. The Velichchapād's movements became quicker, and, suddenly seizing his sword (nāndakam), he ran round the courtyard (against the sun, as sailors say) shouting wildly. He is under the influence of the deity who has been introduced into him, and he gives oracular utterances to the deity's commands. What he said I know not, and no one else seemed to know or care in the least, much interested though they were in the performance. As he ran, every now and then he cut his forehead with the sword, pressing it against the skin and sawing vertically up and down. The blood streamed all over his face. Presently he became wilder and wilder, and whizzed round the lamp, bending forward towards the kalasam. Evidently some deity, some spirit was present here, and spoke through the mouth of the Velichchapād. This, I think, undoubtedly represents the belief of all who were present. When he had done whizzing round the kalasam, he soon became a normal being, and stood before my camera. The fee for the self-inflicted laceration is one rupee, some rice, etc. I saw the Velichchapād about three days afterwards, going to perform elsewhere. The wound on his forehead had healed. The careful observer can always identify a Velichchapād by the triangular patch over the forehead, where the hair will not grow, and where the skin is somewhat indurated."

Velivēyabadina Rāzu.—The name, denoting Rāzus who were thrown out, of a class said to be descended from Rāzus who were excommunicated from their caste.[131]

Veliyam.—Recorded, in the Travancore Census Report, 1901, as a title of Nāyars. In the same report Veliyattu is described as synonymous with Pulikkappanikkan, a sub-division of Nāyar.

Vellaikāran (white man).—A Tamil name for European.

Vellāla.—"The Vellālas," Mr. H. A. Stuart writes,[132] "are the great farmer caste of the Tamil country, and they are strongly represented in every Tamil district. The word Vellālan is derived from vellānmai [vellam, water, anmai, management?] meaning cultivation, tillage. Dr. Oppert[133] considers Vellālan to be etymologically connected with Pallan, Palli, etc., the word meaning the lord of the Vallas or Pallas. The story of their origin is as follows. Many thousands of years ago, when the inhabitants of the world were rude and ignorant of agriculture, a severe drought fell upon the land, and the people prayed to Bhūdēvi, the goddess of the earth, for aid. She pitied them, and produced from her body a man carrying a plough, who showed them how to till the soil and support themselves. His offsprings are the Vellālas, who aspire to belong to the Vaisya caste, since that includes Gōvaisyas, Bhūvaisyas, and Dhanavaisyas (shepherds, cultivators and merchants). A few, therefore, constantly wear the sacred thread, but most put it on only during marriages or funerals as a mark of the sacred nature of the ceremony."

---

[131] Rev. J. Cain, Ind. Ant., VIII, 1879.

[132] Madras Census Report, 1891, and Manual of the North Arcot District.

[133] Madras Journal of Literature and Science, 188–788, p. 134, where the etymology of the name Vellāla is fully discussed.

VELICHCHAPĀD.

The traditional story of the origin of the Vellālas is given as follows in the Baramahal Records.[134] "In ancient days, when the God Paramēsvaradu and his consort the goddess Parvati Dēvi resided on the top of Kailāsa Parvata or mount of paradise, they one day retired to amuse themselves in private, and by chance Visvakarma, the architect of the Dēvatas or gods, intruded on their privacy, which en-

____

[134] Section III. Inhabitants, Government Press, Madras, 1907.

raged them, and they said to him that, since he had the audacity to intrude on their retirement, they would cause an enemy of his to be born in the Bhūlōka or earthly world, who should punish him for his temerity. Visvakarma requested they would inform him in what part of the Bhūlōka or earthly world he would be born, and further added that, if he knew the birth place, he would annihilate him with a single blow. The divine pair replied that the person would spring up into existence from the bowels of the earth on the banks of the Ganga river. On this, Visvakarma took his sword, mounted his aerial car, and flew through the regions of ether to the banks of the Ganga river, where he anxiously waited the birth of his enemy. One day Visvakarma observed the ground to crack near him, and a kiritam or royal diadem appeared issuing out of the bowels of the earth, which Visvakarma mistook for the head of his adversary, and made a cut at it with his sword, but only struck off the kiritam. In the meantime, the person came completely out of the earth, with a bald pate, holding in his hand a golden ploughshare, and his neck encircled with garlands of flowers. The angry Visvakarma instantly laid hold on him, when the Gods Brahma, Vishnu and Siva, and the supporters of the eight corners of the universe, appeared in all their glory, and interceded for the earth-born personage, and said to Visvakarma thou didst vow that thou wouldst annihilate him with a single blow, which vow thou hast not performed; therefore with what justice hast thou a second time laid violent hands on him? Since thou didst not succeed in thy first attempt, it is but equitable that thou shouldst now spare him. At the intercession and remonstrance of the gods, Visvakarma quitted his hold, and a peace was concluded between him and his enemy on the following stipulation, viz., that the pancha jāti, or five castes of silversmiths, carpenters, ironsmiths, stone-cutters, and braziers, who were the sons of Visvakarma, should be subservient to the earth-born person. The deities bestowed on the person these three names. First Bhūmi Pālakudu or saviour of the earth, because he was produced by her. Second, Ganga kulam or descendant of the river Ganga, by reason of having been brought forth on her banks. Third, Murdaka Pālakudu or protector of the plough, alluding to his being born with a ploughshare in his hand, and they likewise ordained that, as he had lost his diadem, he should not be eligible to sovereignty, but that he and his descendants should till the ground with this privilege, that a person of the caste should put the crown on the king's head at the coronation. They next invested him with the yegnōpavitam or string, and, in order that he might propagate his caste, they gave him in marriage the daughters of the gods Indra and Kubēra. At this time, the god Siva was mounted on a white bullock, and the god Dharmarāja on a white buffalo, which they gave him to plough the ground, and from which circumstance the caste became surnamed Vellal Wārus or those who plough with white bullocks. After the nuptials, the deities departed to their celestial abodes. Murdaka Pālakulu had fifty-four sons by the daughter of the god Indra, and fifty-two by the daughter of the god Kubēra, whom he married to the one hundred and six daughters of Nala Kubarudu, the son of Kubēra, and his sons-in-law made the following agreement with him, viz., that thirty-five of them should be called Bhūmi Pālakulu, and should till the ground; thirty-five of them named Vellal Shetti, and their occupation be traffic; and thirty-five of them named Gōvu Shetlu, and their employment breeding and feeding of cattle. They gave the remaining one the choice of three orders, but he would not have any connexion with any of them, from whence they surnamed him Agmurdi or the alien. The Agmurdi had born to him two thousand five hundred children, and became a separate caste, assuming the appellation of Agmurdi Vellal Wāru. The other brothers had twelve thousand children, who intermarried, and lived together as one caste, though their occupations were different.... During the reign of Krishna Rāyalu, whose capital was the city of Vijayanagaram or city of victory, a person of the Vellal caste, named Umbhi or Amultan Mudaliyar, was appointed sarvadhikari or prime minister, who had a samprati or secretary of the caste of Gollavāru or cowherds, whose name was Venayaterthapalli. It so happened that a set of Bhāgavata Sēvar, or strolling players, came to the city, and one night acted a play in the presence of Krishna Rāyalu and his court. In one of the acts, a player appeared in the garb and character of a female cowherd, and, by mimicking the actions and manners of that caste, afforded great diversion both to the Rāja and his courtiers. But no person seemed to be so much pleased as the prime minister, which being perceived by his secretary, he determined on making him pay dear for his mirth by turning the Vellal caste into ridicule, and thus hurt his pride, and take revenge for the pleasure he expressed at seeing the follies of the cowherd caste exposed. For that purpose, he requested the players, when they acted another play, to dress themselves up in the habit of a female of the Vellal caste. This scheme came to the ears of the prime minister, who, being a proud man, was sadly vexed at the trick, and resolved on preventing its being carried into execution; but, having none of his own caste present to assist him, and not knowing well how to put a stop to the business, he got into his palanquin, and went to a Canardha Shetti or headman of the right-hand caste, informed him of the circumstance, and begged his advice and assistance. The Shetti replied 'Formerly the left-hand caste had influence enough with Government to get an order issued forbidding the right-hand caste to cultivate or traffic; therefore, when we quarrel again, do you contrive to prevent the ryots of the Vellal caste from cultivating the ground, so that the public revenue will fall short, and Government will be obliged to grant us our own terms; and I will save you from the disgrace that is intended to be put on you. The prime minister agreed to the proposal, and went home. At night, when the players were coming to the royal presence to act, and one of them had on the habit of a female of the Vellal caste, the Canardha Shetti cut off his head, and saved the honour of the prime minister. The death of the player being reported to the Rāja Krishna Rāyalu, he enquired into the affair, and finding how matters stood, he directed the prime minister and his secretary to be more circumspect in their conduct, and not to carry their enmity to such lengths.' Since that time, the Vellal castes have always assisted the right-hand against the left-hand castes." (*See* Kammālan.)

At the time of the census, 1871, some Vellālas claimed that they had been seriously injured in reputation, and handled with great injustice, in being classed as Sūdras by the Municipal Commissioners of Madras in the classification of Hindus under the four great divisions of Brāhmans, Kshatriyas, Vaisyas, and Sūdras. In their petition it was stated that "we shall first proceed to show that the Vellālas *do* come exactly within the most authoritative definition given of Vysias, and then point out that they do *not* come within the like definition of Sūdras. First then to the definition of Vysia, Manu, the paramount authority upon these matters, says in paragraph 90 of his Institutes:—'To keep herds of cattle, to bestow largesses, to sacrifice, to read the scripture, to carry on trade, to lend at interest, and to cultivate land, are prescribed or permitted to a Vysia.'" In the course of the petition, the Vellālas observed that "it is impossible to imagine that the Vellālas, a race of agriculturists and traders, should have had to render menial service to the three higher classes; for the very idea of service is, as it needs must be, revolting to the Vellāla, whose profession teaches him perfect independence, and dependence, if it be, upon the sovereign alone for the protection of his proper interests. Hence a Vellāla cannot be of the Sūdra or servile class. Besides, that the Vellālas are recognised as a respectable body of the community will also appear from the following. There was a ceremony called tulabhāram (weighing in scales) observed by the ancient kings of, at some part of their lives, distributing in charity to the most deserving gold and silver equal to the weight of their persons; and tradition alleges that, when the kings of Tanjore performed this ceremony, the right to weigh the king's person was accorded to the Vellālan Chettis. This shows that the Vellālas have been recognised as a respectable body of mercantile men in charge of weights and measures (Manu 30, chap. 9). So also, in the Halasya Purānam of Madura, it is said that, when the King Somasundara Pandien, who was supposed to be the very incarnation of Siva, had to be crowned, there arose a contention as to who was to put the crown on his head. After much discussion, it was agreed that one of the Vellālas, who formed the strength of the community (note the fact that Manu says that Vysia came from the thighs of the Supreme Deity, which, as an allegory, is interpreted to mean the strength of the State) should be appointed to perform that part of the ceremony. Also, in Kamban's Rāmayana, written 1,000 and odd years ago, it is said that the priest Vasista handed the crown to a Vellāla, who placed it upon great Rama's head."

In 'The Tamils eighteen hundred years ago,' Mr. V. Kanakasabhai writes that "among the pure Tamils, the class most honoured was the Arivar or Sages. Next in rank to the Arivar were the Ulavar or farmers. The Arivars were ascetics, but, of the men living in society, the farmers occupied the highest position. They formed the nobility, or the landed aristocracy, of the country. They were also called Vellālar, 'lords of the flood,' or 'Karalar,' 'lords of the clouds,' titles expressive of their skill in controlling floods, and in storing water for agricultural purposes. The Chera, Chola and Pandyan Kings, and most of the petty chiefs of Tamilakam, belonged to the tribe of Vellālas. The poor families of Vellālas who owned small estates were generally spoken of as the Veelkudi-Uluvar or 'the fallen Vellālas,' implying thereby that the rest of the Vellālas were wealthy land-holders. When Karikāl the Great defeated the Aruvālar, and annexed their territory to his kingdom, he distributed the conquered lands among Vellāla chiefs.[135] The descendants of some of these chiefs are to this day in possession of their lands, which they hold as petty zamindars under the British Government.[136] The Vellāla families who conquered Vadukam, or the modern Telugu country, were called Velamas, and the great zamindars there still belong to the Velama caste. In the Canarese country, the Vellālas

[135] Thondai-nandalap-paddiyam.

[136] The zamindars of Cheyur, Chunampet, etc., in the Chingleput district.

founded the Bellāl dynasty, which ruled that country for several centuries. The Vellālas were also called the Gangakula or Gangavamsa, because they derived their descent from the great and powerful tribe named Gāngvida, which inhabited the valley of the Ganges, as mentioned by Pliny and Ptolemy. A portion of Mysore which was peopled mostly by Vellālas was called Gangavādi in the tenth and eleventh centuries of the Christian era. Another dynasty of kings of this tribe, who ruled Orissa in the eleventh and twelfth centuries, was known as the Gangavamsa.... In the earliest Tamil grammar extant, which was composed by a Brāhman named Tholkāppiyan, in the first or second century B.C., frequent allusions are made to the Arivar or Sages. But, in the chapter in which he describes the classes of society, the author omits all mention of the Arivar, and places the Brahmins who wear the sacred thread as the first caste. The kings, he says, very guardedly, and not warriors, form the second caste, as if the three kings Chera, Chola and Pāndy could form a caste; all who live by trade belong to the third caste. He does not say that either the kings or the merchants wear the sacred thread. Then he singles out the Vellālas, and states that they have no other calling than the cultivation of the soil. Here he does not say that the Vellālas are Sudras, but indirectly implies that the ordinary Vellālas should be reckoned as Sudras, and that those Vellālas who were kings should be honoured as Kshatriyas. This is the first attempt made by the Brahmins to bring the Tamils under their caste system. But, in the absence of the Kshatriya, Vaisya, and Sudra castes in Tamilakam, they could not possibly succeed; and to this day the Vellāla does not take meals at the hands of a Padaiyadchi, who calls himself a Kshatriya, or a merchant who passes for a Vaisya." In speculating on the origin of the Vellālas, Mr. J. H. Nelson[137] states that "tradition uniformly declares them to be the descendants of foreign immigrants, who were introduced by the Pāndyas: and it appears to be extremely probable that they are, and that an extensive Vellāla immigration took place at a rather remote period, perhaps a little before or after the colonization of the Tonda-mandala by Adondai Chakravarti. The Vellālas speak a pure dialect of Tamil, and no other language. I have not heard of anything extraordinary in the customs prevailing among them, or of any peculiarities pointing to a non-Tamil origin.... With regard to the assertion so commonly made that the Pāndyas belonged to the Vellāla caste, it is observable that tradition is at issue with it, and declares that the Pāndyas proper were Kshatriyas: but they were accustomed to marry wives of inferior castes as well as and in addition to wives of their own caste; and some of their descendants born of the inferior and irregularly married wives were Vellālans, and, after the death of Kūn or Sundara Pāndya, formed a new dynasty, known as that of the pseudo-Pāndyas. Tradition also says that Arya Nāyaga Muthali, the great general of the sixteenth century, was dissuaded by his family priest from making himself a king on the ground that he was a Vellālan, and no Vellālan ought to be a king. And, looking at all the facts of the case, it is somewhat difficult to avoid coming to the conclusion that the reason assigned for his not assuming the crown was the true one. This, however, is a question, the settlement of which requires great antiquarian learning: and it must be settled hereafter."

In the Madras Census Report, 1871, the Vellālas are described as "a peace-lov-

[137] Manual of the Madura district.

ing, frugal, and industrious people, and, in the cultivation of rice, betel, tobacco, etc., have perhaps no equals in the world. They will not condescend to work of a degrading nature. Some are well educated, and employed in Government service, and as clerks, merchants, shop-keepers, etc., but the greater part of them are the peasant proprietors of the soil, and confine their attention to cultivation." In the Madura Manual, it is recorded that "most Vellālans support themselves by husbandry, which, according to native ideas, is their only proper means of livelihood. But they will not touch the plough, if they can help it, and ordinarily they do everything by means of hired servants and predial slaves. In the Sathaga of Nārāyanan may be found a description of their duties and position in society, of which the following translation appears in Taylor's work, the Oriental MSS. The Vellālans, by the effect of their ploughing (or cultivation), maintain the prayers of the Brāhmans, the strength of kings, the profits of merchants, the welfare of all. Charity, donations, the enjoyments of domestic life, and connubial happiness, homage to the gods, the Sāstras, the Vēdas, the Purānas, and all other books, truth, reputation, renown, the very being of the gods, things of good report or integrity, the good order of castes, and (manual) skill, all these things come to pass by the merit (or efficacy) of the Vellālan's plough. Those Vellālans who are not farmers, husbandmen, or gardeners, are employed in various ways more or less respectable; but none of them will condescend to do work of a degrading nature. Some of them are merchants, some shop-keepers, some Government servants, some sepoys, some domestic servants, some clerks, and so forth." In the Tanjore Manual, it is stated that "many Vellālars are found in the Government service, more especially as karnams or village accountants. As accountants they are unsurpassed, and the facility with which, in by-gone days, they used to write on cadjan or palmyra leaves with iron styles, and pick up any information on any given points from a mass of these leaves, by lamp-light no less than by daylight, was most remarkable. Running by the side of the Tahsildar's (native revenue officer) palanquin, they could write to dictation, and even make arithmetical calculations with strictest accuracy. In religious observances, they are more strict than the generality of Brāhmans; they abstain from both intoxicating liquors and flesh meat." In the Coimbatore Manual, the Vellālas are summed up as "truly the backbone of the district. It is they who, by their industry and frugality, create and develop wealth, support the administration, and find the money for imperial and district demands. As their own proverb says:—The Vellālar's goad is the ruler's sceptre. The bulk of them call themselves Goundans." In the Salem Manual, the Vellāla is described as "frugal and saving to the extreme; his hard-working wife knows no finery, and the Vellālichi, (Vellāla woman) willingly wears for the whole year the one blue cloth, which is all that the domestic economy of the house allows her. If she gets wet, it must dry on her; and, if she would wash her sole garment, half is unwrapped to be operated upon, which in its turn relieves the other half, that is then and there similarly hammered against some stone by the side of the village tank (pond), or on the bank of the neighbouring stream. Their food is the cheapest of the 'dry' grains which they happen to cultivate that year, and not even the village feasts can draw the money out of a Vellālar's clutches. It is all expended on his land, if the policy of the revenue administration of the country be liberal, and the acts of Government such as to give confidence to the ryots or husbandmen; otherwise their hoarded gains are buried. The new moon, or some high holiday, may perhaps see the head of the house enjoy a platter of rice and a little meat, but such extravagance is rare." The Vellālas are summed up by 'A Native,'[138] as being "found in almost every station of life, from the labourer in the fields to the petty zamindar (landholder); from the owner of plantations to the cooly who works at coffee-picking; from the Deputy Collector to the peon in his office." It is recorded, in the Census Report, 1871, that a Vellāla had passed the M.A. degree examination of the Madras University. The occupations of the Vellālas whom I examined in Madras were as follows:—

Cart-driver.	Cultivator.
Bricklayer.	Gardener.
Cooly.	Compositor.
Varnisher.	Railway fireman.
Painter.	Peon.
Watchman.	Student.

In an excellent summary of the Vellālas[139] Mr. W. Francis writes as follows. "By general consent, the first place in social esteem among the Tamil Sūdra castes is awarded to them. To give detailed descriptions of the varying customs of a caste which numbers, as this does, over two and a quarter millions, and is found all over the Presidency, is unnecessary, but the internal construction of the caste, its self-contained and distinct sub-divisions, and the methods by which its numbers are enhanced by accretions from other castes, are so typical of the corresponding characteristics of the Madras castes, that it seems to be worth while to set them out shortly.

"The caste is first of all split up into four main divisions, named after the tract of country in which the ancestors of each originally resided. These are (1) Tond-amandalam, or the dwellers in the Pallava country, the present Chingleput and North Arcot districts, the titles of which division are Mudali, Reddi and Nainar; (2) Sōliya (or Sōzhia), or men of the Chōla country, the Tanjore and Trichinopoly districts of the present day, the members of which are called Pillai; (3) Pāndya, the inhabitants of the Pāndyan Kingdom of Madura and Tinnevelly, which division also uses the title of Pillai; and (4) Konga, or those who resided in the Konga country, which corresponded to Coimbatore and Salem, the men of which are called Kavandans. The members of all these four main territorial divisions resemble one another in their essential customs. Marriage is either infant or adult, the Purānic wedding ceremonies are followed, and (except among the Konga Vellālas) Brāhmans officiate. They all burn their dead, observe fifteen days' pollution, and perform the karumāntaram ceremony to remove the pollution on the sixteenth day. There are no marked occupational differences amongst them, most of them being cultivators or traders. Each division contains both Vaishnavites and Saivites, and (contrary to the rule among the Brāhmans) differences of sect are not of them-

[138] Pen and Ink Sketches of South India.
[139] Madras Census Report, 1901.

selves any bar to intermarriage. Each division has Pandārams, or priests, recruited from among its members, who officiate at funerals and minor ceremonies, and some of these wear the sacred thread, while other Vellālas only wear it at funerals. All Vellālas perform sraddhas (memorial services), and observe the ceremony of invoking their ancestors on the Mahālaya days (a piece of ritual which is confined to the twice-born and the higher classes of Sūdras); all of them decline to drink alcohol or to eat in the houses of any but Brāhmans; and all of them may dine together. Yet no member of any of these four main divisions may marry into another, and, moreover, each of them is split into sub-divisions (having generally a territorial origin), the members of which again may not intermarry. Thus Tonda-mandalam are sub-divided into the Tuluvas, who are supposed to have come from the Tulu country; the Poonamallee (or Pundamalli) Vellālas, so called from the town of that name near Madras; and the Kondaikattis (those who tie their hair in a knot without shaving it). None of these three will intermarry. The Sōliya Vellālas are sub-divided into the Vellān Chettis, meaning the Vellāla merchants (who are again further split up into three or four other territorial divisions); the Kodikkāls (betel-garden), who grow the betel-vine; and the Kānakkilināttār, or inhabitants of Kānakkilinādu. These three similarly may not intermarry, but the last is such a small unit, and girls in it are getting so scarce, that its members are now going to other sub-divisions for their brides. The Pāndya Vellālas are sub-divided into the Kārkattās or Kāraikātus, who, notwithstanding the legends about their origin, are probably a territorial sub-division named from a place called Kāraikādu; the Nan-gudis and Panjais, the origin of whom is not clear; the Arumbūrs and Sirukudis, so called from villages of those names in the Pāndya country; the Agamudaiyans, who are probably recruits from the caste of that name; the Nīrpusis, meaning the wearers of the sacred ashes; and the Kōttai Vellālas or fort Vellālas. These last are a small sub-division, the members of which live in Srīvaikuntam fort (in Tinnevelly), and observe the strictest gōsha (seclusion of females). Though they are, as has been seen, a sub-division of a caste, yet their objection to marry outside their own circle is so strong that, though they are fast dying out because there are so few girls among them, they decline to go to the other sub-divisions for brides. [*See* Kōttai Vellāla.] The Kongas are sub-divided into the Sendalais (red-headed men), Paditalais (leaders of armies), Vellikkai (the silver hands), Pavalamkatti (wearers of coral), Malaiyadi (foot of the hills), Tollakādu (ears with big holes), Attangara-is (river bank), and others, the origin of none of which is clearly known, but the members of which never intermarry. In addition to all these divisions and sub-divisions of the Vellāla caste proper, there are nowadays many groups which really belong to quite distinct castes, but which call themselves Vellālas, and pretend that they belong to that caste, although in origin they had no connection with it. These nominally cannot intermarry with any of the genuine Vellālas, but the caste is so widely diffused that it cannot protect itself against these invasions, and, after a few generations, the origin of the new recruits is forgotten, and they have no difficulty in passing themselves off as real members of the community. The same thing occurs among the Nāyars in Malabar. It may be imagined what a mixture of blood arises from this practice, and how puzzling the variations in the cranial measurements of Vellālas taken at random are likely to become. Instances of members of other castes who have assumed the name and position of the Vellālas are the Vēttuva Vellālas, who are really Vēttuvans; the Pūluva Vellālas, who are only Pūluvans; the Illam Vellālas, who are Panikkans; the Karaiturai (lord of the shore) Vellālas, who are Karaiyāns; the Karukamattai (palmyra leaf-stem) Vellālas, who are Shānāns; the Gāzulu (bangle) Vellālas, who are Balijas; the Guha (Rāma's boatman) Vellālas, who are Sembadavans; and the Irkuli Vellālas, who are Vannāns. The children of dancing-girls also often call themselves Mudali, and claim in time to be Vellālas; and even Paraiyans assume the title Pillai, and trust to its eventually enabling them to pass themselves off as members of the caste." The name Acchu Vellāla has been assumed by some Karaiyans, and Pattanavans call themselves Varunakula Vellāla or Varunakula Mudali, after Varuna, the god of the waters. At times of census, many hill Malayālis return themselves as Vellālas, in accordance with their tradition that they are Vellālas who migrated to the hills. Some thieving Koravas style themselves Aghambadiar Vellāla or Pillai, and have to some extent adopted the dress and manners of the Vellālas.[140] In Travancore, to which State some Vellālas have migrated, males of the Dēva-dāsi (dancing-girl) caste sometimes call themselves Nanchinād Vellālas. There is a Tamil proverb to the effect that a Kallan may come to be a Maravan. By respectability he may develop into an Agamudaiyan, and, by slow degrees, become a Vellāla. According to another proverb, the Vellālas are compared to the brinjal (*Solanum Melongena*) fruit, which will mix palatably with anything.

The account of the divisions and sub-divisions of the Vellālas recorded above may be supplemented from various sources:—

1. Arampukutti, or Arambukatti (those who tie flower-buds). According to Mr. J. A. Boyle,[141] the name indicates Vellālas with wreaths of the aram flower, which is one of the decorations of Siva. They are, he writes, "a tribal group established in a series of villages in the Ramnad territory. The family tradition runs that they emigrated five centuries ago from the Tondamandalam, and that the migration was made in dēvendra vimānam or covered cars; and this form of vehicle is invariably used in marriage ceremonies for the conveyance of the bride and bridegroom round the village. The women never wear a cloth above the waist, but go absolutely bare on breast and shoulders. The two rivers which bound this district on the north and south are rigid limits to the travels of the women, who are on no pretext allowed to cross them. It is said that, if they make vows to the deity of a celebrated temple in Tanjore, they have to perform their pilgrimage to the temple in the most perfect secrecy, and that, if detected, they are fined. Intermarriage is prohibited 'beyond the rivers.' It is, with the men, a tradition never to eat the salt of the Sirkar (Government), or take any service under Government."

2. Chetti. The members of the Vellālan subdivision of Chetti are "said to be pure Vellālas, who have taken the title of Chetti. In ancient times, they had the prerogative of weighing the person of kings on occasion of the Tulabhāram ceremony. (*See* Tulabhāram.) They were, in fact, the trading class of the Tamil nation in the south. But, after the immigration of the more skilful Telugu Kōmatis and

---

[140] M. Paupa Rao Naidu. History of Railway Thieves, 1900.
[141] Ind. Ant. III, 1874.

other mercantile classes, the hereditary occupation of the Vellān Chettis gradually declined, and consequently they were obliged to follow different professions. The renowned poet Pattanattār is said to have belonged to this caste."[142]

3. Kāraikkāt or Kārkātta. The name is said to mean Vellālas who saved or protected the clouds, or waiters for rain. Their original profession is said to have been rain-making. Their mythological origin is as follows.

"In old times, a quarrel happened between the Rāja of Pāndya dēsa and the god Dēvendra, and things went to such lengths that the angry god commanded the clouds not to send down any rain on Pāndya dēsa, so that the inhabitants were sorely distressed by the severe drought, and laid their complaints before the Rāja, who flew into a rage, marched his army against Dēvendra, defeated him in battle, seized on the clouds and put them in prison, in consequence of which not a drop of rain fell on any part of the Bhūloka or earthly world, which threw the people into a great consternation, and the whole with one accord addressed their prayers to Dēvendra, the god of the firmament, and beseeched him to relieve them from their present distress. Dēvendra sent an ambassador to the Rāja of Pāndya dēsa, and requested that he would release the clouds, but he refused to do it unless they gave security for their future good behaviour, and likewise promise that they would never again withhold the rain from falling in due season on his kingdom. At this juncture, the Vellal caste of Pāndya dēsa became security for the clouds, and, from that circumstance, were surnamed Kārakāva Vellal Wāru, or redeemers of the clouds."[143] In an interesting account of the Kāraikat Vellālas of the Palni hills by Lieutenant Ward in 1824,[144] it is recorded that "their ceremonies, it is said, are performed by Pandārams, although Brāhmans usually officiate as priests in their temples. They associate freely with the Kunnavans, and can eat food dressed by them, as also the latter can eat food dressed by a Kārakat Vellālan. But, if a Kunnavan is invited to the house of a Kārakat Vellālan, he must not touch the cooking utensils, or enter the cooking-room. Wives are accustomed, it is supposed, to grant the last favor to their husband's relations. Adultery outside the husband's family entails expulsion from caste, but the punishment is practically not very severe, inasmuch as a Kunnavan can always be found ready to afford protection and a home to the divorcée. A man who disgraces himself by an illicit connection with a woman of a lower caste than his own is punished in a similar manner. Formerly the punishment was in either case death." It is recorded[145] that "in 1824 the Kārakat Vellālas were accustomed to purchase and keep predial slaves of the Poleiya caste, giving thirty fanams for a male, and fifty for a female. The latter was held to be the more valuable, as being likely to produce children for the benefit of her owner." It is said that, among the Kāraikkāt Vellālas, a peculiar ceremony, called vilakkidu kalyānam, or the auspicious ceremony of lighting the light, is performed for girls in the seventh or ninth year or later, but before marriage. The ceremony consists in worshipping Ganēsa and the Sun at the house of the girls' parents. Her mater-

---

[142] Madras Census Report, 1891.
[143] Baramahal Records.
[144] Manual of the Madura district.
[145] Manual of the Madura district.

nal uncle gives her a necklace of gold beads and coral, and a new cloth. All the relations, who are invited to be present, make gifts to the girl. The women of this section wear this ornament, which is called kodachimani (hooked jewel), even after marriage.

4. Kondaikatti. Said[146] to consider themselves as the highest and proudest of the Vellālas, because, during the Nabob's Government, they were employed in the public service. They are extremely strict in their customs, not allowing their women to travel by any public conveyance, and punishing adultery with the utmost severity.

Kondaikatti literally means one who ties his hair in a knob on the top of his head, but the name is sometimes derived from kondai, a crown, in connection with the following legend. A quarrel arose between the Kōmatis and Vellālas, as to which of them should be considered Vaisyas. They appeared before the king, who, being unable to decide the point at issue, gave each party five thousand rupees, and told them to return after trading for five years. The Vellālas spent one-fifth of the sum which they received in cultivating land, while the Kōmatis spent the whole sum in trading. At the end of the allotted time, the Vellālas had a bumper crop of sugar-cane, and all the canes contained pearls. The Kōmatis showed only a small profit. The king was so pleased with the Vellālas, that he bestowed on them the right to crown kings.

5. Kumbakōnam. Vellālas, who migrated from Kumbakōnam in the Tanjore district to Travancore.

6. Kummidichatti. Recorded, in the Manual of the North Arcot district, as a sub-division, regarded as low in position, which carried the pot (chatti) of fire at Vellāla funerals. It is said that, in default of Kummidichattis, ordinary Vellālas now have to carry their own fire at funerals.

7. Nangudi or Savalai Pillaimar. (*See* Nangudi.)

8. Tendisai (southern country). They are found in the Coimbatore district, and it has been suggested that they are only a branch of the Konga Vellālas.

9. Tenkānchi. Vellālas, who migrated from Tenkāsi in the Tinnevelly district to Travancore. (*See* Todupuzha Vellāla.)

10. Tuluva. Immigrants from the Tulu country, a part of the modern district of South Canara. Mr. Nelson[147] is of opinion that these are the original Vellālas, who were invited to Tondamandalam after its conquest by the Chōla King Adondai Chakravarti. They are now found in all the Tamil districts, but are most numerous in North and South Arcot and Chingleput. It is noted, in Carr's "Descriptive and historical papers relating to the Seven Pagodas," that "Adondai chiefly distinguished Kānchīpuram (Conjeeveram) and Tripati as his place of residence or capital. The era of Adondai is not higher up than the seventh century of our reckoning. He is said to have brought the Brāhmans from Srī Sailam in Telingāna, and certainly attracted a large colony of Sūdra Vellālas, or agriculturists, from Tuluva

[146] Manual of the North Arcot district.
[147] Manual of the Madura district.

or northern Canara." At Conjeeveram, there are a Nāttar and a Dēsayi, whose authority, in olden times, extended over the whole Presidency. The Nāttar must be a Tuluva Vellāla, and the Dēsai a Ralla Balija. The two offices conjointly are known as the Nādu Dēsam. The authority of these officers has in great measure ceased, but some still go to the Nādu Dēsam for appeal. For purposes of caste organisation, Conjeeveram is regarded as the head-quarters. All sections of the Tondamandalam Vellālas are divided into twenty-four kōttams and seventy-nine nādus. The latter are subject to the former.

The following legendary account of the Tondamandalam Vellālas is given in the Baramahal Records. "During the reign of a certain Rāja of Chōladēsa, a kingdom supposed to have comprised the present provinces south of the river Kāvēri, the countries between the Kistna and Kāvēri were quite a wilderness, in which many families of the Kurbavar caste or shepherds resided here and there in villages surrounded by mud walls. On a time, the Rāja came forth into the wilds to take the diversion of hunting, and, in traversing the woods, he came to a place in the vicinity of the present town of Conjeeveram in the Kingdom of Arcot, where he met with a Naga Kanya or celestial nymph, fell in love with her, and asked her to yield to his embraces. She replied, 'If I consent to your proposal, and bear you a son, will you make him your successor in the kingdom?' He rejoined 'I will,' and she asked him who should witness his promise. He answered 'the earth and sky,' but she said that two witnesses were not sufficient, and that there must be a third. There happened to be a tree called adhonda near them, and the Rāja replied 'Let the fruit of this adhonda tree be the third witness.' When she was satisfied respecting the witnesses, she granted the Rāja his desires, and, after he had remained with her a short time, he took his leave, and returned to his metropolis, and, in a little while, abdicated his throne in favour of his eldest son, who managed the affairs of the kingdom. To return to the Naga Kanya, she conceived and brought forth a son, who remained with her three or four years, and then visited the different Rishis or hermits who resided in the forest, and learnt from them to use the sword, the bow and arrow, and the art of war, and obtained from them a knowledge of the whole circle of sciences. By this time he had attained the age of sixteen years, and, coming to his mother, he requested her to tell him who was his father. She answered 'Thy father is the Chōla Rāja.' He replied 'I will go to him, but who is to bear witness to the truth of your assertion?' She rejoined 'The earth, sky, and the fruit of the adhonda tree are witness to what I have told you.' The son plucked one of the berries of the adhonda tree, hung it by a string to his neck, took his sword and other weapons, and set out for his father's capital. He one day took an opportunity of accompanying some of the nobles to the darbar, and called out to the old Rāja 'Behold your son.' The Rāja replied 'I know nothing of thee;' upon which the young man repeated everything which his mother had told him, but it had no effect on the Rāja. When the son found that his father was determined not to acknowledge him he challenged him to single combat, but the Rāja, not thinking it proper to accept a challenge from a rash youth, demanded if he had any witnesses to prove his claim. He answered 'The earth and sky, and the fruit of the adhonda tree, which I wear suspended from my neck, are witnesses to the truth of my assertion.' This circumstance brought the old occurrence to the Rāja's recollection, and he owned his son, and told him that, as he had already abdicated the throne, he trusted he would not insist upon the fulfilling of the promise which had been made to his mother, but consent to live in a private station under the dominion of his elder half-brother. The young man nobly replied 'I with pleasure waive the performance of your promise, but point out to me your enemy, and assist me with some troops, and I will conquer a kingdom for myself.' The Rāja gave him an army, and directed him to subdue the Kurubavāru or shepherds, to clear the woods, and to form himself a kingdom between the rivers Kistna and Kāvēri. He accordingly advanced into the wilderness, and, without meeting much opposition, soon subjected the Kurubavāru, who, knowing nothing of cultivation or sinking of tanks or watering the country from the rivers, and the conqueror wishing to introduce agriculture among them, he was obliged to repair to his father, and make known his difficulties. The Rāja was much pleased with the enterprising spirit of his son, conferred on him the title of Adhonda Chakra, wrote and permitted him to take with him such of the Vellāla caste as chose to emigrate. The young Rāja held out great encouragement, and got a number of adventurers of that caste to accompany him back, to whom he gave large grants of waste land, and told them to pitch upon such spots of ground as met with their approbation, and they fixed upon the forts, districts, and villages belonging to the Kurubavāru caste, which consisted of twenty-four forts, eighty-one districts, and one thousand and nine hundred villages. This country was formerly named Dandaka Aranya. Dandaka is the name of a famous Rakshasa or Giant, who is mentioned in the Rāmāyana, and Aranya signifies a wilderness. It was also called Dhuntra Nādu, or the middle country, and the new Rāja named it Dhanda Mandalam, or country of the tree dhonda, alluding to the fruit of the adhonda or dhonda tree, which bore testimony to his descent. The emigrants of the Vellāla caste surnamed themselves Dhonda Mandala Vellāla vāru, and are now corruptly called Tondamandala Vellāla vāru."

VELLĀLAS WORSHIPPING LINGAM, SNAKE-STONES AND GANĒSA.

In connection with the sub-divisions of the Vellālas, Mr. Hemingway, in a note on the Vellālas of the Trichinopoly district, gives some still further information. "The Kondaikattis are so-called from the peculiar way in which they used to wear their hair—a custom no longer observed. They are split into two sections, called Mēlnādu and Kīlnādu (westerns and easterns). The Dakshināttāns (south country men) are immigrants from Tinnevelly. The members of the Kāraikkāttar sub-division in the Udaiyarpālaiyam tāluk are rather looked down on by other Vellālans as being a mixed race, and are also somewhat contemptuously called Yeruttu-māttu (pack-bullocks), because, in their professional calling, they formerly used pack-bullocks. They have a curious custom by which a girl's maternal uncle ties a tāli (marriage badge) round her neck when she is seven or eight years old. The Panjukkāra Chettis live in the Udaiyarpālaiyam tāluk. The name is an occupational one, and denotes cotton-men, but they are not at the present day connected with the cotton trade. The Sōlapūram (or Chōlapūram) Chettis are apparently called after the village of that name in the Kumbakonam tāluk of Tanjore. The Sōlias (or Chōlias) are numerous and ubiquitous. They are generally regarded as of doubtful descent, since *parvenus*, who wish to be considered Vellālans, usually claim to belong to this sub-division. The more respectable Pandārams, the Thambirans who own temples and matams, and the Oduvar or Ādi Saivāl, belong to the Sōzhia section. The Uttunāttu sub-division is local in origin. Its head-quarters is the country round Uttatūr. The members thereof are the special devotees of the Siva of that place. The Arunāttus (six nādus) are also called Mottai (shaved) Vellālans, apparently because they always shave their moustache, and wear only a very small kudumi (hair-knot). Some of their customs are unlike those of the rest of the caste. They have exogamous septs, their widows always dress in white and wear no ornaments (a rule not universally observed in any other sub-division), they never marry their sister's daughter, and their wives wear the tāli (marriage badge), like the Panta Reddis, on a golden thread. Of their six nādus, three of which are supposed to have been located on each side of the Aiyār river, only two are now recognised. These are the Sērkudi nādu in Nāmakkal tāluk and the Omandūr nādu of Musiri. The Yēlūr (seven villages) Vellālas are very few and far between. There is a small colony of Tuluvas, engaged in dyeing, at Illuppūr. The Malaikandas are only found near the Ratnagiri hill in the Kulittalai tāluk. They take their name from the fact that they are required to look at the Ratnagiri hill when they get up in the morning. They are devotees of the god there. The Kāni-yālans (landowners) are scarce, but widely distributed, since the man who carries the pot of blood, when animals are sacrificed at festivals to the village goddesses, must belong to this sub-division. The Kodikkal Vellālans are so-called from their occupation of betel cultivation, which they still pursue largely."

The Konga Vellālas differ so strikingly from the rest in many of their customs that a separate account of them is given. (*See* Konga Vellāla.)

It is noted by Mr. Hemingway that some Vellālas "observe a curious custom (derived from Brāhmans) with regard to marriage, which is not unknown among other communities. A man marrying a second wife after the death of his first has to marry a plantain tree, and cut it down before tying the tāli, and, in the case of a third marriage, a man has to tie a tāli first to the erukkan (arka: *Calotropis gigantea*) plant. The idea is that second and fourth wives do not prosper, and the tree and the plant are accordingly made to take their places."

A peculiar ceremony, called Sevvai (Tuesday) Pillayar, is performed by some

Vellāla women. It is also called Avvai Nonbu, because the Tamil poetess observed it. The ceremony takes place twice in the year, on a Tuesday in the months of Thai (February-March) and Audi (August-September). It is held at midnight, and no males, even babies in arms, may be present at it, or eat the cakes which are offered. A certain number of women club together, and provide the necessary rice, which is measured on the back of the hand, or in a measure similar to those used by Madras milk-sellers, in which the bottom is fixed high up in the cylinder. At the house where the ceremony is to be performed the rice is pounded into flour, and mixed with leaves of *Pongamia glabra* and margosa (*Melia Azadirachta*). The mixture is then made into cakes, some flat, and some conical, to represent Pillayar (Ganēsa). Flowers, fruits, betel, turmeric, combs, kunkumam (red powder), and other articles required in connection with the Pillayar worship, are also taken to the room in which the rites are performed. Of these it has been impossible to gather an account, as the women refused to describe them, lest ruin should fall on their families. Some say that, during the ceremony, the women are stark-naked.

In an account of an annual ceremony at Trichinopoly in connection with the festival of Kulumai Amman, who is the guardian deity against epidemics, Bishop Whitehead records[148] that "a very fat pujāri (priest) of the Vellāla caste is lifted up above the vast crowd on the arms of two men. Some two thousand kids are then sacrificed, one after the other. The blood of the first eight or nine is collected in a large silver vessel holding about a quart, and handed up to the pujāri, who drinks it. Then, as the throat of each kid is cut, the animal is handed up to him, and he sucks, or pretends to suck the blood out of the carcase."

Of proverbs relating to the Vellālas, the following may be cited:—

Agriculture is no agriculture, unless it is performed by the Vellālas.

The Vellāla ruined himself by gaudy dress; the courtesan ruined herself by coquetry and affectation.

Of all the sections of the Sūdras, the Vellāla is foremost; and, of all the thefts committed in the world, those of the Kallans are most notorious.

Though you may face an evil star, never oppose a Vellāla.

Though apparently the Vellāla will not ruin you, the palm leaf, on which he writes about you, will certainly ruin you for ever.

In the Madras Census Report, 1891, Vellāla is recorded as a caste of Jains. In this connection, it is noted by Mr. Hemingway that the Naināns or Nāyinārs (*q.v.*) and the Kāraikkāttans of the Udaiyarpālaiyam tāluk are thought to be descended from Jains who were converted to the Hindu faith.

Vellān Chetti.—A name, denoting Vellāla merchant, taken by some Vellālas.

Velli (silver).—*See* Belli.

Velnāti.—A sub-division of Kāpu, named after the old Velnādu division of the Telugu country.

Veloma.—Defined as "one of the two classes of Sūdras, viz., Anuloma and

[148] Madras Museum Bull., V. 3, 1907.

Veloma. The term Veloma is applied to those born of a lower caste male and higher caste female."

Veluttēdan.—The Veluttēdan is defined in the Madras Census Report, 1891, as "the washerman of the Nāyars and higher castes in Malabar. He calls himself a Nāyar, and, in many cases, was returned as of that main caste, but these have been separated in abstraction. The caste is called Vannattān in North Malabar. The Veluttēdans follow the marumakkatāyam law of inheritance in the north, and makkatāyam in the south. They have tāli-kettu and sambandham separately. Their dress and habits are the same as those of Nāyars." In the Madras Census Report, 1901, Bannata is given as a Canarese synonym for the caste name. In the Travancore and Cochin Census Reports, 1901, Veluttētan and Veluthēdan are given respectively as an occupational title and sub-division of Nāyars.

For the following note on the Veluttēdans of Travancore, I am indebted to Mr. N. Subramani Aiyar. The name is believed to signify a place where clothes are bleached. In the early Settlement Records the designation recorded is Ayavu, in all probability an old synonym for washing. The South Travancore Veluttēdans are said to be divided into two endogamous septs, Paravūr and Attingal, with four exogamous septs in each; but these distinctions may be said to have now lost their vigour and force. There is a current tradition that once upon a time a Brāhman was washing cloths for a friend, and was on that account thrown out of caste by Parasurāma. The occupation of the Veluttēdans is washing cloths for all high-caste Hindus down to the Sūdras, in which profession, for neatness and purity at any rate, if not for promptitude, they stand above the Vannāns and Chayakkārans of the east coast, both of whom have now entered the field in competition with them, and, at least in the most civilised parts of the State, not entirely without success. In no case do the castemen receive cloths from classes lower in social rank than the Sūdras, and this is pointed to with pride as one of the causes which keep them in their present elevated scale. It need hardly be said that, in their traditional occupation, the Veluttēdans are largely and materially assisted by their females, the Veluttēdathis. They do not live in a group together, but are conveniently scattered about, so as to avoid competition one with another. Their main profession is, in many cases, supplemented by agriculture. There are absolutely no educated men among them, and, as long as machine-laundries are not introduced into the country, they have no reason to abandon the profession of their forefathers in pursuit of alien ones. In the matter of food and drink, as also in their dress and ornaments, they resemble the Nāyars. Clothes, it may be mentioned, are never bought by Veluttēdans, as they are always in possession, though temporarily, of other peoples' apparel. Tattooing prevails only in South Travancore. They cannot enter Brāhmanical shrines, but are permitted to stand outside the talakkal or stone-paved walk round the inner sanctuary, by which the image is taken in daily procession. Besides standing here and worshipping the higher Hindu deities, they also engage in the propitiation of the minor village deities. There are two headmen in each village, who punish social delinquents, and preside over caste ceremonials. On the twenty-eighth day after the birth of a child, the name-giving ceremony is performed, and a thread is tied round the infant's neck. Those who can afford it celebrate the first food-giving. The tāli-tying and sambandham ceremonies are performed separately, just like Nāyars. The former is known as muhurtham or auspicious occasion. The marriage badge is called unta minnu or puliyilla minnu. The details of the marriage ceremony do not differ from those of the Nāyars. The ayani unu, bhūtakkalam, appam poli, and avaltitti are all important items, and, at least in South Travancore, seldom failed to be gone through. In poor families the mother, without any formal ceremonial, ties the tāli of the girl before she is twelve years old, after an oblation of cooked food to the rising sun. This is called Bhagavan tāli, or god's marriage ornament. Freedom of divorce and remarriage exist. The pulikuti (tamarind) is an indispensable ceremonial, to be gone through by a pregnant woman. Inheritance devolves in the female line (marumakkattāyam). The clothes washed by Veluttēdans are used by Nambūtiri Brāhmans, without previous washing as on the east coast, for all religious purposes; and clothes polluted by a member of a low caste are purified by the Veluttēdan sprinkling ashes and water over them.

Vēmu (margosa or nīm: *Melia Azadirachta*).—An exogamous sept of Mūka Dora.

Vēngai Puli (cruel-handed tiger).—An exogamous section of Kallan.

Veralu Ichē Kāpulu or Vēlu Ichē Kāpulu (those who dedicate their fingers).—*See* Morasu.

Vēshya (Sansk: Bēshya).—A name denoting prostitute, applied to dancing-girls.

Vētagiri.—A Tamil class found in the Chingleput district. The members thereof are employed in hunting, cultivation, and the manufacture of wild date baskets. Their title is Nāyakan.

Vettaikāran (hunter).—An occupational name of Bōyas, Irulas, and Koravas, returned at times of census.

Vettile (betel vine: *Piper Betle*).—A kothu or tree of Kondaiyamkotti Maravans.

Vettiyān.—Vettiyān is the name applied to one of the officials of a Tamil Paraiyan settlement, who is also called Tōti or Thōtti. The former title is said to be more respectful as an appellation than the latter, but this is a distinction without a difference.[149] The name Vettiyān is said to be equivalent to Bittiyān (bitti, for nothing), or one who does service, *e.g.*, collecting grass, firewood, etc., without remuneration. Tōti is derived from thott, to go round, as he is the purveyor of news, and has to summon people to appear before the village tribunal, or from tondu, to dig.

The duties of the Vettiyān are multifarious. He it is who goes round the rice fields, and diverts the water-courses to the various fields, according to the rights of the ryots (agriculturists). The Vettiyān beats the drum for public notices and ceremonies. As a servant of Government, he has to carry the revenue which has been collected to the treasury. He is sometimes entrusted with large sums of money, and has never been known to abscond with it. It is said that the Village Munsiff will trust the Vettiyān, but not the Taliāri, who is never sent alone with money.

[149] Manual of the Salem district, 1883.

The Vettiyān is in charge of the burial ground, and those who repair thither have to pay him for his services. He is also the grave-digger, and officiates when a Paraiyan corpse is burnt or buried. Hence the Tamil proverb against meddling in what ought to be left to some one else:—"Let the Vettiyān and corpse struggle together." At a Paraiyan funeral, the Vettiyān, in some places, carries the pot of fire to the grave. To bring down rain, some of the lower classes, instead of addressing their prayers to the rain-god Varuna, try to induce a spirit or dēvata named Kodumpāvi (wicked one) to send her paramour Sukra to the affected area. The belief seems to be that Sukra goes away to his concubine for about six months, and, if he does not return, drought ensues. The ceremony consists in making a huge figure of Kodumpāvi in clay, which is placed on a cart, and dragged through the streets for seven to ten days. On the last day, the final death ceremonies of the figure are celebrated. It is disfigured, especially in those parts which are usually concealed. Vettiyāns, who have been shaved, accompany the figure, and perform the funeral ceremonies. This procedure is believed to put Kodumpāvi to shame, and to get her to induce Sukra to return and stay the drought.

At Paraiyan marriages certain pots are worshipped, and it is, in some places, the Vettiyān who says "The sun, the moon, the pots, and the owner of the girl have come to the marriage booth. So make haste, and fill the pots with water."

The office of the Vettiyān village official is hereditary, and the holder of it is entitled to some respect among his brethren, and to certain emoluments in kind, *e.g.*, grain at the harvest season. There is a proverb that "whatever may be the wealth of the lord who comes to rule over him, his duty of supplying him with a bundle of grass is not to cease." This relates to the demands which were, and perhaps are still, made on him in rural parts of the country. In some places, lands, called Vettiyān Māniyam, are given rent-free to Vettiyāns.

The Vettiyān is said to possess the right of removing dead cattle from villages, and in return to supply leather for agricultural purposes. He is further said to make drum heads and tom-toms from raw hides.[150]

The Vettiyāns belong to the right-hand section during disputes between the right and left hand factions.

Vēttuvan.—The Tamil Vēttuvans are described, in the Madras Census Report, 1901, as "an agricultural and hunting caste, found mainly in Salem, Coimbatore, and Madura. The name means 'a hunter.' They are probably of the same stock as the Vēdans, though the exact connection is not clear, but they now consider themselves superior to that caste, and are even taking to calling themselves Vēttuva Vellālas. Tradition says that the Konga kings invited Vēttuvans from the Chōla and Pāndya countries to assist them against the Kēralas. Another story says that the caste helped the Chōla king Aditya Varma to conquer the Kongu country during the latter part of the ninth century. In paragraph 538 of the Census Report, 1891, reference is made to the belief that the Vēdans are identical with the Veddahs of Ceylon. In connection with this supposition, it is reported that the Vēttuvans worship a goddess called Kandi-Amman, which may possibly mean 'the

---

[150] A. Chatterton. Monograph on Tanning and Working in Leather, 1904.

goddess of Kandy' (in Ceylon). Of the endogamous sections into which the caste is divided, the most numerically important are Venganchi, Kilangu (root), Pasari, Viragu (firewood), Pannādai (sheath of the cocoanut leaf), and Villi (bow). They have their own barbers, who seem also to form a separate sub-division, and are called Vēttuva Ambattans or Nāvidans, both of which words mean barber. They are said to refuse to serve any one lower than a Konga Vellāla. Nominally they are Hindus, but they are said to worship the seven Kannimars, or aboriginal goddesses, to whom the Irulas also pay homage. They eat meat and drink alcohol, though some of those who are endeavouring to increase their social repute are taking to vegetarianism. Widow marriage is forbidden. They either burn or bury the dead, but no ceremonies are performed for deceased ancestors. Their customs are thus a curious mixture of those followed by high castes and low ones. Their ordinary title is Kavandan."

Of the Malayālam Vēttuvans, who live in Malabar and the southern portion of the South Canara district, it is recorded, in the Madras Census Report, 1901, that they are "agricultural serfs, shikāris (hunters), and collectors of forest produce, who live in the Malabar jungles. They have two endogamous sub-divisions, called Kodi and Peringala. The former keep their hair long, and their women wear a cloth. The latter have top-knots, and their women dress in leaves, which they wear only round their waists, and renew daily. The latter are an unclean set of people, who live in rude bamboo and reed huts, and will eat anything down to carrion. Yet they consider themselves superior to Cherumans and Pulaiyans, and are careful not to be polluted by them. This same name is also borne by a class of masons and salt-workers in the low country in Malabar."

The Malabar Vēttuvans are said to have a fantastic legend, showing that they were not originally as low as they are at the present day in the social scale. "It is related that one of their tribe went and asked a high-caste Nāyar to give him a daughter in marriage. The Nāyar offered to do so on condition that the whole tribe would come to his place and dance on berries, each one who fell to be shot with arrows. The tribe foolishly agreed to the condition, and went and danced, with the result that, as each one tripped and fell, he or she was mercilessly shot dead with arrows. A little girl who survived this treatment was secretly rescued, and taken away by a compassionate Nāyar, who married her into his family. From this union, the present day Vēttuvans affirm their origin is to be traced. Up to this day they hold the caste of that particular Nāyar in very great veneration."[151] The costume of these Vēttuvans has been described as follows.[152] "The men wear a short loin-cloth, secured round the waist by a belt which is also used as a sling during hunting expeditions. They also wear brass ear-rings, and grow a bit of moustache, and a little stumpy beard. The dress of the women consists of three clusters of long leaves, suspended from the waist and tied on by a cheap girdle. According to a tribal legend, when, in the morning of time, costumes were being distributed by the deity to the various races of the earth, the Vettuva women, being asked to choose between a costume which needed to be changed daily, and one

[151] Madras Mail, 1907.
[152] *Ibid.*

which needed to be changed only yearly, readily expressed a preference for the former, and the deity, considering this an unpardonable piece of vanity, decreed that thenceforth the women should dress in leaves gathered fresh every morning. Whenever it is suggested to them that they should adopt some more lasting apparel, the Vettuva women answer that they are carrying out the mandate of the deity, and can abandon their present dress only if the deity appears in person, and sanctions a change."

On the occasion of a recent visit of the Governor of Madras to South Canara, a party of Vēttuvans was paraded before him. One of the men was wearing an aluminium coronation medal, and, on being asked by the Collector who had given it to him, he folded his arms obsequiously, and replied 'My Tamburan' (landlord).

In a recent note on the leaf-wearing Vēttuvans, it is stated that "they believe that the sun travels, after it has set, through a hole in the bowels of the earth, and emerges at morning in the east. The way they calculate time is interesting. A Vēttuvan says that his children were born when his master sowed paddy (rice) on such and such hills. They are a very truthful lot, of good moral character, the chastity of their womankind being held very sacred."

The Malabar Vēttuvans are summed up by Mr. T. K. Gopal Panikkar[153] as being "not exactly slaves, but their social position justifies their classification amongst the slave races. They live on the cocoanut plantations of the Nairs, and other well-to-do classes. They lead a hand-to-hand existence on the wages which they obtain for hedging and fencing cocoanut plantations, plucking cocoanuts, tilling, and other allied work. They live, with their wives and children, and sometimes other relations as well, in houses small but more decent-looking than the mere huts of the other lower classes. In point of caste restrictions they are certainly better circumstanced; and their daily contact with the higher classes in the ordinary concerns of life affords them greater facilities for increased knowledge and civilisation than their brother citizens of the slave races enjoy. They are much addicted to toddy-drinking, but their principal food is rice. Their condition is never so intolerably wretched as that of the other classes. They are sometimes employed by cultivators for agricultural purposes. Their females occupy themselves in the fields during the harvest season, but they also make thatch for houses of cocoanut leaves woven after a set model during the thatching season about December or January. Their males wear ear-rings of brass, and their females adorn themselves with nose, finger, and neck ornaments of brass or beads. The one piece of cloth supplied annually by the masters, to whose plantations they are attached, forms the dress both for males and females, which they tie round their waists. They do not eat carrion, but are exceedingly fond of fish, the flesh of the civet, and the rat, and of some other animals not generally eaten by other classes. They observe death pollution like the higher classes of Malabar, and the period of observance varies according to the particular class or caste, to which their masters belong. For instance, if they belong to a Nair's plantation, such period is fifteen days, and, if to a Brahmin's, it is ten days; Nairs and Brahmins observing pollution for these periods respectively. The priests who officiate at their ceremonials are selected

[153] Malabar and its Folk, 1900.

from among their own tribesmen or Enangers, whose express recognition is necessary to give validity to the performance of the ceremony. Their marriage customs are very like those of the Tiyyars, excepting that the feasting and revelry are not so pompous in their case. Like the Nairs, they retain the front knot. The only offences of general occurrence among them are petty cases of theft of cocoanuts, plantains, areca nuts, and roots of common occurrence. The Vettuvans believe in a Supreme Creator, whom they name and invoke as Paduchathampuram, *i.e.*, the king who created us. Likewise, they believe in certain evil deities, to whom they make offerings at particular times of the year. They are not, like the other classes, distinguished by loyalty to their masters, but are a very ungrateful sect, and their very name, viz., Nambu Vettuvan, has passed into a bye-word for ingratitude of all kinds."

It is recorded, in the Gazetteer of Malabar, that "the Vēttuvans of Chirakkal taluk are a low caste of jungle cultivators and basket makers, distinguished by the survival amongst their women of the custom of dressing in leaves, their only clothing being a kind of double fan-shaped apron of leaves tied round the waist with a rolled cloth. They live in huts made of split bamboo and thatched with elephant grass, called kudumbus. The Vēttuvans are divided into fourteen illams, which seem to be named after the house names of the janmis (landlords) whom they serve. Their headmen, who are appointed by their janmis, are called Kirān, or sometimes Parakutti (drummer). Amongst the Vēttuvans, when labour begins, the woman is put in a hole dug in a corner of the hut, and left there alone with some water till the cry of the child is heard." For the following note on the Vēttuvans of the Cochin State, I am indebted to Mr. L. K. Anantha Krishna Aiyar.[154]

"The Vettuvans are also called Vettuva Pulayas. They are pure agricultural labourers, taking part in every kind of work connected with agriculture, such as ploughing, sowing, weeding, transplanting, pumping water, and reaping. They are more day labourers. The males get two edangazhis of paddy (hardly worth 2 annas), and the females an edangazhi and a half. In times of scarcity, they find it difficult to support themselves.

"When an unmarried woman becomes pregnant, her parents, as soon as they become aware of the fact, inform their local headman (Kanakkan or Kuruppan), who convenes a meeting of the elderly members of the community for the purpose of summoning the secret lover, and prosecuting the necessary enquiries. In the event of the confession of the charge, he is asked to marry her. The matter does not end there. They go to the local Thandan, and relate to him the incident, who thereupon gives him water in a vessel (kindi vellam). The woman is asked to drink this as well as some cow-dunged water, and is then made to let flow a few drops of blood from the body. After this he says 'dhosham thirnu' (free from guilt). Should, however, the lover be unwilling to marry her, he is thrashed and placed under a ban. If they are related to each other, they are both turned out of caste. The woman who is freed from guilt can marry again. The Thandan gets as his perquisite four annas out of the fine imposed, four packets of betel leaf, eight areca nuts, and three tobacco leaves. Their headman also has a share of the fine, etc. The balance which

[154] Monograph, Ethnological Survey of Cochin, 1905.

then remains is spent on toddy, and beaten rice for those assembled.

VĒTTUVANS.

"The Vettuvans profess the lower forms of Hinduism. Their chief gods are Chevva, Chathan, Karinkutti, Parakutti, Kappiri and Kandakaranan, and also Namburi Thamburan. They give regular offerings to them, lest the gods should become angry, and cause serious calamities to the members of their families. Images of gods are made of bell-metal, and worshipped in their huts. The deceased ancestors are also worshipped as gods, to whom are given a different kind of offerings. Toddy is an indispensable item in their offerings to them. In Ooragam and its neighbourhood, when I took my notes on the Vettuvans, I was told that there was no tree-tapping, and that toddy brought to them for sale was largely adulterated with water, and very costly. Their gods were very angry, for they were not satisfied with it. They caused fever, deafness, blindness, and other disorders. They worship Kāli also. Kumbhom Bharani is an important festival to them. On the morning of this day, tunes are played in honour of the goddess. There are special songs called Thottampattu. Sacrifices are offered to the deity very early. A pūja (worship) is also performed for the sword, anklets, and bells worn round the loins, all placed in front of the deity, and songs are again sung. One of them turns a Velichchapād (oracle), who speaks as if by inspiration. Wearing the above ornaments, they go to a temple, in front of which they empty out on a mat a few paras of paddy, and again play and sing.

"The funeral ceremonies of the Vettuvans are somewhat elaborate. When a member of the caste breathes his last, his relations, friends, and other castemen of the kara (settlement) are all informed of the event. They attend, and take part in the obsequies. The dead body is bathed, and dressed in a piece of new cloth. Some gold, rubbed on a stone in water, is poured into his mouth by his sons and daughters. Karuvanguka, or Gurutvam Vanguka, is an important ceremony performed by his sons and daughters. It consists in taking sixteen small bits of plantain leaves, with some rice on each, and placing them on the forehead, neck, chest, loins, thighs, hands, legs, feet, etc., washing the last two, and collecting the water, which is taken in by the members junior to him in the family. After this, the dead body is placed on the bier, which is carried by four persons to the grave. The nearest relatives of the family, four in number, called Bhedakars, with a mundu (cloth) tied round their heads, walk in front of the procession. The grave is dug, and a new cloth is spread, and the corpse laid on it. It is filled in with layers of earth and stones, to prevent dogs and jackals from disturbing the dead body. All those who have accompanied the chief mourner bathe, and return home. The members of the family fast for the night. The eldest son, who is the chief mourner, bathes in the early morning, and offers the pinda bali (offering of rice) to the spirit of the departed for fifteen days. On the seventh day, the chief mourner, and the Enangan, go to the graveyard, and level the slightly raised part of the grave. A piece of stone, kept near the foot, is taken, and placed on a leaf. Some toddy, arrack (alcoholic liquor) and water of the tender cocoanut, are poured over it as offerings. By some magic, the spirit is supposed to be living in it. It is brought home, and placed in a cocoanut shell containing oil mixed with turmeric, and kept outside the hut until the pollution is over. The pollution lasts for fifteen days, and on the night of the fifteenth day they fast. On the morning of the sixteenth day, all the castemen of the kara who are invited bring with them rice, curry-stuffs, and toddy. Rubbing themselves with oil, they all go to bathe, after which the Enangan sprinkles cowdunged water, to show that they are freed from pollution. The stone is also purified by a dip in water, and then brought home. Those who have assembled are fed, and then depart. The chief mourner, who has to perform the diksha, does not shave for a year, bathes in the early morning, and offers the bali before going to work. This he continues for a year, at the end of which he gets himself shaved, and celebrates a feast called masam in honour of the departed. The stone, representing the deceased, is placed on a seat in a conspicuous part of the hut. An image of wood or copper sometimes takes its place. It is thenceforward worshipped, and believed to watch over the welfare of the family. Regular offerings are given to it on Karkadagom and Thulam Sankranthi, Ōnam, Vishu, and the festival day of the local temple.

"The castes below the Vettuvans are Pulayan, Nayādi, and Ullatan. They consider themselves superior to Pulayas, and are careful not to be polluted by them. A Vettuvan who is polluted by a Nayādi or Ulladan fasts for seven days, subsisting on water, tender cocoanuts, and toddy. On the eighth day he bathes, and takes his regular meals. As the Vettuvans are Chandalars, any distance less than sixty-four feet will pollute the higher castes. They stand at a distance of twenty-four feet from Kammālar. Nayādis and Ullatans stand far from them. Owing to their disabilities and low wages, many turn either Christians or Muhammadans, and work for wages of two and a half to three annas a day."

There is a class of people in Malabar called Vettan or Vettuvan, which must not be confused with the jungle Vēttuvan. These people were, it is said,[155] "once salt-makers, and are now masons, earth-workers, and quarrymen. They are said to be divided into two classes, the marumakkattāyam (with inheritance in the female line) regarded as indigenous to Malabar, and the makkattāyam (with inheritance from father to son), said to be immigrants from the south."

Vibhāka Gunta.—Recorded in the Madras Census Report as "a low class of wandering beggars; clubbed with Māla." Some Mālas in the Vizagapatam district possess gunta mānyams, or petty fields, and supplement their income by begging.

Vignēsvara.—A synonym for the elephant god Ganēsa, which occurs as a gōtra of Nagarālu. The equivalent Vināyaka is a gōtra of Mēdara.

Vilkurup.—The Vilkuruppu or Vilkollakuruppu are the priests and barbers of the Malayālam Kammālans, and also makers of umbrellas and bows (vil) and arrows. In former times they supplied the latter articles for the Malabar Infantry. Malabar and Travancore are, par excellence, the home of the palm-leaf umbrella, which still holds its own against umbrellas of European manufacture, which were, in 1904–1905, imported into India to the value of Rs. 18,95,064. A native policeman, protecting himself from the sun with a long-handled palm umbrella, is a common object in towns and villages on the west coast.

Concerning the Vilkurups of the Cochin State, Mr. L. K. Anantha Krishna Aiyar writes as follows.[156] "In former times, their occupations were training low caste men to arms and athletic feats, to use sticks in fighting, and also to the use of bows and arrows, and pial school teaching. In these days of civilisation, their services are no longer required for these purposes, and they are employed in shampooing, umbrella making, and quarrying laterite stones for building purposes. In Nāyar families, during tāli-tying ceremonies, they have to give a bow and a few

---

[155] Gazetteer of Malabar.
[156] Monograph, Eth. Survey of Cochin.

arrows. During the Ōnam festival also, they have to give a bow and arrows to every Nāyar house, for which they get some paddy (rice), curry stuffs, a cocoanut, and some oil. When they are called in for shampooing, three oils are well boiled, and cooled. The patient lies on a plank, oil is poured over him, and every part of his body is well shampooed, and afterwards he is bathed in water boiled with medicinal herbs. The Vilkurups eat at the hands of Brāhmans, Nāyars, Izhuvans, and Kammālans, but abstain from taking the food of barbers, washermen, Pānāns, Kaniyans, and other low castes. They have to stand at a distance of thirty-two feet from Brāhmans and Nāyars. Pulayans and Parayans have to stand at a great distance. They live in localities occupied by the Izhuvans. They cannot approach the Brāhman temples, but have to stand far away from the outer wall. They are their own barbers and washermen."

Villasan (bowmen).—A synonym of Malayalām Kammālans, who formerly had to supply bows and arrows for the Travancore army.

Villi.—Villi (bow) or Villiyan (bowmen) has been recorded as a synonym of the Irulas of Chingleput. Villi also occurs as a sub-division of Vēttuvan, a hunting caste of the Tamil country.

Villu Vēdan (huntsmen using bows).—A synonym of Eravallar.

Vīlyakāra.—Recorded, in the Madras Census Report, 1901, as "a sub-caste of Sērvēgāra or Kōtēgāra." Vīlyakāra, Vālēkāra and Olēkārā are names indicating the occupation of a servant under Government or a private individual.

Vinka (white-ant: *Termites*).—An exogamous sept of Jātapu.

Vipravinōdi.—In a note on the Vipravinōdis, Mr. C. Hayavadana Rao writes that they are said to be the descendants of a Brāhman by a Lingāyat woman. They are Lingāyats, and are called Vipravinōdi because they perform acrobatic feats before Vipras, or Brāhmans. They generally travel about the country with their wives and children. One of their favourite feats is throwing up three stone or wooden balls in the air, and catching them, or rolling them over various parts of the body. When they perform before a mixed audience, they call themselves Nar-avidya vāru, which is said to be an abbreviated form of Narulu Mechchē Vidyalu Chēsē vāru, or those who perform feats which men praise. The dead are buried in a sitting posture.

Vīrabhadra.—A synonym of the Tamil washermen (Vannān), whose patron deity is Vīrabhadra, from whom they claim descent.

Viragu (firewood).—A sub-division of Vēttuvan.

Virakudiyān.—A synonym of Panisavans, who are engaged in blowing the conch shell on ceremonial occasions.

Vīrala (heroes).—An exogamous sept of Golla and Kāpu.

Vīra Māgāli (a god).—An exogamous section of Kallan.

Vīramushti.—For the following account of the Vīramushtis in the Vizagapatam district, I am indebted to Mr. C. Hayavadana Rao.

They are Lingāyats, but do not, as a rule, wear the lingam, as it is the custom to postpone initiation until death, when the linga is tied on the corpse by a Jangam before it is buried. Those who are initiated during life wear the linga suspended from the neck. The Vīramushtis seem to have several sub-divisions, *e.g.*, Nāga Mallika (*Rhinacanthus communis*), the roots of which are believed to cure snake-bite, Puccha Kaya (*Citrullus Colocynthis*), Triputa (*Ipomœa Turpethum*), and Ramadosa (*Cucumis Melo*).

Girls are married before or after puberty. The mēnarikam custom, according to which a man should marry his maternal uncle's daughter, is observed. A vōli (bride-price) of sixteen rupees, or half a tola of gold, in the form of jewelry, is given to the bride.

The Vīramushtis are professional acrobats and mendicants, and are attached to the Dēvāngas and Kōmatis. The following legends are current to account for their connection with these castes. In days gone by, there was, in a big town, a great Lingāyat mutt (monastery) named Basavanna Mandiram, presided over by a Jangam priest named Basavanna. The mutt contained three hundred crores of Lingāyat priests, and great wealth was stored in it. This the Vīrāmushtis guarded against thieves. A Telaga, Chikayya by name, who was a professional thief, determined to plunder the mutt, in order to satisfy his mistress. One night, when the Vīramushtis were fast asleep, he entered the mutt, but, when he saw a number of Jangams engaged in devout worship, he abandoned his project, and determined to turn Lingāyat. Accordingly, at day-break, he advanced to the place where the head of the mutt was seated, made known to him who he was, and informed him of his resolution. Opinions were divided as to the fitness of receiving such an applicant, but it was finally decided that, if a man repented, he was a fit person to be received into the Lingāyat fold, as the linga recognises no caste. The linga was accordingly tied on his neck. From that time Chikayya became a new man and a true Jangam, and went from place to place visiting sacred shrines. One day he happened to be at a place where lived a merchant prince, who never dined except in the company of a Jangam. On the suggestion of his wife Nīlakuntaladēvi, an invitation to dine was sent to Chikayya, who accepted it. After dinner, the merchant went out on business, and Nīlakuntaladēvi, noticing what a beautiful man Chikayya was, fell in love with him. He, however, rejected her advances, and ran away, leaving his knapsack behind him. Nīlakuntaladēvi cut off her golden necklace, and, having placed it in the knapsack, ran after Chikayya, and threw it at him, asking him to accept it. She then inflicted several cuts on herself, and, as soon as her husband returned home, complained that the Jangam had stolen her necklace, and attempted to ravish her. Information was sent to Basayya, the head of the mutt, and a council meeting summoned, at which it was decided that Chikayya should have his head cut off. The order to carry out this act was given to the Vīramushtis, who went in search of him, and at last found him beneath the shade of a tree overhanging the bank of a river, engaged in worshipping his linga, which was in his hand. On searching the knapsack, they found the necklace, and proceeded to cut off Chikayya's head, which went several hundred feet up into the air, and travelled towards the mutt, whither the headless trunk followed on foot. On their return to the mutt, the Vīramushtis found that the three hundred crores of priests had been miraculously beheaded, and the place was a vast pool of blood. As soon, however, as the head and body of Chikayya approached, they became re-united, and Siva, appearing on the scene, translated him to kylās (heaven). At the same time, he restored the priests to life, and inflicted the following four curses on the Vīramushtis:—(1) they were not to build or use houses, and are consequently found living under trees outside villages; (2) they were not to sleep on a cot; (3) they were not to use the wild broom-stick; (4) they were not to set up permanent ovens for cooking purposes, but to make impromptu stoves out of three stones. Taking compassion on them, the Dēvāngas promised to give the Vīramushtis a small sum of money annually, and to contribute towards their marriage expenses.

VIRAMUSHTI.

The Vīramushtis are said to have become attached to the Kōmatis subsequent to the above incident. The story goes that some Kōmatis asked them to delay for three and half hours the march of Vishnuvardhāna Rāja, who was advancing with a view to marrying the daughter of one of them, named Vasavakanya (now deified into Kanyakamma). This the Vīramushtis did by entertaining the Rāja with their acrobatic feats. Meanwhile, the Kōmatis made a number of fire-pits, and put an end to themselves. Vishnuvardhāna arrived too late, and had his head cut off. The Vīramushtis prayed to Vasavakanya, inasmuch as they had lost both the Rāja, who promised them a grant of land in return for their performance, and herself, who had promised to give a lump of gold to each gōtra. The Kōmatis replied in a body that each family of their caste would in future give the Vīramushtis an annual present of money, and help in defraying the expenses of their marriages.

In accordance with the above legends, the Vīramushtis usually beg only from Dēvāngas and Kōmatis. When they approach a village, they generally halt under a tree, and, early in the morning, dress up as acrobats, and appear with daggers, sticks, etc., crying Good luck! Good luck! They caper about as they advance, and, when they reach a Dēvānga or Kōmati house, perform their acrobatic feats, and wind up with a eulogium of the caste. Money and food are then doled out to them.

Whenever a Dēvānga, Lingayat Kōmati, or other Lingāyat wants to make a hero (vīra) of a deceased member of his family, he sends for a Vīramushti (or hero-maker), and has a slab planted, with a recognised ceremonial, at the spot where he is buried.

In a further note on the Vīramushtis I am informed that they correspond to the Vīrabhadra Kāyakams of the Canarese Lingayats, like whom they dress up, and adorn themselves with small lingams, the figure of Vīrabhadra, a sword, a plate bearing a star, and heads of Asuras (demons). Every important Saivite temple has one or two Vīramushtis attached to it, and they are supposed to be servants of the god Siva. One of their chief duties is to guard the idol during processions, and on other occasions. If, during a car procession, the car will not move, the Vīramushtis cut themselves with their swords until it is set in motion. There is a Tamil proverb that the Siva Brāhman (temple priest) eats well, whereas the Vīramushti hurts himself with the sword, and suffers much. The custom is said to be dying out.

The principal occupation of the Vīramushtis is begging from Bēri Chettis, Dēvāngas, Kōmatis, and washermen. In former days, they are said to have performed a ceremony called pāvadam. When an orthodox Lingāyat was insulted, he would swallow his lingam, and lie flat on the ground in front of the house of the offender, who had to collect some Lingāyats, who would send for a Vīramushti. He had to arrive accompanied by a pregnant Vīramushti woman, pūjāris (priests) of Draupadi, Pachaiamman and Pothurāja temples, a Sembadava pūjāri, Pambaikārans, Udukkaikārans, and some individuals belonging to the nearest Lingayat mutt. Arrived at the house, the pregnant woman would sit down in front of the person lying on the ground. With his sword the Vīramushti man then made cuts in his scalp and chest, and sprinkled the recumbent man with the blood. He would then rise, and the lingam would come out of his mouth. Besides feeding the people, the offender was expected to pay money as pāvadam to the Vīramushtis and mutts.

Some Vīramushtis style themselves Vastād, or athletes, in reference to their professional occupation.

Vīrānattān.—The name denotes those who play on a drum called vīrānam. It is recorded, in the Madras Census Report, 1901, that the Vīrānattāns "were originally temple servants, but now do miscellaneous day labour. Their females are prostitutes. Their titles are Mēstri and Mudali."

Vīranollu.—Vīranollu and Viththanollu are gōtras of Gānigas, who may not cut the wood-apple (*Feronia elephantum*).

Vīrasaiva.—A synonym for Lingāyat. Some Lingāyats claim to be Vīrasaiva Brāhmans.

Visālākshiamma.—Recorded, in the Manual of the North Arcot district, as a sub-division of Vāniyan. Visālākshiamma is the goddess of Benares, who is said to be the sister of Minākshi of Madura and Kāmākshi of Conjeeveram. Visālākshi means literally one with beautiful eyes, and is a name of Parvati, who is described as possessing large and beautiful eyes.

Viswakarma.—Viswakarma and Viswa Brāhman are synonyms for Kammālan, the members of which class claim descent from the five faces of Viswakarma, the architect of the gods.

Vitugula-vāndlu.—A fanciful name, meaning hunters or gallants, adopted by Bōyas.

Vodāri.—*See* Odāri.

Vodda.—*See* Oddē.

Vōdo.—A small caste of Oriya basket-makers and cultivators in the Vizagapatam agency.

Vōjali.—*See* Ojali.

Vokkiliyan (cultivator).—A sub-division of Kāppiliyan, and Tamil form of Vakkaliga. (*See* Okkiliyan.)

Vudupulavallu.—An occupational name for Balijas, Velamas, etc., who paint chintzes.

Vyādha (forest men).—A synonym of Myāsa Bēdars.

Vyāpāri.—A trading section of Nāyar.

Vyāsa (the name of a sage or rishi).—A sub-division of Balija.

W

Wahābi.—The Wahābis are a sect of Muslim revivalists founded by Muhammad ibn 'Abdu'l Wahhāb, who was born in A.D. 1691. Wahābyism has been defined as the Puritanism of Islām, "hated by the so-called orthodox Musalmāns, as the Lutherans were hated by Leo, and the Covenanters by Claverhouse."[157] It is recorded, in the Manual of North Arcot (1895), that since 1806 (the year of the Vellore mutiny) "two alarms have been raised in the district, both at Vellore, which is largely inhabited by Muhammadans. The last alarm occurred in 1869. Early in May of that year, anonymous petitions were received by the Joint Magistrate and the Assistant Superintendent of Police, stating that the Wahābi Muhammadans of Vellore were in league against Government, and had arranged a plot for the massacre of all the European residents, in which the 28th Regiment of Native Infantry, then stationed at Vellore, was deeply implicated. An East Indian subordinate of the Public Works Department also reported that he had overheard a Muhammadan munshi of the Small Cause Court speaking to a shopman of his faith about the seditious preaching of a certain Khāzi. The munshi was sent for, and described what he said had occurred in a certain mosque, where sedition had been openly advocated by a Wahābi missionary who had recently arrived from Hyderabad, as well as by others." It appeared, from the investigations of the Inspector-General of Police, that the whole affair had been nothing more than a conspiracy among the orthodox Muhammadans to arouse alarm regarding the designs of the Wahābis, and to prevent these sectarians from frequenting their mosques.

Wudder.—*See* Oddē.

Wynād.—Returned, at times of census, as a territorial division of Chetti. There are at Gudalūr near the boundary between the Nīlgiri district and Malabar, and in the Wynād, two classes called, respectively, Mandādan Chettis (*q.v.*) and Wynādan Chettis.

The following account of the Wynādan or Wynaadan Chettis is given in the Gazetteer of the Nīlgiris. "They speak Malayālam, and follow marumakkatāyam (inheritance in the female line). They say they were originally Vellālas from Coimbatore, followed makkatāyam (inheritance from father to son), spoke Tamil, and wore the Tamil top-knot. In proof of this, they point out that at their weddings they still follow certain Tamil customs, the bridegroom wearing a turban and a red cloth with a silver girdle over it and being shaved, and the woman putting on petticoats and nose-rings. They have headmen called Kolapallis, subordinate to whom are Mantiris, but these are liable to be overruled by a nād council. No

---

[157] Ind. Ant., X, 1881, p. 69.

wedding may take place without the headman's leave. Two forms of marriage are recognised. In one, the couple exchange garlands after the Tamil fashion, and the father (a relic of the makkatāyam system) conducts the ceremony. Preliminaries are arranged by go-betweens, and the chief of the numerous rites is the placing of a bracelet on the girl's upper arm under a pandal (booth) before the priest and the assembled relatives. The other form is simpler. The bridegroom goes to the girl's house with some men friends, and, after a dinner there, a go-between puts on the bangle. Before marriage, a tāli-kettu ceremony resembling that of the Nāyars is often gone through, all the girls of a family who are of marriageable age having tālis tied round their necks on the same day by a maternal uncle. Married women are allowed intimacy with their husbands' brothers. Widows are permitted to marry again. The dead are usually burnt, but those who have met their deaths by accidents and epidemics are buried. Water from a vessel containing rice and a gold coin is poured into a dying person's mouth. Should the spirit of the dead disturb the dreams of the relatives, a hut for it is built under an astrologer's directions close to the house, and in this lights are lit morning and evening, and periodical offerings of food are made. The Wynaadan Chettis reverence the deities in the Ganapati, Mahāmāri and Kalimalai Tambirān temples near Sultan's Battery, Airu Billi of the Kurumbas, and one or two others. The women wear in their distended ear-lobes gold discs which are so characteristic of the Nāyars, and many necklaces. They wear two white cloths, tying one round the waist and another across their breasts."

It is recorded, in the Gazetteer of Malabar, that the Wynād or Wynaadan Chettis "claim to be Sūdras, and are in appearance and customs very similar to the Nāyars. They are polluted by all castes below Nāyars. Their marriage customs seem to be a mixture of east and west coast practices. They follow the marumak-kattāyam system, and perform the tāli-kettu kaliānam; but this is done on the tenth day after puberty, and two tālis have to be tied on the girl, one by her maternal uncle, and one by the senior female of her house. They also celebrate a regular marriage ceremony, at which a bracelet is put on the bride's right arm, and bride and bridegroom garland each other; while next morning a kānam or bride-price has to be paid to the bride's karnavan (senior male in a family). They are bold shikāris (sportsmen), and tiger spearing is a favourite pastime, closely connected with their religion.

"The tiger is encircled by a wall of netting six feet high, which is gradually closed up, and then speared. The carcass is not skinned, but is stretched on a pole, and hung up as a sacrifice to their deity."

Y

Yādava.—Yādava, meaning descendants of king Yādu, from whom Krishna was descended, has been recorded as a synonym or title of Idaiyan, and a sub-division of Golla and Koracha. There is a tradition among the Idaiyans that Krishna was brought up by their caste.

Yākāri.—*See* Ekāri.

Yānādi.—The Yānādis are a dark-skinned, platyrhine tribe, short of stature, who inhabit the Telugu country. The name has been the subject of much etymological speculation. Some derive it from a (privative) and nathu (lord or protector), and it may mean those who are not included in the ruling or principal caste. Again, it has been derived from yanam (boat) and adi (means). But the Yānādis are not known to have plied, nor do they now ply boats at Srīharikota, their chief place of residence, which is on the coast. The word would seem to be derived from the Sanskrit anadi, or those whose origin is not traceable. The people perhaps elongated the vowel-sound, so that it became Yānādi. In like manner, the Native graduate of the Madras University talks of himself as being, not a B.A. or M.A., but B.Ya. or M.Ya. And a billiard-marker will call the game yeighty-yeight instead of eighty-eight.

The tradition of the Yānādis as to their origin is very vague. Some call themselves the original inhabitants of the wilds in the neighbourhood of the Pulicat lake, where they hunted and fished at will, until they were enslaved by the Reddis. Others say that the Reddi (or Manchi?) Yānādis were originally Chenchus, a small but superior class, and that they fled from oppression and violence from the mountains in the west, and amalgamated themselves with the common Yānādis. The common deity of both Chenchus and Manchi Yānādis is Chenchu Dēvudu. Between the Yānādi and the Chenchu, however, there is no love lost. They can be seen living close together, but not intermingling, on the Nallamalais, and they differ in their social customs. Yānādi Chenchu is said to be the name given by Brāhmans to the Chenchus.[158] The following legend concerning the Yānādis is narrated by Mackenzie.[159] "Of old, one named Rāghava brought with him sixty families from Pācanātti district, locating himself with them at Sriharicotta, and, clearing the country, formed Rāghavapuram. The people by degrees spread through a few adjoining districts. A rishi, who came from Benares, and was named Ambikēsvarer, resided in Mad'hyāranya (or the central wilderness), and there, daily bathing in a river, paid homage to Siva. These wild people of their own accord daily brought

---

[158] Manual of the Kurnool district.
[159] Catalogue Raisonné of Oriental Manuscripts, III, 1862.

him fruits and edibles, putting them before him. At length he inquired of them the reason. They replied that their country was infested by a terrible serpent, and they wished to be taught charms to destroy it, as well as charms for other needful purposes. He taught them, and then vanished away."

It is an advantage for a European to have a Yānādi as a camp servant, as he can draw water from any caste well. The Yānādi can also wash, and carry water for Brāhmans.

The animistic nature of their religion; the production of fire by friction; the primitive hunting and fishing stage in which a number remain; the almost raw animal food which they eat, after merely scorching or heating the flesh of the game they kill, indicate that the Yānādis have not yet emerged from a primitive stage of culture. They make fire by friction with sticks from the following trees:—

> *Protium caudatum* (konda rāgi).
> *Bauhinia racemosa* (aree chettu).
> *Ficus. sp.* (kallu jeevee chettu).
> *Ptereospermum suberifolium* (tada).
> A tree belonging to the Nat. Order Laurineæ.
> *Cordia monoica* (female tree).

Two sticks are prepared, one short, the other long. In the former a square cavity is scooped out, and it is held firmly on the ground, while the long stick is twisted rapidly to and fro in the cavity. No charcoal powder is used, but a rag, or even dried leaves are set fire to.

The head-quarters of the Yānādis is the island of Srīharikota in the Nellore district. Their primitive condition attracted notice in 1835, when the island came into the possession of the Government, which endeavoured to ameliorate their position by supplying them with a liberal allowance of grain, clothing, tobacco, and money, in return for the jungle produce, which they collected. The demand for labour naturally rose, and the Government offered to pay to parents 2 annas 6 pies on the birth of a male, and 1 anna 3 pies on the birth of a female child—a bounty on productivity justified by special local causes. In 1858, the Government opened a school for the teaching of Telugu, which was rendered attractive by offers of rice and clothing to those who attended it. An industrial department gave lessons in basket-making, and land was assigned for the cultivation of chay-root (*Oldenlandia umbellata*), which yields the beautiful red dye formerly much employed in the dyeing of cotton fabrics, but has had its nose put out of joint by the introduction of aniline and alizarin dyes. But the industries proved unsuccessful, and the strength of the school gradually declined, so that it was abolished in 1877.

YĀNĀDIS MAKING FIRE.

At the census, 1891, the Yānādis returned as many as 89 sub-divisions, of which the two most important numerically were Chenchu and Manchi. A division into classes exists according to dietary, occupation, residence, etc. There are, for example, the Reddi Yānādis, the Challa (refuse-eating), Adavi, and Kappala (frog-eaters). The Reddi Yānādis are a settled class, employed chiefly as cooks by the Panta Reddis. They do not mingle with the Challa and Adivi sections, whom they regard as out-castes. If a Reddi Yānādi woman's husband dies, abandons, or divorces her, she may marry his brother, and, in the case of separation or divorce, the two brothers will live on friendly terms with each other. The Challas are also known as Garappa (dry-land) or Chatla (tree). They reside in huts on the borders of villages in the service of the community, and live on jungle produce, and by snaring and hunting game. The Reddi and Challa Yānādis are occasionally employed as kāvalgars, or village watchmen, in the Kistna and Godāvari districts. In the Venkatagiri Zemindāri the Yānādis are among the recognised servants of the village community as procurers of charcoal for the blacksmith. The Adavi Yānādis are, as the name implies, jungle-men. The Manchi or good Yānādis are a small superior class. The Yānādis of the North Arcot district, it may be noted, are Chenchu worshippers, and go by that name. They are non-frog-eaters, and do not permit the Kappala, or frog-eaters, even to touch their pots. Some Yānādis of the Nellore district feed on the refuse of the table. The Somari, or idle Yānādis, live in the Kavali tāluk of that district. They do scavenging work, and eat the refuse food thrown away by people from the leaf plate after a meal.

The following are some of the house-names of families living in Nellore, Sriharikota, Tada, and Kāmbakam: —

(*a*) Manchi Yānādis —

Bandi, cart.	Mēkala, goat.
Chembetti, hammer.	Mānikala, measure.
Chilakala, paroquet.	Pāmula, snake.
Dhoddi, sheep-fold.	Tenkayala, cocoanut.
Īgala, house-fly.	Totla, garden.
Enthodu, a village.	Tupākala, gun.
Illa, of a house.	Udamala, water-lizard.
Kathtlula, sword.	Jandayi, flag.
Kānūr, a village.	Marrigunta, pond near a fig-tree.
Kotlu, cow-shed.	

(*b*) Challa Yānādi —

Nerigi Mēkala, a kind of goat.
Elugu, bear.
Thirlasetti, name of a Balija Chetti.

All these names represent exogamous septs. In every case, the house-name was known only to old men and women, and they, as a rule, did not know the house-names of their neighbours or relations. Many of the names are derived from villages, or persons of other castes, on whose land they may live, and are probably new names adopted instead of the original ones. For the purpose of their register, Forest officers invent prefixes by which Yānādis with the same family name can be distinguished, *e.g.*, Kee Chenchugadu, Permadu Budthagadu, to distinguish them from other Chenchugadus, and Budthagadus. The same practice is resorted to by planters, who give "estate names" to their coolies.

Yānādis will not eat with Mādigas or Paraiyans, and observe some principle in partaking of the refuse of the table. Thus, for a Chinna Yānādi to eat the refuse of the Mondis, Oddes, or Yerukalas, would involve excommunication, which is always pronounced by a Balija Chetti, whose decision is final and binding. Restoration to caste can be secured by undergoing a personal ordeal, by giving a feast, and promising good behaviour in the future. The ordeal takes the form of scalding of the tongue with hot gold by the Balija Chetti. It is curious that there has recently grown up a tendency for members of other castes to join the Yānādi community. There are instances of barbers, weavers, fishermen, and even Kōmatis being admitted into the Yānādi fold.

The headman, who goes by the name of Kulampedda or Pedda Yānādi, exercises general social control over a group, known as a guddem, ordinarily of about twenty huts. He decides social questions, sometimes on his own responsibility, by excommunicating or fining; sometimes acting on the advice of a council of his castemen. Until quite recently, the tribe remained under the guidance of a hereditary leader of Srīharikota, who wielded immense power. The Paraiyans have risen superior to the Yānādis as a community, supplying among themselves their own artisans, weavers, carpenters, barbers, priests, teachers, etc., while the Yānādis are only just beginning to move in this direction.

The language of the Yānādis is Telugu, but some words are compounds of Telugu and Tamil, *e.g.*, artichedi for plantain, pandikutti for pig.

The Yānādis know the forest flora well, and the uses of the various trees and shrubs, which yield good firewood, etc. They call the roller (*Coracias indica*) the milk bird, in the belief that, when a cow goes dry, she will yield milk if a feather of the roller is put in the grass for her to swallow. The crow-pheasant (*Centropus sinensis*) is to them the prickly-pear crow; florikin the ground peacock; the fan-tail snipe the pond snipe; and the pin-tail the rice field snipe.

At the census, 1891, 84,339 Yānādis were returned as Hindus, and 549 as animists. Their places of worship are not temples, but houses, called dēvara indlu (houses of the gods), set apart for every centre. They worship a household god, a village goddess of local importance, and a deity of wider repute and influence. Chenchu Dēvudu is invariably the household god. Poleramma or Ankamma is in charge of a local area for weal or woe. Subbarāyudu, Venkatēswaralu, Panchala, Narasimhulu, and others, are the gods who control destinies over a wider area. The Yānādis are their own priests. The objects of worship take various forms: a wooden idol at Srīharikota; bricks; stones; pots of water with margosa (*Melia Azadirachta*) leaves; images of gods drawn on the walls of their houses; or mere handfuls of clay squeezed into shape, and placed on a small platform erected under an aruka tree, which, like other Hindus, they hold sacred. They use a red powder, flowers, turmeric, etc., for worship; burn camphor and incense; and distribute fruit, dhāl (pulse of *Cajanus indicus*), and the like. In worshipping ancestors, they resemble the Kurumbas. The house of the gods is a sanctum, into which no polluting object is allowed to enter. The most pious perform rites every Friday. At Srīharikota they do so once a fortnight, or once a month. The ordinary Yānādi only worships on occasion of a marriage, funeral, etc. A belief lingers that the pious are *en rapport* with the deity, who converses with them and even inspires them. The goddess receives animal sacrifices, but Chenchu Dēvudu is a strict vegetarian, whose votaries are bound, at times of worship, to subsist on a single daily meal of roots and fruits. The Yānādis, like Hindus, wear sect marks, and are even divided into Vaishnavites and Saivites. They are supposed, during worship, to endow inanimate objects, and the spirits of geographical features, with life and mind, and supernatural powers. Some Yānādis are converts to Christianity.

The Yānādis live in low conical huts, rudely built of bamboo and palmyra leaves, grass, or millet stalks, with a small entrance, through which grown-up people have to creep. The hut affords protection from the sun and rain, but the Yānādis generally cook, eat, and sleep outside. The staple food of the Yānādis, apart from bazar purchases, consists of the following:—

Animals:—Sāmbar deer, wild goat, bear, porcupine, boar, land tortoise, hare, bandicoot and jerboa rat, *Varanus* (lizard), mungoose, and fish.

Vegetables and fruit:—*Dioscorea* (yams); pith and fruit of *Phœnix sylvestris* (date palm); fruit kernel of *Cycas circinalis*, eaten after thorough soaking in water; and fruits of *Eugenia alternifolia* and *Jambolana* (black plum), *Carissa Carandas* and *spinarum, Buchanania acuminata,* and *Mimusops hexandra.*

They are, like the Irulas of Chingleput, very partial to sour and fermented rice-water, which is kept by the higher classes for cattle. This they receive in exchange for headloads of fuel. For some time past they have been stopped by the Forest officers from drinking this pulusunīllu, as it makes them lazy, and unfit for work.

The marriage ceremony is no indispensable necessity. The Adavi Yānādis, as a rule, avoid it; the Reddi Yānādis always observe it. The parents rarely arrange alliances, the parties concerned managing for themselves. Maturity generally precedes marriage. Seduction and elopement are common occurrences, and divorce is easily obtained. Adultery is no serious offence; widows may live in concubinage; and pregnancy before marriage is no crime. By nature, however, the Yānādis are jealous of conjugal rights, and attached to their wives. Widowhood involves no personal disfigurement, or denial of all the emblems of married life.

A widow has been known to take, one after another, as many as seven husbands. The greater the number of her husbands, the more exalted is the status of a widow in society, and the stronger her title to settle disputes on questions of adultery, and the like. Polygamy is common, and a Yānādi is known to have had as many as seven wives, whom he housed separately, and with whom he lived by turns. The marriage ceremony is undergoing change, and the simple routine developing into a costly ceremonial, the details of which (*e.g.,* the "screen scene") are copied from the marriage rites of higher castes in the Telugu country. Until quite recently, the flower of the tangēdu (*Cassia auriculata*) did duty for the tāli, which is now a turmeric-dyed cotton thread with a gold bottu suspended from it. The auspicious hour is determined by a very simple process. The hour is noon, which arrives when a pole, two feet high, stuck vertically on the marriage platform, ceases to throw a shadow. The pole has superseded the arrow used of old, and sometimes a purōhit is consulted, and gives the hour from his calendar.

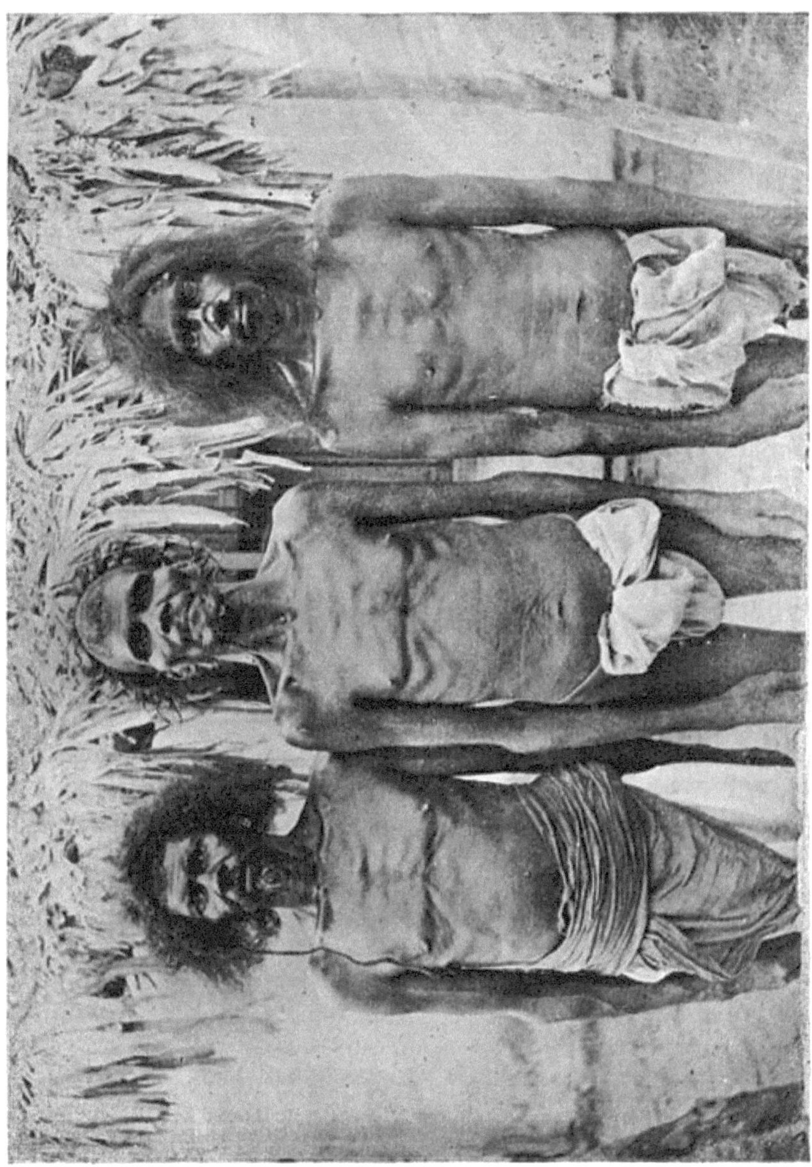

YĀNĀDIS.

As a punishment for adultery, the unfaithful woman is, at Srīharikota, made to stand, with her legs tied, for a whole day in the sun, with a basket full of sand on her head.

The maternal uncle receives a measure of rice, a new cloth, and eight annas, at the head-shaving ceremony of his nephew. At this ceremony, which is a borrowed custom, the uncle plucks a lock of hair from the head of the lad, and ties it to a bough of the aruka tree. The head is shaved, and the lad worships the village goddess, to whom a fowl is offered. The guests are feasted, and the evening is spent in a wild torch-light dance.

At the first menstrual period, a Yānādi girl occupies a hut erected for the purpose, which must have within it at least one stick of *Strychnos Nux-vomica*, to drive away devils. On the ninth day the hut is burnt down, and the girl cleanses herself from pollution by bathing. A woman, after confinement, feeds for three days on the tender leaves, or cabbage of the date palm (*Phœnix sylvestris*), and then on rice. Margosa leaves, and sometimes the leaves of other trees, and the knife with which the umbilical cord was cut, are placed under the infant's head for six days. A net is hung in front of the door, to keep out devils. The baby is given a name by the soothsayer, who pretends to be in communication on the subject with the god or goddess.

The Yānādis pose as prophets of human destinies, and, like the Nīlgiri Kurumbas, pretend to hold intercourse with gods and goddesses, and to intercede between god and man. Every village or circle has one or more soothsayers, who learn their art from experts under a rigid routine. The period of pupilage is a fortnight spent on a dietary of milk and fruits with no cooked meat, in a cloister in meditation. The god or goddess Ankamma, Poleramma, Venkatēswaralu, Subbaroyadu, or Malakondroyadu, appears like a shadow, and inspires the pupil, who, directly the period of probation has ceased, burns camphor and frankincense. He then sings in praise of the deity, takes a sea bath with his master, gives a sumptuous feast, and becomes an independent soothsayer. The ardent soothsayer of old wrought miracles, so runs the story, by stirring boiling rice with his hand, which was proof against scald or hurt. His modern brother invokes the gods with burning charcoal in his folded hands, to the beat of a drum. People flock in large numbers to know the truth. The word is rangampattedhi in North Arcot and sodi in Nellore. The soothsayer arranges Chenchu Dēvudu and the local gods in a separate dēvara illu or house of god, which is always kept scrupulously clean, and where worship is regularly carried on. The auspicious days for soothsaying are Friday, Saturday, and Sunday. The chief soothsayer is a male. The applicant presents him with betel nuts, fruit, flowers, and money. The soothsayer bathes, and sits in front of his house smeared with black, white, red, and other colours. His wife, or some other female, kindles a fire, and throws frankincense into it. He beats his drum, and sings, while a woman from within repeats the chant in a shrill voice. The songs are in praise of the deity, at whose and the soothsayer's feet the applicant prostrates himself and invokes their aid. The soothsayer feels inspired, and addresses the supplicant thus: "You have neglected me. You do not worship me. Propitiate me adequately, or ruin is yours." The future is predicted in song. In these predictions the rural folk place abundant faith.

YĀNĀDI HUT.

The Yānādis bury their dead. The corpse is laid on leaves in front of the hut, washed and clad. Pēlalu (parched rice) is thrown over the corpse by the son and all the agnates. It is eventually placed on a bier, covered with a new cloth, and carried to the burial ground, by the sons, or, in the absence thereof, the sapindas. At a fixed spot near the grave, on which all corpses are placed, a cross is drawn on the ground, the four lines of which represent the four cardinal points of the compass.

Close to the corpse are placed betel leaves and nuts, and a copper coin. All present then proceed to the spot where the grave is to be dug, while the corpse is left in charge of a Yānādi called the Bathyasthadu, who, as a rule, belongs to a different sept from that of the deceased. The corpse is laid on a cloth, face downwards, in the grave. The eldest son, followed by the other relatives, throws three handfuls of earth into the grave, which is then filled in. On their return home, the mourners undergo purification by bathing before entering their huts. In front of the dead man's hut, two broken chatties (pots) are placed, whereof one contains ash-water, the other turmeric-water. Into each chatty a leafy twig is thrown. Those who have been present at the funeral stop at the chatties, and, with the twig, sprinkle themselves first with the ash-water, and then with the turmeric-water. Inside the hut a lighted lamp, fed with gingelly oil, is set up, before which those who enter make obeisance before eating.

The chinnadinamu ceremony, whereof notice is given by the Bathyasthadu, is usually held on the third day after death. Every group (gudem) or village has its own Bathyasthadu, specially appointed, whose duty it is to convey the news of death, and puberty of girls, to all the relatives. Tupākis will never nominate a Tupāki as their Bathyastha, but will select from a Mēkala or any sept except their own.

On the morning of the chinnadinamu, the eldest son of the deceased cooks rice in a new pot, and makes curries and cakes according to his means. These are made up into six balls, which are placed in a new basket, and taken to the burial-ground. On reaching the spot where the cross-lines were drawn, a ball of rice is placed thereon, together with betel leaves and nuts and a copper coin. The Bathyasthadu remains in charge thereof, while those assembled proceed to the grave, whereon a pot of water is poured, and a stone planted at the spot beneath which the head lies. The stone is anointed with shikai (fruit of *Acacia Concinna*) and red powder, and milk poured over it, first by the widow or widower and then by the relations. This ceremony concluded, the son places a ball of rice at each corner of the grave, together with betel and money. Milk is poured over the remaining ball, which is wrapped in a leaf, and buried over the spot where the abdomen of the deceased is situated. Close to the grave, at the southern or head end, three stones are set up in the form of a triangle, whereon a new pot full of water is placed. A hole is made in the bottom of the pot, and the water trickles out towards the head of the corpse. This concludes the ceremony, and, as on the day of the funeral, purification by bathing, ash-water and turmeric-water, is carried out.

The peddadinamu ceremony is performed on the sixteenth, or some later day after death. As on the chinnadinamu, the son cooks rice in a new pot. Opposite the entrance to the hut a handful of clay is squeezed into a conical mass, representing the soul of the deceased, and stuck up on a platform. The eldest son, taking a portion of the cooked rice, spreads it on a leaf in front of the clay image, before which incense is burnt, and a lamp placed. The image, and the remainder of the food made up into four balls, are then carried by the son to a tank (pond). As soon as the relatives have assembled there, the recumbent effigy of a man is made, close to the edge of the tank, with the feet towards the north. The conical image is set up close to the head of the effigy, which is anointed by the relatives as at the chinnadinamu, except that no milk is poured over it. The four balls of rice are placed close to the hands and feet of the effigy, together with betel and money, and the son salutes it. The agnates then seat themselves in a row between the effigy and the water, with their hands behind their backs, so as to reach the effigy, which is moved slowly towards the water, into which it finally falls, and becomes disintegrated. The proceedings conclude with distribution of cloths and cheroots, and purification as before. The more prosperous Yānādis now engage a Brāhman to remove the pollution by sprinkling water over them. During the peddadinamu incessant music and drum-beating has been going on, and is continued till far into the night, and sometimes the ceremonial is made to last over two days, in order that the Yānādis may indulge in a bout of music and dancing.

The Yānādis are expert anglers, catching fish with a triangular net or wicker basket. They also excel in diving for and catching hold of fish concealed in crevices of rocks or buried in mud, and assist European sportsmen by marking down florikin. Those who are unable to count bring in a string with knots tied in it, to indicate the number of birds marked. They catch bandicoot rats by a method known as voodarapettuta. A pot is stuffed with grass, into which fire is thrown. The mouth of the pot is placed against the hole made by the bandicoot, and smoke blown into the hole through a small slit in the pot. The animal becomes suffocated, and tries to escape through the only aperture available, made for the occasion by the Yānādi, and, as it emerges, is killed. They are fearless in catching cobras, which they draw out of their holes without any fear of their fangs. They pretend to be under the protection of a charm, while so doing. A correspondent writes that a cobra was in his grounds, and his servant got a Yānādi, who had charge of the adjoining garden, to dislodge it. The man was anxious to catch it alive, and then, before killing it, carefully removed the poison-sac with a knife, and swallowed it as a protection against snake-bite.

The Yānādis are good shikāris (huntsmen), and devoid of fear in the jungle. They hold licenses under the Arms Act, and being good shots, are great at bagging tigers, leopards, porcupines, and other big and small game. After an unsuccessful beat for spotted deer, a friend informs me, the Yānādis engaged therein erected a cairn of twigs and stones several feet high, round which they danced with gradually quickening step, to the refrain in Telugu 'Nothing comes.' Then, to the same tune, they danced round it in the opposite direction. The incantation concluded, the beat was continued and a stag duly appeared on the scene—and was missed!

They gather honey from bee-hives on hill tops and cliffs which are precipitous and almost inaccessible, and perilous to reach. The man climbs down with the help of a plaited rope of pliant bamboo, fastened above to a peg driven firmly into a tree or other hard substance, and takes with him a basket and stick. He drives away the bees at the first swing by burning grass or brushwood beneath the hives. The next swing takes him closer to the hive, which he pokes with the stick. He receives the honey-comb in the basket, and the honey flows out of it into a vessel adjusted to it. When the basket and vessel are full, he shakes the rope, and is drawn up by the person in charge of it, who is almost always his wife's brother, so that there may be no foul play. He thus collects a considerable quantity of honey and wax, for which he receives only a subsistence wage from the contractor, who makes a big profit for himself.

The following list of minor forest products, chiefly collected by Government Yānādis, is given in the Nellore District Gazette:—

> Chay root (*Oldenlandia umbellata*), which, by a quaint misprint, appears as cheroot.
> Kanuga (*Pongamia glabra*).
> Sarsaparilla (*Hemidesmus indicus*).
> Nux vomica (*Strychnos Nux-vomica*).
> Tangēdu (*Cassia auriculata*).
> Soap nut (*Sapindus trifoliatus*).
> Achilla weed (lichens).
> Ishwarac (*Aristolochia indica*).
> Vishabuddi (*Sida carpinifolia*).
> Kukkapala (*Tylophora asthmatica*).
> Honey.
> Rattan (*Calamus Rotang*).
> Tamarind (*Tamarindus indicus*).
> Neredu (*Eugenia Jambolana*).
> Surati bark (*Ventilago Madraspatana*).

In the interests of the Yānādis it is laid down, in the Gazette, that "the Yānādi villages must be encouraged, and the people paid at least once a week for the produce they collect. This must be done by the maistry (overseer) going up and down the main ride every day during the collection season, checking the collections, and paying for them on the spot. The Yānādis will, of course, camp out in the reserve when collecting produce, and not return, as heretofore, every three days to Sriharikota, thus wasting 45 per cent. of their time in the mere coming and going, apart from the fact that, under the old system, the produce from some parts of the reserves was never collected at all, as no one visited them."

The Yānādis dance on festive occasions, at ceremonies, and occasionally for begging, smearing the body with turmeric, wearing flowers, singing meaningless songs, and drumming in rude fashion "dambukku, dambukku." Their only wind instrument is the bag-pipe, but they play on the snake charmer's reed as an accompaniment. Their dance is full of indecent suggestion. They have of late trained themselves for the stage, and there are several troupes of Bhāgavathulu.

To the Rev. G. N. Thomssen, of the Telugu Mission, Bapatla, I am indebted for the following account of a Yānādi dance. "Especially at night, they love to gather in some part of the jungle where they have their huts, and, having gathered a pile of palmyra leaves, burn them one by one as torches, while a number of men and women begin to dance their quaint, weird jungle dance, which is to represent the experiences of the hunters in their wanderings. The chief actors, or dancers, are dressed fantastically. They are almost nude, but dangling from their loins are palmyra baskets, in which they gather edible bulbs and roots, dead rats, snakes, etc., which are prized as something to fill the stomach. Suddenly the actors fell on the ground. One of them cries out 'thēlu' (scorpion). Then the other asks where, and is shown the place where the scorpion is supposed to have stung the sufferer, while the choir sing:—

> Alas! the scorpion stings.
> O! O! the scorpion stings.
> Which finger? Ah! the middle one.
> As soon as I was stung,
> The poison into my head ascends.
> Ayo! Ayo! What shall I do?
> Bring down the poison with yilledu.

This chant is kept up for a long time, when suddenly another of the actors falls on the ground, and writhes like a snake. The Yānādis are a very supple race, and, when dancing, especially when writhing on the ground, one sees a display of muscular action that makes one believe that the human body is capable of all the twists and turns of a serpent. When the actor is representing the man bitten by a snake, one hears quaint cries while the snake is sought in the hair, ears, and nose, basket and loin-cloth. The choir now sings the following:—

> Come down to catch the snake,
> O! snake-charmer, behold the standing snake.
> Be sure the pipe sounds well.
> Come, come, with the big snakes in the basket,
> And the little ones in the lock of your hair.
> When I went down the bank of the Yerracheru,
> And saw the harvest cut,
> The cobra crawled beneath the harvester.
> Ayo! Ayo! Ayo!

To see this action song, and to hear these strange people, is one of the queerest experiences of native aboriginal life. The dancers, and the spectators who form the choir, all become very excited, and even the European, seeing the tamāsha (spectacle), is infected with the excitement. The actors are bathed in perspiration, but the dance is kept up nevertheless, and only when their large stock of palmyra leaf torches is exhausted will they stop and take their rest."

In their nomadic life the Yānādis have learnt by experience the properties and uses of herbs and roots, with which they treat fever, rheumatism, and other diseases. They have their own remedies for cobra bite and scorpion sting. It is said that the Yānādis alone are free from elephantiasis, which affects the remaining population of Sriharikota.

It is noted by the Rev. G. N. Thomssen that "while it has been impossible to gather these people into schools, because of their shyness and jungle wildness, Christian missionaries, especially the American Baptist missionaries, have succeeded in winning the confidence of these degraded children of nature, and many of them have joined the Christian Church. Some read and write well, and a few have even learned English. We have a small, but growing settlement of Christianised Yānādis at Bapatla."

To sum up the Yānādi. It is notorious that, in times of scarcity, he avoids the famine relief works, for the simple reason that he does not feel free on them. Nevertheless, a few are in the police service. Some are kāvalgars (watchmen), farm labourers, scavengers, stone-masons or bricklayers, others are pounders of rice, or domestic servants, and are as a rule faithful. They earn a livelihood also in various subsidiary ways, by hunting, fishing, cobra-charming, collecting honey or fuel, rearing and selling pigs, practicing medicine as quacks, and by thieving. "An iron implement," Mr. F. S. Mullaly writes,[160] called the sikkaloo kōl, is kept by them ostensibly for the purpose of digging roots, but it is really their jemmy, and used in the commission of burglary. It is an ordinary iron tool, pointed at both ends, one end being fitted in a wooden handle. With this they can dig through a wall noiselessly and quickly, and many houses are thus broken into in one night, until a good loot is obtained. House-breakings are usually committed during the first quarter of the moon. Yānādis confess their own crimes readily, but will never implicate accomplices.... Women are useful in the disposal of stolen property. At dusk they go round on their begging tours selling mats, which they make, and take the opportunity of dropping a word to the women of cheap things for sale, and the temptation is seldom resisted. Stolen property is also carried in their marketing baskets to the village grocer, the Kōmati. Among the wild (Adavi) Yānādis, women are told off to acquire information while begging, but they chiefly rely on the liquor-shopkeepers for news, which may be turned to useful account."[161]

Yanāti.—The Yānātis, Yēnētis, or Ēnētis, are a class of cultivators in the Ganjam and Vizagapatam districts, between whom and the Yānādis some confusion has arisen. For example, it is noted, in the Madras Census Report, 1891, that it is curious to find the Yānādi sub-division of the Velamas so strongly represented, for there is at the present day a wide gulf between Velamas and Yānādis. Again, in the Census Report, 1901, it is noticed under the heading Yānāti that "entries of this name were clubbed with Yānādi, but it has since been reported that, in Bissumcuttack taluk of the Vizagapatam Agency, there is a separate caste called Yānāti or Yēnēti Dora, which is distinct from either Yānādi or Konda Dora."

It is said that the Yānātis of Ganjam also go by the name of Entamara and Gainta or Gayinta.

Yāta.—The Yātas are the toddy-drawers of Ganjam and Vizagapatam. The caste name is a corrupt form of ita, meaning date palm, from which the toddy is secured. It is noted, in the Gazetteer of the Vizagapatam district, that "toddy is obtained from the palmyra (*Borassus flabellifer*) and date palm (*Phœnix sylvestris*). The toddy-drawers are usually of the Yāta and Segidi castes. The palmyra is tapped by cutting off the end of the flower spathe, and the date palm by making an incision, like an inverted V, close under the crown of leaves. In the zamindaris, little care is taken to see that date trees are not over-tapped, and hundreds of trees may be seen ruined, and even killed by excessive tapping." Many members of the caste are

----

[160] Notes on Criminal Classes of the Madras Presidency, 1892.
[161] This note is based on an article by Mr. Ranga Rao, with additions.

engaged in the manufacture of baskets and boxes from palm leaves. The Yātas are said to be responsible for a good deal of the crime in portions of the Vizagapatam district.

For the following note on the Yātas of the Vizagapatam district, I am indebted to Mr. C. Hayavadana Rao. They are a Telugu-speaking people, and the caste is organised on the same lines as many other Telugu castes. In each locality where they are settled, there is a headman called Kulampedda, who, with the assistance of the caste elders, settles disputes and affairs affecting the community. The caste is, like other Telugu castes, divided up into numerous intipērus or exogamous septs. The custom of mēnarikam, according to which a man marries his maternal uncle's daughter, is the rule. If the girl, whom a man claims in accordance with this custom, is not given to him, his mother raises such a howl that her brother is compelled by the castemen to come to terms. If he still refuses to give up his daughter, and bestows her on another man, the protest of his sister is said to destroy the happiness of the pair. Girls are married before or after puberty. The marriage ceremonies last over three days, and are carried out either at the house of the bride or bridegroom, the former if the parents are prosperous and influential people in the community. A Brāhman officiates, and ties the satamānam on the bride's neck. On the evening of the third day, at the bride's house, presents called katnam, in the shape of rings, waist-bands, and a gold bangle for the right upper arm, are given to the bridegroom. The value of these presents bears a fixed proportion to that of the vōli or bride-price. The pair live for three days at the bride's house, and then proceed to the house of the bridegroom, where they stay during the next three days. They then return to the home of the bride, where they once more stay for three days, at the end of which the bridegroom returns to his house. The consummation ceremony is a separate event, and, if the girl has reached puberty, takes place a few days after the marriage ceremony. The remarriage of widows is permitted. The satamānam is tied on the bride's neck by the Kulampedda. Divorce is also recognised, and a man marrying a divorced woman has to pay twelve rupees, known as moganāltappu, or new husband's fine. The divorced woman has to return all the jewellery which was given to her by her former husband.

The dead are cremated, and a man of the washerman caste usually assists in igniting the pyre. There is an annual ceremony in memory of the dead, at which the house is cleaned, and purified with cow-dung. A meal on a more than usually liberal scale is cooked, and incense and camphor are burnt before the entrance to the house. Food is then offered to the dead, who are invoked by name, and the celebrants of the rite partake of a hearty meal.

The usual caste titles are Naidu and Setti.

Yeddula (bulls).—An exogamous sept of Bōya and Kāpu.

Yēdu Mādala (seven madalas).—The name of a section of Upparas, indicating the amount of the bride-price. A mādala is equivalent to two rupees.

Yelka Mēti (good rat).—An exogamous sept of Bōya.

Yemme.—Yemme, Emme, or Yemmalavāru, meaning buffalo or buffalo people, has been recorded as an exogamous sept of Bēdar or Bōya, Kurni, Kuruba,

Mādiga, and Vakkaliga.

Yenne (oil).—A sub-division of Gāniga.

Yēnuga.—Yēnuga or Yēnigala, meaning elephant, has been recorded as an exogamous sept of Kāpu, the members of which will not touch ivory.

Yēnumala.—Yēnumala or Yēnamaloru, meaning buffalo or buffalo people, has been recorded as an exogamous sept of Balija, Bōya, Mādiga, and Oddē.

Yeravallar.—*See* Eravallar.

Yerlam.—A division of Kāpus, so called after a Brāhman girl named Yerlamma, who was excommunicated for not being married, and bore children to a Kāpu.

Yerra (red).—A sub-division of Golla and Kāpu, and an exogamous sept of Dēvānga.

Yerudāndi.—*See* Erudāndi.

Yōgi Gurukkal.—The Yōgi Gurukkals are described in the Madras Census Report, 1891, as "a Malayālam-speaking beggar caste. They are also priests in Kāli temples, and pial schoolmasters. They bury their dead in a sitting posture (like Sanyāsis)." The pial, it may be noted, is a raised platform under the verandah, or on either side of the door of a house, in which village schools are held.

The Yōgi Gurukkals are scattered about Malabar, and their chief occupation seems to be the performance of worship to Kāli or Durga. They officiate as priests for Mukkuvans and Tiyans. Among the Mukkuvans, pūja (worship) to Kāli at the annual festival has to be done by a Yōgi Gurukkal, whereas, on ordinary occasions, it may be done by a Mukkuvan, provided that he has been initiated by a Yōgi Gurukkal. In their customs, the Yōgi Gurukkals closely follow the Nāyars.

It is recorded, in the Gazetteer of Malabar, that "the Yōgi Gurukkals of North Malabar are a caste which, though low in the social scale, is not regarded as conveying distance pollution. They perform sakti pūja in their own houses, to which no one outside the caste is allowed to attend; they also perform it for Nāyars and Tiyans. They are celebrated sorcerers and exorcists, and are also schoolmasters by profession."

Z

Zonnala (millet: *Sorghum vulgare*).—Zonnala, or the equivalent Zonnakūti, has been recorded as an exogamous sept of Kāpu. The Kōyis hold a festival when the zonna crop is ready to be cut, at which a fowl is killed in the field, and its blood sprinkled on a stone set up for the purpose.

END OF VOL. VII.

Lector House believes that a society develops through a two-fold approach of continuous learning and adaptation, which is derived from the study of classic literary works spread across the historic timeline of literature records. Therefore, we aim at reviving, repairing and redeveloping all those inaccessible or damaged but historically as well as culturally important literature across subjects so that the future generations may have an opportunity to study and learn from past works to embark upon a journey of creating a better future.

This book is a result of an effort made by Lector House towards making a contribution to the preservation and repair of original ancient works which might hold historical significance to the approach of continuous learning across subjects.

HAPPY READING & LEARNING!

LECTOR HOUSE LLP
E-MAIL: lectorpublishing@gmail.com

9 789390 058921